To See the Buddha

To See the Buddha

A Philosopher's Quest for the Meaning of Emptiness

Malcolm David Eckel

HarperSanFrancisco
A Division of HarperCollins*Publishers*

To Leslie and Leslie

A detail of this illustration appears on page 130.

FIRST EDITION

Library of Congress Cataloging-in-Publication Data

Eckel, Malcolm David
To see the Buddha : a philosopher's quest for the meaning of emptiness / Malcolm David Eckel.
p. cm.
Includes bibliographical references and index.
ISBN 0-06-062126-5
1. Buddha (The concept) 2. Bhāvaviveka. 3. Śūnyatā. I. Title.
BQ4180.E25 1991
294.3'63—dc20 90-56448
CIP

92 93 94 95 96 RRD(H) 10 9 8 7 6 5 4 3 2 1

This edition is printed on acid-free paper that meets the American National Standards Institute Z39.48 Standard.

Contents

Abbreviations

Full publication information for particular works can be found in the bibliography. When the works are listed under the name of the author or translator rather than the name of the text itself, the name of the author or translator is printed in **bold type**.

AA	Abhisamayālaṃkāra of **Maitreyanātha**
Ālokā	Abhisamayālaṃkārālokā Prajñāpāramitāvyākhyā of **Haribhadra**
BBh	Bodhisattvabhūmi of **Asaṅga**
BCA	Bodhicaryāvatāra of **Śāntideva**
BEFEO	Bulletin de l'École Française de l'Extrême Orient
BHSD	Buddhist Hybrid Sanskrit Dictionary, by Franklin **Edgerton**
DBh	Daśabhūmika Sūtra
HR	History of Religions
IIJ	Indo-Iranian Journal
JAOS	Journal of the American Oriental Society
JAS	Journal of Asian Studies
JIABS	Journal of the International Association of Buddhist Studies
JIP	Journal of Indian Philosophy
JRAS	Journal of the Royal Asiatic Society
Kośa	Abhidharmakośa of **Vasubandhu**
Life	The Life of Hsüan-tsang, by **Hui-li**, trans. Beal
MCB	Mélanges chinois et bouddhiques
MHK	Madhyamakahṛdayakārikās of **Bhāvaviveka**

MMK	Mūlamadhyamakakārikās of **Nāgārjuna**
Mppś	Le traité de la grande vertu de sagesse, trans. **Lamotte**
MS	Mahāyānasaṃgraha of **Asaṅga**
MSA	Mahāyānasūtrālaṃkāra of **Maitreyanātha**
MV	Mahāvyutpatti
PEW	Philosophy East and West
Prasannapadā	Prasannapadā Mūlamadhyamakavṛtti of **Candrakīrti**
Records	Buddhist Records of the Western World, by Hsüan-tsang, trans. Beal
RGV	Ratnagotravibhāga of **Maitreyanātha**
Śgs	Śūraṃgamasamādhi Sūtra
Siddhi	Vijñaptimātratāsiddhi of **Hsüan-tsang**
WZKS	Wiener Zeitschrift für die Kunde Süd- und Ost-Asiens

Acknowledgments

Mahāyāna philosophers tell us that the study of Emptiness is a study of interdependence, and this book, happily, is no exception. It has been enhanced and enriched by the comments of many colleagues and friends. I am grateful to Wilfred Cantwell Smith who challenged me, when I was a student in the Center for the Study of World Religions at Harvard, to look within the Buddhist intellectual tradition for qualities of mind and heart that can genuinely be called religious. That challenge was echoed in other conversations about the relationship between Emptiness and Buddhist ethical or devotional life. I remember with particular vividness a question Margaret Miles asked at the end of a seminar at Harvard Divinity School on the concept of God, "Is it is possible to have trust in Emptiness?" These questions and others like them helped give a sense of urgency and clarity to the intellectual project that lay behind this book.

The book also has been enriched by a series of important encounters with Tibetan scholars who are the modern heirs of the Madhyamaka tradition that can be traced back to the early centuries of the Common Era in India. I am grateful again to Acharya Doboom Tulku of Tibet House in Delhi for his help in introducing me not only to the works of Bhāvaviveka but to the tradition of Tibetan exegesis that keeps Bhāvaviveka's insights alive. The Venerable Tulku Thondup did me the great service of reading through the crucial portion of Bhāvaviveka's work with me when he was a Visiting Scholar at the Center for the Study of World Religions in the early 1980's. My knowledge of Madhyamaka epistemology was greatly enhanced by a series of conversations with the late Tsultrim Gyatso, abbot of Gomang.

I am particularly grateful to Douglas Brooks, John Carman, William Graham, Christian Lindtner, John McRae, Masatoshi Nagatomi, Jan Nattier, and Olle Qvarnstrom for the care they took with early versions of the manuscript; to Gregory Schopen for many stimulating conversations about the use of relics in classical India; to Susan and John Huntington for long and informative discussions of what is sometimes called the "aniconic" images of the Buddha; to William Newell for his editorial wisdom; and to Steven Rockefeller for his encouragement, on many long walks in the Adirondacks, to explore the religious meaning of classical Buddhist thought. Thanks are due also to the students who responded to the book with such critical intelligence, particularly Stephen Jenkins and Suzanne Mrozic at Harvard and the students in Religion 254 in the fall of 1991 at the University of Rochester.

The research for this book was funded in part by a grant from the National Endowment for the Humanities. Preliminary versions of parts of the book have appeared in the *Bulletin* of the Center for the Study of World Religions, and *Journal of Ritual Studies,* Summer 1990.

Introduction

Those who saw me by my form and those who followed me by my voice have acted incorrectly. Those people will not see me.

One should see the Buddha through the Dharma, for the Dharma Bodies are the guides. The nature of the Dharma cannot be discerned, and it is not capable of being discerned.

(The Diamond Sūtra)

What does it mean to see the Buddha? This question confronts anyone who has looked at a physical image of the Buddha or heard a story of the Buddha's life and wondered how these images and stories have served Buddhists as sources of power or comfort, how they have taught a lesson of moral discipline or mental cultivation, or how they have challenged a person to peel away layers of illusion and look more deeply into the nature of reality. The question is not necessarily a difficult one. Members of Buddhist communities have ways of taking in basic lessons in "seeing" as if they were absorbing them from the air they breathe. But this question also draws a person inexorably into contact with some of the deepest dilemmas of Buddhist thought. Many of the most sophisticated thinkers in the history of Buddhism have struggled with the ambiguities of the act of "seeing" in all its many ramifications—not just the cool, analytical vision that allows a person to take the structure of reality apart and distinguish its most minute constituents but also the emotional vision of a beloved object that fills the eyes with tears of joy, sadness, frustration, or satisfaction.

This book is an attempt to re-vision the Buddha through the eyes of a classical Indian philosopher. It is not intended to revise (although any attempt to grasp an ancient pattern of thought and feeling involves inevitable distortions) but to see again what it meant for an Indian intellectual, in a period when the Indian Buddhist tradition was in full flower, to gaze on the figure of the Buddha and examine its meaning. To reflect on such a person's act of seeing has a number of crucial components. There is the Indian intellectual himself, a personality who has to be seen as clearly as the sources allow us to see him. There is the figure of the Buddha that he sees. There is the act of seeing itself, an action that is shaped by different cultural presuppositions about the relationships between the senses and the world they perceive.

There is the larger cultural world within which this single act of seeing is located. Finally, there is our own act of seeing, through which we try to gain access to a sense of reality that in so many respects is different from our own. All of these components—from the personality and work of a particular Indian scholar to the imaginative re-visioning of a lost intellectual world—play a role in the study that follows.

The scholar through whose eyes this book attempts to see is Bhāvaviveka (also known as Bhavya), a sixth-century exponent of the school of Mahāyāna philosophy known as Madhyamaka, the school of the "Middle Way."[1] The distinctive ideas of the Madhyamaka tradition were formulated by Nāgārjuna in the early centuries of the Common Era and had wide and lasting influence in India, China, Japan, and Tibet. Like many of his fellow intellectuals in the sixth and seventh centuries, Bhāvaviveka had the instincts of a commentator. One of his best-known works is a commentary on Nāgārjuna's *Root Verses on the Middle Way (Mūlamadhyamakakārikās)*, and his greatest independent work, *The Verses on the Essence of the Middle Way (Madhyamakahṛdayakārikās)* with the commentary known as *The Flame of Reason (Tarkajvālā)*, contains an encyclopedic summary of the philosophical opinions of not only his own school but also of others.[2] Bhāvaviveka's work is striking in its completeness. There are moments when he gives the impression of being the Indian tradition's earliest and most diligent collector of philosophical trivia. But he was also sensitive to the systematic aspect of other schools. Unlike many of his contemporaries, he was not content just to tear an opponent's argument out of context and set it up for refutation. He organized his opponents' arguments into a systematic whole and then analyzed that system from his own critical perspective.

Bhāvaviveka's most important attribute for this study lies not in the breadth of his work, however, but in the quality of his imagination. This scholar and philosopher was a shrewd and dedicated logician, so dedicated that one of his critics accused him of being scorched by the flame of his own logic. But he was not just a logician. He also had the ear of a poet. He cast the arguments of the Madhyamaka tradition in the most precise and up-to-date logical form, but he also framed his vision of the Buddha in images and metaphors that reached outside his narrow philosophical circle and reflected the themes and preoccupations of Buddhist culture at large. For someone who is only interested in the logical structure of Buddhist thought, this characteristic is not much help. In some situations it can even be a distraction. But for someone who wants to know how a Buddhist philosopher struggled to reconcile the abstract dimension of Buddhist thought with the richness and diversity of life in medieval India, images and metaphors are precious evidence. As Steven Collins has pointed out in his fine study of the Buddhist concept of no-self, metaphors provide important clues to the philosopher's sense of the ordinary.[3] They bring the complex and abstract concepts of Buddhist philosophy down to earth.

Bhāvaviveka struggled, like many other philosophers in the Mahāyāna tradition, to find an adequate account of the concept of Emptiness *(śūnyatā)*, a concept that defies simple expression but can be summarized by saying that everything, in the end, is empty *(śūnya)* of individual identity *(svabhāva)* and depends for the appearance of its own existence on an infinite network of other equally empty things. Bhāvaviveka's images not only bring this concept down to earth but also reveal the metaphorical structure of the concept itself. For there to be Emptiness, there has to be a place that is empty. Strictly speaking, the place where Emptiness is located is every place, since there is nothing that is not empty. But, in a practical sense, not every place is equally revealing of its own true nature, nor is every experience equally open to the reality it is trying to grasp. For the ordinary practitioner who is struggling to grasp Emptiness more fully, there will be particular moments in time and particular points in space where Emptiness is known or felt more deeply than it could be otherwise, and these places and moments can be the focus of powerful religious actions and feelings.

For Bhāvaviveka and other Buddhist philosophers of the sixth century, the logic of place that lay embedded in the concept of Emptiness led inevitably to the location where Emptiness was preeminently present, the figure of the Buddha. The Buddha was the one who understood in the most definitive way what Emptiness was and the one who made it present in the experience of others. Bhāvaviveka's philosophical struggle with the concept of Emptiness brought him, along with many other like-minded thinkers in his time, through the negative and critical aspects of Emptiness to a contemplation of the figure of the Buddha, a contemplation that was deeply touched by the negative implications of Emptiness but one that was also filled with the warmth and energy of Mahāyāna devotion. This contemplation of the Buddha gave Bhāvaviveka's return to ordinary experience what seems to our eyes a most extraordinary cast. It summoned up for him an image of the Buddha that was embroidered with extraordinary virtues, a Buddha who emitted innumerable rays of light from the pores of his skin and who could shake the universe simply by opening his mouth to speak. But beneath the extraordinary imagery lay a conviction that was as important for Bhāvaviveka's understanding of Emptiness as it is for the modern study of his tradition: the concept of Emptiness found its location inside a structure of religious symbolism and religious practice that led a person naturally to confront the figure of the Buddha.

For Bhāvaviveka, the concept of Emptiness and the concept of the Buddha were inseparable: to see Emptiness was to see the Buddha, and vice versa. But the Buddha could also be visualized in a number of different forms (or, as the philosophers in Bhāvaviveka's tradition would prefer to say, in a number of different "bodies"), and the philosopher had to learn not just how the different forms of the Buddha are distinguished from one another but how they come together and are related. In addition to this examination of the object of vision, the philosopher had to examine the act of vision itself in order to understand how the seeing that is the peculiar property of the process of philosophy relates to other more familiar kinds of vision. To see the Buddha could mean to analyze the Buddha's true nature. It could mean to engage in a form of concentration in which a person has a vision of the Buddha's physical form.

It could mean to be illuminated by the power of the Buddha's presence. Or the vision of the Buddha could be a combination of all these varieties of vision in a single philosophical and devotional act.

To bring the metaphorical dimension of Bhāvaviveka's thought into the foreground, I have divided the book into three parts and used each part to explore a particular image that shaped Bhāvaviveka's vision of the Buddha. Since these images are so deeply related to the act of seeing and since Bhāvaviveka's own imagination was so dominated by visual metaphors, I have keyed each part of the book to a visual image drawn from the visual field of classical Indian Buddhism preserved for us in the tradition of Buddhist art. The first part, called "The Palace of Reality," explores the implications of a series of verses in Bhāvaviveka's philosophical work that compares the structure of reality (equated with Emptiness, and through Emptiness with the Buddha) to a series of palaces, some of which are real, some illusory, and some balancing on the narrow line that separates illusion from reality. This part is illustrated by the image of a structure that played a crucial role in Bhāvaviveka's understanding of the relationship between illusion and reality, a "peaked dwelling" *(kūṭāgāra)* from the representation of the last stages of Sudhana's pilgrimage on the walls of the great monument at Barabuḍur in Java. The second part of the book, called "The Empty Throne," explores the significance of absence in Bhāvaviveka's concept of the Buddha. This part is illustrated by an image of an empty throne from the stūpa or reliquary mound at Amarāvatī. The third part, called "The Buddha Eye," explores the significance of vision itself as a devotional phenomenon and as a metaphor for the way a person gains access not only to the Buddha but also to the reality that the Buddha knows and represents. This part is illustrated by the image of an eye on a bronze representation of a stūpa from ninth-century Kashmir.

To relate the conceptual images embodied in these three objects to the cultural background of Bhāvaviveka's work, I have introduced each of the three parts with an episode drawn from the travels of the great Chinese monk Hsüan-tsang. In the year 629, perhaps seventy years after the end of Bhāvaviveka's career, Hsüan-tsang left his home in China to travel to India and the lands to the west. Like a number of other Chinese pilgrims before him and unlike most of his Indian contemporaries, Hsüan-tsang attempted to record what he saw, and he left behind a voluminous account of the state of Buddhism as he knew it in the early years of the seventh century. Hsüan-tsang was not completely free from the impulse to embellish his tales, and there is little independent confirmation for many of his stories. But the narrative of Hsüan-tsang's journey gives a point of entry into Bhāvaviveka's world that is lively, rich, and almost impossible to duplicate from an Indian source. It also resonates with the narrative dimension of Bhāvaviveka's philosophy and helps draw out the implications of Bhāvaviveka's metaphors in ways that are difficult to duplicate from a strictly philosophical text.

Jonathan Smith began a recent book by saying, "For the self-conscious student of religion, no datum possesses intrinsic interest. It is of value only insofar as it can serve as an exemplum for some fundamental issue in the study of religion."[4] The same can be said of this study of Bhāvaviveka's vision of the Buddha. The Indian thinkers of the sixth and seventh centuries have already received a great deal of attention from specialists in Indian philosophy. But scholars who feel at home in the works of Bhāvaviveka and his contemporaries are far outnumbered by people who find the style and idiom of Indian philosophy almost insurmountable barriers to understanding. What basic issue can someone who is not a specialist in Indian philosophy expect to confront by looking at the Buddha through Bhāvaviveka's eyes? One way to answer this question would be to see this study of Bhāvaviveka as another example of the movement in contemporary philosophy and anthropology that wants to see philosophy itself as simply one more artifact of human culture. It has become commonplace in recent years to argue that philosophy is affected as much by the preoccupations of particular historical settings and particular images of the world as the rest of human culture, and philosophers cannot claim to hold a privileged or timeless vantage point on other people's controversies.[5] To show that mental pictures hold captive not just the people who have never had the desire or the opportunity to study philosophy but also the philosophers themselves changes the way a person sees the role of philosophy. And it does this not just for the study of seventh-century India but also, by example, for the study of times and cultures that are closer to our own.

A clear picture of the lines of continuity that tie Bhāvaviveka's vision of the Buddha to other aspects of Indian culture can also force us to look in new ways at some of the most basic distinctions made by the modern study of Buddhism. The first of these is the distinction between theory and practice. It is common in modern Western studies of the Buddhist tradition to treat the works of philosophers like Bhāvaviveka as if they were "theoretical" and divorced from the world of "practice." To speak of Bhāvaviveka as a "philosopher" as opposed to a practitioner, an adept, a devotee, or a sage is one manifestation of this distinction. His works and the works of others like him in the Indian intellectual tradition are treated as secondary reflections on the primary experience of Buddhist practitioners, even though Bhāvaviveka's own words make it difficult to state, let alone to defend, such a distinction. Bhāvaviveka's word for a "philosopher," someone who practices the analysis that he sets forth in his text, is simply an "intelligent" person, and he often refers to these "philosophers" as *yogins*, a word that could just as well be translated "practitioners." When Bhāvaviveka's "theorizing" is viewed as Bhāvaviveka himself saw it—as an inclusive system for the discipline of thought rather than as a piecemeal presentation of individual arguments—it is much closer to the *theoria* in Plato's contemplation of the Good than it is to "theory" in the modern distinction between theory and practice.[6] It is not a pale shadow of reality but a direct confrontation with reality itself. Bhāvaviveka included both the analysis and the contemplation of reality under the category of vision, and both were parts of the philosopher's "vision" of the Buddha.

A second distinction that needs to be reexamined is that between elite and popular modes of practice. Hsüan-tsang and Bhāvaviveka clearly represented an intellectual elite. Not only did they master the scholarly texts that were authoritative in their day but they also acquired the power and prestige necessary to generate texts that became authoritative for others. The fact that we can walk into libraries thirteen centuries later and take their works down from the Chinese and Tibetan canons is a testament to their mastery of the procedures and the technology of an elite culture. But their works were also capable of reflecting the habits of people quite different from themselves. Hsüan-tsang was a scholar and a learned monk, but he was also a pilgrim and a devotee. When he visited the great Indian pilgrimage sites, he rubbed shoulders with people who had little access to the discipline of philosophy. He must have heard the same stories and confronted the same signs and symbols that ordinary pilgrims used to make sense of their experience. Whether Hsüan-tsang and Bhāvaviveka interpreted those stories and signs as others did is difficult to know. Judging from the diversity of interpretation modern pilgrims encounter in similar situations, it is not likely that they did. But the stories and symbols gleaned from Buddhist sacred sites still spoke a common language, a language that they shared with others outside the circles of the learned elite. In this book I have deliberately shifted attention away from the discursive and analytical elements in these two scholars' work in favor of the narrative and the metaphorical. The point of this shift is to reveal the lines of continuity that tie scholars like Hsüan-tsang and Bhāvaviveka to those who lacked the benefit of philosophical study but who still could learn to "see" the Buddha through the stories and symbols that were present at Buddhist holy sites.

The last distinction that this book intends to challenge is the distinction between philosophy and religion. I follow what has now become common practice in the study of Indian thought and use the word "philosophy" to describe the content of Bhāvaviveka's work. The reasons for this choice are not difficult to see. Bhāvaviveka criticizes many of the categories that are associated with religion, and he criticizes them from a self-consciously rational and analytical perspective. In their analytical dimension, his works are a warning not only to those who think that the categories of Western theology can be applied to Mahāyāna thought but also to those who think that this tradition can be represented in the dualistic categories, such as the sacred and the profane, found in the phenomenology of religion. Bhāvaviveka criticizes dualities of all kinds, and the duality of sacred and profane is as vulnerable as the duality of God and creation. Nor does he spare the seemingly "religious" categories of traditional Buddhism. His approach to the concept of nirvana is epitomized by the famous statement, "There is no difference between nirvana and samsara," and his approach to the Buddha follows Nāgārjuna's equally negative claim that "the nature of the Buddha is the nature of the world: the Buddha has no nature and the world has no nature."[7] Nāgārjuna's verses do not seem to leave much room for such religious impulses as the aspiration for nirvana or the veneration of the Buddha. In fact, these verses make it easy to see why one of the greatest European scholars of Mahāyāna thought described Nāgārjuna's philosophy as "Nihilism (Buddhist)."[8]

But the negations of nirvana and the Buddha are not all they seem. It is clear, if we read Bhāvaviveka's version of the Madhyamaka critique in the context of his philosophy as a whole, that the critique supports and promotes what can rightly be called a religious vision of the world. When Bhāvaviveka has the opportunity to define Buddhist philosophy (or, in Bhāvaviveka's words, the Buddhist "vision of reality") without having to comment on the works of someone else, he brings his account of Madhyamaka thought to a climax with a devotional vision of the Buddha. This final vision is not the same as the vision of God in the tradition of Christian theology,[9] but there are enough similarities and points of congruence to suggest the possibility of a common vocabulary. Bhāvaviveka is hardly a cryptotheologian—his critique of the concept of God is too strong to let anyone make that very basic mistake—but his final description of the Buddha bespeaks all the majesty and power of great divinity. There may ultimately be no difference between the Buddha and the world, but the Buddha without qualities and distinctions is not the one that appears at the end of Bhāvaviveka's argument. Instead, it is a Buddha who overwhelms the gods with his power, cools the fire of suffering in the minds of sentient beings, plucks beings from the ocean of samsara, illuminates their minds with his radiance, and wakes them from the sleep of ignorance with the sound of his teaching. To all outward appearances (and the word "appearance" is a crucial qualification), Bhāvaviveka's Buddha is the apotheosis of power and grace.

With this final image of the Buddha in mind, we cannot help but be suspicious of interpretations of Madhyamaka thought that pit the "philosophical" and "religious" aspects of the tradition against one another. It is true that there are moments in Bhāvaviveka's work, as there are in the works of other Madhyamaka philosophers, when a strict analysis of epistemological and ontological categories overwhelms everything else. Bhāvaviveka considers the rational analysis of things to be an *ultimate* analysis, by which he means that there is no higher level from which it can be contradicted. But the *logos* of Bhāvaviveka's rational investigation is embedded in its own *mythos*. It is part of a story of liberation and illumination, a story that leads out of ignorance to wisdom and out of blindness to sight. To understand this mythic dimension of Bhāvaviveka's work takes a clear awareness of the context and the narrative movement of his thought. Like the events of a complex and open-ended journey, no single statement in Bhāvaviveka's work is ever quite what it seems. When he speaks of the Buddha's overwhelming virtues, he is talking about the same Buddha whom he describes elsewhere as the no-arising of no-thought about no-thing. Only the perspective changes, not the Buddha himself. To understand the relationship of these different perspectives and to see how the majesty of the Buddha is related to the awareness of the Buddha as nothing in itself, we only need to adjust our eyes to the distinctive modalities of Bhāvaviveka's philosophical vision. The chapters that follow are a guide to that exercise in imaginative seeing.

Part I

The Palace of Reality

It is impossible to climb the tower of the palace of reality without the steps of correct, relative [wisdom].

(The Verses on the Essence of the Middle Way)

At the beginning of Bhāvaviveka's presentation of his own philosophy, he pictures reality as a palace and invites the practitioner of philosophy to climb its tower as if ascending a ladder. As the practitioner climbs the rungs of the ladder, he gains more and more control over the structure of the palace itself. First he learns to see through it, like the palace seen in a dream, and then he learns to shape it into a magnificent "peaked dwelling," a dwelling that functions simultaneously as an offering to the Buddha and as a tool to demonstrate the fragility of reality itself.

The pilgrim Sudhana with the Bodhisattva Maitreya at the door of a peaked dwelling, as illustrated on the wall of the Buddhist monument at Barabuḍur in Java. Photograph by John E. Huntington

Chapter 1

The Story of the Asuras' Cave

The Chinese monk Hsüan-tsang, in an account of his travels through seventh-century India, tells a story about the philosopher Bhāvaviveka.[1] The story seems to have become encrusted with legend even in the few decades that passed between Bhāvaviveka's time and the travels of Hsüan-tsang, but it is a story that gives rare insight into the life of philosophers in sixth- and seventh-century India. Hsüan-tsang describes Bhāvaviveka as a master of learned texts, "renowned for his elegant scholarship and for the depth of his vast attainments." In this respect Hsüan-tsang's description coincides nicely with the image of Bhāvaviveka that has come down to us from other sources. Bhāvaviveka is known in the Tibetan tradition as a powerful and original interpreter of that branch of the Mahāyāna tradition known as Madhyamaka (the philosophy of the Middle Way), which stems from the second-century philosopher Nāgārjuna. His surviving works show that he had an eye for controversy and a shrewd grasp of the issues that divided his own tradition from the traditions of other Indian schools, both Buddhist and Hindu. To a modern eye, his works show the signs of a brilliant professorial mind—a mind that, with a few changes in style and idiom, would be as much at home in a modern university as it was in the monasteries of ancient India. But it is not just Bhāvaviveka's academic brilliance that is celebrated in Hsüan-tsang's story. The story also pictures a philosopher who was in touch with some of the deep religious currents of his age, a philosopher who controlled the forces of illusion through the manipulation of magical phrases and who turned in moments of frustration to figures such as Avalokiteśvara and Maitreya, the celestial bodhisattvas who functioned as the great saving deities of the Mahāyāna.[2]

According to Hsüan-tsang, Bhāvaviveka, in the process of his academic labors, discovered that another philosopher was making thousands of disciples in Magadha, the region in the center of the Ganges basin that once had been the homeland of the Buddha. The other philosopher was Dharmapāla, a representative of the Yogācāra school (the school of the "Practitioners of Yoga") of which Hsüan-tsang himself was a member.[3] Hsüan-tsang does not tell us how Bhāvaviveka felt when he heard this report, but it is not unlikely that he was moved by a sense of rivalry and perhaps even of jealousy. In his own philosophical writings, Bhāvaviveka took great pains to argue that the Yogācāras had not only misinterpreted the Buddha's teaching but had read it with an arrogant disregard for the truth.[4] We can well imagine that Bhāvaviveka was provoked by the reports of Dharmapāla's success into trying to test him in debate. In any case, Hsüan-tsang tells us that Bhāvaviveka took up his staff and traveled to Magadha to meet with Dharmapāla in person. When Bhāvaviveka arrived, he was told that Dharmapāla had gone to teach at the Bodhi tree, the spot where the Buddhas of the present age go to attain enlightenment. Bhāvaviveka traveled in the direction of the Bodhi tree but stopped short of the site itself, saying that he was constrained by a previous vow not to visit the scene of the Buddha's enlightenment until he was ready to attain enlightenment himself.[5] He sent a group of disciples ahead to ask Dharmapāla for a meeting, and Dharmapāla responded with a message that could just as easily have come from an overworked member of a modern philosophy department: "The lives of men . . . are like a phantom; the body is as a bubble. The whole day I exert myself. I have no time for controversy; you may therefore depart—there can be no meeting."

When his plans to meet with Dharmapāla failed to bear fruit, Bhāvaviveka went back to the south of India and resolved to find someone who could talk with him about the teaching of Dharmapāla's school. Hsüan-tsang tells us that Bhāvaviveka decided to settle for nothing less than a confrontation with Maitreya, the great celestial bodhisattva who was waiting in Tuṣita Heaven for the time when he would appear as the future Buddha. There must have been other, lesser representatives of the Yogācāra school for Bhāvaviveka to engage in conversation, especially if Dharmapāla was as successful in attracting disciples as Hsüan-tsang claims, but Hsüan-tsang tells us that Bhāvaviveka decided to wait and speak directly with the source. According to a legend that was well known in Hsüan-tsang's time, it was Maitreya himself who had transported Asaṅga, the first exponent of the Yogācāra tradition, to his palace in Tuṣita Heaven and set the teaching of the Yogācāra tradition in motion.[6]

It is hard to see, through the veil of Hsüan-tsang's words, exactly what he means when he says that this great critic of the Yogācāra hoped to study with Maitreya. These words might very well be meant to carry a subtle tone of mockery, with the suggestion that this querulous defender of the tradition of Nāgārjuna actually thought that he could challenge the future Buddha in debate. It is more likely, however, that Hsüan-tsang is drawing Bhāvaviveka into a pattern of devotional practice that transcends the divisions between the two philosophical schools. Hsüan-tsang himself was deeply devoted to

Maitreya, and not just in his capacity as the founder of Hsüan-tsang's own philosophical lineage. According to his biographer, Hsüan-tsang turned to Maitreya at moments of great crisis, especially when his life was in danger, and he carried the hope of being reborn in the presence of Maitreya with him to his deathbed.[7] It does not seem unnatural for Hsüan-tsang to extend this same devotional orientation to an Indian sage like Bhāvaviveka.

After Bhāvaviveka had decided to wait for the coming of Maitreya, Hsüan-tsang tells us, he visited an image of Avalokiteśvara—the celestial bodhisattva who for many Mahāyāna Buddhists in South and East Asia has served as the paragon of compassion—and asked Avalokiteśvara to help him bring his hopes to reality. Bhāvaviveka fasted and chanted in front of the image and at the end of three years was granted a vision of Avalokiteśvara himself. The bodhisattva at first seemed unimpressed by Bhāvaviveka's desire to remain in his present body until the coming of Maitreya, and he advised him instead to develop a pure aspiration and seek rebirth in Tuṣita Heaven where he could see Maitreya face to face. But Bhāvaviveka persevered, and Avalokiteśvara finally told him of a nearby mountain where a spirit by the name of Vajrapāṇi could help him obtain what he desired.[8]

At the mountain, Bhāvaviveka repeated a second chant to summon Vajrapāṇi. After three more years of waiting, Vajrapāṇi appeared and asked Bhāvaviveka to explain what he wanted. When Bhāvaviveka said that he hoped to remain in his present body until he could meet Maitreya in the flesh, Vajrapāṇi told him of a cave inside the mountain. Inside the cave was an Asuras' palace—a palace of demons—where Bhāvaviveka could wait for the coming of Maitreya. After another period of three years, Bhāvaviveka brought a crowd of people to the mountain, spoke another formula, and struck the face of the mountain with charmed mustard seed. When the mountain opened in front of him, he turned to the crowd of followers and urged them to join him inside. Only six of them were confident enough to accept his invitation. The story ends with a description of Bhāvaviveka and his six companions walking into the Asuras' palace to enter a state of suspended animation and wait for the future Buddha.[9]

It is a rare scholar who can suspend the normal process of aging and continue in physical form for a long time into the future, but this ability is not without parallel in other Buddhist traditions. Hsüan-tsang's account of Bhāvaviveka recalls another well-known story about the Buddha's disciple Mahākāśyapa.[10] According to Hsüan-tsang's version of this story, Mahākāśyapa was commissioned by Śākyamuni, the Buddha of the present era, to take custody of his cloak and convey it to the Buddha of the future. When Mahākāśyapa finished his own career as a teacher, he took the cloak and withdrew to a remote mountain range. At the end of a long defile, he struck the wall of a mountain with his staff and, like Bhāvaviveka, saw the wall of the mountain open in front of him. He walked inside, and the mountain closed over him. Hsüan-tsang ends the story with the prediction that the mountain will remain closed until the next Buddha comes to collect the cloak. At the proper moment, Maitreya will lead a band of disciples to the mountain, the mountain will open, and Mahākāśyapa will place the cloak in Maitreya's hands, soar into the air, and pass directly into nirvana.

The story of the sage buried in the mountain also has variants outside the Indian subcontinent. Hsüan-tsang encountered another version of the story on his return to China along the Silk Road.[11] As Hsüan-tsang drew near a great mountain in the vicinity of Kashgar, he saw a particularly awesome and mysterious shrine. When he asked the inhabitants of the region about the shrine's significance, they told him a story of a great storm that had split the mountain and revealed the figure of a saint seated inside. The first person to see the saint was a solitary hunter, and the hunter hurried off to tell his story to the local king. The king brought a group of people to visit the saint and pay him homage. When they drew near, they found that the saint's body was so dry and shriveled with age that they had to rub his skin with oil to keep him from disintegrating. When they had finished their restorative efforts, they carefully roused the saint from his concentration. The saint opened his eyes, saw the crowd that had gathered around him, and explained that he was a disciple of Kāśyapa, the Buddha who preceded Śākyamuni. When the people told him that he had not only outlived his master but had also lived through the career of the next Buddha, the saint rose into the air, displayed a variety of extraordinary manifestations, and disappeared in a blaze of fire. All he left behind was a pile of bones, and it was around these bones that the awesome and mysterious shrine had been constructed.

The parallels between the stories of these other extraordinary saints and the story of Bhāvaviveka make the figure of Bhāvaviveka seem somewhat larger than life. Bhāvaviveka may have been a great master of dialectic and argument, but it takes more than an armchair philosopher to suspend the processes of bodily deterioration and lie quietly behind mountain walls until the appearance of a future Buddha. Hsüan-tsang's story gives a strong warning to anyone who would like to reduce the complex figure of a sage like Bhāvaviveka to the mechanics of scholarly commentary and the fabrication of a string of syllogisms. When Hsüan-tsang looked at Bhāvaviveka, through eyes that had become accustomed in some fashion to the Indian intellectual and religious landscape, he saw a philosopher whose quest for wisdom operated side by side with a quest for the powers of mental concentration, and he saw a sage who depended as much on the intervention of the great savior figures of the Mahāyāna as he did on his own capacity for logical analysis.

The most tantalizing element in Hsüan-tsang's story—and the one that seems to draw us most deeply into Bhāvaviveka's own ambiguous vision of the world—is not, however, Bhāvaviveka's great devotion or his mastery over the process of meditation; it is the image of his final resting place, the Asuras' palace. What clues can we find in Hsüan-tsang's narrative to unlock the meaning of this strange image? In the account of another episode in his journey, Hsüan-tsang describes an Asuras' palace near the Vulture Peak, where the Buddha is said to have delivered the teaching that constituted the Mahāyāna.[12] This particular Asuras' palace was located in a cave behind the walls of a stone house that once had been occupied by the Buddha himself. When

Hsüan-tsang visited the site, monks were using the house to practice meditation. It seems that this remote house was quiet and peaceful enough, most of the time, to allow the monks freedom from mental distraction. The only problem came from the cave itself. Hsüan-tsang says that the Asuras' palace sometimes overwhelmed the monks with frightening visions of serpents and lions. When monks were not well disciplined or in full control of their faculties, they often saw strange and terrifying forms issuing from the cave. In some cases, the forms dazzled their minds and drove them mad.

Just how these bewildering forms might cause a meditating monk to lose touch with reality is illustrated by another story in Hsüan-tsang's text. Somewhat earlier in the account of his travels, Hsüan-tsang describes a small hill, near a forest known as Yaṣṭīvana, in which a large assembly hall had been excavated.[13] The southwest corner of the hall was said to conceal a cavern holding an Asuras' palace. Local tradition told of a man who was skilled in magic and took a group of companions for a journey into the cavern. After they had walked some distance, the cavern lit up with a great light, and they saw a walled city with towers that glowed with silver and gold. As the men drew near the city, they were greeted by a group of young women and then by a group of slave girls who offered them a bowl full of flowers and told them that they could only enter the city after they bathed themselves in a pond. When the men entered the pond, their minds became confused: they forgot everything that had happened to them, and they woke up to find themselves sitting in the middle of a rice field outside the cavern.

This story is reminiscent of some of the tales of illusion that Wendy Doniger O'Flaherty tells so masterfully in her *Dreams, Illusions, and Other Realities.*[14] There is the popular Indian story, for example, of the sage Nārada who makes the mistake of saying to the god Viṣṇu that he has conquered illusion. To teach him a lesson about the power of illusion, Viṣṇu invites Nārada to bathe in a pond. When he enters the pond, Nārada suffers a loss of memory that is even more extreme than the one suffered by the men who wandered up to the Asuras' palace: he loses all sense of his former identity and comes out of the pond in the form of a woman. In this new identity, he (or she) lives an entirely new life, marrying a king, raising a family, and then watching the family destroyed in a cataclysmic battle. Finally, as Nārada lies lost in grief, Viṣṇu visits him in the form of a Brahman and reminds him that everything he has experienced is a mistake. Viṣṇu asks him to perform the rituals for the dead, beginning with the proper ritual bath. When Nārada goes into the water for the bath, his memory is restored and he returns to the spot where he left his former identity behind.

The Asuras' illusory palace is reminiscent also of the illusory palaces and cities that appear from time to time in the Buddhist sūtras from which Bhāvaviveka drew much of his inspiration. At the beginning of *The Descent to Laṅkā (Laṅkāvatāra) Sūtra*, for example, the Buddha pays a visit to the island of Laṅkā (modern Śrī Laṅkā), and when he gets there, the demon Rāvaṇa asks the Buddha to teach him a lesson.[15] The Buddha accepts Rāvaṇa's invitation, climbs aboard Rāvaṇa's flying chariot, and travels to the city of Laṅkā.

As the two of them look over the city, the Buddha multiplies the scene in which they are standing. He creates the illusion of multiple cities, and in the illusory image of each city stands the image of the Buddha and Rāvaṇa's entire entourage. With this apparition shimmering before their eyes, the Buddha disappears and leaves Rāvaṇa wondering what it was that he saw and what it is that distinguishes the "illusory" cities of the Buddha's creation from the city whose reality he took so much for granted.

What does it say about the character of Bhāvaviveka, then, for Hsüan-tsang to leave him wrapped in a pattern of such exquisite illusion? Hsüan-tsang's other stories show that the most powerful sages are not the ones who flee the structures of illusion but are those who possess the knowledge to manipulate it and bring it under their control. The monk who led the excursion through the walls of the assembly hall and into the Asuras' cavern was said to be skilled in magic. Was it this skill that allowed him to return as the one person in the whole band able to tell the tale? Hsüan-tsang does not say, but he does indicate that this skill in magic made it possible for the man to pass fearlessly through the walls that separated the realm of conventional reality from the bewildering realm of the palace. The same skill appears in the story of another monk who chose to meditate in the stone house that lay near the Vulture Peak.[16] In this story, Hsüan-tsang says that the monk was warned not to use a place associated with such calamities, but the monk persisted, saying that he wanted to follow the Buddha's example and conquer any distractions that could be thrown in his path. To guard himself, he set up an altar and began to recite "magic protective sentences." When ten days had passed, a young woman came out of the cave and asked the monk why he, as a follower of the Buddha, would be so cruel to an innocent band of Asuras. The monk's reaction carried a tone of righteous indignation: "Here I am in the mountains trying to avoid distractions, and you come along and harass me with your accusations. What am I doing wrong?" The young woman explained that his protective sentences were causing fire to burst out in the Asuras' house, and she and her family were being burned. The monk said that he was just trying to protect himself against the problems that had afflicted other monks at the same place, and the woman agreed to wall up the mouth of the cave in return for a promise from the monk to stop reciting his powerful formulas.

Powerful formulas also play a crucial role in Hsüan-tsang's story of Bhāvaviveka. The appearance of Avalokiteśvara depends on a process of fasting and the recitation of a particular formula. When Avalokiteśvara has delivered his response to Bhāvaviveka's request, the cavern is opened with a formula that controls Vajrapāṇi. Finally, when Vajrapāṇi makes his appearance, he gives Bhāvaviveka another formula, a formula that we can guess is used to control the forces of illusion inside the Asuras' palace itself. Thus, the formulas bring mastery and make of Bhāvaviveka not a bumbling philosopher who puts himself inadvertently in the clutches of illusion but a careful practitioner who gathers the mental and verbal forces he needs to meet the illusion on its own ground and overcome it. It is this element of mastery that is the key to

Hsüan-tsang's final image of Bhāvaviveka, the key to Bhāvaviveka's position within the illusory world of the Asuras' palace, and the key that unlocks Bhāvaviveka's own attitude toward the illusory palaces that symbolize his own conception of reality.

When we read Bhāvaviveka's account of his own philosophy and adjust our eyes to the images he uses to visualize and structure his conception of reality, we find that he sees reality as a series of palaces. Like the Asuras' palace in Hsüan-tsang's story, these palaces demonstrate the delicate and shadowy line that separates illusion from reality. Sometimes Bhāvaviveka's palaces are meant to give an impression of solidity, allowing a practitioner to chart a passage through the philosophical maze with firm signposts and a clear destination. Sometimes the palaces have no more solidity than a dream from which one suddenly and inexplicably awakes. Finally, however, they are palaces that fall under the practitioner's control, that are spun out by a great bodhisattva's illusion-making power, and yet that share the solidity of the ordinary world to such a degree that, for all ordinary purposes, they can be conceived of as "real."

When Bhāvaviveka introduces the image of the palace into the structure of his own philosophy, he does it with the presumption of reality, as if he were looking at the palace from the point of view of a person who has never been able to escape from its spell. At the beginning of the third chapter of *The Flame of Reason,* he says:

> It is impossible to climb the tower of the palace of reality without the steps of correct relative [wisdom].[17]

The terminology of the verse shows that Bhāvaviveka thinks of the world as a palace or temple (Bhāvaviveka's term, *prāsāda,* can mean either one) and the philosopher as a person who scales its tower by analyzing the categories of ordinary experience.[18] The gradual ascent of the tower corresponds to the gradual process of distinguishing and testing the categories of conventional reality. As Bhāvaviveka moves through the stages of analysis and finds that no conventional categories can stand up to his analytical test, the palace reappears in the guise of a dream. This time Bhāvaviveka pictures a palace like the dream-palaces of *The Descent to Laṅkā Sūtra,* a palace that is much more elaborate, much more explicitly enmeshed in the ordinary world, and fraught with much more dazzling images:

> Someone who feels drowsy and falls asleep sees such things as young men, women, and a palace, but does not see them when he wakes up.
>
> Likewise, someone who has opened the wisdom-eye, stopped the sleep of ignorance, and woken up does not see things as they are seen conventionally.[19]

The commentary expands these two verses into an alluring picture of the pleasures of a royal palace, a picture that absorbs the dreamer in an experience involving all of the senses. There are young men with crowns and soft voices, young women with shiny black hair and eyes like lotus petals. Surrounding the palace are gardens with herds of deer, sweet-sounding birds, and groves of tall trees. The palace courtyard is full of the trappings of war: chariots, elephants, cavalry, foot soldiers, and a mass of victory banners. The person who experiences such a dream feels that it is intensely real, but when the person wakes up, the scene disappears in the blink of an eye.

Bhāvaviveka's image of the dream-palace illustrates the evanescent quality of ordinary experience, but it lacks the element of mastery. The dreamer can only escape from the dream of reality, not yet bend it to express his or her own will. To see a palace that can be manifested as a deliberate fiction, we have to move to the last stages in Bhāvaviveka's presentation of his own philosophy. In his account of the tenth stage of the path, Bhāvaviveka pictures a bodhisattva who can manipulate reality at will. The beings who have achieved this stage (among whom Bhāvaviveka mentions Avalokiteśvara, Maitreya, Samantabhadra, and Mañjuśrī) can display the appearance of their own body in world systems as numerous as the grains of sand in the Ganges. Each of these manifestations is capable of displaying an equally vast number of hands, heads, and tongues. To honor the Buddha, these manifestations offer sweet-smelling flowers, parasols, canopies that sparkle with jewels, and magnificent palaces that Bhāvaviveka refers to by the name "peaked dwelling" (*kūṭāgāra*).[20]

Why do the great bodhisattvas of the tenth stage use these peaked dwellings as their final offering to the Buddha? What associations did they carry for Bhāvaviveka and his potential readers? The best way to explore the answers to these questions is to turn to the Mahāyāna sūtras out of which Bhāvaviveka spun many of his literary images. The structure of the peaked dwelling plays an important and exemplary role in the story of the young Buddhist hero called Sadāprarudita ("Perpetually Weeping") at the end of *The Perfection of Wisdom in Eight Thousand Lines.*[21] In this story, Sadāprarudita goes on a long journey to meet the teacher, Dharmodgata, who is destined to teach him the meaning of the Mahāyāna. When he arrives in his teacher's presence, he finds that Dharmodgata has constructed an elaborate peaked dwelling as a sign of worship to the text of the Perfection of Wisdom.[22] Later Sadāprarudita and a group of disciples lay an offering of flowers at Dharmodgata's feet. The text tells us that Dharmodgata's power causes the flowers to rise up and form a peaked dwelling over Dharmodgata's head, just as the flowers offered at the feet of the Buddha were said in earlier literature to rise up to form a canopy over the Buddha's head.[23]

The same sequence of symbolic actions is played out in the presence of the Buddha himself at the beginning of *The Large Sūtra on the Perfection of Wisdom.* The passage in question describes a series of transformations the Buddha experiences as he prepares to teach the Perfection of Wisdom. Seated on the lion throne of enlightenment, the Buddha enters into the "king of concentrations," and his body begins to glow. From his pores he emits rays of light, illuminating the universe in every direction. He stretches out his tongue to cover the whole universe, and from his tongue also pour a vast number of rays. In each ray sits a jeweled lotus with thousands of petals, and in each jeweled lotus sits the image of a Buddha teaching the Dharma. Entering another concentration called "the lion's play," the Buddha begins to shake the entire universe. Again, without moving from his throne, he manifests a body that towers over the universe. When the gods who live in the Realm of Desire and the Realm of Form see this "natural body" of the Buddha, they throw a great mass of flowers at the Buddha's feet. By the Buddha's power, these flowers rise up over his head and form a peaked dwelling with the dimensions of the universe itself. Out of this great structure of celestial flowers, the glow of the Buddha's body streams into every corner of the universe, and every being who is touched by the glow thinks, "The Buddha is teaching the Dharma to me."

In both these passages from the Perfection of Wisdom Sūtras, the peaked dwelling serves a double purpose. From the point of view of the worshiper, the dwelling functions as an expression of devotion: devotees offer it to the Buddha (or to the text that stands in place of the Buddha) as a sign of worship. From the point of view of the one to whom it is offered, it can (but does not always) provide an opportunity for an expression of power. In both the stories, there is a group of devotees who present the raw materials for the structure. Bodhisattvas and Buddhas then perfect the action and fashion the flowers into a finished act of worship.

Both of these elements—devotion and power—are present in Bhāvaviveka's account of the peaked dwellings at the end of the bodhisattva path, but in a slightly different way. Using the word *bhakti*, the same word that is used to speak of devotion to God in a Hindu context, Bhāvaviveka says that the bodhisattvas in the tenth stage make their offerings to the Buddha with eyes "moist with devotion" (*bhaktyārdra*). These tears of devotion reflect the tears of compassion (*karuṇā*) that the bodhisattvas shed at an earlier stage of the path.[24] But here the emotions are turned in another direction: the bodhisattvas' multiple hands, arms, faces, and tongues are directed not backward toward the suffering beings who lie behind them on the path but forward toward the Buddha who still lies ahead. This devotion is also wrapped in an aura of power. Bhāvaviveka introduces the peaked dwellings at the end of a series of verses on the powers (*ṛddhi*) of the bodhisattva in the tenth stage. These powers are similar to the ten masteries (*vaśitā*) that were associated with the eighth stage, but they transcend them in at least one crucial respect: the powers of the tenth stage allow bodhisattvas to project the appearance of becoming Buddhas themselves. Here at the pinnacle of the bodhisattva's career, it is as if the bodhisattva not only can shape reality on a vast scale into an act of worship but also can manifest the being to whom the worship is directed. The bodhisattvas function simultaneously as the subject and object of worship—the paragons of devotion and power in the same personality.

The relationship between the peaked dwelling and the bodhisattvas' power to control illusion appears in its most direct form in the famous story of the pilgrim Sudhana, a story that is narrated in *The Gaṇḍavyūha Sūtra* and illustrated on the walls of the Buddhist monument of Barabuḍur in Java.[25] In the text of the sūtra, Sudhana undertakes a long journey to a series of "spiritual friends" (*kalyāṇa-mitra*) to receive a series of distinctive teachings about the Mahāyāna. At the beginning of the climactic episode of the text, Sudhana finds himself in front of an enormous peaked dwelling called "[The Dwelling that] Contains the Ornament of the Magical Arrays of Vairocana" (*vairocana-vyūhālaṃkāra-garbha*).[26] Sudhana pictures the structure in his mind's eye and throws himself down in front of the door. With a concentration that obliterates the distinction between mind and body, he then visualizes himself prostrate in front of all Buddhas, bodhisattvas, teachers, and saints. After he has spent a period of time contemplating the peaked dwelling in this way, the bodhisattva Maitreya appears in front of him and uses the dwelling as a device to teach him a lesson about the nature of reality. The lesson has to do first with the interdependence of all things but finally with the pervasive power of illusion. Sudhana first sees the dwelling from the outside as a vast interconnected representation of reality; then he enters the dwelling and sees it filled with reflections of hundreds of thousands of other dwellings, all equally magnificent and vast. The reflections of the different dwellings fuse with one another so that each of them maintains its own distinctive identity, yet is identified with every other. Under the influence of Maitreya, Sudhana then sees himself entering all the different dwellings and watches the events in the career of Maitreya acted out before his eyes. Finally, Maitreya himself enters the dwelling and, with a snap of his fingers, makes the vision disappear. When Sudhana asks where the vision has gone, Maitreya says, "Exactly where it came from." And where did it come from? Maitreya says, "It came from the application of the bodhisattva's knowledge and power."[27]

Here the devotional function of the peaked dwelling is no longer an issue. Maitreya uses the peaked dwelling simply as a three-dimensional device to teach Sudhana about the relationship between illusion and reality. The appearance of the dwelling demonstrates that everything, including the events in the career of Maitreya and the personality of Sudhana, is part of an interconnected network of being. Each item and each personality reflected in the vast structure of the dwelling mirror and in turn are mirrored by every other. The separate identity of any single element in the universe is an illusion, but it is an illusion supported by a relationship with every other element in the universe. Through this crucial lesson about the nature of things, Maitreya also teaches what it means for a bodhisattva to manipulate reality in a positive way. The structure is created and maintained by Maitreya's illusion-making power, and all it takes at the end of the story is a snap of Maitreya's fingers to make the structure disappear.

Bhāvaviveka's palaces and palacelike structures—from the palace of reality at the beginning of the chapter to the peaked dwellings at the end—are hard to confuse with Hsüan-tsang's image of the Asuras' palace: they clearly are not the dwellings of a being who projects frightening and bewildering shapes and drives solitary monks to madness. But both the Asuras' palace and the three palaces in Bhāvaviveka's text function as symbols of the nature of reality and convey similar messages about the process through which a person can learn to recognize and dominate illusion. Bhāvaviveka's first palace is a structure that a person can climb and use to gain a dominant perspective on the environment that surrounds it. Bhāvaviveka's second palace—the palace of dreams—wraps the mind in a web of illusion but also evaporates when a person has the insight to wake up from the dream. The final palace—the peaked dwelling—represents illusion in its most positive aspect: the illusion that bodhisattvas create to bend what others see as reality to their own ends.

The passage from one palace to another in Bhāvaviveka's thought sets up a three-part movement (from a state in which one sees illusion as reality, to a state in which one sees illusion as illusion, and then to a state in which one can use the illusion as reality and make it serve one's own ends), and this three-part movement not only shapes Bhāvaviveka's vision of reality but it also allows Bhāvaviveka to balance the competing and sometimes contradictory aspects of the Mahāyāna vision of the Buddha. The next step in this study of Bhāvaviveka's philosophical vision is to follow the direction suggested by the sequence of these three palace images in order to explore the deeper structures of Bhāvaviveka's thought. We now know that Bhāvaviveka thought of reality as if it *were* a structure. We will also find that he thought reality *had* a structure, and this structure gives shape to Bhāvaviveka's conception of the Buddha's elusive form.

Chapter 2

The Structure of Bhāvaviveka's Thought

The images of palaces and palacelike structures in Bhāvaviveka's writings raise a serious question about the role of metaphor in the analytical process of Indian philosophy. It is obvious that Indian philosophers illustrate their arguments with examples from ordinary life, and we know that their texts are enlivened from time to time with metaphors, but how deep do the metaphors go? Are they just isolated embellishments on the surface of the text, or are they an integral part of the philosopher's understanding of the world? If we were speaking about poetry, the answer to this question would be easy. The metaphorical dimension of poetic language is impossible to separate from the poetry itself. But philosophical discourse gives the impression of being different. Argument seems to take precedence over rhetoric, and the metaphorical devices that distinguish poetry seem to be added as an afterthought, if they are added at all. They may be used to make the argument more vivid or more palatable, but they do not make it more clear. At least this is what we are led to believe by the conventional distinction between philosophy and more overtly metaphorical modes of discourse.

In practice it is not so easy to rid philosophy of the influence of metaphor.[1] Some of the most basic words in the language of philosophy, words like "concept," "foundation," or "theory," may have had their metaphorical dimension effaced by constant use, but they still derive their meaning, respectively, from the physical gesture of grasping an object, from the experience of putting something down on solid ground, or from the experience of gazing at a physical object. These metaphors are the building blocks (to use another metaphor) out of which the language of philosophy is constructed.

Even when the rough edges of the metaphors have been worn away and their meaning seems perfectly "clear" (another metaphor), the shape of the blocks still determines how they fit together in the construction of a philosophical system. One of Nietzsche's more memorable remarks is that "truths are illusions of which one has forgotten that they *are* illusions; worn-out metaphors which have become powerless to affect the senses; coins which have their obverse effaced and now are no longer of account as coins but merely as metal."[2] The words of philosophy may have had their metaphorical values worn away, but they still enter into a network of relationships that derive from their original functions. They may no longer have the appearance of coins, but they still function as tokens of value.

If we chose to, we could read Bhāvaviveka's palace metaphors as nothing more than illustrations or embellishments on the surface of his argument. We could take the palace with its tower simply as an illustration of the idea that reality has a predictable structure, and we could take the dream palace as an illustration of the idea that reality is an illusion. But as Bhāvaviveka elaborates his understanding of reality, it becomes clear that his images of palaces and palacelike structures reflect deeper patterns of thought, where the metaphors are more difficult to separate from the argument itself. One way to identify these patterns and draw them to the surface is to look at the relationship between the physical structure of the palace and the sense of motion that is present in Indian representations of the quest for philosophical knowledge. As we have seen, Bhāvaviveka starts his analysis of reality with a reference to the steps of a palace. The steps that lead to the top of the palace represent stages in a process of reasoning that leads from the realm of ordinary thought to the realm of ultimate truth. The goal of the philosopher is to "climb" to the top of the palace and see reality as it truly is. When the image of the palace next appears, it represents reality with the ordinary values reversed: the structure that the philosopher once had to climb through a laborious process of conventional study becomes a palace seen in a dream. The physical act of climbing gives way to an instantaneous cognitive transformation. All a person has to do is wake up from the palace image as if waking up from a dream. When the palace image appears for the last time, it represents conventional reality regained in the form of illusion. The advanced bodhisattva uses the palace as it would be perceived in ordinary consciousness—once again it is a palace that functions as a site for worship—but now the bodhisattva has the ability to create the palace out of thin air.

Philosophy as a Cognitive Quest

If the movement through these three stages of thought has the appearance of an imaginative journey, this is not entirely accidental. One of the most basic metaphors in Indian philosophy is that of the path or quest. This image is embedded in the language of Indian philosophy just as deeply as the image of reality as a palace, and its effect on Bhāvaviveka's thought is just as important. Bhāvaviveka attacks one of his philosophical rivals, for example, by saying:

> Everything the Buddha taught is authoritative for us because a good person *makes progress* from the authoritative teaching of someone who is worthy of trust.
>
> Our opponent's mind has been confused and misled by other scriptures, so, for him to *make progress*, it is necessary to *follow* a rational *approach*.[3]

The struggle between Bhāvaviveka and his opponent is cast in the form of a metaphorical journey, and the point of the argument is to force the opponent to make "progress" (*pratipatti*). The word "progress" could just as easily be translated "understanding," if we were willing to overlook the sense of motion in the root *pad-*.[4] *Pratipatti* ("progress") is related etymologically to the word *pratipad*, a word that is often translated "path" but that could just as well be translated "the way to proceed."[5] In the second verse, the word "approach" (*naya*) indicates a way of "leading" (*nī-*) toward a goal.[6] Bhāvaviveka reinforces the element of motion in the word by saying that the approach has to be "followed" (*mṛgya*), just as a deer is stalked on the hunt. Bhāvaviveka's title for the chapter, "The Quest for the Knowledge of Reality" (*tattvajñānaiṣaṇā*), does not use the language of a journey directly, but it does suggest the quest for a new form of knowledge. It is only when he begins the chapter itself that Bhāvaviveka gives the quest a spatial location and speaks of it as a way of climbing the steps of ordinary knowledge in order to get to the top of the palace of reality.

The sense of motion is common in Indian words for knowledge—so common, in fact, that the metaphor almost disappears from view in ordinary usage.[7] But in the hands of a philosopher and poet like Bhāvaviveka, the word pictures come back to life. When Bhāvaviveka speaks of the philosophers *climbing* palace steps in order to know reality or *following* a rational *approach* the way hunters would search for a wild animal, the philosophy moves out of the realm of abstract argument and takes on the dramatic structure of a story. It is an abstract story, of course, without names and places, but the development of the metaphors marks a process of intellectual development that someone might actually follow—a passage from a state of ordinary, deluded consciousness to a state of consciousness where it is possible to shape reality to one's own will.

The "desire for knowledge" that sets this quest in motion often is important enough to appear in the title or in the language of the first line. In Bhāvaviveka's chapter on his own philosophy, it is part of the title, "The Quest [or the Desire] for the Knowledge of Reality" (*tattvajñānaiṣaṇā*). In the root text of the Vedānta school, the *Brahmasūtras*, the element of desire is present in the first line: "Now then [there is] a desire for the knowledge of Brahman" (*athāto brahmajijñāsā*).[8] This line from the *Brahmasūtras* shows, in schematic form, the desire for knowledge follows a narrative sequence.

Knowledge grows from a preparatory discipline and confronts the reader as a goal that needs to be realized by an extended course of study.[9] In the introduction to his commentary on the *Brahmasūtras*, Śaṅkara starts the narrative of the quest in what seems to be a confrontation between two people. Thibaut's standard translation of Śaṅkara's opening line goes like this: "It is a matter not requiring any proof that the object and the subject whose respective spheres are the notion of the 'Thou' (the Non-Ego) and the 'Ego,' and which are as opposed to each other as much as darkness and light are, cannot be identified."[10] But Śaṅkara's Sanskrit has almost a colloquial flavor, especially when the words are read in their original order. In a conversational style, the Sanskrit would sound something like this: "When it comes to a consideration of you and me (*yuṣmad-asmat-pratyaya-gocarayor*), the object and the subject (*viṣaya-viṣayiṇos*), like darkness and light (*tamaḥ-prakāśa-vad-*), are contradictory (*viruddha-svabhāvayor*) and cannot be identified (*itaretarabhāvānupapattau*)—this is established (*siddhāyām*)." It is as if Śaṅkara were starting by pointing at the student and then pointing at himself. The effect is to say, "First there is you, then there is me. We are what people refer to as the object and the subject, and we are as different as darkness and light."

By putting this opening phrase in the locative case, Śaṅkara makes it the presupposition for the argument that follows. As Thibaut's translation shows, the distinction between "you" and "me" corresponds to the distinction between the nonself and the self, the distinction on which the Vedānta arguments about the individual self (*jīva*) and the absolute Self (*ātman*) are based. But behind this philosophical point is another point about a personal relationship—the encounter between a student and a teacher—where the quest for knowledge of Brahman is actualized and given concrete shape. "You" brings to mind all the anxious students who feel as if they are groping in the darkness while their teacher is bathed in light. To seek the knowledge of Brahman is implicitly to place oneself inside this relationship. A student has to find a teacher, with all of the social and psychological requirements that this relationship implies, and has to enter into a dialogue with the teacher about the meaning of the scriptures. Stripped down to its bare pedagogical essentials, this requirement does not suggest a complex story, but the lives of Indian saints show that the encounters between teachers and students could involve intense personal journeys in both a literal and a metaphorical sense. Simply to find the right teacher could take a lifetime, and to discover within oneself the right sense of conviction and receptivity could require purification for many lives.

Wendy Doniger O'Flaherty has argued that Indian narrative texts carry their own philosophical commentary with them the way a turtle carries its own shell, and she has pointed out that Western readers often find this combination of narrative and philosophy a source of confusion.[11] Someone whose assumptions about the nature of narrative have been formed by the traditions of European and American literature may come to Indian narrative texts expecting a continuous story. If this is the ideal model, Indian narrative texts like the *Mahābhārata* seem to be woefully disappointing. Instead of a continuous, unified story line, the reader finds a narrative that is perpetually broken and interrupted by arguments and philosophical digressions. Western scholars of Indian literature have often been tempted to treat these digressions as interpolations precisely because they seem to break the continuity of the story itself. O'Flaherty argues that the problems of digression and interpolation are not a function of the text but of the reader's Western expectations. Readers who come to the text from an Indian perspective, on the other hand, are well aware that it contains a mixture of what we in the West would call "philosophy" and "narrative," and they have no trouble treating the philosophical digressions as integral parts of the epic itself. What seems to us to be a story about the rivalry between two clans, punctuated by long digressions about the nature of Dharma, strikes Indian audiences as a long philosophical reflection punctuated by moments when the reflection crystallizes into narrative.

It is notoriously difficult to maintain arguments that are based on the concept of an ideal reader.[12] Whether the reader is "Western" or "Indian," he or she always seems to bear a suspicious resemblance to the person who constructs the argument. And the act of reading itself is not as simple as it seems, especially if it is broadened to include the dramatic enactments through which so many people in the Indian subcontinent have come to know the stories of the Indian epics. But there is no question that the modes of discourse we identify as "narrative" and "philosophy" are more deeply interwoven in Indian culture than they are in the literary traditions of the West. It is also clear that O'Flaherty's point about the Indian epics can be applied to the literature of Indian philosophy, but with the values reversed; in other words, if it is true to say that a "narrative" text like the *Mahābhārata* has an essential component of philosophy, it is just as true to say that a "philosophical" text like Bhāvaviveka's has an essential component of narrative. Our conventional expectations about literary genres tempt us to treat Bhāvaviveka's text as an example of what we call "philosophy" and to mine it for the epistemological and ontological arguments that establish his connection with other recognizable "philosophers." But this expectation obscures the narrative context in which the arguments are placed. It is not that the narrative element in the text is necessarily easy to see. Bhāvaviveka does not identify specific individuals, and he does not locate the characters in a specific temporal setting. But he does tell a story by reporting a sequence of events: he charts a passage and marks the stages of an intellectual quest. The quest is one that Buddhas have already enacted and one that can be enacted again by the reader who uses the narrative as a guide to his or her own illumination. In this respect, Bhāvaviveka's "story" is similar to the story of Sudhana's quest in *The Gaṇḍavyūha Sūtra*, or the story of Christian in John Bunyan's *The Pilgrim's Progress*, but without the same specificity of character and place.

A good way to see how deeply the idea of the quest is woven into the metaphorical texture of Bhāvaviveka's thought is to watch how he develops his image of philosophical "insight" or "illumination." Here we have to use the words for "vision," "insight," and "illumination" quite deliberately. They now seem lifeless in English, but they correspond precisely to the language Śaṅkara used to characterize the relationship between teacher and student, and they also correspond to metaphorical features in Bhāvaviveka's own philosophical quest. Both philosophers saw (or understood) understanding as vision, as you would expect in a philosophical tradition where the word we customarily translate as "philosophy" (*darśana*) literally means an act of "seeing."[13] It is not surprising to discover that Bhāvaviveka develops the metaphor of seeing through precisely the same stages we have already identified in his elaboration of the metaphor of the palace.

He starts "The Quest for the Knowledge of Reality" with a description of the philosopher's eyes:

> The one who has the eye of knowledge, not some other [eye], is the one who sees. So an intelligent person concentrates on the quest for the knowledge of reality.
>
> An intelligent person, even one who is blind, sees the three worlds without any obstruction. Such a person sees the things that he wants to see, whether they are far away, subtle, or concealed.[14]

The first mention of the eyes corresponds to the palace with its steps and tower. Here the eye of knowledge plays the role of the tower. It is the goal to which the intelligent readers of the text are meant to aspire but which is not yet within their grasp. In the second stage of Bhāvaviveka's argument, the function of the philosopher's eyes is reversed in a way that reflects the transformation of the palace of reality into a palace of dreams: the eyes become those that see nothing at all.

> Someone who gets rid of an eye disease and has eyes that are pure and clear does not see spots, hairs, flies, or a double image of the moon.
>
> Likewise, someone who gets rid of the eye disease of defilements and objects of cognition and has the clear eye of true knowledge does not see anything at all.[15]

In the last stage of the argument, the philosopher's eyes become the eyes of a bodhisattva who understands the illusory nature of things but who feels sympathy for the people who are caught in the web of their own illusions:

> [The bodhisattva] has climbed the mountain peak of wisdom and is free from grief, but looks with compassion on ordinary people who suffer and are burned by grief.
>
> Then, with an eye that is moist with compassion, [the bodhisattva] sees that [the wisdom-eyes of] ordinary people have been covered by an imaginary net created by the art of conceptual thought.[16]

The circle is completed, just as it was with the image of the palace, but here the final stage is a state of awareness rather than of action. The bodhisattva whose eyes fill with the tears of compassion sees the world the way others see it and is moved by its suffering, but also realizes that the vision is nothing but an illusion.

These verses about the bodhisattva's eyes bring us back to the traditional image of the saint on the mountain, but in this version the saint's attention is not focused inward toward the cavern. It moves outward toward the confusion and suffering in the valley below. This image of the saint on the mountaintop lies behind the generic cartoon saints with long beards and flowing robes who dispense wisdom to the few pilgrims hardy enough to make their way into their presence. But it is also a common image in the religious literature of India, as we find in the twelfth book of the *Mahābhārata:*

> When he has climbed the palace of wisdom, he [looks down on] people who grieve, without grieving himself, as if he were standing on a mountain and looking down on ignorant people on the earth [below].[17]

The *Mahābhārata* seems to be indebted to a nearly identical verse from an early Buddhist source, the *Dhammapada:*

> When the wise one by awareness expels unawareness,
> Having ascended the palace of wisdom,
> He, free from sorrow, steadfast,
> The sorrowing folk observes, the childish,
> As one standing on a mountain
> [Observes] those standing on the ground below.[18]

The verse descriptions of the saint on the mountaintop derive much of their impact from the symbolic identification of "palace," "mountain," and "temple," an identification that is implicit in Bhāvaviveka's verses about the eye of wisdom. At the beginning of the chapter, Bhāvaviveka speaks of "climbing the tower [or peak] of the palace of reality" (*tattva-prāsāda-śikharārohaṇam*). Near the end, he speaks of "climbing the peak of the Mount Meru of wisdom" (*prajñā-meru-śekharam ārūḍhaḥ*). The second formula is a transposition of the first, with "wisdom" substituted for "reality" and "Meru" substituted for "palace." The substitution would make little sense without the assumption that the palace or temple is a replica of the cosmic mountain.[19] I will say more in a later chapter about the other significant transposition in these two verses, the substitution of the word "wisdom" for the word "reality." (The equation of knowledge and reality is a symptom, among other things, of Bhāvaviveka's identification of the Buddha's awareness with reality itself.) For the moment, it is enough just to recognize how closely the metaphor of vision repeats the pattern established by the metaphor of the palace. To ascend the tower of the palace of reality is also to develop a standpoint or a mode of vision that makes all of reality become clear.

The Three-Part Structure of Bhāvaviveka's Argument

To make this point another way, we could say that the structure of cognition mirrors the structure of reality and mirrors it in two ways. Bhāvaviveka's metaphors involve a physical structure—a palace or a monumental feature of the natural landscape—where a person can have the experience of physical or cognitive ascent. To know reality is to "climb" it, and reality itself is the "structure" that is climbed. But the metaphors also involve structure in another sense. They chart a passage through three distinct stages of thought. The structures (or physical objects) on which the philosopher climbs also represent the structure (or logical pattern) that Bhāvaviveka uses to organize his own thought about knowledge and reality. It is as if Bhāvaviveka's understanding of reality *has* a structure because it *is* a structure, and vice versa. He thought of reality as a palace, a temple, and a mountain because he thought of the cognitive process as an ascending series of graded stages, and he thought of cognition as an ascent because of the spatial images that were built into the metaphorical structure of his own thought.

To name the three stages in Bhāvaviveka's thought, we could say that first there is a point for Bhāvaviveka where a person has to *assume* distinctions drawn from ordinary life. In the development of the palace metaphor, this is the moment when people notice that they are at the bottom of the steps and begin to reach for the top. In the metaphor of the eye, this is the moment when people realize they have to reach for a clarity of vision that they do not yet have. Then there is a stage where a person *denies* these distinctions. This is the stage that is associated with the palace of dreams and the eyes that see nothing at all. Finally, there is a stage in which a person *reappropriates* the distinctions of the first stage but in a transformed way. The palace becomes an object for a bodhisattva to use as an expression of devotion to the Buddha, and the eyes make it possible for a bodhisattva to see the suffering of others (and also to weep the tears of devotion). Reduced to a single, three-part formula, these are the stages of Bhāvaviveka's quest: there is an *assumption* of distinctions, followed by a *denial* of distinctions, and then by a *reappropriation* of distinctions that brings the quest to its conclusion and at the same time returns it to the point from which it began.

Simply naming the stages does not tell us, however, why Bhāvaviveka's metaphors fall so clearly into this three-part pattern. What is it about the movement of Bhāvaviveka's thought that expresses itself so naturally in these three stages? To understand the reasoning behind this pattern requires a look through the metaphors to the arguments they express. The chapter where these metaphors appear includes a total of 360 verses. In these 360 verses, Bhāvaviveka discusses almost all the major categories that a Buddhist philosopher of his era and scholastic affiliation would be expected to consider. The verses move from the gross elements, such as earth and fire, to nirvana, and from the simple practice of breath control to the attainment of the three

Bodies of a Buddha. The chapter is an impressive, detailed account of Madhyamaka thought. But for all its detail, the argument of the chapter follows precisely the same stages suggested by Bhāvaviveka's treatment of the two metaphors. The chapter has a section that assumes ordinary distinctions. It has a section that denies distinctions. Then it shows how Buddhas and bodhisattvas reappropriate distinctions as they situate themselves on the path toward enlightenment.

The first stage of the argument is covered by the first twenty verses, two of which I have already quoted. Bhāvaviveka starts with his description of the eye of knowledge, then goes on to distinguish between the vision of ordinary people and the vision that belongs to someone who is wise:

> The one who has the eye of knowledge, not some other [eye], is the one who sees. So an intelligent person concentrates on the quest for the knowledge of reality.
>
> An intelligent person, even one who is blind, sees the three worlds without any obstruction. Such a person sees the things that he wants to see, whether they are far away, subtle, or concealed.
>
> Without intelligence, even the one who has a thousand eyes is blind because he does not see the right and wrong paths to heaven and liberation.
>
> Someone who has opened the eye of wisdom does not enter into [the practice of] generosity and so forth as if they were thorns poisoned with the desire for visible, invisible, special, or desirable results.
>
> Such a person is disciplined in generosity and so forth, pure in three ways, with compassion as the motivation and omniscience as the goal, yet such a person does not fix the mind on that [goal].
>
> Wisdom is the ambrosia that brings satisfaction, the lamp whose light cannot be obscured, the steps on the palace of liberation, and the fire [that burns] the fuel of the defilements.[20]

It would be difficult to tell from the first three of these verses what kind of knowledge Bhāvaviveka has in mind. The "knowledge eye" only refers to knowledge (*jñāna*) in the generic sense. This knowledge might just as well be the skill of an artisan or the learning that comes from studying any of the other Indian philosophical schools. The word "intelligence" also refers to knowledge in the general sense rather than to a form of knowledge that is associated with a particular Buddhist discipline or school.[21] But in the fourth verse, Bhāvaviveka begins to fill the concept of knowledge with a distinctively Buddhist meaning. To be truly "intelligent," a person has to open the eye of "wisdom" (*prajñā*)—and not just any wisdom but the specific wisdom that completes the virtues, which begin with "generosity" (*dāna*), and that turns them into "perfections" (*pāramitā*).

To Bhāvaviveka's Buddhist readers, the image of wisdom as the completion of the perfections would have been immediately recognizable. A number of the most basic sūtras of the Mahāyāna speak of the perfection of wisdom (*prajñā-pāramitā*) as the eye or guide that leads the other perfections to their goal. A particularly charming pair of verses describes the perfection of wisdom not only as the guide that leads the other perfections to the city of enlightenment but also as the eye that brings the painting of a deity to life.

> How could a vast number of people ever find their way into a city when they have been blind from birth, have no guide, and do not know the way? Without wisdom the five perfections are blind, have no guide, and cannot reach enlightenment.
>
> When they have gotten hold of wisdom, they receive their sight and can be called by the name ["perfection"]. They are like a painting that is finished in every way except for the eyes: [the painter] receives no payment until [he] paints the eyes.[22]

Bhāvaviveka must have had this idea of wisdom as the eye of the perfections in mind when he wrote his own verses, but he gives the image a distinctive twist. The five perfections that begin with generosity are not just a group of blind people waiting for a leader but a place where people without wisdom risk being torn apart by poisoned thorns. In the commentary, Bhāvaviveka explains that some people engage in generosity out of hope that they will receive some immediate benefit in this life. Others are generous in the hope that they will benefit in a future life. But even the greatest acts of generosity cause suffering if they are based on a desire for reward. They inevitably turn around and wound the person who performs them. Only the person who has wisdom can "enter" (*pravartate*) these thorns and not be torn apart. It is not just that the would-be perfections risk going astray; they are also a vicious snare. They are like the jaws of samsara itself. Without wisdom, one cannot engage in even the most elementary acts of altruism and come out unscathed.

After Bhāvaviveka has focused his attention on the perfection of wisdom, he distinguishes wisdom into two separate types: the conventional and the ultimate. Conventional wisdom he defines as the wisdom that is "consistent with the distinction of real things" (*bhūtārtha-pravivekānuguṇya*).[23] The key phrase, "the distinction of real things," is reminiscent of the definition of wisdom in the Abhidharma ("the distinguishing of *dharmas*"),[24] but Bhāvaviveka develops the distinctions involved in conventional wisdom in a way that is more characteristic of the Mahāyāna. He explains that conventional wisdom is the wisdom that fulfills the "accumulation" (*saṃbhāra*) of merit and knowledge. By this he means that a bodhisattva uses conventional wisdom to assemble the qualities necessary to attain perfect enlightenment. Then he adds two more characteristics to the list: conventional wisdom is used to discriminate causes and effects and to practice the Mahāyāna virtues of great compassion and commiseration. To define ultimate wisdom, he simply turns the approach he used for conventional wisdom upside down. Whenever conventional wisdom creates distinctions, ultimate wisdom breaks them down. Ultimate wisdom negates all concepts and confronts reality in a way that is free from all distinctions.

It is only at this point in the argument, after he has laid out the distinction between the two kinds of wisdom, that Bhāvaviveka introduces his description of reality as a palace. Conventional wisdom, with its distinctions between different categories, is the staircase, and ultimate wisdom is the top of the tower itself. He has already planted the suggestion that the ascent of this tower will not be an easy one, but he avoids any possible misunderstanding by explaining that the palace cannot be climbed all at once. No one fulfills the perfections (in the first six bodhisattva stages), the masteries (in the eighth stage), and the superknowledges (in the tenth stage) without practicing for seven countless eons on the steps of correct relative wisdom.[25]

Bhāvaviveka brings the introductory stage of his argument to a close with several verses on the mental discipline that prepares for the contemplation of ultimate truth:

> An intelligent person should be disciplined in the concentration of the mind and also in the knowledge that comes from hearing [the teaching of others] because this is [the knowledge] that causes other forms of knowledge.
>
> No one sees [his or her] face [reflected] in muddy or turbulent water, and [no one sees] reality in a mind that is unconcentrated and covered with obstructions.
>
> When the mind strays like an elephant from the right path, it should be bound to the post of the object [of meditation] with the rope of mindfulness and brought slowly under control with the hook of wisdom.[26]

In his commentary on these verses, Bhāvaviveka explains what he means by mental concentration by giving a short outline of the discipline of breath control. He says that practitioners should start concentrating the mind by counting the exhaled breaths from ten to a hundred, then back to ten. As the breath flows out, they should be mindful that the exhaled breath carries with it the musty smell of the body. As the breath flows in, they should be aware that the breath is sweet, short, and cold. As the breath flows back and forth, they should be aware that it moves from the navel to the tip of the nose and circulates through the entire body. When people have clarified the mind by controlling the breath, they can move on to the next step in the development of wisdom, the step of study and analysis. Bhāvaviveka mentions explicitly only the first part of this process, the wisdom that comes from hearing the teaching of others (*śrutamayī prajñā*). In the traditional scheme of the three forms of wisdom, this has to be followed by the wisdom that comes from analysis (*cintāmayī prajñā*) and the wisdom that comes from repeated practice (*bhāvanāmayī prajñā*). The second and third of these three forms of wisdom are what Bhāvaviveka means when he speaks of "other forms of knowledge."

The barrage of distinctions in the opening section of Bhāvaviveka's chapter may seem odd to someone who associates Madhyamaka philosophy with a doctrine of rigid nondualism. But the tone of these verses is not unlike the tone of introductory passages in the texts of other philosophical schools. In some ways, it is essential to begin a philosophical argument, whether it is written in the Indian or the Western style, by saying that there are different ways of understanding reality and that some of these ways are more true than others. It would be difficult to find a precise parallel between Bhāvaviveka's regimen for the concentration of the mind and the normal prerequisites for a philosophy course in a Western university, but it should be clear that analytical philosophy does not yield its secrets to an unfocused mind. In any case, it is common, even in the schools of Indian philosophy that are formally characterized as nondualistic, to assume that a student must begin philosophical study by distinguishing right knowledge from wrong. In Śaṅkara's nondualistic Vedānta, the more advanced stages of nondualistic understanding presuppose an ability to "distinguish" (*viveka*) what is eternal from what is not.[27] Students have to be clear about *this* distinction before they can go on to learn how distinctions do not apply. The same is true in the works of the Yogācāra philosophers who were Bhāvaviveka's chief Mahāyāna opponents. In the text known as *The Distinction Between the Middle and the Extremes* (*Madhyāntavibhāga*), there is a claim that all dualities are unreal, but the title of the text itself shows that correct understanding of nonduality requires the right distinction—the distinction between a view that is correctly balanced and a view that is subject to extremes. The text argues that some positions go too far in denying the dualities of ordinary consciousness and that some do not go far enough, but the correct position strikes a balance between these two extremes.[28]

The most important preliminary distinction in Bhāvaviveka's Madhyamaka system is the distinction between the two truths, as Nāgārjuna explains in *The Root Verses on the Middle Way*:

> Buddhas rely on two truths when they teach the Dharma: ordinary relative truth and ultimate truth.
>
> Those who do not understand the distinction between these two truths do not understand the profound point of the Buddhas' teaching.
>
> No one can teach the ultimate without relying on conventional usage, and no one can attain nirvana without understanding the ultimate.[29]

When Bhāvaviveka speaks of "climbing" the steps of correct relative wisdom to reach the tower of the palace of reality, he is elaborating Nāgārjuna's idea of "relying" on conventional usage. The image Bhāvaviveka uses is more concrete and suggests a more complex series of stages, but the spatial dimension of the metaphor is the same. A person has to assume or be "based upon" (*āśritya*) the distinctions of conventional usage in order to understand or "come to" (*āgam-*) ultimate truth. Exactly what it means to say that someone has to "assume" conventional distinctions posed a considerable problem for Madhyamaka philosophers in Bhāvaviveka's time and in later centuries. In fact, it was one of the problems that led eventually to the division of the Madhyamaka tradition into rival factions.[30] But it is true to say that all Mādhyamikas, regardless of their scholastic affiliation, have to assume (in some sense of the word) that there is a distinction between right and wrong knowledge before they can go on to show that all distinctions are ultimately false.

Bhāvaviveka's next step, after he has assumed the necessary preliminary distinctions, is to scrutinize the different categories that philosophers in his tradition used to build their philosophical systems. The point of the scrutiny is to show that all these categories, including the positive categories of his own school, are ultimately false. Bhāvaviveka frames his arguments in the mechanical, syllogistic style that eventually got him into trouble with his Madhyamaka critics, and the demands of philosophy in his own day often take him far beyond the arguments Nāgārjuna left behind, but his feet are still firmly planted in the central doctrines of the Madhyamaka tradition. It would be possible to understand almost all the arguments in this section of his chapter as an extended footnote on the first verse of Nāgārjuna's *Root Verses on the Middle Way*:

> Nothing ever arises anywhere from itself, from something else, from both, or from no cause at all.

Nāgārjuna's verse is a critique of the idea of real causation, although it does not actually use the Sanskrit equivalent of the word "causation." It is common in Madhyamaka texts to speak of "origination" or "arising" (*utpāda*), or the longer formula "dependent origination" or "dependent arising" (*pratītya-samutpāda*), rather than to speak of causation directly. But the point is the same. Nothing can come into being from itself, from anything else, or from any combination of itself and anything else. When Bhāvaviveka applies this point to specific cases, he uses two more critical terms. To say that things do not arise is to say that they have no "identity" or "own-being" (*svabhāva*), and something that does not arise with any "identity" or "own-being" is "empty" (*śūnya*) of "identity." The last term is the one that gives the distinctive doctrine of the Madhyamaka school its name. Madhyamaka philosophers are called Śūnyavādins, "the ones who hold the doctrine of Emptiness." When Bhāvaviveka shows that the categories of reality do not arise and thus cannot stand up to rational analysis, he is working out the critical implications of the doctrine of Emptiness.

Bhāvaviveka begins his consideration of Emptiness with some remarks about what it means to analyze something from the ultimate point of view; then he constructs a formal syllogism about the nature of earth:

> After concentrating the mind, a person should wisely ask the following question: One grasps the identity of things conventionally, but when this [identity] is analyzed intelligently, is it [also grasped] ultimately? If so, it is [ultimate] reality. If [ultimate reality] is something other than this, it should be sought [elsewhere]. . . .

> The aggregate of material form is investigated first because of its coarseness, and in the category [of material form] the gross elements are [investigated] first for the same reason.
>
> Here [among the gross elements], earth and so forth do not ultimately have the identity of elements because they are conditioned or because they have causes and so forth, as in the case of cognition.[31]

The syllogism is only the first step in Bhāvaviveka's quest for ultimate truth, but it gives a clear example of the way he plays the varieties of wisdom off against each other to move from the conventional view of reality to the ultimate. He argues that earth and the other gross elements do not have the identity of gross elements (which is to say that they are *not* gross elements) precisely because they depend on causes other than themselves to come into existence. But how do they come into existence, if they ultimately have no identity? The answer is that they arise only from the conventional point of view. The two different perspectives meet and overlap in the same argument. The elements do not come into existence from the standpoint of ultimate wisdom, but they do come into existence from the standpoint of conventional wisdom. (Remember that Bhāvaviveka earlier defined conventional wisdom as the wisdom that grasps the causal connection between things.) From the point of view of ultimate wisdom, or from the point of view of someone who uses rational analysis to determine the actual "identity" of a thing, the elements do not come into existence at all.[32]

The relationship between ultimate and conventional truth is one of the most difficult points to follow in Madhyamaka thought, and it is hard to be precise about it without going further into the doctrines of the school than most people have either the time or inclination to do. But it is not difficult to understand the symmetry in the relationship between the two truths that made Bhāvaviveka develop his argument the way he did. Bhāvaviveka bases his analysis on the claim (some might call it an assumption) that if something actually has "identity" as an object in its own right, it cannot change. It simply is what it is and cannot become anything else. The only way to account for the apparent causal connection between things and for all the possible changes a person can experience, from rebirth in the lowest hell to the attainment of nirvana, is to assume that nothing that seems to change or to enter into causal relationships is anything in its own right. Things only arise conventionally, like a dream, by depending on other things that are just as conventional and illusory as themselves.

This concept of reality had a number of important consequences for Bhāvaviveka. It meant first that things can be approached from two different perspectives, and the two different perspectives yield different results. You can ask about the events of conventional reality the way you can ask about the configuration of a palace in a dream. How many floors does it have? What is the shape of the courtyard? Who built the palace? What materials were used to build it? The questions can go on and on, and as long as you stay within the limits of the dream, all the questions can have an answer. But as soon as you step out of the dream, the questions no longer produce the same kind of answer. To someone who is awake, there is no palace. It has no floors and no courtyard. No one built it, and nothing was used to build it. Whether the palace "exists" or not depends on the perspective from which you ask the questions. The opponents of the Madhyamaka school sometimes seize on the contrast between these two perspectives to make some easy debating points at the Mādhyamikas' expense. They accuse the Mādhyamikas of contradicting themselves by saying that something exists and does not exist at the same time.[33] Admittedly this position does require some explanation, but it is not that difficult to defend. There are any number of things in ordinary experience whose identity depends on the perspective from which they are approached. As one of Bhāvaviveka's successors said some centuries later, "What is ultimate for one is relative for another, just as one person's mother is considered another person's wife."[34]

It is easy to see how the doctrine of two truths grows from the application of two different perspectives. What is more difficult to understand is how the two perspectives are related. If the two perspectives are as different as dreaming and waking, how can the experience of one have any relationship to an experience of the other? In a sense the answer to this question is simple. The conventional experience of a palace is radically different from the ultimate experience of a palace. In fact, even the claim that there can be an "ultimate" experience of a palace is nothing more than a reflection of conventional experience. Ultimately there is no "ultimate" experience of a palace. But, while there is no relationship in reality between the two perspectives, there is a logical relationship that tells a great deal about both. If something arises conventionally, it has to be subject to change, and something that is subject to change cannot exist ultimately. If something does exist ultimately, it cannot change and thus cannot arise conventionally. So the relationship between the two truths can be understood to mean not only that the palace both *is* (conventionally) and *is not* (ultimately) but that it *is* (conventionally) *precisely because it is not* (ultimately) and vice versa. It is sometimes said that Madhyamaka philosophers affirm the conventional reality of things *in spite of* the fact that they are ultimately unreal. Actually, the Madhyamaka claim is stronger than this. It is precisely *because* things are unreal ultimately that they are real conventionally, as Nāgārjuna said in *The Root Verses on the Middle Way*: "Everything is possible for someone for whom Emptiness is possible. Nothing is possible for someone for whom Emptiness is not possible."[35]

In his elaboration of the concept of Emptiness, Bhāvaviveka extends his critique step by step from the category of earth and the gross elements to other categories accepted by other schools of Indian thought. After he has denied the identity of material form (*rūpa*), he denies the existence of the sense organ that takes material form as its object:

> The eye does not ultimately see form because it is different from the mind and the phenomena that are associated with the mind, like the sense of taste.

> Or the eye does not ultimately see form because [the act of seeing] cannot arise in something that is unconscious, like skin and so forth.[36]

He then constructs a series of arguments to deny the identity of three other constituents of the personality, "feeling" (*vedanā*), "ideas" (*saṃjñā*), and "consciousness" (*vijñāna*). He criticizes the existence of motion, bondage and liberation, the person and the self, passion and nirvana, and "identity" itself. When he has finished his critique of conditioned (*saṃskṛta*) things, he moves on to the category of things that are not conditioned (*asaṃskṛta*), a category in which he lists a total of four items: two types of cessation, space, and Thusness.[37]

When Bhāvaviveka has finished his critique of individual categories, he turns his attention to causation itself. Through a series of verses too long to repeat here, he denies that there can be any coherent explanation of the causal relationship, whether it is the explanation, associated with the Sāṃkhya school, that things arise from themselves or an explanation that results arise from causes that are different from themselves. He singles out the doctrine of God (*īśvara*) for special criticism in a group of nine verses.[38] Then he summarizes his own understanding of causation:

> Ultimately nothing is existent, nonexistent, or anything else, and nothing arises or is manifested in any way from itself, from something else, from both, or from nothing at all, from Viṣṇu, from Śiva, from Puruṣa, from Primal Matter, from atoms, and so forth.
>
> All concepts of this [dependent arising] also [do not arise], just as a whip stroke, a painting, or a sprout do not appear in the sky. [These concepts] are based on identities, actions, the things that possess certain characteristics, and the characteristics themselves. They are based on identity and difference, and the actions of defilement and purification.[39]

It is at this climactic point in the argument, when Bhāvaviveka has made his most inclusive statement about the possibility of causation, that he returns to the metaphor of the eye and says that true vision is the vision that is no vision.

Bhāvaviveka's choice of the imagery of vision at this point in the text is partly a function of his fondness for visual metaphors, but he is also influenced by traditional formulas that appear in the texts of the sūtras. Bhāvaviveka introduces the concept of dependent arising through the words of an opponent who takes literally the scriptural statement that someone who "sees" dependent arising "sees" the Dharma.[40] The opponent argues that if there is no dependent arising, it is impossible for anyone to see the Dharma. Without dependent arising, not only would the sūtras be contradicted but the whole cognitive quest that is expressed in the metaphor of vision would be meaningless. Bhāvaviveka pursues the point about the vision of dependent arising in a way that mirrors the point he made about material form earlier in the chapter. Material form is the object of the sense of sight; so, if there is nothing for the eye to see, there can be no seeing. The same is true of dependent arising. If nothing arises, then to see dependent arising correctly is not to see. The verses that introduce and follow Bhāvaviveka's final definition of dependent arising thus contain his most elaborate reflection on what it means, in the ultimate sense, to see.

> If [dependent] arising does not exist, does not not exist, and does not both [exist and not exist], what kind of thing can it be? How can anyone think that he sees the Teacher by seeing this [dependent arising]?
>
> . . . By removing the stains of errors [others] have made and being illuminated by the rays of the true Dharma, one sees the Buddha in a relative and beneficial way.
>
> [But] ultimately [this seeing] is no seeing because whatever is illusory is nonexistent. [Dependent arising] cannot be analyzed, discerned, compared, or specified.
>
> It has no cognitive marks, no image, no concept, and no expression. Someone who sees it and understands it with wisdom sees it by not seeing. . . .
>
> Someone who gets rid of an eye disease and has eyes that are pure and clear does not see spots, hairs, flies, or a double image of the moon.
>
> Likewise, someone who gets rid of the eye disease of defilements and objects of cognition and has the clear eye of true knowledge does not see anything at all.
>
> Someone who feels drowsy and falls asleep sees such things as young men, women, and a palace, but does not see them when he wakes up.
>
> Likewise, someone who has opened the wisdom-eye, stopped the sleep of ignorance, and woken up does not see things as they are seen conventionally.
>
> On a dark night someone may see ghosts that are unreal, but when the sun comes up and he opens his eyes, he does not see [them].
>
> Likewise, when an intelligent person has destroyed all the traces of ignorance with the sun of true knowledge, he does not see mind and associated mental phenomena as real.
>
> He does not see things as having any individual identity, because they have no absolute identity and do not arise in their own right, like a magic elephant.
>
> He does not see things as having any individual identity, because they do arise conventionally and have a cause, like a magic elephant.[41]

At the end of this discussion of dependent arising, Bhāvaviveka turns his attention to the concept of Emptiness itself:

> Emptiness is empty of any identity such as "Emptiness," so someone who is wise does not see Emptiness as "Emptiness."[42]

By this time, the argument has developed such powerful momentum that its meaning is hard to miss, even when the formulation of individual verses is obscure. When Bhāvaviveka gets to this verse about Emptiness, he has just finished saying that everything is empty. He has even shown that the absence of anything is also empty. Finally, he turns the argument on Emptiness itself, and he shows that Emptiness is no less empty than anything else. The process of negation seems so relentless and so complete that it is difficult to imagine what could possibly be said next, much less fill the more than ninety verses left in the chapter, but the question "What comes after Emptiness?" is one about which Bhāvaviveka and his fellow Mādhyamikas had a surprising amount to say.

The form of the answer is suggested by an episode in the life of one of Bhāvaviveka's Mādhyamika successors, the philosopher Śāntideva. Legendary accounts of Śāntideva's life tell us that he was devoted to mental concentration and "meditated on the light" without interruption, even while he was walking, eating, and sleeping.[43] One of Śāntideva's fellow monks took his constant meditation as a sign of laziness and decided to challenge him to a public test. On a particular day of the year when the monastery gathered to recite the Dharma, the monk had a high seat set up outside the monastery and invited Śāntideva to sit down and demonstrate his understanding of the scriptures. Śāntideva agreed and asked whether the monks wanted to hear a compendium of selections from the scriptures, the work that became his *Compendium of Instruction* (*Śikṣāsamuccaya*), or his own interpretation of the meaning of the scriptures, the work that became his *Introduction to the Bodhi[sattva] Practice* (*Bodhi[sattva]caryāvatāra*).[44] His fellow monks asked him, perhaps with some derision, to recite his own interpretation. Śāntideva began to recite a text that has become one of the most honored, poetic accounts of the bodhisattva path in the Sanskrit language. When he reached the thirty-fifth verse of the ninth chapter, he said, "When neither being nor nonbeing is present before the mind, then, because there is no other possibility, [the mind] has no object and is at peace."[45] At that moment, the bodhisattva Mañjuśrī appeared in front of him, and the two of them rose into the heavens together. Normally you would think that Śāntideva's extraordinary exit would mark the end of the text, but the text in fact does not end. The monks in Śāntideva's audience left the assembly where Śāntideva had been teaching, went to his cell, and discovered that Śāntideva had left behind a text that continued for well over a hundred verses.

When they opened the leaves Śāntideva had left behind, they found that he went on from his statement about nothing (and no nothing) being present to the mind to talk about the vision of the Buddha:

> Like a wishing jewel or a wishing tree that grants desires, the form of the Buddha is seen because someone is ready to be taught and because of a [previous] vow.

> A dealer in antidotes may die after consecrating a pillar, but [the pillar] cures [the effect of] poison and so forth long after his death.
>
> A Buddha is like such a pillar. He is created by following the practice of enlightenment, and he accomplishes everything that needs to be accomplished, even after the bodhisattva [who followed the practice of enlightenment] has ceased.[46]

The leap from the analysis of Emptiness to the image of a wishing jewel or an antidote to cure snakebite may seem strange, perhaps even incomprehensible, but not if we remind ourselves that Śāntideva is not talking about Emptiness merely as an abstract concept. He is talking about the powers that come to the person who understands it. Emptiness is the nature of things (and the fact that things have no nature), but it is also the content of the Buddha's understanding at the moment of enlightenment. In the story of the Buddha's career, the final understanding of Emptiness may mark the end of one phase of activity, but it also marks the beginning of another. The Buddha does not understand Emptiness and then fade gently from the scene. By understanding the nature of things and making this understanding present in a particular place, the Buddha creates a source of revelation, a locus of power, and an object of worship. This, at least, is what Śāntideva implies when he speaks of the Buddha's body as a wishing jewel or wishing tree that grants all desires.

Bhāvaviveka makes the same move in his own account of Emptiness. After the verse on the emptiness of Emptiness, he takes up the discussion of the Buddha. There may not be much more to say about Emptiness directly, but Bhāvaviveka still has a lot to say about what he calls "the innumerable, immeasurable, astonishing abundance of virtues" associated with the being who perfectly understands Emptiness.[47] He starts his account of the Buddha in a critical style that grows directly from the description of Emptiness in the previous section. Then he shifts to a discussion of the bodhisattva path, as if he were returning to the distinctions out of which the concept of Buddhahood arises. Finally, at the end of the chapter, he takes up the effect Buddhas have on others through the manifestation of the Buddha Bodies.

It is not necessary to quote the verses from this part of the chapter in detail. Unlike the verses in the two earlier parts, these verses are all found in the translation at the end of this book. But it is worth noting how the flavor of this section of the chapter differs from the flavor of the earlier sections. Bhāvaviveka starts his account of the Buddha in verse 266 with a definition of reality (*tattva*) that sounds like an extension of the argument about dependent arising. He defines reality as "that of which no cognition arises."[48] The formula is one that occurs frequently in Madhyamaka texts at precisely the point where the philosopher denies any reality even to reality itself. Here the formula functions as a bridge between the emptiness of Emptiness in verse 265 and the discussion of Buddhahood that follows. Verse 267 then defines the Buddha simply as the no-arising of any cognition:

> The no-arising of cognition that is called "Buddha" because it is the understanding of this [reality] is the primary [Buddha] because it is the understanding that is no-understanding and because it dispels the sleep of concepts.[49]

In the next few verses, he extends the same negative mode of definition to a series of common epithets for the Buddha, such as Sambuddha, Tathāgata, and Sugata. The Sambuddha (the one who has "understood equally") is one whose equal understanding is no-understanding, and the Sugata (the one who has "understood well") is one whose good understanding is no-understanding.[50] After discussing a series of adjectives that are sometimes used to describe the Buddha in the negative mode, adjectives such as "immeasurable," "incalculable," and "inconceivable," he brings his definition of the Buddha to a close with a verse about the uniqueness of the Buddha's enlightenment:

> [We] consider [The Dharma Body] to be the Tathāgata's Body because it is not different in nature from [the Tathāgata] and because it is the reality that [the Tathāgata] has understood. And [we] do not [consider] it to be anyone else's [body] because [others] do not understand it.[51]

The next fifty-four verses contain Bhāvaviveka's description of the bodhisattva path, including a discussion of the six perfections (developed in the first six stages of the path), the ten masteries (developed in the eighth stage), and the six superknowledges (developed in the tenth stage). When the account of the path is over, we get another fifteen verses describing the Buddha from the point of view of a devotee who sees the Buddha's form and hears his teaching. From this perspective the Buddha appears not as the no-arising of thought but as a being who can open the mind with the rays of his teaching the way the sun brings a pond of lotuses to flower.[52]

The cumulative effect of these verses, from the definition of the Buddha in verse 267 to the final description of the Buddha's miraculous body and voice in verses 356–359, is quite different from the effect of earlier sections, especially when Bhāvaviveka warms to his description of the Buddha's and bodhisattvas' miraculous powers. Instead of the relentless march of syllogisms, there is a flood of elaborate imagery, the kind of imagery that is more often associated with hymns of praise than with works of philosophy.[53] When Bhāvaviveka stops to consider a particular category in greater detail, it is not to analyze it more carefully or to criticize it but to pile up layers of description and give an even more exalted impression of the Buddha's and bodhisattvas' attainments. He also adjusts his treatment of the path to emphasize the bodhisattvas' most impressive virtues. From all of the qualities a bodhisattva develops in innumerable eons on the path, Bhāvaviveka selects two lists that emphasize the element of power (*ṛddhi*)—the bodhisattvas' masteries (*vaśitā*) and superknowledges (*abhijñā*)—and he rearranges the elements in the lists to give power the most prominent place. He dismisses nine of the ten masteries, for example, in only five verses, then spends seventeen verses on the mastery of power (*ṛddhi-vaśitā*). In his account of the superknowledges, he dismisses four in only five verses, then devotes ten verses to the superknowledge of power (*ṛddhy-abhijñā*).[54] The ten verses on the superknowledge of power are the ones that give us, among other things, the image of the peaked dwellings offered by bodhisattvas to the Buddha.

It is no accident that the language of these final verses seems reminiscent of the language of Buddhist hymns. Bhāvaviveka has already said that Avalokiteśvara, Maitreya, Samantabhadra, Mañjuśrī, and the other great bodhisattvas of the tenth stage are worthy of sincere homage. In this section he says that the bodhisattvas themselves praise the Buddhas continually with hymns.[55] These final verses on the superknowledge of power—verses that also function as the final verses on the bodhisattva path—are Bhāvaviveka's last words of praise for the great celestial bodhisattvas of the Mahāyāna. Implicitly, of course, they are a way of giving the highest possible praise to the Buddha as well.

Points of Transition from One Stage in the Argument to Another

Now that we have the three-part pattern in Bhāvaviveka's argument in front of us, can we also identify the intellectual impulse that drives Bhāvaviveka through these stages? What is it that moves him so relentlessly, on both the metaphorical and the analytical level, through this process of assumption, denial, and reappropriation? To answer this question, we must focus more closely on the points where Bhāvaviveka makes the transition from one stage in the argument to another.

The first transition takes place when Bhāvaviveka asks this question: Are any of the things that are assumed in the first stage of the argument possible as things in their own right? The transition from the assumption of distinctions to their denial, or from conventional to ultimate truth, is difficult to define, but, for Bhāvaviveka himself, the move clearly involves an "analysis" (*vicāra*) in which he asks whether anything "ultimately" (*paramārthena*) has any "identity" (*svabhāva*).[56] What the words "analysis," "ultimately," and "identity" actually meant became the subject of great disagreement in the later history of the Madhyamaka school,[57] but Bhāvaviveka's question is not difficult to grasp on an intuitive level. It is just a reflection of the perennial question, "Is this all there is?" or "Is this really true?" The question comes from the desire to look at things more closely, analyze them in a more rational or consistent way, and find out what they really are. Concepts like "analysis," "reason," and "consistency," of course, are laden with presuppositions. What is consistent for one person is not necessarily consistent for another. But Bhāvaviveka's impulse at this stage of the argument is not so different from the impulse that drives the analytical tradition in Western philosophy. It is an impulse to penetrate beneath the surface of things and to do it with a sense of rational consistency that cuts through the errors and misconceptions of ordinary experience. As Bhāvaviveka works his way through the second stage of his argument, he forces this analytical project to its logical conclusion and shows that none of the distinctions assumed in conventional experience can finally be defended.

The problem with the analysis that occupies the second stage of Bhāvaviveka's argument is that it is intrinsically unstable. Following the argument through to its conclusion feels a bit like the game of "Chutes and Ladders." You make your way to the top of the board by a series of steps, each one of which follows directly from the last, and suddenly a trap door opens under your feet and drops you back where you started. From the point of view of Emptiness, none of the normal distinctions between things applies. But Emptiness itself is a distinct position, too, and when it is analyzed from the point of view of Emptiness, it also has to be empty. So the "intelligent" readers who have followed the argument faithfully through all of its stages finally see the last distinction, the distinction between distinction and no-distinction, vanish before their eyes. At the end they are left where they began. It is not that they can plunge into the distinctions of ordinary consciousness with the same naïveté as before, but they are aware that Emptiness ultimately is not different from the process of distinction-making with which they began. Nāgārjuna had this point in mind when he said, "Dependent arising is what we call Emptiness. It is a dependent designation, and it is the middle path."[58] Other Mādhyamikas make the point in a different way. But no matter how it is made, the point is crucial to Madhyamaka thought. Without denying the distinction between distinction and no-distinction, the concept of Emptiness would be essentially sterile. It would leave the philosopher trapped in a world of Emptiness *as opposed to* something else. But with the emptiness of Emptiness, the argument not only pushes the concept of Emptiness to its final limit; it also forces the transition from the stage of denial to the stage of reappropriation, the transition that returns the argument to the world of distinctions out of which it came.

This process may seem uncomfortably abstract, but it reflects the narrative movement of the journey toward enlightenment. Buddhas (or Buddhas-to-be) also go through a process that has three stages. They move out of the realm of suffering into a realm of insight, where they see through the illusions of conventional experience and understand the world for what it is; then they reengage the world they have left behind.[59] The different elements in this quest for enlightenment are crucial in shaping Bhāvaviveka's own response to Emptiness. As an abstraction, Emptiness is difficult to respond to with devotion, no matter how much freedom the logic of Emptiness may allow a philosopher in the world of ordinary experience. But Emptiness comes down to earth when it is embodied in a particular person. As Bhāvaviveka often points out when he is interpreting the verses of Nāgārjuna, Emptiness is a state of awareness, not just a state of being.[60] And it is a state of awareness that can be embodied in particular persons at particular times. When the analysis of Emptiness has moved to its conclusion, it is a natural consequence of the argument for Bhāvaviveka to turn his attention from Emptiness itself to the Buddha, the being in whom Emptiness is perfectly embodied.

Bhāvaviveka sets the stage for the transition with an objection about logical procedure. He has an opponent ask, "Is it not a form of philosophical nihilism to reject your opponent's position and not maintain a position of your own?"[61] But Bhāvaviveka does not confine his answer to the level of logical method. He takes the objection as a challenge to explain who the person is who understands and teaches the doctrine of Emptiness. He says that Mādhyamikas have a responsibility to explain not only what they think reality is but who the teacher is who understands reality. The definition of reality takes only a verse. The explanation of the teacher occupies, in one way or another, the rest of the chapter.

Bhāvaviveka's Ironical Point of View

Seeing the stages of the argument as a narrative process helps explain why Bhāvaviveka moves from one step to another, but it does not answer all the questions that could be raised about the three-part pattern that dominates his thinking about Buddhahood. If the pattern is so important and so pervasive in his reasoning, what kind of pattern is it? Is it a familiar pattern? Does it have any relationship to similar patterns of thought in other intellectual traditions? It is customary in Madhyamaka studies to speak of this way of thinking as a dialectic, for obvious reasons.[62] The assumption of conventional distinctions seems to function as a thesis, the denial of distinctions seems to function as an antithesis, and the reappropriation of distinctions seems to resolve the two antithetical positions in a new synthesis. The problem with this interpretation is the suggestion that there *is* a third position different from the other two. Bhāvaviveka certainly is not content to let the argument rest in Emptiness, and he clearly uses the third stage of the argument to reappropriate the distinctions that were denied in the second stage, but he does it in a way that is as much a step back as a step forward. The distinctions he goes back to are just the ones he left behind. The movement of the argument could just as well be understood as the interplay of two separate and contradictory points of view, rather than three. In the first stage, everything is viewed from a conventional perspective. In the second stage, everything is viewed from an ultimate perspective. In the last, the ultimate itself is viewed from a conventional perspective. What seems from one angle to be the third stage of a dialectic may, from another angle, be nothing more than the balancing of two different perspectives on the same thing.

This sense of balance and symmetry in Bhāvaviveka's approach to reality is reminiscent in some respects of the long struggle in modern French philosophy with the influence of Hegel.[63] His argument holds the perspectives of the two truths together simultaneously in a kind of double vision or, as Jacques Derrida would say, in a double register that permits no synthesis.[64] The Madhyamaka critique "deconstructs" in the sense that it brings to the surface the contradictions that lurk within particular systems of thought. It does not resolve the differences in a higher synthesis but unmasks the differences for what they are. Instead of the Hegelian *Aufhebung* that negates a previous position and conserves it by "lifting it up" to a higher level, there is a *différance* that "differs" and "defers" the contradiction without leading it to a higher synthesis.[65] The parallels between the two traditions of thought are intriguing, but there is no need to leave the Buddhist world to make the same critical point about the logic of dialectic. The Japanese philosopher Nishida Kitarō has also shown how misleading it is to assimilate the system of negations in Mahāyāna literature to a dialectical pattern.[66] Nishida argues that Mahāyāna texts like the *Diamond Sūtra* have a logic of their own—one that he calls the logic of "is" and "is not" (*soku hi*).[67] To say, "Because all dharmas are not all dharmas, therefore they are called all dharmas" or "Because there is no Buddha, there is Buddha," is not to transcend the contradiction between the two positions but to leave the contradiction in place. There is a claim that the opposites imply each other, as there is in Derrida's understanding of *différance*, but there is no claim of a resolution.

The best way to name this bipolar aspect of Madhyamaka thought might be to call it paradox rather than dialectic, particularly when we confront it in the language of the verses themselves. The structure of the Sanskrit language makes it particularly easy to transform a concept into its own negation by adding a single negative particle, *a-*. The rules of euphonic combination often make it possible to absorb the negative particle into a verse without changing the metrical structure of the verse itself. This allows an author to carry out a simple, symmetrical conversion of a verse in order to change an opponent's argument into its own negation. Nāgārjuna uses this linguistic device in a number of important places in *The Root Verses on the Middle Way* to convert his opponent's argument into an argument of his own, while still leaving the structure of the verse intact.[68] He begins the chapter on the four Noble Truths, for example, with an opponent's objection: "If everything is empty, there is no arising and no cessation, and it follows for you that the four Noble Truths do not exist." Several verses later he gives his own reply: "If everything is *not* empty, there is no arising and no cessation, and it follows for you that the four Noble Truths do not exist." He is able to make the change from one argument to the other just by changing *yadi śūnyam* in the first verse to *yady aśūnyam* in the second.

Bhāvaviveka sometimes uses the same rhetorical device to give different perspectives on the same concept within the limits of a single verse. He begins his definition of the Buddha in verse 267, for example, with the phrase "Because he understands this (*tad-bodhāt*) . . . he is called 'Buddha.'" The definition itself is a traditional formula that appears in Nāgārjuna's *Hymn to the Inconceivable* (*Acintyastava*): "This is considered reality, the ultimate, Thusness, and the real. It is an indisputable fact, and it is because he understands this that he is called 'Buddha.'"[69] In the hymn, Nāgārjuna leaves the concept of understanding intact, but Bhāvaviveka turns the concept upside down. In the second half of the verse, he explains that the Buddha is literally a Buddha because he has the understanding that is no-understanding (*abodha-bodha*). The effect of the formula is the same as the equation of "seeing" and "no-seeing" in his account of dependent arising. It is not that seeing or understanding are obliterated. We still can distinguish conventionally between true seeing and false seeing. But from the ultimate perspective, true seeing is no-seeing and true understanding is no-understanding.

When the conventional and ultimate perspectives operate side by side as they do in this verse, they also make possible multiple levels of paradox. It is not just that seeing is interchangeable with no-seeing but that the distinction between seeing and no-seeing is interchangeable with no-distinction between seeing and no-seeing. Bhāvaviveka plays on this possibility with great subtlety at the end of his most negative and critical account of the Buddha. The verse is one I have already quoted:

> [We] consider [the Dharma Body] to be the Tathāgata's Body because it is not different in nature from [the Tathāgata] and because it is the reality that [the Tathāgata] has understood. And [we] do not [consider] it to be anyone else's [body] because [others] do not understand it.

The closing formula of the verse ("because [others] do not understand it": *tad-abodhataḥ*) is a direct echo of the formula that began the definition of the Buddha ("because he understands this": *tad-bodhāt*). "Understanding" was the quality that made the Buddha a Buddha at the beginning; "no-understanding" is now the quality that makes others not Buddhas at the end. The same formula, with the simple insertion of a negative particle, frames the whole section and gives it a sense of balance and closure. But in between the two formulas, Bhāvaviveka has explained that the Buddha's understanding is precisely the understanding that is no-understanding. So, hidden in the last verse, but not so deeply hidden as to be imperceptible, is a message that those who have no understanding would be Buddhas themselves if they only knew what it meant truly not to understand.

The structure of paradox within paradox in so many of Bhāvaviveka's key verses makes it important to read the whole text with an ironical eye. It is as if Bhāvaviveka has embedded in the rhetorical structure of his language reminders always to look for another, contradictory level of meaning. The meaning is often quite clear, as it is in his comments about seeing and understanding. It may seem odd at first to hear that true seeing is no-seeing and that no-seeing is seeing, but the structure of the contrast is hard to miss. The point gets more complex when he says that true understanding is no-understanding and that no-understanding (if the no-understanding is understood correctly—that is, by no-understanding) is true understanding, but it is still comprehensible. There are moments, however, when Bhāvaviveka's meaning seems to recede into indeterminacy.

At one point in his account of the Buddha,[70] he equates the Dharma Body with the supreme Brahman of the Upaniṣads. The equation seems utterly foreign in a Buddhist text, even in one that is as inclusive of other perspectives as this. At least it seems foreign until Bhāvaviveka begins to add layers of irony. If Brahman is equivalent to the Dharma Body, how does a Buddhist go about worshiping it? Bhāvaviveka says that Avalokiteśvara and the great bodhisattvas of the tenth stage worship it by the discipline of no-worship. On one level, the point seems perfectly straightforward. Bhāvaviveka seems to be saying that anyone who thinks a Buddhist would worship Brahman is sadly mistaken. The only way to approach Brahman correctly is not to worship it. But we also know that Bhāvaviveka's negations can be carried to another level. He could be saying, by a negation of his negation, that Avalokiteśvara *does* worship Brahman in precisely the same way he worships, sees, and understands the Dharma Body of the Buddhas, by the discipline of no-worship. Which of these two meanings is the "true" meaning? In the end, the answer is a matter of perspective. To someone who thinks there is such a thing as Brahman and an action called "worship," the sentence says, "There is no worship." To someone who understands that there is no worship and nothing to be worshiped, the sentence says that there *is* an appropriate worship, the worship that is no-worship. The two perspectives are mutually contradictory, but they have to be held together to have a complete view of what it means to worship.[71]

Wayne Booth distinguishes between two kinds of irony.[72] In stable irony, there is a surface level of meaning that yields to another level in a solid and predictable way. The ironical meaning may at first be hidden, but when a competent reader discovers it, it is as hard as a rock. When Hamlet says, "Thrift, thrift, Horatio! the funeral bak'd meats / Did coldly furnish forth the marriage tables" to explain the seeming haste of his mother's remarriage, there is no doubt about his irony. There is also no doubt that he is pointing by indirection to his mother's affection for Claudius as the real explanation. The interpretation of the line is stable in the sense that the movement from the surface meaning to the deeper, truer meaning reaches a solid conclusion. In unstable irony, the new interpretation seems to undermine itself so that a reader is never sure of having reached the final meaning. In Chuang-tzu there is the famous story of Chuang Chou and the butterfly.[73] When Chuang Chou dreamed that he was a butterfly, we are told that he fluttered around, happy with himself, doing as he pleased, and did not know that he was Chuang Chou. When he woke up, he found himself in the same familiar body, as the same familiar person, but he did not know whether he was the one who had dreamed the butterfly or whether the butterfly was the one who had dreamed Chuang Chou. When the dreamer is part of the dream, it is impossible any longer to find a vantage point that can establish the real identity of either the dreamer or the dream.

Some of Bhāvaviveka's irony has the stability of Hamlet's comment about his mother. When Bhāvaviveka says that seeing is actually no-seeing, he makes it clear that no-seeing is meant to be the primary or literal (*mukhya*) meaning of the word "seeing" and that seeing is the secondary or metaphorical (*upacāra*) meaning.[74] He also explains that no-understanding is the literal (*mukhya*) meaning of the word "understanding."[75] But we also know that no concept is immune from the analysis of Emptiness. No-seeing and no-understanding are only "literally" true from one perspective (the perspective of conventional truth). From another perspective (the perspective of ultimate truth), they are just as empty as anything else.[76] Whether Bhāvaviveka's irony in a particular phrase is stable or unstable depends in the end on one's interpretive point of view. When he is denying distinctions in the second stage of the argument, we know that positive concepts have to yield to their negation: seeing has to yield to no-seeing, and understanding has to yield to no-understanding. But when we step back to another frame of reference and view these negations from the point of view of the argument as a whole, we also know that the negation itself has to be negated. At this point the irony becomes unstable. The negation of the negation can also be negated, and there is no place for the process of negation to stop.

In the beginning of his account of the bodhisattva path, Bhāvaviveka mentions one of the most basic paradoxes in the practice of the Mahāyāna. He speaks of the bodhisattva as a person who dwells in the nirvana where there is no foundation (*apratiṣṭhita-nirvāṇa*).[77] In the standard English translation of this term, the paradox is almost completely obscured. To "dwell" is literally to "stand," and nirvana-without-foundation is literally the nirvana where there is no "standing." To dwell in nirvana-without-foundation is thus to stand in the nirvana where there is no standing. Bhāvaviveka develops this concept by relating it to a number of standard contrasts in the practice of the bodhisattva path. A bodhisattva does not leave samsara, for example, but a bodhisattva is free from the harm of samsara; a bodhisattva does not attain nirvana, but it is as if a bodhisattva were standing in nirvana. To know in an experiential sense what it means to stand in the nirvana where there is no standing, one would, of course, have to be an accomplished bodhisattva, but the concept is still a fine metaphor for the process of understanding that we have used to plot the stages of Bhāvaviveka's thought. From one perspective, the stages form a dialectic: the second stage is the antithesis of the first, and the third takes up both of the first two stages and carries them to a higher level. From another perspective, the third stage is not different from the first two. It simply represents the ability to hold the first two stages together simultaneously. To tread comfortably in this conceptual structure, to climb its measured steps, to gaze without gazing from the peak that is no-peak requires the soft tread of a bodhisattva in order to stand precisely where it is necessary to stand and yet stand nowhere at all.

Part II

The Empty Throne

O Śāntamati, between the night in which he attained perfect Buddhahood and the night in which he attained parinirvana without remainder, the Tathāgata did not utter a sound. He did not speak, he does not speak, and he will not speak. But all sentient beings, with different dispositions and interests and in accordance with their aspirations, perceive the Tathāgata's diverse teaching as if it were coming forth [from the Tathāgata himself]. And each of them thinks, "The Lord is teaching the Dharma to me, and I am hearing the Lord teach the Dharma." But the Lord has no concept of this and makes no distinction. O Śāntamati, this is because the Tathāgata is free from all conceptual diversity, consisting of the traces of the network of concepts and distinctions.

(The Tathāgataguhya Sūtra)

Bhāvaviveka's theory of the Buddha grew out of a radical conception of the Buddha's absence, an absence of speech, of action, and ultimately of real identity. What made it possible for the Buddha's absence to influence the lives of the disciples and followers of the Mahāyāna was the fact that this absence was located in space and time. The form of the Buddha functioned like the Buddha's empty throne beneath the tree of the Buddha's enlightenment. It was an empty center where a person could appropriate the Buddha's power, be reminded of the Buddha's message, and gain a paradoxical vision of the Buddha's manifested presence.

A group of worshipers at the Buddha's empty throne. Behind the throne is the tree that marks the site of the Buddha's enlightenment. In front of the throne are the marks of the Buddha's feet. From Amarāvatī, reproduced by courtesy of the Trustees of the British Museum.

Chapter 3

Interpreting the Signs of the Buddha

Hsüan-tsang's Encounter with the Indian Landscape

When Hsüan-tsang traveled through the towns and villages of seventh-century India, collecting copies of the scriptures and studying with his Indian teachers, he learned to look at the Indian landscape with the eyes of a pilgrim. The account of his travels shows a topography that is marked in both a literal and a metaphorical sense by the traces of the Buddha. Every town seems to have its own shrine bearing a relic or image and telling a story that links the site to an event in the life of Śākyamuni, the Buddha of this era, to one of Śākyamuni's disciples, or to the Buddha of a previous era. Hsüan-tsang's narrative is not only a rich source of information about the practice of Buddhism in medieval India but it also clarifies an aspect of Buddhist thought that is almost invisible in the works of Indian philosophers themselves, even though it must have been as obvious to the philosophers as the ground beneath their feet. To see the evidence of the Buddha and hear his teaching did not require an elaborate study of texts. All it took was the stamina to travel in the steps of the Buddha, see the remnants of his presence, and hear the stories that placed each site in the sacred narrative of the Buddha's life.

It is possible to carry the point even further and argue that the landscape[1] was the dominant factor in determining Hsüan-tsang's understanding of the Buddha, more important than the texts we now use to study the narrative of the Buddha's life. Hsüan-tsang had an idea of what the Buddha was before he even came to India, but his understanding was framed and the details were painted in by the stories he heard in the towns and villages that preserved traces of the Buddha's presence. This is true not just because Hsüan-tsang was able to fill out his knowledge of episodes in the Buddha's life by tracing the Buddha's steps but also because his prior understanding of the Buddha—the understanding that he had inherited in China as part of the common lore of the Buddhist tradition—was fashioned out of the narratives of events in the life of the Buddha preserved at different pilgrimage sites. As Alfred Foucher has pointed out in his life of the Buddha, before the details of the Buddha's life were collected in scriptural form, they existed as common memories attached to particular places or objects, and the memories continued to affect the consciousness of the community as long as there were physical objects that could call them to mind.[2] When we compare the standard accounts of the Buddha's life in texts such as the *Lalitavistara* with the record of Hsüan-tsang's travels, the texts give the impression of a pastiche of stories gathered from the major sacred sites, either by firsthand experience or from the ancient equivalent of modern pilgrimage manuals.[3]

To understand how Hsüan-tsang and his contemporaries conceived of the Buddha, on either a practical or a philosophical level, requires an understanding of the way the sacred landscape of India shaped the community's collective memory of its founder. By this I mean not just that we need to know what the Buddha is said to have done at particular places. By now the traditions about the actions of the Buddha are well known and have been subjected to intense historical analysis.[4] I mean that we need to ask even more fundamental questions about the way communication through sacred objects and stories affected the way Buddhists understood not just what the Buddha *did* but what a Buddha *is*. Pilgrims who visited Buddhist sites in Hsüan-tsang's day heard stories about the Buddha's actions that allowed them to piece together a rough conception of the Buddha's life, just as we might piece together a biography of the Buddha today from different textual sources. But, along with specific information about the Buddha, Buddhist pilgrims also imbibed a certain way of thinking that allowed them to interpret the stories and sacred objects as signs of a particular kind of being. Whether they thought of it explicitly or not, they developed the elements of an instinctive "Buddhology"—an idea of the powers, attainments, levels of being, and so forth that made it possible for the Buddha to affect the lives of followers even after he was gone.

In this chapter, I would like to trace the essential elements in this logic of Buddhahood by looking not just at the philosophical sources but at evidence buried in the sacred objects and stories through which even the philosophers, at some time in their lives, would have become acquainted with the Buddha. The question I am posing is in part a question about grammar—or, as a semioticist might say, it is a question about the code that makes it possible for knowledgeable Buddhists to interpret certain objects or symbols as signs of a Buddha. But the question grows out of concerns that are also central to the study of religion. If we want to understand how Christians perceive the nature of Christ, it is just as important to understand the symbols or the interpretive habits that make "the body of Christ" into a sacrament for a community of believers as it is to understand the theological categories of traditional Christology. The logic of worship or iconography shapes a Christian's perception of Christ, and the logic is so deeply engrained in Christian tradition that it is difficult to conceive of a theologian working without it. The same is true in a different way for Buddhist philosophers. The fact that the logic of worship is not more visible in the study of Buddhist thought is due more to our fragmentary knowledge of the tradition and the difficulty of mastering more than a small portion of the sources than to any failure of imagination on the part of the Buddhist philosophers themselves.

To focus on the logic rather than the content of Buddhist conceptions of the Buddha requires even more attention than usual to the form of the questions we ask. It is tempting to approach the definition of the Buddha directly and search the literature for passages that answer the question, "What is a Buddha?," just as someone might begin a study of Christology by searching the literature of the Church for passages about the nature of Christ. Passages that respond to this question do exist in Buddhist literature, but they are not always useful. Buddhist sources have a tendency to deflect direct questions about the identity or "selfhood" of any being, and questions about the identity of the Buddha are no exception. A direct question often provokes a negative answer or a response so impenetrable that it suggests a problem with the question itself. A Pali text, "The Group of Discourses" (*Sutta-nipāta*), says of the Buddha, "I am certainly not a brahman, nor a prince, nor a *vessa*, nor am I anyone [else]. Knowing [and renouncing] the clan of the common people, I wander in the world, possessing nothing, being a thinker. Wearing a robe, houseless, I wander with shaven hair, with self quenched, not clinging here to [other] men. You have asked me an unfitting question about my clan, brahman."[5] Another Pali text, "The Discourse to Vacchagotta on Fire," deals with a question about the identity of the Buddha by saying, "The Tathāgata is deep, immeasurable, and unfathomable like the great ocean. It is not appropriate to say that he arises, does not arise, both arises and does not arise, or neither arises nor does not arise."[6] The two passages are responding to different questions, but they both suggest that a direct approach to the identity of the Buddha will lead to frustration and may even be misleading.

A more useful way to frame the question is to combine the perspective of a pilgrim with the perspective of a philosopher and ask, "Where do I look to find the Buddha?" For a pilgrim the question could be nothing more than a way of asking directions to a sacred site (or directions about how to approach or interpret a sacred object). For a philosopher the question asks how to define the "place" (*āśraya*) where the attributes of a Buddha are located.[7] The passages from "The Group of Discourses" and "The Discourse to Vacchagotta" suggest that the correct experience of a Buddha may be an experience in which one seeks and does *not* find a Buddha, but it is still possible to say to a pilgrim or a philosopher that there is a *place* where this experience occurs more directly, more easily, or more profoundly than other places, and this place shapes the idea of what a Buddha is in the mind of the person who seeks him.[8]

Foucher mentions eight major sites that contributed cycles of stories to the legend of the Buddha,[9] but there is surprising disagreement in the sources about the way these sites are ranked and interpreted. The Pali account of the Buddha's death in "The Discourse on the Great Decease" (*Mahāparinibbāna Sutta)* mentions four places that a person should "see and be moved by" (*dassanīyāni saṃvejanīyāni*): the place where the Buddha was born, the place where he attained enlightenment, the place where he delivered his first sermon, and the place where he passed away.[10] Hsüan-tsang's predecessor Fa-hsien, who visited India in the early decades of the fifth century, reports that there are four sites regularly associated with the appearance of the Buddha: the place where he becomes enlightened, the place where he delivers his first sermon, the place where he preaches and confronts opponents, and the place where he comes back to earth after preaching to his mother in heaven.[11] *The Treatise on the Great Perfection of Wisdom* (*Mahāprajñāpāramitāśāstra*) stresses that there are two cities that had particular importance in the Buddha's career: Śrāvastī and Rājagṛha.[12] The sources clearly have different ideas of what made a site important. The *Mahāparinibbāna Sutta* seems to reflect an early pilgrimage tradition associated with the places where key moments of transition occurred in the Buddha's life. These were places that should be "seen" (that is, visited) either in person or by an act of remembrance. The author of *The Treatise on the Great Perfection of Wisdom* seems to be more interested in explaining why the Buddha delivered his teaching more frequently in one place rather than another. In Fa-hsien, the peripatetic and the textual interests seem to have been merged to create a single list. But in spite of their differences, all three sources share an awareness that the land has a sacred shape: some sites are made more significant than others by the remnants they bear or the stories they bring to mind.

The actual stories associated with these sites are quite varied. In the region of Śrāvastī, where the Buddha is said to have spent a large part of his teaching career, Hsüan-tsang describes more than twenty locations associated in some way with the life of the Buddha.[13] In the area of the city itself there are ruins of a great hall erected by King Prasenajit for the Buddha. A nearby stūpa marks the spot where the king built a monastic compound for the Buddha's aunt. Outside the city there is a series of sites surrounding one of the early Buddhist monastic centers, the Jeta Grove. By the time of Hsüan-tsang's visit, the original monastic buildings had fallen to ruin, but the site was still marked by the presence of several pillars and a number of small stūpas. One stūpa marked the spot where the Buddha had ministered to a sick monk. Another marked the spot where the Buddha's disciple Maudgalyāyana, a monk who was known for his extraordinary magical powers, tried and failed to lift his more learned colleague Śāriputra off the ground. Still another stūpa is said to contain physical relics of the Buddha and to create a "mysterious sense of awe." Outside the city in another direction there was a town associated with the Buddha Kāśyapa, one of the predecessors of the historical Buddha, Śākyamuni. The worship of Kāśyapa was focused on a stūpa similar to the shrines of Śākyamuni, and it too contained physical relics.

The impression these sites made on Hsüan-tsang seems to have varied considerably from place to place. Hsüan-tsang says that some of the sites, particularly the sites that housed relics of Śākyamuni (or of previous Buddhas), displayed a sacred aura that might very well cause someone, in the words of the *Mahāparinibbāna Sutta*, to tremble or be strangely moved. Hsüan-tsang often reports that the sites manifest a mysterious light or heavenly music, or have the power to bring about miraculous cures. The sites also functioned as reminders of edifying stories. The Jeta Grove, for example, did not contain relics per se, but it was associated with the story of the Buddha's lay disciple Anāthapiṇḍika. Hsüan-tsang pauses long enough in his description of the physical features of the site to tell how Anāthapiṇḍika bought the grove for the Buddha by covering the ground with gold pieces and in the process set a standard of generosity to which future lay disciples, with a few notable exceptions, could merely aspire. Hsüan-tsang also describes deep ravines near the monastery where the earth was said to have opened and swallowed a number of unfortunate individuals who attempted to persecute or slander the Buddha. In the ruins of the monastery itself, Hsüan-tsang tells of an image of the Buddha that combined the miraculous quality of a relic with the ability to remind a visitor of an edifying story. Fa-hsien had reported that King Prasenajit, the king who ruled the region during the life of the Buddha, had become so attached to the Buddha's presence that when the moment came for the Buddha to travel to heaven to teach the Dharma to his mother, the king commissioned an image to occupy the Buddha's empty seat. When the Buddha returned to the monastery, the image got up and went out to greet him. The Buddha directed the image back to its place and explained that the image would serve as a prototype for the creation of similar Buddha images in the future.[14]

Hsüan-tsang's account of the area associated with Śrāvastī gives it the look and feel of a major Buddhist site, with a rich overlay of stories and monuments, but there are other sites in Hsüan-tsang's narrative that are encrusted even more heavily with the traces of the Buddha's presence. Hsüan-tsang's description of Sārnāth, the town on the outskirts of Vārāṇasī where the Buddha is said to have preached his first sermon, depicts a much more active pilgrimage site than a visitor would find today. In Hsüan-tsang's time, the site was dominated by a large monastery.[15] Inside the monastery was a temple that housed a famous image of the Buddha in teaching posture. To the south and west of the monastery there was a stūpa that marked the spot where the bodhisattva who many lives later became the Buddha was born as a partridge to teach his companions respect for elders.[16] In a nearby forest another stūpa marked the spot where the bodhisattva was born as the king of a herd of deer and offered to sacrifice himself for the other members of the herd.[17]

Hsüan-tsang lists these sites in no apparent order, along with other shrines that commemorate Kāśyapa Buddha's prediction of the enlightenment of Śākyamuni and Śākyamuni's prediction of the enlightenment of Maitreya.[18]

In other sections of the narrative, Hsüan-tsang's emphasis seems to fall less on stories of the Buddha's career than on veneration of the Buddha's remains. In the early stages of his trip through the northwest of India, he passed through a region where even the smallest villages seemed to boast their own stūpas containing the hair and nail clippings of the Buddha. These shrines do not necessarily relate to a distinctive legend about the life of the Buddha, but they are often associated with miraculous or extraordinary events. Hsüan-tsang tells the story of a stūpa that exudes a black, scented oil and on quiet nights echoes with the sound of music.[19] According to local legend, the oil was the remainder of a man who came to deposit a relic in the stūpa. When the man approached the stūpa with the relic in his hands, the stūpa is said to have opened miraculously to let him in, but when the man tried to leave, he caught the hem of his garment on a rock, and he was crushed between the stones of the stūpa. Fortunately not all monuments in the northwest were this grisly. The region also boasted the presence of stūpas honoring the Buddha's robe and staff and the ruins of a shrine that was said to have held the Buddha's begging bowl.[20]

The central region of the Ganges basin, where the Buddha's active teaching career was focused, was also fertile ground for the veneration of relics and other marks of the Buddha's presence. Here the remnants often took the form of marks left by the Buddha's robe or feet.[21] Hsüan-tsang describes a spot near Sārnāth where the impression of the Buddha's robe was engraved on rocks in the bed of a river, and the marks in the riverbed were accorded the same respect as a stūpa. Hsüan-tsang also notes the existence of a number of stūpas associated with the relics of the Buddha's cremation. By the time of Hsüan-tsang's visit, these relics had been divided and redivided several times, and each division had given rise to a complicated series of legends. Hsüan-tsang did what he could to unravel their history. When the relics were present, he commented on their distinctive characteristics and tried to account for the story that brought each one to its present resting place.[22]

Hsüan-tsang's account of different sacred sites is a reminder that what we loosely call "relics" could come in different varieties.[23] Relics could be the actual remnants of the Buddha's body, or they could be objects such as a footprint, a begging bowl, and a mark on a wall that are associated with the Buddha in only a conventional or accidental sense. Relics could also function quite differently in different contexts. Some clearly were treated as if they had power in their own right and were worthy of worship. Others seem to have had more of a teaching function: they marked events in the life of the Buddha and reminded a visitor of an edifying story. Some levels of the tradition have attempted to bring order to this proliferation of holy objects by grouping them in a series of categories. Some objects are said to consist of the physical remnants of the Buddha's body (*sārīrika*), some are objects that the Buddha used during his life (*pāribhogika*), such as the begging bowl that once was housed in the Northwest, and some are simply depictions or representations of the Buddha's form (*uddesika*).[24] It is clear from Hsüan-tsang's travels, however, that the diversity is even greater than this, especially when one includes the relics of Buddhist saints, relics of the bodhisattva who became the Buddha, relics of previous Buddhas, and marks of extraordinary events (such as the stūpa that emitted scented oil) that convey a message about the worship of the Buddha but are associated only indirectly with the Buddha himself. By Hsüan-tsang's own account, his journey led him through a landscape that was richly endowed not only with signs of the Buddha's power but also with a series of reminders that showed how these signs functioned in a complex system of worship and religious instruction.

To say that Hsüan-tsang traveled only as a pilgrim would be misleading.[25] Hsüan-tsang was attracted to India as much by the open-ended search for texts and sacred knowledge as he was by the lure of sacred sites. But there still was a sense in which Hsüan-tsang experienced the landscape as a conventional pilgrim. When he stood on the ground of a sacred site, he was on the same footing, literally and figuratively, as an ordinary Buddhist devotee. Whether Hsüan-tsang's learning would have caused the guides to have been more thorough about transmitting local traditions or more generous in embellishing them with detail, we do not know. (To judge from his own record, Hsüan-tsang's learning does not seem to have restrained their imagination much, if at all.) But Hsüan-tsang would have walked the same ground, seen the same ruined foundations, and heard many of the same stories about the Buddha's bones or the marks of the Buddha's robe as an ordinary pilgrim. And he would have used those signs and stories to construct a framework for understanding the being who left those marks behind.

How can we begin to reconstruct the framework of understanding that lies behind Hsüan-tsang's account of these signs and stories? In a paper called "Exploratory Observations on Some Weeping Pilgrims," T. H. Barrett suggests that we can start by trying to understand why Hsüan-tsang was reduced to tears when he first laid eyes on the site of the Buddha's enlightenment.[26] In Samuel Beal's translation, the story of Hsüan-tsang's visit to the Bodhi tree goes like this:

> The Master of the Law, when he came to worship the Bodhi tree and the figure of Tathāgata at the time of his reaching perfect wisdom, made (*afterwards*) by (*the interposition of*) Maitreya Bodhisattva, gazed on these objects with the most sincere devotion, he cast himself down with his face to the ground in worship, and with much grief and many tears in his self-affliction, he sighed, and said: "At the time when Buddha perfected himself in wisdom, I know not in what condition I was, in the troublous whirl of birth and death; but now, in this latter time of image (*worship*), having come to this spot and reflecting on the depth and weight of the body of my evil deeds, I am grieved at heart, and my eyes filled with tears."[27]

Barrett traces the sense of grief in this passage to a combination of factors in the intellectual and cultural world of seventh-century China. Like many of the lyric poets of the late T'ang Dynasty, Hsüan-tsang approached the tree of the Buddha's enlightenment with a sense of melancholy about the inevitable loss of the splendor of the past,[28] and his sense of melancholy was deepened by a Buddhist sense of karmic unworthiness. Like the saint who was hidden in the mountain in Central Asia, Hsüan-tsang missed the auspicious historical moment to make his appearance, and he missed it not because of the depth of his concentration but because he was buried in the web of his previous actions. Instead of visiting the site of the Buddha's enlightenment when the Buddha was present to explain its meaning, Hsüan-tsang was condemned to arrive centuries later, when the signs of the Buddha's enlightenment were already beginning to decay and disappear.

The key element in Hsüan-tsang's experience, and the one that seems to have triggered his emotional response, was the sense of absence. Hsüan-tsang had an acute sense that the Buddha he longed to see was not there. This is not to say that the shrine itself was in an unusual state of decay during Hsüan-tsang's time. Hsüan-tsang saw many monastic compounds in other parts of India that had been reduced to ruins, but the site of the Buddha's enlightenment was still an active focus of worship. Nor was the shrine lacking in physical representations of the Buddha. Hsüan-tsang's biographer points out that the shrine contained a "figure of Tathāgata at the time of his reaching perfect wisdom." But the activities of worship and the physical image of the Buddha took second place in Hsüan-tsang's mind to a feeling that the crucial object of his devotion was absent. It is as if Hsüan-tsang had placed himself inside the devotional scene represented by the so-called aniconic images of the empty throne at sites such as Amarāvatī.[29] His tears seem to invert (or are they simply another way of expressing?) the joy that radiates from the faces of devotees as they kneel before the place of the Buddha's absence in the image of the empty throne with which this part of the book began. Even though Hsüan-tsang saw an image of the Buddha, he perceived the image as a sign of absence, and he responded to the absence with tears.

How can we probe more deeply into the meaning of these tears? It is hard to ask this question and not be overwhelmed by the feeling of cultural distance—not just the chronological gap of nearly fourteen hundred years that separates us from Hsüan-tsang but also the gap that separates Hsüan-tsang as a representative of the Chinese literati from the world of an Indian sage. It is encouraging to know, however, that Hsüan-tsang was not unique when he responded to this emotional sight with tears. Hsüan-tsang's reaction reflects not only the tears that are shed by the great bodhisattvas in Bhāvaviveka's text—tears that Bhāvaviveka saw first as expressions of compassion, then finally as expressions of devotion—but also the tears of other Indian devotees who struggled like Hsüan-tsang in a quest for insight.

The name of the young pilgrim whose quest consumes the last few chapters of *The Perfection of Wisdom in Eight Thousand Lines* is Sadāprarudita,

"Perpetually Weeping." Sadāprarudita's journey leads eventually to the vision of the teacher he is seeking, but in its early stages his journey shares Hsüan-tsang's sense of sadness and self-reproach.[30] Sadāprarudita starts with a dim feeling that he is surrounded and led by the power of a teacher, a teacher who functions as a surrogate for the Buddha, but whose identity Sadāprarudita does not know and whose presence he has not yet seen. His journey then brings him slowly and painfully into the teacher's presence. The journey starts when Sadāprarudita hears a voice saying, "Go east, son of good family!," but Sadāprarudita soon dissolves in tears.

> Before long it occurred to him that he had not asked the voice how far he ought to go. He stood still just where he was, cried, sorrowed, and lamented. For seven days he stayed in that very spot waiting to be told where he could hear the perfection of wisdom, and all that time he paid no attention to anything else, and took no food, but simply paid homage to the perfection of wisdom.[31]

After weeping for seven days, he finally had a vision of the form of the Buddha and was given a description of the town where his teacher lived. When he heard about his teacher, he became "contented, elated, overjoyed, and jubilant" and began to hear the voice of his teacher speaking to him. Eventually, after Sadāprarudita has learned to visualize Buddhas and bodhisattvas in countless world systems and to sense the encompassing power of his teacher, even when the teacher is absent, he finally makes his way physically into the teacher's presence.

Why do these two travelers seem to feel such melancholy? I doubt that there can be any definitive answer to a question that depends so much on literary conventions and matters of taste that the ensuing centuries have only obscured. But it is clear that both travelers respond with deep emotion to the absence of the person who is the goal of their quest. For Hsüan-tsang, the signs of the Buddha are present but the Buddha himself is absent, and the absence is an occasion for lament. For Sadāprarudita, the teacher's power is present but the teacher himself is absent, and the teacher's absence is a cause for weeping. In both cases it is the sense of absence that brings the tears. For both of the travelers, the sense of absence also changes over time. As they travel on their separate journeys, they have the experience of reaching toward or falling away from the presence of the Buddha (or, in Sadāprarudita's case, from the teacher who is the surrogate for the Buddha). The Buddha or teacher has not always been or will not always be absent. If Hsüan-tsang had been present at the tree of enlightenment during the career of Śākyamuni, he would have been able to stand in the Buddha's presence. It was just his own bad luck or his own past actions that denied him that opportunity. In Sadāprarudita's case, the teacher's absence may have been discouraging, but he still could look forward to a time in the future when he could stand in the teacher's presence. For Hsüan-tsang and for

Sadāprarudita, the sense of absence was diachronic: it changed over time. What had been present in the past or might be present in the future was not present to them at the moment when they wept their tears.

By itself, the diachronic sense of absence is not surprising or even complex. It is a common experience to lament the loss of a more wonderful age or long for the appearance of an age that is more perfect or fulfilling than the present. But this sense of absence takes on more complexity of meaning when it is expanded in another direction. It is not only possible for the Buddha to be present at one moment and absent at another; the Buddha can also be present and absent simultaneously. The *diachronic* sense of the Buddha's absence can be combined with a sense of absence that is *synchronic*: the relationship between the presence and absence of the Buddha can be manifested over time, and it can be manifested at a single moment. The classic example of this *synchronic* sense of absence is the well-known passage in the *Saṃyutta Nikāya* about the relationship between the physical Buddha and the Buddha's teaching: "What is there, Vakkali, in seeing this vile body? Whoever sees Dhamma sees me; whoever sees me sees Dhamma. Seeing Dhamma, Vakkali, he sees me; seeing me he sees Dhamma." But it is not necessary to search the scriptures to find an example of such a basic idea. For the last few years, students in introductory courses in Buddhism have learned to "see" the Buddha through the film *Footprint of the Buddha*.[32] In this film the narrator starts his search for the Buddha by visiting a sculptural representation of the Buddha's parinirvana in Śrī Laṅkā. As he stands in front of the stone image, he hears a sermon about the virtues of mindfulness; then he turns his search for the Buddha to one of the Buddhist pilgrimage sites in northern India. Standing in front of the ruins of the great stūpa at Sārnāth, he voices the suspicion, "It is not exactly that the venerable Anandamaitreya [the monk who had interpreted the statue for him in Śrī Laṅkā] disapproved of my trip to India, but I had the distinct impression that he preferred a living teaching to a dead relic."

Anyone who has encountered Buddhist teaching on more than the most superficial level will have a favorite story to illustrate the idea that a Buddha who is present to the senses also in some sense is absent—and vice versa. But it is worth reminding oneself how many different variations can be generated out of this simple contrast. A well-known example is Hsüan-tsang's visit to the cave of the Buddha's shadow. Legends known to Hsüan-tsang associated the cave with a Nāga who was converted by the Buddha and became a protector of the Dharma.[33] When the Nāga realized that the Buddha would not stay with him permanently, he told the Buddha that he was afraid he would fall back into his old, violent ways. To restrain the Nāga and remind him of what he had been taught, the Buddha agreed to leave his shadow on the wall of a cave. The Buddha went on to predict that all future Buddhas would appear in the same place and leave behind their shadows in the same way. By the time Hsüan-tsang visited the cave, the shadow was no longer visible. Only after strenuous and tearful recitation of scripture and many prostrations was Hsüan-tsang able to see the form of the Buddha appear as a momentary flash of light. It took more prostrations and ardent promises before the cave finally was filled with light and Hsüan-tsang had a full vision of the Buddha's form "as when the opening clouds suddenly reveal the golden Mount and its excellent indications."[34]

With all of the different personalities in the story, including the Nāga, the living Buddha, the Buddha's form, Hsüan-tsang, and the Buddhas of the future, the passage elaborates the contrast of presence and absence in an almost endless series of permutations. The Nāga fears the absence of the Buddha, so he is given a reflection of the form that reminds him of the Buddha's presence. When the form itself has begun to disappear, a visitor like Hsüan-tsang has to engage in acts of religious discipline to make the form of the past Buddha become present. Finally, all of these events anticipate a story that will be played out again and again in the future as more Buddhist travelers and Buddhas come and go. Added to these diachronic relationships, there is a play on the relationship between the Dharma and the Buddha's physical form. Before Hsüan-tsang gets to the cave, he is already a learned and accomplished monk. In a sense, he already understands and is in possession of the Dharma. What he lacks is the Buddha's physical form. When he confronts the absence of the Buddha's form, his learning allows him to reverse the relationship in the *Saṃyutta Nikāya* between the Dharma and the Buddha's form. He does not use the physical form as a sign to point to the Dharma; instead, he chants the Dharma to make manifest the physical form.

One way to account for the range of meanings that comes from combining the diachronic and synchronic modes of absence is to use the interpretive model that Stanley Tambiah has developed to describe the use of amulets in modern Thailand.[35] Amulets are blessed by a forest saint, stamped with the saint's image, and distributed in a complex system of exchanges to collectors and devotees throughout the country. Tambiah argues that the amulets are signs that take on the functions of a symbol and of an index simultaneously. As he uses these terms (following the tradition of semiotics that stems from Peirce), a *symbol* is associated with its object only by a conventional rule, while an *index* stands in a direct existential relationship to its object. To say that an amulet is simultaneously a symbol and an index means that it stands for the saint in a conventional or symbolic sense (the way the wheel stands for the Buddhist Dharma) and that it also makes present, in an existential sense, the saint's power. In other words, an amulet makes a double statement about the saint it signifies: by functioning as a symbol, it shows that the saint is absent, and by functioning as an index, it shows that the saint (through his power) is present.

This double message, however, is only a part of the amulet's meaning. When Tambiah asked his Thai informants to explain how amulets could give protection and prosperity to the person who wears them, he received a range of answers that suggested more complex modes of interpretation. A businessman said that the amulet brought him good luck because it reminded him to be diligent and to practice morality in his business dealings.[36] A monk said that the amulet recalled the Buddha's virtues and reminded him not to do evil. The two responses suggest, among other things, that the function of amulets as signs of a Buddhist saint cannot be reduced to a simple act of reference. They do *symbolize* the saint, and they do *indicate* the saint by making present his power, but they also shift attention away from the saint toward a moral message. The message for the businessman was one of diligence and virtue. For the monk it was a message of "Go and do likewise." The message could not be confused either with the saint himself or with the saint's power, but it still was a natural part of the amulet's function, at least in the minds of the businessman and monk who provided Tambiah with his information.

It is a long way from Hsüan-tsang in the cave of the Buddha's shadow to a collector of amulets in modern Thailand, but there is a model of interpretation that ties them together. In each case there is a physical image that stands for and at the same time embodies the power of a saint, even when the saint is absent. In addition to this symbolic and indexical relationship to the absent saint, there is also an assumption that the physical image is related to a teaching. Someone who wants to interpret the signs fluently and relate one type of signification to the other has to grasp the complex relationship of presence and absence. To "use" an amulet or "see" the Buddha's shadow, a person has to be aware that they embody the power (which may be present, as in the case of the amulet, or absent, as in the case of the shadow) of an absent saint, and a person also has to know that the physical object is related to a teaching (which also may be present or absent). What is present can be used to call to mind what is absent, and vice versa. In the case of the amulet, the teaching is not present as a physical object; it is only the object that reminds someone of the teaching. For Hsüan-tsang in the cave, the teaching is even more present than the object, and he uses the teaching to make present a vision of the Buddha's physical form.

Tambiah's concept of the *indexical symbol* helps open up some of the complexity involved in interpreting the signs of Buddhist saints, but there are other possibilities as well. Another concept that has been used to interpret similar signs in other cultures is Mikhail Bakhtin's concept of the *chronotope* (literally, a "time-place"). Like the road in a picaresque novel or the salon in a novel by Stendhal or Balzac, a chronotope is a place where space and time intersect to give a particular interpretive structure to a series of events. Bakhtin himself explains a chronotope by saying, "In the literary and artistic chronotope, spatial and temporal indicators are fused into one carefully thought-out, concrete whole. Time, as it were, thickens, takes on flesh, becomes artistically visible; likewise, space becomes charged and responsive to the movements of time, plot, and history."[37] We are not likely to confuse Hsüan-tsang's cave with the drawing room in a French novel, but Bakhtin's concept is still helpful in two ways. First, it shows how important it is to have a particular point in space or a particular spatial structure in order to focus and symbolize a particular act of understanding. This is the aspect of Bakhtin's chronotope that caught Keith Basso's eye as a way of describing the attitude of the Western Apache toward the geographical features of their landscape.[38] Basso found that the Apache tied particular features of the landscape to particular stories and used the landscape, like the features of the sites Hsüan-tsang visited in India, to fix the stories in a person's mind—to "shoot" a person with a story—and drive home a moral point. A second suggestive aspect of Bakhtin's definition of the chronotope is the connection between a particular point in space and a community's perception of its own history. The Bodhi tree had such great impact on Hsüan-tsang because it forced him to stop for a moment and reflect not only on his own history but on his relationship to the larger historical movements within the Buddhist community as a whole.[39]

Another way to approach some of the ironies and incongruities that lurk beneath the surface in these signs of the Buddha might be to use Michel Foucault's concept of a *heterotopia*. Foucault himself introduces the heterotopia through the medium of a second concept, the *heteroclite*. He defines a heteroclite as a state in which "things are 'laid,' 'placed,' 'arranged' in sites so different from one another that it is impossible to find a place of residence for them, to define a *common locus* beneath them all."[40] A heterotopia is a place where there is a heteroclite. It is a place where concepts lie in radical disjunction so that not only are incongruous elements linked together but the idea of any common conceptual space is radically challenged. Foucault associates this shattering of our familiar conceptual space with Borges's fictional quotation from "a certain Chinese encyclopedia":

> Animals are divided into: (a) belonging to the Emperor, (b) embalmed, (c) tame, (d) sucking pigs, (e) sirens, (f) fabulous, (g) stray dogs, (h) included in the present classification, (i) frenzied, (j) innumerable, (k) drawn with a very fine camelhair brush, (l) *et cetera*, (m) having just broken the water pitcher, (n) that from a long way off look like flies.

Foucault sees Borges's passage itself as a place where certain concepts are juxtaposed that cannot go harmoniously together. As a result, the passage is also a place that figuratively is a no-place, since the concepts that purport to reside there cannot be set in any conceivable relation. Heterotopias like this undermine not only the concepts they seemingly contain but also the relationship of container and contained. As Foucault says, they "dessicate speech, stop words in their tracks, contest the very possibility of grammar at its source."[41]

To transpose Foucault's concept from a literary context to the places that reveal the Buddha's simultaneous absence and presence may seem to stretch his concept to the breaking point, but there is something to be said for considering the signs of the Buddha's absence as points of incongruity that challenge the stability of conceptuality itself. The sites where someone discovers the Buddha's presence in his absence, and vice versa, are like the room in *The Teaching of Vimalakīrti* where the bodhisattva Vimalakīrti greets a group of visitors in a state of feigned illness. When the visitors come to inquire about his health, they expect to find his room filled with all the trappings of a wealthy and urbane lay disciple. Instead, they find that Vimalakīrti has stripped the room of everything but a single cot. Vimalakīrti then uses the empty room as a device, a *topos*, to challenge the idea that there can be any space where anything can be located:

> Mañjuśrī: Householder, why is your house empty and why have you no retinue?
>
> Vimalakīrti: Mañjuśrī, all the Buddha-fields themselves also are empty.
>
> Mañjuśrī: Of what are they empty?
>
> Vimalakīrti: They are empty of emptiness.
>
> Mañjuśrī: What is empty of emptiness?
>
> Vimalakīrti: Imaginings are empty of emptiness.
>
> Mañjuśrī: Can emptiness be imagined?
>
> Vimalakīrti: Imagination itself is also empty, and emptiness does not imagine emptiness.
>
> Mañjuśrī: Householder, where is this emptiness found?
>
> Vimalakīrti: Mañjuśrī, emptiness is found in the sixty-two kinds of false views.
>
> Mañjuśrī: Where are the sixty-two kinds of false views found?
>
> Vimalakīrti: They are found in the deliverance of the Tathāgatas.
>
> Mañjuśrī: Where is the deliverance of the Tathāgatas found?
>
> Vimalakīrti: It is found in the first thought activity of all beings.[42]

When this bewildering conversation is over, Vimalakīrti uses his supernatural power to transport thirty-two hundred thousand thrones from the Merudhvajā universe and place them in his room, leaving his own town and the continent of India "as they were before." The act is meant to be a palpable demonstration of the malleability of space, or of space as no-space. Vimalakīrti's "inconceivable liberation" includes the ability to use space to undermine the notion of space itself.

Perhaps the best way to name the point where the Buddha's absence intersects with his presence, however, is with a modern Buddhist concept, the "locus" of absolute nothingness, developed first by Nishida Kitarō and extended by his disciple Nishitani Keiji. In *Religion and Nothingness*, Nishitani thinks of the understanding of Emptiness as a way of "standing" correctly on the ground beneath one's feet: "Only when the self breaks through the field of consciousness, the field of *beings*, and stands on the ground of nihility is it able to achieve a subjectivity that can in no way be objectivized."[43] But Nishitani also makes it clear that this "standing" is not simply a matter of exchanging one standpoint for another: "In standing subjectively on the field of nihility (I use the term 'stand' and refer to nihility as a 'field,' but in fact there is literally *no place* to stand), the self becomes itself in a more elemental sense."[44] This "standing" is a standing that is no-standing. Speaking about Emptiness, Nishitani says, "The standpoint of śūnyatā is another thing altogether. . . . As a standpoint assumed at the far side itself, it is, of course, an absolute conversion from the mere near side. But it is also an absolute conversion from a near side looking out at a far side beyond. The arrival at the far side is nothing less than an absolute near side."[45]

All of these concepts, from Bakhtin's chronotope to Nishitani's locus of absolute nothingness, have in common the idea of "place." Whether we think of a sign of the Buddha as a place where the consciousness of a community becomes particularly vivid and apparent, a place where conceptual systems clash and reveal their incompatibility, or a place that is no place but around which it is possible to have a distinctive form of "conversion," the sign is still a specific location, a "place" that can be understood by someone who has the right interpretive knowledge. Part of this interpretive knowledge is the ability to perceive and respond to the absence that is given spatial location in that particular place.

The Buddha as a Place Where an Absence Is Present

If we look beyond the travelers' accounts of Buddhist sites to philosophical accounts of the Buddha, especially the accounts that were current in the time of Hsüan-tsang and the centuries immediately thereafter, we find that they bear an uncanny resemblance to the pilgrim's question: "Where does someone look to find the Buddha?" And to search for the Buddha in an analytical sense is often to search, as Hsüan-tsang did, for the place where the Buddha is not present.

Sometimes the idea of place is reflected in a simple formula, as in the definition of the Dharma Body of the Buddha by the eighth-century Mādhyamika Jñānagarbha:

> When [the Buddha] takes no notice of subject, object, or self, no signs of cognition arise [in his mind]. His concentration is firm, and he does not get up.
>
> The place where he sits is a locus (*sthāna*) of every inconceivable virtue. It is incomparable, worthy of worship, a guide, and utterly beyond thought.
>
> This is the Dharma Body of the Buddhas, because it is the body of all the qualities (*dharma*) [that constitute a Buddha], the locus (*āśraya*) of every inconceivable virtue, and rational in nature.[46]

When Jñānagarbha says that a Buddha "does not get up," he means that a Buddha stays in a perpetual state of concentration without being affected by any discursive thought and without uttering a sound. It is this Buddha, the visible absence of conceptuality, that is the object (the "locus") of the epithets traditionally applied to the Dharma Body of the Buddha. It is "incomparable," a "guide," "worthy of worship," and "inconceivable."[47]

Behind Jñānagarbha's formulaic account of the Dharma Body lies a traditional image of the Buddha as a silent teacher, one who remains on his throne in a state of constant concentration but who manages to create in his disciples the impression that he is actually teaching. Madhyamaka philosophers often trace this image of the silent teacher to a passage in the *Tathāgataguhya Sūtra*:

> O Śāntamati, between the night in which he attained perfect Buddhahood and the night in which he attained parinirvana without remainder, the Tathāgata did not utter a sound. He did not speak, he does not speak, and he will not speak. But all sentient beings, with different dispositions and interests and in accordance with their aspirations, perceive the Tathāgata's diverse teaching as if it were coming forth [from the Tathāgata himself]. And each of them thinks, "The Lord is teaching the Dharma to me, and I am hearing the Lord teach the Dharma." But the Lord has no concept of this and makes no distinction. O Śāntamati, this is because the Tathāgata is free from all conceptual diversity, consisting of the traces of the network of concepts and distinctions.[48]

It is not uncommon in Buddhist literature to hear that the Buddha remained silent on certain occasions or in response to certain questions, but to hear that the Buddha said nothing from the time of his enlightenment to the time of his parinirvana is relatively rare.[49] This radical conception of the Buddha's silence became dominant, however, in Madhyamaka thought from the time of Nāgārjuna to the eighth century and beyond. Nāgārjuna refers to the Buddha's silence in one of his hymns: "O Lord, you have not uttered even a single syllable, yet everyone who needs to be taught is sprinkled by the rain of Dharma,"[50] and his commentators elaborate the image in their commentary on the definition of nirvana in the twenty-fourth verse of the twenty-fifth chapter of *The Root Verses on the Middle Way*. What makes this particular image of silence so attractive? It is not just that the image is shrouded with an aura of scriptural authority. There are many other scriptural accounts of the Buddha's teaching that put less stress on his silence. But this particular image allows the Mādhyamikas to bridge the gap between two sides of their philosophy that otherwise would be difficult to reconcile. They can insist that the Buddha's enlightenment is rigorously nonconceptual, but also give that nonconceptuality a local habitation and a form. The Buddha's awareness may ultimately be indescribable and in that sense inaccessible, but it is located in a place, and that place can function for those who gather around it (those who are "ready to be taught": *vineya*) as a locus of revelation and an object of worship.

The logic of place takes on a very distinctive character when one asks, as philosophers do, not just about the location of the Buddha but about the location of Emptiness. Emptiness can be defined as the absence of the identity that people mistakenly attribute to things: when analyzed, fire is found to be empty of the identity "fire," Buddha of the identity "Buddha," and even Emptiness of the identity "Emptiness." Buddhist logicians, unlike the logicians of other Indian schools, did not think that it was possible, however, to perceive such an absence directly. A perception of the absence of something like a pot on a particular spot of earth had to be based on the perception of the empty spot of earth. Perception of Emptiness also had to be based on a perception of the thing that is empty. But if all things are empty of identity, in what does Emptiness reside? Jñānagarbha explains that it is the "thing itself" (*vastu-mātra*) in its mere conventionality: merely to see a conventional entity as it is, without superimposing on it any ultimate identity, is the same as seeing its Emptiness.[51] Not all the Madhyamaka philosophers who came after Jñānagarbha have been comfortable with his way of expressing this insight,[52] but it represents a type of thinking that had enormous aesthetic significance in Mahāyāna literature, especially in East Asia. The imaginative power of a poet like Bashō flows from his ability to capture in each fleeting moment not just a symbol of Emptiness, as if Emptiness were something different from the moment, but Emptiness itself.

The logic of place also creeps into the more traditional account of the Buddha that is found in Vasubandhu's *Treasury of the Abhidharma* (*Abhidharmakośa*). At one point in the text, Vasubandhu raises a question that, like many questions about the Buddha, combines the preoccupations of worship and philosophy. He asks, "What does someone take refuge in who takes refuge in the Buddha?" His answer is reminiscent of the interpretive movement from the Buddha's physical body to the Buddha's Dharma in traditional statements about the Dharma Body:

> Someone who takes refuge in the Buddha takes refuge in the qualities (*dharmas*) that constitute a Buddha. These are the qualities that belong to someone who no longer needs training (*aśaikṣa*). It is because of the dominance of these [qualities] that a body is called a 'Buddha.' Or it is by attaining these [qualities] and by understanding all things that one becomes a Buddha.[53]

The "qualities" (*dharmas*) Vasubandhu mentions at the beginning of this passage are the qualities of awareness that distinguish the Buddha from unenlightened beings. Vasubandhu argues that people direct their act of "refuge" toward the Buddha's distinctive qualities rather than toward the Buddha's physical body. To take refuge in the *Buddha* and not in a physical body, a person has to take refuge in the qualities that make the Buddha's awareness unique.

This shift of focus away from the Buddha's physical form makes good traditional sense, but it also presents a number of problems. As Vasubandhu says, "If the Buddha is nothing more than the qualities that belong to someone who no longer needs training, how can a desire to injure the Buddha be a deadly sin?" Vasubandhu answers this question by arguing that the Buddha's body can also legitimately be called the Buddha because it is the *place* where the qualities that constitute the Buddha are located:

> The text does not say that the qualities that belong to someone who no longer needs training *are* the Buddha. It says that [they] *constitute* the Buddha. So it is wrong to say that [the text] denies [the claim] that the place [that is, the

> Buddha's physical body] is the Buddha. Otherwise, [the place] where ordinary thoughts are located could not become a Buddha.

Here Vasubandhu finds himself falling into the language of place for reasons that are similar to those that led the philosophers in the Madhyamaka tradition toward the scriptural image of the silent Buddha. The qualities that constitute a Buddha in the deepest sense are not qualities that have extension in space and time. They cannot be seen or touched. But they still have to *take place*, in part because there are moments, as rare as they may be, when a being becomes a Buddha at a particular time and place, but also because the veneration of the Buddha focuses on a particular form. The physical form may not be the characteristic that sets the Buddha apart from other beings, but it still *is* the Buddha through the logic of place.

Perhaps the most challenging exploration of the logic of place in Mahāyāna literature is found in the Yogācāra concept of Buddhahood as a "change of standpoint" (*āśraya-parāvṛtti*). At the end of the *Thirty Verses* (*Triṃśikā*), one of the fundamental texts of the Yogācāra tradition, Vasubandhu (in his Yogācāra mode) explains that the "change of standpoint" is another name for the Dharma Body of the Buddha:

> As long as consciousness does not stand in ideation-only, the propensity for duality does not cease. . . .
>
> But when consciousness does not perceive an object, it stands in consciousness-only, because that [consciousness] is not grasped [as a subject] if there is no object.
>
> This nonperception, in which there is no subject, is extraordinary insight. The change of standpoint is of two kinds depending on which difficulties are removed.
>
> It is the pure element that is inconceivable, virtuous, permanent, and pleasurable. It is the liberation body and also what is called the Dharma [Body] of a Great Sage.[54]

To someone who is not already well versed in this particular tradition of thought, the condensed, elliptical mode of expression makes the verses difficult to read. But my point has to do more with the metaphorical structure of the verses than with the technical details of Yogācāra philosophy. I have tried to bring this structure to the surface by translating the term *āśraya* as "standpoint" rather than using the more common equivalents such as "place," "locus," or "substratum." If we understand *āśraya* as "standpoint," it is easier to recognize Vasubandhu's use of the verb "to stand" as part of the metaphorical structure of his thought. The term seems to be a deliberate exploration of the metaphor of place: to be enlightened (that is, to achieve the Dharma Body of a Great Sage) is to change one's cognitive standpoint from "standing" in consciousness as subject and object to "standing" in consciousness alone. It is almost as if "the practice of yoga" from which the school gets its name (a practice in which it is essential for the participant to be firmly fixed in the posture of meditation) were dictating the choice of language. To be caught in ignorance, for Vasubandhu, is to "stand" or "be fixed" in a state of duality or distraction. To be enlightened is to "change the standpoint" and be fixed in the state of lucidity and concentration that Vasubandhu calls "consciousness-only."

Bhāvaviveka captures the structure of the metaphor very clearly in his own account of Vasubandhu's philosophy at the beginning of the fifth chapter of *The Flame of Reason*:

> As long as one does not stand in the store-consciousness (*ālaya-vijñāna*) as the nature of the mind itself (*svacitta-dharmatā*) . . . , but stands instead in a state of perception (*upalabdhi*), one does not eliminate the seeds of objects and does not remove the seeds of the perception of cognitive marks. But when one no longer perceives objects such as form as other than the mind, one stands in the nature of the mind itself. With this change of standpoint, all obstacles are removed. One is then the master of all qualities and achieves nonconceptuality.[55]

To say that one "masters all qualities and achieves nonconceptuality" is to say that one achieves Buddhahood. We could read Bhāvaviveka's account of the "change of standpoint" as suggesting a movement from one place to another, but the change is actually more a question of becoming clear, as Nishitani indicated, about the ground beneath one's feet. It is not that the previous standpoint needs to be abandoned; it needs to be transformed. In Bhāvaviveka's words, the place to stand is consciousness itself in its role as store-consciousness (*ālaya-vijñāna*). The term *ālaya* in this compound is often translated "storehouse," because it suggests a place where the "seeds" of various mental defilements are stored. (This is why Bhāvaviveka associates the "change of standpoint" with the elimination of the "seeds" of different kinds of faulty cognition.) But the more fundamental meaning of the word *ālaya* is simply "locus" or "place."[56] It is by "transforming" or "purifying" this locus and removing various imperfections that one "changes standpoint." The metaphor indicates that the transformation has negative as well as positive aspects. There is something that needs to be removed and something that remains. A person has to free the mind from the duality, defilements, and distractions that should not be present. In the process the person is firmly established in what remains, which is "the nature of the mind itself."[57]

The Yogācāra awareness of place also makes its influence felt in definitions of Emptiness. Yogācāra philosophers, like their Madhyamaka counterparts, found themselves speaking of Emptiness as a particular kind of absence that occurs in a particular place. *The Distinction Between the Middle and the Extremes* (*Madhyāntavibhāga*), an early and influential Yogācāra text, defines Emptiness like this: "The imagination exists, and in it there is no duality. But Emptiness is in it, and it is in that [Emptiness]."[58] Here the word "imagination" (literally "the imagination of what is unreal:" *abhūta-parikalpa*) refers to the mind in its constructive, imaginative aspect, or, to use the language of the text itself, the mind overlaid with the duality of subject and object. According to the verse, this active, functioning consciousness exists, and *in it* exists Emptiness. The mind, in other words, is the *locus* of Emptiness. In the verse, the metaphor of location is present only in the case endings of the words themselves. Vasubandhu's commentary, however, adds flesh to the grammatical bones.

> The right way to define Emptiness is to say, "One perceives correctly, when one thing is not present in another, that the latter is empty of the former, and one understands correctly that whatever remains there is actually present."[59]

As is often the case with Vasubandhu's brief commentaries, the explanation seems to do no more than replace one cryptic formula with another, but there are elements in these cryptic formulas that tell a great deal about Vasubandhu's understanding of Emptiness.

One significant addition in the commentary is the word "remain." Vasubandhu thinks of Emptiness as an absence (the absence of the duality of subject and object) that occurs in a particular locus (the imagination), and this locus is something that *remains* when duality is removed. To make the point another way, Vasubandhu thinks that the imagination is the place where Buddhahood (the understanding of Emptiness) occurs and a place that continues when the understanding of Emptiness has taken place. The word "remain" introduces an element of sequence: it marks a temporal transition from ordinary consciousness to enlightened consciousness. So it also introduces into the language of abstract ontology an element of practice. It suggests that the relationship between the three categories of the original verse —imagination, duality, and Emptiness—can be read as a meditative process. A person begins with the imagination, the ordinary state of mind where the categories of life have their ordinary meaning ("the imagination exists"). Then one realizes that the dualities in ordinary consciousness are not real ("in it there is no duality"). Then, by realizing the absence of duality in the mind, one realizes the Emptiness that *is* present ("But Emptiness is in it"). Finally, by understanding Emptiness, one can understand in a new way the imagination from which the whole meditative process began ("and in that [Emptiness] is this [imagination]"). The circular sequence is like the sequence in the famous line from the *Heart Sūtra* ("Form is Emptiness, and Emptiness is Form"), but it is expressed in a distinctively Yogācāra style, a style that is related to the practice of concentration itself.

The element of sequence was also important in the passage on the Buddha's silence in the *Tathāgataguhya Sūtra*. The sūtra pictured the Buddha as a locus of perfect nonconceptuality. The place where the Buddha was located did not break forth into speech in a literal sense because it no longer was subject to the concepts that generate words. But because the Buddha's enlightenment was located in a particular place and time, words could coalesce around him, and a disciple who had the appropriate preparation could hear him "teaching the Dharma." Reduced to his most essential features, this silent Buddha is simply a place that remains when concepts are absent. While the Buddha is alive, the place (*āśraya*) can be thought of as the physical body (*ātma-bhāva*) of the Buddha. It can also be conceived as the consciousness (or imagination) where the understanding of nonconceptuality occurs. After parinirvana, the "remainder" can be thought of as a relic or some other sign that continues to signify the Emptiness that is the content of the Buddha's enlightenment. But no matter how the achievement of Buddhahood is pictured, there is something that "remains" after the experience has taken place.

Vasubandhu's commentary on *The Discrimination Between the Middle and the Extremes* also expands the concept of Emptiness in another direction by connecting the Yogācāra understanding of Emptiness to an early scriptural account of meditation on Emptiness. The quotation that begins "One perceives . . ." is not Vasubandhu's own fabrication; it is a formula drawn from a traditional discourse about a form of meditation on Emptiness.[60] The "Lesser Emptiness Sutta" (*Cūḷasuññata Sutta*) of *The Middle Length Sayings* describes a type of concentration in which a monk focuses on the Emptiness of a series of different locations.[61] The monk begins his meditation in a forest, focuses his attention on the forest itself, and becomes aware that it is empty of the distractions associated with a village. With this realization of the absence of distractions comes a sense of satisfaction and freedom. The monk then focuses on the earth and becomes aware that it is empty of forest. Then he focuses on space and becomes aware that it is empty of earth. The process continues until he realizes the Emptiness of the plane in which there is neither perception nor nonperception. At each level, the monk's realization is expressed in the same formula: "He perceives correctly, when one thing is not present in another, that the latter is empty of the former, and he understands correctly that whatever remains there is actually present."[62] In each case, the final form of realization (which is expressed with the verb *prajānāti* or *pajānāti*—"to have wisdom") is one in which the meditator is aware of a real substratum or locus that remains when distractions are removed.

The terminology that Vasubandhu shares with the "Lesser Emptiness Sutta" suggests one of the truly vexing problems of Mahāyāna metaphysics. When Vasubandhu speaks of the imagination as the locus of Emptiness and says that it *actually exists* (*sad asti*), he raises "the problem of the Absolute."[63] The problem has generated as much controversy among modern interpreters of Buddhism as it did centuries ago among the Mahāyāna philosophers themselves. This is not the time or place to consider what it means to say that the Absolute does (or does not) exist. What we are concerned with here is the spatial metaphor that underlies the different Mahāyāna conceptions of Buddhahood. On the level of metaphor, the philosophers of the different Mahāyāna schools shared deep continuities. Whether the Absolute existed ultimately or not (assuming that we could agree on what it meant for something to exist "ultimately"), the Madhyamaka and Yogācāra authors began their philosophical reflection on the Buddha with the same image:

the image of a place where an absence is present. This image has its ontological implications, but it is essentially prereflective or prephilosophical. It is not the result of ontological speculation but the framework in which ontological speculation operates. And since it is not the result of philosophical speculation, it is not the special property of the philosophers. It belongs as much to the casual visitor to a Buddhist shrine as it does to a philosopher of Emptiness. What brings it to mind is simply a sign (which can be as different as the forest for a meditating monk, the marks of the Buddha's feet for a visiting pilgrim, or the nature of the mind itself) of an absence.

These philosophical passages speak in a more abstract language than the passages about Hsüan-tsang at the Bodhi tree or Sadāprarudita on the road to pay homage to the Perfection of Wisdom, but they respond in their own way to the problem of "the empty throne." To give an account of the Buddha, philosophers have to deal with the problem of absence. And they have to represent the problem of absence in two separate dimensions. There is a diachronic problem posed by the fact that the Buddha once was active in a certain way and now is not, and there is a synchronic problem posed by the fact that any particular representation of the Buddha (including the physical Buddha himself) is inadequate to represent the Buddha in the deepest sense. In the experience of a Buddhist traveler like Hsüan-tsang, the two aspects of the problem may be difficult to separate. Perhaps in the end they are not decisively different, in the sense that Hsüan-tsang's struggle to interpret the remnants of the Buddha as signs of his past presence forces him to confront the present meaning of the Buddha as well. But a complete theory of the Buddha has to confront the problem of absence in these two ways. The next two chapters will take up these two dimensions of the Buddha's absence, the diachronic and the synchronic, before bringing the two dimensions together in a discussion of Bhāvaviveka's doctrine of the Buddha Bodies.

Chapter 4

The Diachronic Dimension of the Buddha's Absence

How does the Buddha continue to influence the life of the Buddhist community after his career has come to an end? For many commentators and historians of the Buddhist tradition, this question has been the key to unlock not only the philosophical and doctrinal speculation about the Buddha but the devotional attitudes toward the Buddha that are expressed in Buddhist worship.[1] It was also a key question for philosophers who worked in the tradition of Bhāvaviveka. Philosophers seldom mentioned the Buddha's relics, and only rarely did they discuss the concrete details of Buddhist worship, but it was impossible for Bhāvaviveka to work out an effective conception of the Buddha without taking up the problem of the Buddha's powerful remains.[2] If anything, his philosophical point of view made him feel the problem more acutely. Traditional accounts of the Buddha's life focused the question on the event of the parinirvana: when the Buddha's teaching career came to an end at the moment of his death, the community had to find new devices to maintain a sense of direction in his absence. But for Bhāvaviveka the problem of absence did not wait for the Buddha's parinirvana. The picture of the Buddha's silence in the *Tathāgataguhya Sūtra*, the picture that Bhāvaviveka used as the basis for his own analysis of the Buddha's career, showed that the Buddha withdrew from active teaching not just at the end of his life but at the moment of his enlightenment. To account for the continuing appearance of the Buddha's teaching, Bhāvaviveka had to explain not just how the Buddha could influence his disciples after his death but how the Buddha's actions during his life could flow from influences that were set in motion even before he achieved enlightenment.

Whether the problem of influence and continuity is focused at the moment of the parinirvana or at some earlier point in the Buddha's career, the problem is still essentially *diachronic*. There is a time when the Buddha (or the being who is to become the Buddha) is present and capable of influencing the lives of his followers in an active way, but there comes a time when the Buddha can no longer affect them directly. For the philosophers to explain how the Buddha's influence continues, there has to be a causal mechanism or a device that will make it possible for the Buddha to act even in his absence. We find, when we look at Bhāvaviveka's account of the Buddha, that there are three principal concepts that deal with the diachronic problem: the idea of a "previous vow" (*pūrva-praṇidhāna*), the idea of the Buddha's "manifestations" (*nirmāṇa*), and the idea of the Buddha's "sustaining power" (*adhiṣṭhāna*). This chapter will discuss these three categories in turn.

The Buddha's Previous Vows

Nāgārjuna closes the twenty-fifth chapter of his *Root Verses on the Middle Way* with a verse that defines nirvana and at the same time gives a picture of what it means for the Buddha to teach the Dharma: "It is bliss to cease all objectification and bring conceptual diversity to an end: the Buddha taught no Dharma anywhere to anyone."[3] Taken out of context, the verse seems incongruous: it seems to bring together two ideas that do not belong together. To speak in an abstract way about the bliss someone feels when the habit of grasping things as objects (*upalambha*) has been laid to rest does not necessarily bring to mind the action of the Buddha's teaching. But the sequence that governs the selection of topics in the verse comes from treating nirvana not merely as an abstract concept but as a moment in the career of the Buddha. When the Buddha has reached the cognitive state described in the first half of the verse, when he has made his way to the Bodhi tree and achieved enlightenment, the next step in the narrative sequence is to ask how the Buddha will make that experience of enlightenment available to others. The Buddha has to step down from the throne, in a figurative sense, and wrap his experience in words. Nāgārjuna's verse about the experience of nirvana raises the diachronic question about the Buddha's action in its most direct form: if all of the Buddha's conceptual activity has ceased, not only at the moment of parinirvana but also at the moment of enlightenment, how can he get up from the seat of enlightenment and teach? Nāgārjuna's answer is that the Buddha did *not* get up: he taught no Dharma anywhere to anyone at all.

There are venerable traditions, however, that the Buddha did teach—or at least gave his disciples the impression that he was teaching. *How* could he have managed to be silent and still be the source of such a rich and varied body of tradition? Bhāvaviveka tackled the problem in his own commentary by elaborating the scriptural image of the Buddha's silence.

> [An opponent objects:] A Buddha who is free from concepts cannot have a Mahāyāna because such a Buddha ultimately does not teach any Dharma. . . .
>
> [Bhāvaviveka replies:] The Tathāgata Body is free from concepts, but because of a promise to seek the welfare and happiness of others and because of a previous vow, a Manifestation Body arises from it that is capable of assisting everyone. On this basis, a teaching arises that consists of syllables, words, and sentences. [This teaching] reveals to the followers of the excellent vehicle the selflessness of *dharmas* and persons—[a doctrine that is] not shared by heretics, disciples, and solitary Buddhas—in order to complete the perfections. This [teaching] is called the Mahāyāna. The teaching arises in spoken form when the ultimate Buddha is present, so [we] consider the Teacher to be the agent of this teaching.[4]

The passage contains many concepts that deserve further comment. For the moment, it is enough to concentrate on the description of the causal sequence that gives rise to the Buddha's teaching and particularly on the role of the "previous vow" (*praṇidhāna*).

The "previous vow" comes up often in Bhāvaviveka's works, particularly in passages that deal with the Buddha's act of teaching. He mentions it in his commentary on verse 6 in chapter 18 of *The Root Verses on the Middle Way*, where Nāgārjuna says, "The Buddhas used the term 'self,' they taught no-self, and they taught neither self nor no-self."[5] In his explanation, Bhāvaviveka says that the Buddhas' teaching arises from "a vow to seek the welfare of others." He uses almost the same formula in his explanation of the "Tathāgata Body" in *The Flame of Reason*: "By the power of a previous vow, nurtured by conduct that brings benefit to others, a Manifestation Body arises from the nonconceptual Tathāgata Body."[6] Bhāvaviveka does not dwell on the concept in detail in either of these two passages, but he makes it clear that the "previous vow" plays a crucial role in connecting the silence of the Buddha with the appearance of the Buddha's teaching.

One can sense the difficulty of this connection by focusing on the formula Bhāvaviveka uses to define the causal relationship between the two aspects of the Buddha that he calls by the names "Tathāgata Body" and "Manifestation Body." Bhāvaviveka identifies the Tathāgata Body with the state of awareness that makes the Buddha an enlightened being.[7] Someone who wants to understand the Buddha's teaching at the deepest level would want somehow to get in touch with this aspect of the Buddha's experience. The problem is that the Tathāgata Body is free from all concepts and does not speak. The aspect of the Buddha that does speak is the Manifestation Body. As Bhāvaviveka explains it, the Manifestation Body is conceptual and produces a teaching that fits the needs of the disciples. But the Manifestation Body is not identical to the Tathāgata Body. It is a conceptual expression of it, and in the end the concepts that create the Manifestation Body mean that it is a falsification. So how can disciples of the Buddha be confident that the teaching they receive from one aspect of the Buddha also comes from the other? How can they know that an encounter with the Manifestation Body brings them in contact with the Tathāgata Body itself?

Bhāvaviveka answers the question with a precise causal formula: "The teaching arises in spoken form when the ultimate Buddha is present." The formula is a direct reflection of the traditional Buddhist formula of dependent arising:

> When this is present, that comes to be;
> From the arising of this, that arises.
> When this is absent, that does not come to be;
> On the cessation of this, that ceases.[8]

The formula is meant to express a pragmatic or empirical association between two separate things. To say that one thing has a rigid connection with the other would be to say too much. To say that they are not connected at all would be to say too little. Instead of a definitive causal relationship, there is simply a pragmatic observation that the appearance of one phenomenon is associated in a temporal sequence with the appearance of the other. With this formula, Bhāvaviveka can suggest that the Tathāgata Body (or the ultimate Buddha) is the "agent" of the teaching without giving it the role of a formal cause. When the Tathāgata Body is present, the teaching arises.

But the chronological association between the Tathāgata Body and the Manifestation Body is not enough to account for all aspects of the teaching. It may explain why the teaching arises at a particular time in a particular place, but it cannot explain the conceptual form of the teaching itself. What makes the variety of the teaching possible from the Buddha's side is the lingering effect of the "previous vow." By "previous" Bhāvaviveka means that the vow was made before the enlightenment, as part of the career that brought the Buddha to his seat at the foot of the Bodhi tree. Until the bodhisattva who becomes the Buddha finally achieves enlightenment, conceptual distinctions are inescapable. Whether it is a question of "achievement for the bodhisattva's own sake" (*svārtha-sampad*) or "achievement for the sake of others" (*parārtha-sampad*), a bodhisattva has to set goals and make choices. To bring the understanding of Emptiness to bear in a way that helps others ("to teach all sentient beings"), a bodhisattva has to prepare the environment in an appropriate way ("purify the Buddha-field") and set the right karmic influences in motion ("bring all vows to completion").[9] To focus the bodhisattva's general aspiration to enlightenment in the specific way that will be of most help to others, the vow is crucial. As *The Treatise on the Great Perfection of Wisdom* says, to get an ox cart to reach its destination, you have to have a driver. The accumulation of merit is like the ox, and the vow is like the driver.[10]

If the vow is necessary to give specific form to the Buddha's actions, how does it bring about its effect? Bhāvaviveka does not give a clear picture of the mechanism, and it is not clear that any formal explanation would be possible without saying more about the causal process than Bhāvaviveka's philosophical scruples would allow. But there are other Mādhyamika philosophers who make good use of comparisons and illustrations to suggest the process he had in mind. Śāntideva uses the example of a dealer in antidotes (*gāruḍika*) who consecrates a post in such a way that it is capable of curing snakebite.[11] The dealer in antidotes can then leave the post behind, and the post is still capable of working its effect. Śāntideva explains that the post is like the form of the Buddha. It is consecrated (the word *sādhita* can also mean "brought to completion") by someone who follows the bodhisattva practice, and it serves the needs of sentient beings even after the bodhisattva is gone. Candrakīrti compares the vow to the motion of a potter's wheel.[12] Once a potter sets the wheel in motion, it keeps turning, and the potter seems to produce pots without expending any effort. The Buddha is like the potter, and his vow is like the wheel. The Buddha remains in the form of the Dharma Body and makes no effort, but he seems to produce actions through the inherent motion of specific previous vows.

Perhaps the most appealing account of the vow in a philosophical source comes not from a Mādhyamika but from the Yogācāra commentator Śīlabhadra.

> The Tathāgata has no concept of effort, either with regard to himself or with regard to something that belongs to himself, but because of a previous vow, he generates insights and manifestations and accomplishes the needs of sentient beings. . . . The Tathāgata does not distinguish what he will do from what he will not do, but he still does what needs to be done, just as someone who is in a state of concentration rises from concentration because of a previous vow. As is said in "The Chapter on the Ocean of Wisdom Bodhisattva," [the Buddha] is like a monk who stays in a state of concentration until a bell is rung. Even though he does not hear the bell ring, he still rises from concentration at the appointed time.[13]

What makes Śīlabhadra's explanation so charming is the quality that is present in so much of the best Yogācāra literature. It relates an abstract concept to a concrete human situation that we can understand without necessarily having had the experience ourselves.

Another fine Yogācāra illustration of the power of the vow is found in *The Ornament of the Mahāyāna Sūtras* (*Mahāyānasūtrālaṃkāra*). The illustration does not address the problem of action directly, but it does show how Buddhas can experience liberation in different ways even when the Emptiness they experience is always the same. The Buddha's liberation is compared to a tie-dyed cloth. Before it is dyed, the cloth is all the same color, and the dye also is the same color. But when the cloth is dipped into the dye, it takes on a distinctive pattern of colors from the knots that were tied in the cloth before it was dyed. Here the cloth is the Buddha, the dye is Emptiness, and the knots are the vows that were made in the Buddha's previous bodhisattva career.[14]

We can understand the human dimension of the vow even more clearly by looking at the role it plays in the career of a bodhisattva. For most people,

Buddhahood is such an exalted state that they can only aspire to it at the end of many lives. But even to "aspire" to Buddhahood is to form the beginning of a "vow," and a vow is one of the crucial marks of the career that eventually brings a bodhisattva to enlightenment. For an ordinary practitioner of the Mahāyāna, this means that even the humblest aspiration to seek Buddhahood, whether it takes the form of a pious wish or functions as a formal promise, anticipates the experience of enlightenment. Bhāvaviveka uses the word *dīkṣā* ("initiation" or "dedication") to capture some of the different meanings that come together in the bodhisattva's aspiration. Near the beginning of *The Flame of Reason*, Bhāvaviveka says that he wrote the text "with a *dedication* to bring benefit to others."[15] When he first mentions his own "dedication," he does it with a sense of humility: he says that he can only write on subjects that fall within the range of his own modest abilities. But when he uses *dīkṣā* again, he applies the term to accomplished bodhisattvas: "They did not stay in ordinary existence, because they have seen its faults; nor did they [stay] in nirvana, because of their compassion. They stay in ordinary existence because of a *dedication* to bring benefit to others."[16] The word does not appear again in the text until Bhāvaviveka begins his formal description of the bodhisattva path in chapter 3: "An accomplished [bodhisattva], who is tormented by compassion and *dedicated* to the welfare of these [ordinary people], has a mind as hard as a diamond and is the greatest of beings."[17] The use of the same word to apply to accomplished bodhisattvas and also to himself generates a sense of contrast and a hint of irony. His own dedication at the moment when he acknowledges his limitations is impossible to confuse with the mature dedication of the bodhisattvas in the advanced stages of the bodhisattva path. But the impulse is still the same. It is not that Bhāvaviveka is immediately raised to a high level of spiritual attainment the moment he sets pen to palm leaf, but he anticipates that attainment and also shares its dignity by dedicating himself to the same goal that characterizes the greatest bodhisattvas.[18]

It is possible that Bhāvaviveka uses the word *dīkṣā* for himself so that he can reserve the word *praṇidhāna* for the more formal discussion of the Buddha, but Buddhist literature in general does not observe such a distinction. The word *praṇidhāna* can be used to refer to anything from a pious wish to a ritual promise, and it can apply to everyone from an ordinary practitioner of the bodhisattva path to a Buddha. In its verb form, the word can mean "to fix the mind firmly," "to make an earnest wish," "to cherish an ardent desire," or "to assume a vow."[19] A related noun (*praṇidhi*) is often used to name the element of "wishing" in "the mind of enlightenment" (*bodhicitta*) that is generated in successive stages by a bodhisattva on the path to Buddhahood. In *The Introduction to the Bodhisattva Practice*, for example, Śāntideva says, "In brief, the mind should be understood to be of two kinds: the mind that wishes (*praṇidhi*) for enlightenment and [the mind] that starts out (*prasthāna*) toward enlightenment. The difference between them is like the difference between someone who wants to go and someone who goes."[20]

The "wish" is a simple aspiration, but it can be dignified and transformed into a formal commitment when it is made in a ritual context, as Kamalaśīla does in *The Stages of Practice* (*Bhāvanākrama*):

> The mind of enlightenment is of two kinds: the mind that wishes and the mind that starts out. In the Holy *Gaṇḍavyūha* it says, "O son of good family, it will be hard for you to find any beings who wish for supreme perfect enlightenment. It will therefore be extremely difficult to find any who have started out for supreme perfect enlightenment." The mind that wishes [for enlightenment] is the first aspiration: "May I become a Buddha for the sake of all beings!" The mind that sets out [for enlightenment] is the one that undertakes the accumulation [of merit and wisdom] after taking a vow. A person should take the vow in front of a preceptor (*kalyāṇa-mitra*) whose vow is recognized as being firmly established. If there is no suitable sponsor, one should visualize (*āmukhīkṛtya*) Buddhas and bodhisattvas and generate the mind of enlightenment just as Mañjuśrī did when he was King Ambara. When the mind of enlightenment has been generated, the bodhisattva undertakes the practice of generosity and so forth, realizing that when one does not discipline oneself one cannot discipline others.[21]

Some of the same ritual elements are repeated in Atiśa's short text on the bodhisattva path, *The Lamp for the Path to Enlightenment* (*Bodhipathapradīpa*).[22] Atiśa says that, to confirm the mind of enlightenment in a ritual way, people should start by taking refuge in the Buddha, Dharma, and Saṃgha, then make offerings to the three jewels and to the teacher (*guru*) who functions as their preceptor (*kalyāṇa-mitra*). As they lay the offerings down in the mandala in front of the teacher, they treat the teacher as an embodiment of the Buddha and resolve to accomplish all the great deeds of the Buddhas. Then they kneel down, offer a flower, and recite the following words:

> O Omniscient One, epitome of wisdom,
> Purifier of the wheel of life,
> I have no refuge in any Lord,
> Except at your lotus feet.
> O Hero of creatures, may the Great Sage
> Bestow his kindness upon me!
> May the Holy One grant to me the
> Supreme and Highest Enlightenment Thought![23]

These verses are followed by the recitation of two other texts, and the teacher closes the ceremony by saying how wonderful it is that someone has come forward in such a degenerate age to make a commitment to the practice of enlightenment.

These ceremonies show how much the practice of the later Mahāyāna was characterized by what Stephan Beyer calls the ritualization of moral attitudes.[24] But the ritualized expression of the aspiration to enlightenment is not by any means confined to the late phases of Indian Buddhist history. There are clear indications in Mahāyāna literature that the "wish" (*praṇidhi*) or "vow" (*praṇidhāna*) had a ritual function at quite an early date. A form of discipline known as The Three Groups (*triskandhaka*), containing a confession of sins, a rejoicing in others' merit, and an invocation of Buddhas, is mentioned in a number of early texts. According to a sūtra known as *The Questions of Ugradatta*, a bodhisattva was expected to recite The Three Groups three times a day and three times a night.[25] The list of three groups was expanded in some texts to seven,[26] and the list of seven could be abbreviated to fit the needs of a particular occasion. But the list seems to have grown out of a context that was genuinely liturgical and not just the product of an author's literary imagination.[27] In Nāgārjuna's *Jewel Garland*, the four elements of "refuge," "confession," "supplication," and "rejoicing" are preceded by specific directions about preparing the proper ritual setting:

> Therefore in the presence of an image
> Or reliquary or something else
> Say these twenty stanzas
> Three times every day.[28]

Vows also played an important role in ritual expression of the bodhisattva's aspirations. They were not always included as a separate element in their own right, but they were often used to elaborate or expand other elements of the ritual. In some particularly well-known and important ritual texts, the vows played the dominant role, and other elements were reduced to the status of preparation.[29]

Nāgārjuna treated the bodhisattva vow as a unique feature of the Mahāyāna.[30] While this may be true in a narrow sense, it is not true to say that aspiration had no role in Theravāda understanding of the career leading to enlightenment or, for that matter, in Theravāda practice as a whole. Richard Gombrich has pointed out that an "earnest wish" (*patthanā*) and an "aspiration" (*paṇidhi*) play important parts in Theravāda conceptions of the path to nirvana.[31] Gombrich compares the aspirations for nirvana to "acts of truth" (*sacca-kiriyā*) that take on a karmic identity of their own and bring about their result without any further interference from the person who made them. Sadāprarudita makes use of a form of the "act of truth" to heal his own mutilated limbs just before he meets his teacher at the end of *The Perfection of Wisdom in Eight Thousand Lines*:

> Sadaprarudita replied: "Do not trouble your mind about the mutilated condition of my body! I shall myself now make it whole again by the magical power of my enunciation of the Truth. As I am in truth irreversible, have been predicted to full enlightenment, and am known to the Tathagatas by my unconquerable resolution,—may through this Truth, through this utterance of the Truth this my body be again as it was before!" That very moment, instant and

second, through the Buddha's might and through the perfect purity of the Bodhisattva's resolution, the body of the Bodhisattva Sadaprarudita became again as it had been before, healthy and whole.[32]

The bodhisattva vow is not fully comparable to an "act of truth," but the two actions do share important characteristics. The vow is a moral commitment (and often a ritual act) that takes on an identity of its own. It has to be developed by the career of the bodhisattva and brought to fruition by the attainment of Buddhahood, but the vow acts as if it had a life of its own. It is like a stone dropped into a karmic pond.[33] The trajectory of the stone is the bodhisattva career, the point of impact is the event of enlightenment itself, and the ripples are the continuing effect of the vow in the minds of the Buddha's disciples after the Buddha is gone.

The idea of the vow is so rich in its associations that it is almost impossible to exhaust its meaning. A thorough study of the concept would have to include situations where bodhisattvas act "through the power of a vow" (*praṇidhāna-vaśena*) even before their enlightenment.[34] It would also have to consider the important lists and classifications of vows that occur in standard accounts of the bodhisattva path.[35] But the particular vows that offer the most help for understanding Bhāvaviveka's theory of the Buddha may also be the ones that are best known. In the larger *Sukhāvatīvyūha Sūtra*, the forty-eight vows of the bodhisattva Dharmākara set in motion a process of compassion that becomes actualized in the enlightenment of the Buddha Amitābha and results in the creation of the "Pure Land."[36] To put these vows in Bhāvaviveka's language, we would say that Amitābha is the "place" where compassion is based, but it takes the vows of the bodhisattva Dharmākara to channel this compassion and express it in Amitābha's distinctive way.

There is another well-known series of vows in the chapter on "The Apparition of the Stūpa" in *The Lotus Sūtra*. The chapter begins with the description of a great jeweled stūpa that hovers in the air and utters sounds of praise to the Buddha who is preaching the Lotus Sūtra. When the bodhisattva Mahāpratibhāna asks the Buddha for an explanation, the Buddha says:

> In this great jeweled stūpa, O Mahāpratibhāna, is the entire body of a Tathāgata, and the stūpa belongs to him. He is the one who emits this sound. Underneath, O Mahāpratibhāna, beyond innumerable hundreds of thousands of *nayutas* of *koṭis* of world systems, is a world system called Ratnaviśuddha. In that [world system] there was a Tathāgata, an Arhant, a perfectly enlightened Buddha named Prabhūtaratna. This Lord made the following previous vow (*pūrva-praṇidhāna*): "Previously, when I was following the bodhisattva practice, I did not attain supreme perfect enlightenment as long as I did not hear the Lotus Sūtra, the discourse that is directed to bodhisattvas. But after I heard the discourse of the Lotus Sūtra, I became perfected in supreme perfect enlightenment." So, Mahāpratibhāna, the Lord Prabhūtaratna, the Tathāgata, the Arhant,

> the perfectly enlightened Buddha, at the moment of his parinirvana, in the presence of the world with its gods, Māras, Brahmās, śramaṇas, and brāhmaṇas, announced, "After I attain my parinirvana, O monks, make a single jeweled stūpa for my Tathāgata Body, and make other stūpas dedicated to me." Then, Mahāpratibhāna, the Lord Prabhūtaratna, the Tathāgata, Arhant, perfectly enlightened Buddha, made the following resolution (*adhiṣṭhāna*): "Let this stūpa with my body appear in any Buddha-field, in any world system in the ten directions, where the discourse of the Lotus Sūtra is revealed. When any Lord Buddha preaches this discourse of the Lotus Sūtra, may [this stūpa] stand above the assembly. And may the stūpa with my body applaud the Lord Buddhas who teach this discourse of the Lotus Sūtra."[37]

In spite of the unmistakably Mahāyāna character of this passage, it is remarkable how many of its conceptual elements would be as much at home in a text of the Pali canon. Even though Prabhūtaratna makes an extraordinary manifestation, there is no requirement in the terminology of the passage that Prabhūtaratna *himself* continue after his parinirvana. He simply leaves the remnant of his body (*ātma-bhāva*) behind and empowers it to manifest itself when certain conditions are present. Strictly speaking, it is the "vow" (*praṇidhāna*) or "resolution" (*adhiṣṭhāna*) that gives the body this power, not the presence of Prabhūtaratna himself.

What seems to break the traditional pattern of the Buddha's powerful remnants and lead toward the Mahāyāna notion of the Buddha's permanent presence is the idea that the Buddha can leave behind the power to manifest his own form. As the story of Prabhūtaratna continues, it becomes clear that the stūpa manifests not only miraculous signs but also the form of Prabhūtaratna himself. When Mahāpratibhāna has seen the stūpa hovering in the air and heard the sound of its voice, he asks the Buddha whether it is also possible to see Prabhūtaratna's "form."[38] In reply, the Buddha describes another of Prabhūtaratna's vows:

> Whenever any Lord Buddhas preach the discourse of the Lotus Sūtra in other Buddha-fields, may the stūpa that possesses the form of my body go to those Buddhas to hear the discourse of the Lotus Sūtra. And whenever those Lord Buddhas want to reveal and show the form of my body to the fourfold assembly, let all those Buddhas come together, along with the bodies they have manifested to teach the Dharma to beings in other Buddha-fields in the ten directions—[bodies] that have the form of a Buddha and their own respective names. Then may the stūpa with[39] the form of my body be revealed and shown to the fourfold assembly.[40]

When he has given this explanation, Śākyamuni gathers his own manifestations together, opens the great stūpa, and shows the figure of Prabhūtaratna seated in a state of deep concentration. Prabhūtaratna then utters praise for the Lotus Sūtra and invites Śākyamuni to join him on the lion throne at the center of the stūpa.

How should we interpret the manifestation of Prabhūtaratna's form? Is it just another miraculous sign associated with Prabhūtaratna's remains, or is it Prabhūtaratna himself? The evidence in the passage is ambiguous and difficult to interpret. When Mahāpratibhāna and the members of the assembly hear the voice from the stūpa, they express astonishment at "seeing someone speak who has been in parinirvana for many hundreds of thousands of *nayutas* of *koṭis* of eons."[41] At this point Prabhūtaratna also begins to function as the active subject of the verb. These signs alone would suggest that Prabhūtaratna himself is present in the center of the stūpa. On the other side is the reference to Prabhūtaratna's vow. Śākyamuni's retelling of the events that lead up to the opening of the stūpa shows that Prabhūtaratna's appearance was made possible by the vow he took at the moment of his parinirvana. In addition, the Prabhūtaratna seated in the stūpa is said to be in a state of deep concentration (*samādhi*). This might suggest that he is no different from the silent figure of the Buddha in the *Tathāgataguhya Sūtra*. Others may "see" him speaking because of his previous vow, but the Buddha himself does not actually rise from his concentration. Then is the Prabhūtaratna who speaks the "real" Prabhūtaratna? At this point we come face to face with one of the great dilemmas in Mahāyāna speculation about the Buddha. The language of the passage does not suggest that Prabhūtaratna's parinirvana was unreal.[42] In fact, the passage assumes its reality. But it transforms the concept of parinirvana by suggesting that Prabhūtaratna was able not only to leave behind powerful and miraculous remnants of his body but to leave behind himself. To ask whether this "self" is the "real" Prabhūtaratna becomes more than a question about the continuation of the Buddha's life: it is a question about "selfhood" itself.

These examples from Mahāyāna literature illustrate why the concept of the Buddha's "previous vow" was so important for Bhāvaviveka's understanding of the Buddha. Behind the concept lay the same problem of absence that confronted the Buddha's followers in the wake of his parinirvana, and the power of the vow meant that this absence was not negative or sterile. The Buddha's enlightenment represented the absence of all concepts, but it could still serve the needs of sentient beings in distinctive ways. What made it possible for enlightenment to have this distinctive impact was the conceptual structure of the vow. The event of enlightenment simply brought the potential of the vow to fruition. So the relationship between enlightenment and the power of the vow is a strong and positive one, perhaps even stronger and more positive than it first appears. The vow needs the event of enlightenment to become active, and enlightenment needs the vow to have its intended effect. It would be true to say that the vow makes it possible for the Buddha to continue acting *in spite of* the absence of conceptuality. But the relationship between the vow and enlightenment is even stronger than this. It is precisely *because* the Buddha has attained the absence of conceptuality that the vow is able to act. As Nāgārjuna said in another context, it is not that everything is possible *in spite of* Emptiness but that "if Emptiness is possible, everything is possible."[43]

The Buddha's Manifestations

If we follow the order of the words in Bhāvaviveka's account of the Buddha quoted at the beginning of this chapter, they lead us to another crucial concept. Bhāvaviveka says, "Because of a promise to seek the welfare and happiness of others and because of a previous vow, a Manifestation Body (*nirmāṇakāya*) arises from [the Body of the Tathāgata] that is capable of assisting everyone." The vow may explain *how* the Buddha is able to speak and still maintain his silence, but it does not tell us *what* speaks. To picture the Buddha's act of teaching as Bhāvaviveka himself did, we need to consider the concept of the Buddha's "manifestations."

The manifestation of ultimate reality is a problematic concept even in theistic traditions where God is thought of as a being who can intervene actively in human affairs. It is even more problematic in a tradition that opposes the concept of God and thinks of ultimate reality as devoid not only of concepts but of any identity of its own. As is often the case, we paper over the difficulties in the act of translation. The word "manifestation" suggests a "someone" who is manifested through a "something." In fact, the meaning of the Sanskrit term *nirmāṇa* comes closer to "an act of magic," and it leaves open the question of the reality not only of the action itself but of the actor who performs the action.[44] To understand the implications of the term, we again have to step behind the text and see what expectations Bhāvaviveka and his readers would have brought from earlier sources to their understanding of the Buddha's "manifestation."

In Nāgārjuna's *Vigrahavyāvartanī,* one of the Madhyamaka tradition's most important works on logic, Nāgārjuna poses a dilemma about the doctrine of Emptiness: If someone tries to establish the doctrine of Emptiness by arguing that everything is empty of "identity" (or "own-being"), the argument itself seems to be self-defeating. If the argument itself has identity, it contradicts itself. But if it has no identity, how can it be used to deny the identity of anything else?[45] Nāgārjuna's answer tells us something about his theory of language, but it also tells us something about his theory of action in general. He starts by conceding that the argument has no identity, but he insists that its lack of identity does not keep it from doing what it is intended to do. As an example, he first cites the use of composite objects, such as a wagon, a pot, or a piece of cloth, to perform meaningful actions. These objects are often cited in Buddhist literature as examples of things that have no identity of their own apart from the identity of their individual components but that can still serve a useful function. They can be used to carry earth, hold water, or protect someone from heat and cold. Each of the objects is "unreal" in itself but can serve a useful purpose as a combination of real components. In a second set of examples, Nāgārjuna says that even *illusory* things—things that are made from nothing at all—can produce significant effects. He says that a person who is "magically created" (*nirmita*) can influence another person who is magically created, and a person who is "illusory" (*māyā-puruṣa*) can create or dissolve another illusory person. In both cases, illusion acts on illusion to bring about a meaningful effect.

The example of an "illusory" or "magically created" person can point in two directions. It is most often used in Buddhist literature to show that someone's ordinary conception of reality is mistaken. In *The Teaching of Vimalakīrti*, a "magically created" person is included in a list of things that are unsubstantial or unreal.[46] Like the moon reflected in water, the reflection in a mirror, the water in a mirage, the sound of an echo, or the shape created by a group of clouds in the sky, the magical creation is simply an illusion. Nāgārjuna begins his argument from this point. He assumes that a "magically created" person is illusory. But he takes the illustration a step further in order to make a different point. He argues that a "magical creation" may be illusory, but it still can be used to do things that others (including perhaps the magicians themselves) recognize are significant. For Bhāvaviveka and other philosophers, the combination of these two points gives the manifestations of the Buddha an ambiguous and fluid sense of reality. They are illusory, but at the same time they have significant effects. A Buddha's manifestation (*nirmāṇa*) is the equivalent, etymologically and ontologically, of a person who is "magically created" (*nirmita*). From one point of view, the manifestation is an illusion, but, in a world where everything finally is an illusion, a manifestation can work just as efficiently as anything else to bring about a "real" effect.

The idea of illusions nested within illusions is one that is associated particularly with the Mahāyāna, but illusory manifestations are not limited to this branch of the tradition. When Bhāvaviveka says that the Buddha acts through a Manifestation Body, he uses a concept that is deeply rooted in the Pali tradition. There is a sutta in the *Dīgha Nikāya* that describes the way Brahmā uses a series of manifestations to appear to the assembly of the thirty-three gods.[47] According to the explanation that accompanies the story, Brahmā's form is too subtle to be perceived by the coarse senses of the gods themselves. When Brahmā wants to pay them a visit, he first announces his presence by displaying an extraordinary radiance, then he rises into the air and "manifests" himself on the seat next to each one of the thirty-three gods. The manifestations then deliver discourses in praise of the Buddha.[48] Brahmā's appearance before the eyes of the lesser gods is like the act of a magician: it is an act of creative illusion making. Brahmā compounds the illusion by manifesting himself thirty-three times and speaking in such a way that each god thinks that only the manifestation seated next to him is speaking.

The power to create manifestations is not limited to gods such as Brahmā. It is also listed in "The Sutta on the Results of Asceticism" (*Sāmaññaphala Sutta*) as one of the powers that come to practitioners who have reached an advanced stage of meditation:

> When the mind is concentrated, purified, cleansed, free from any stain, without a flaw, mild, ready to act, firm, and imperturbable, one applies and bends the mind to manifest (*abhinimmina*) a body that is made of mind (*manomaya-kāya*).

> In this body one creates another body that is material, is made of mind, has every limb and part, and does not lack any of the senses.[49]

The text also mentions a series of powers that involve transformations of the body:

> One experiences various kinds of power. Being one, one becomes many; being many, one becomes one; one becomes visible or invisible; without any obstruction, one moves through a wall, a barrier, or a mountain, as if it were space; one goes up and down through the earth as if it were water; one walks on water without sinking, as if it were earth; one travels cross-legged through the sky like a bird on the wing; even though the moon and sun are great and powerful, one touches and strokes them with the hand; one travels in the body even up to the world of Brahmā.[50]

As the Pali tradition developed, these scriptural images of power and transformation crystallized into a formal system of classification. In *The Path of Discrimination* (*Paṭisambhidāmagga*), we find the abilities to manifest a mind-made body and to transport or transform one's body listed as two of ten "powers" (*iddhi*) that belong to a sage.[51] In Sanskrit literature, the list of powers (*ṛddhi*) is sometimes condensed to two: the power to produce movement (*gamana*) and the power to produce manifestations (*nirmāṇa*).[52]

Bhāvaviveka's treatment of the power to create manifestations can also be located in the framework of a conceptual list. He takes up the topic of manifestation three times in his discussion of the path to Buddhahood. The power to create manifestations (*nairmāṇikī ṛddhi*) appears as part of the list of ten masteries (*vaśitā*) attained by a bodhisattva in the eighth stage of the path. Here it functions as the second of the two kinds of power that constitute the first mastery (the other is the power of transformation—*pariṇāmikī ṛddhi*), and it can be subdivided three ways, into manifestations of body, manifestations of place, and manifestations of voice.[53] The power to create manifestations appears for a second time as part of the superknowledges (*abhijñā*) attained in the tenth stage.[54] Bhāvaviveka then returns briefly to the concept of manifestation in his description of the Buddha Bodies at the end of the chapter.

Lists like these sometimes reveal a great deal about the conceptual system that an author brings to the text. In this case the lists show, for example, that manifestations do not have to come from the Buddha. Manifestations of the Buddha are only a part of a larger body of speculation about the illusion-making powers of a saint. These powers are also represented by the bodhisattvas' ability to create multiple bodies, transform their bodies into Buddha-fields, and miraculously adapt their teaching to the needs of their listeners. These powers come to bodhisattvas even before they reach the final stage of the path. When they finally reach the tenth and final stage (just before the stage of Buddhahood itself), they add the ability to display the twelve acts of a Buddha, an ability that makes even more permeable the barrier between the image of the bodhisattva and the image of the Buddha. But the problem with conceptual lists is that they give the impression that the job of interpretation is over. Pinning down a Buddhist concept by looking at its place in a list is like pinning a butterfly to a collecting tray. It may be easier to identify, but something in the life of the concept is lost.

Fortunately, the lists themselves contain suggestions of stories that can be used to bring the concepts back to life. These suggestions are sometimes only fragmentary, sometimes only a single reference to a long-forgotten personality, but they open up a different world of meaning than the world found in the lists alone. In the description of the ten powers in *The Path of Discrimination*, for example, there is a passage that says:

> Someone who is normally one thinks of himself as many. He thinks of himself as a hundred, a thousand, or a hundred thousand. And with this thought he produces a cognitive resolution: "May I become many!" Even though he is one, he becomes many, like the venerable Cūḷa Panthaka.[55]

Who is Cūḷa Panthaka? The text does not explain, but it suggests that we can discover something of what it means to create miraculous manifestations if we can only discover his identity and learn his story. To trace the venerable Cūḷa Panthaka, we turn to Buddhaghosa, a commentator who was just as fond of good stories as he was of lists. According to Buddhaghosa, Cūḷa Panthaka was an earnest but rather slow monk who had the misfortune to be overshadowed by a successful older brother.[56] The brother had quickly attained the state of arhantship and had tried to pass his own attainment on to his younger brother. But the more the older brother tried, the less successful he became, and his brother's fumbling efforts drove him to distraction. The situation finally came to a crisis, not over a discussion of meditation, but over an invitation to dinner. The older brother had been given the responsibility of allocating invitations to the homes of the monastery's lay supporters. When he received an invitation to a particularly lavish meal at the home of a lay supporter named Jīvika, the brother included himself and five hundred monks but excluded Cūḷa Panthaka. Whether this was out of embarrassment or spite we do not know, but Buddhaghosa does tell us that it reduced Cūḷa Panthaka to tears.

Fortunately for Cūḷa Panthaka, all this took place in sight of the Buddha. With the pedagogical instincts that Cūḷa Panthaka's brother seemed to lack, the Buddha took Cūḷa Panthaka aside and turned his frustration into a tool to teach him a lesson. He gave him a piece of cloth and said, "Keep rubbing this and recite over it, 'Removal of dirt, removal of dirt.'" As Cūḷa Panthaka rubbed it, the cloth became more and more dirty, until he finally grasped the point the Buddha was trying to make. There was nothing wrong with the cloth, and there was nothing wrong with him. It was just his own anxious effort that was causing the problem. Cūḷa Panthaka applied this insight to his meditation on the constituents of the personality and finally found himself making progress.

The next day the scene was played out again, but with a difference. The Buddha, Cūḷa Panthaka's brother, and the rest of the monastery went to

Jīvika's house to be fed, but instead of tagging along behind, Cūḷa Panthaka stayed in the monastery to practice meditation. When the monks were seated, Jīvika approached the Buddha to serve him his meal. To Jīvika's surprise, the Buddha put his hand over his begging bowl and said that he would not accept any food until everyone in the monastery was fed. Jīvika ran to the monastery to invite anyone who had been left behind. When he arrived, he was astonished to find not one monk but a thousand, all glowing with a yellow glow—not a pleasant sight for a layman who had only prepared enough food for five hundred. He hurried back to the Buddha and asked him what to do. The Buddha told him not to worry about the crowd of manifestations but to grab the robe of the first monk he saw and invite him to eat. When Jīvika followed the Buddha's directions, the manifestations vanished, and the real Cūḷa Panthaka rose from his meditation to join the feast. The story ends with Cūḷa Panthaka taking his seat at the head of the congregation and the Buddha allowing the feast to proceed.

What does the story tell us about the Buddha's manifestations? Obviously the story has layers of meaning. As is often the case in his commentaries, Buddhaghosa uses the story to illustrate verses from scripture. In this case, he associates the story with two separate verses. He quotes the first when Cūḷa Panthaka grasps the Buddha's teaching about the cloth and the second when Jīvika sees the thousand manifestations. The first verse makes the point that "dirt" is a metaphor for the desire, hatred, and delusion that the Buddha's teaching is meant to remove.[57] The second describes a monk seated in a mango grove in the midst of a thousand manifestations.[58] The two verses may indicate that Buddhaghosa's story of Cūḷa Panthaka is actually a conflation of two separate stories, or it may be a single story with a double message. In either case, the story can be read as an illustration of two separate points. The first is that effort accompanied by anxious self-concern will not free someone from attachment and illusion. The second is that manifestations are signs of success in meditation. When the story is included in a list of powers, the second point helps explain the meaning of the word "power" itself (Sanskrit *ṛddhi*, Pali *iddhi*). The word comes from a root that means to "prosper" or "succeed."

Buddhaghosa's two verses show the function of the story for Buddhaghosa himself, but they do not exhaust its meaning. In both parts of the story, there is an ironic commentary on the dangers of trying too hard. No matter how much Cūḷa Panthaka tries to practice what his brother taught, his progress is blocked. It is only when the Buddha gives him a palpable demonstration that he understands what has been holding him back. When he sees that all of his diligent effort is part of the problem, he begins to move ahead. There also is an ironic commentary on Cūḷa Panthaka's brother. The brother is an arhant, an accomplished saint, but he still lacks the skill to teach his own brother. When Cūḷa Panthaka is finally given the place of honor at the feast, there is an implied rebuke of the brother, along with a subtle reminder that the race does not always go to the swift. The story also seems to contain a good monastic joke about the earnest merit making of the layman Jīvika.

Here Jīvika puts on a feast for five hundred monks, and what does the Buddha do? He tells Jīvika that he will not eat until he feeds every last monk in the monastery, knowing that Cūḷa Panthaka is wrapped in a shroud of illusion that makes him look like a thousand. It is easy to imagine that this modest twist in the story caused as much amusement in the monastic circles where it was passed down as the figure of Cūḷa Panthaka himself. The message that emerges from each of these elements in the narrative is that success cannot be bought only by diligent effort. It also takes right understanding.

Reading the story as a commentary on the way people mistake diligence for insight makes it more than an illustration of the power to create manifestations, but it also helps interpret the phenomenon of manifestation itself. The story shows that Cūḷa Panthaka's power is a sign of insight. As Tambiah also shows in his study of the forest saints, the monks who are thought to have attained the highest levels of insight are also thought to have the greatest power. The power carries with it a claim to a position of honor in the monastery and also to a position of rank at occasions of merit making for the laity. This combination of three elements—insight, power, and the ability to serve as a focus of merit making—are part of the meaning of the Buddha's manifestations.

But if the power to create manifestations grows out of insight, it also sometimes leads to insight. For Cūḷa Panthaka, the power to create manifestations flowed from the insight he gained from the Buddha. For Jīvika, insight flowed from the encounter with the manifestations. The vision of a thousand manifestations puts his effort at merit making in a different light (both for Jīvika himself and for the monastic audience of the story). It is fair to say that manifestations have a natural teaching function. They are a sign that someone has achieved great insight, but they also point others to a new level of understanding.

When Buddhaghosa turns his attention to the manifestations of the Buddha rather than to the manifestations of the Buddha's disciples, his stories bring the manifestations' teaching function even more fully into the forefront. At the beginning of *The Expositor* (*Atthasālinī*), a commentary on the first book of the Abhidhamma Piṭaka, Buddhaghosa takes up a question that has occurred more than once to commentators on the Buddhist scriptures: how was the Buddha able to teach so much and still get on with the ordinary business of monastic life? Part of the answer is that the Buddha could rely on manifestations. Even without manifestations, the Buddha was capable of doing great things. Buddhaghosa explains that the Buddha's mouth and tongue were so well formed that he could deliver long discourses in the time it would take an ordinary person to thank a host for a meal. But there were moments when the Buddha was called upon to be in two places at once, a problem that even his great eloquence could not solve. One such moment occurred when the Buddha spent three months in heaven teaching the Dharma to his mother. To continue his teaching in this world, Buddhaghosa says that the Buddha created a manifestation (*nimmita*) of himself and resolved that it grasp a robe and begging bowl in a certain way, assume a certain quality of voice, and deliver a certain body of teaching.[59] Fa-hsien and Hsüan-tsang also report a story of the Buddha's trip to heaven as part of their accounts of the holy sites at Śrāvastī, but in their version, the Buddha is replaced by a Buddha image rather than by a manifestation.[60] The Chinese accounts do not indicate that the image teaches in the Buddha's absence, but they do say that it rises from its seat to greet the Buddha when he returns. In any case, the Buddha's manifestations differ in one crucial respect from the manifestations of saints: they can function in the Buddha's absence. With Cūḷa Panthaka, it only took a tug on the edge of his robe to make the real Cūḷa Panthaka appear. But in Buddhaghosa's story of the Buddha, the Buddha is absent—not yet in the definitive sense, but temporarily—and the manifestation has to substitute for the Buddha himself. Buddhaghosa's story anticipates the problem of the parinirvana and suggests a solution: artificial or magical forms of the Buddha can be left behind to substitute, as teaching devices and as objects of veneration, for the presence of the Buddha himself.

The Buddha's Sustaining Power

There is one more concept that needs to be mentioned to complete the picture of the Buddha's enduring influence. It is not a concept that plays a major role in Bhāvaviveka's explanation of the Buddha's speech, but it is so important in other contexts that it should not be overlooked. Bhāvaviveka describes one of the powers of a bodhisattva in the eighth stage as an ability to "sustain" the existence of manifestations:

> [At will, the bodhisattva] sustains (*adhitiṣṭhati*) innumerable past, present, and future bodies, the completion of Buddha-fields, the destruction and creation of innumerable world systems.
>
> Also at will [the bodhisattva sustains] a Buddha-field in [the bodhisattva's] own body, [the bodhisattva's] own body in that [Buddha-field], and a Buddha Body in [the bodhisattva's] own field.[61]

The first verse describes the bodhisattva's power to sustain "manifestations of body" (*kāya-nirmāṇa*), and the second describes the ability to sustain "manifestations of place" (*viṣaya-nirmāṇa*). The categories themselves are easy to locate in the standard outlines of the bodhisattva path and need not detain us.[62] But what should we make of the verb "sustain" (*adhitiṣṭhati*)? How is it related to the act of manifestation? And what kind of agency, power, or influence does it imply?

The word *adhiṣṭhāna* is defined as "standing on or near," "residing in," or "having authority or dominion over."[63] In a political context, the word can be used to name the relationship between a king and the territory over which the king rules. In religious literature, it is sometimes used for the relationship between God and the material reality out of which God creates an incarnation. In the *Bhagavad Gītā* Krishna says, "Exercising control over (*adhiṣṭhāya*) my own nature, I come into being by my own magic."[64] It is tempting to extend the example of the *Gītā* to Bhāvaviveka and say that the bodhisattva "takes control over" (rather than "sustains") innumerable bodies. Certainly the Buddhist use of the term shares the sense of power and authority that is present in the *Gītā*'s picture of the relationship between God and nature. But it is also clear when we dig more deeply into Buddhist literature that the Buddhist use of the term responds to a different set of problems and carries a different meaning. One aspect of the difference is suggested by the source that Bhāvaviveka drew on to describe the "power to manifest bodies." According to *The Bodhisattva Stages* (*Bodhisattvabhūmi*), "[the bodhisattva] sustains (*adhitiṣṭhati*) a manifestation that *continues* when the bodhisattva or Tathāgata has ceased."[65] Here the act of *adhiṣṭhāna* is tied to the problem of continuity. It involves the ability to set something in motion that continues when the original agent is gone. In the *Gītā* there is no serious question about continuity; the text simply assumes that God will continue to act. But in a Buddhist context, where the goal of religious discipline, at least nominally, is one of cessation, continuity is a fundamental issue. To "exercise control" is not just a question of initiating a creative act but of investing it with the power to continue when the actor is gone.

There are some situations in Buddhist literature where the element of continuity in the verb *adhi-sthā* is clearly dominant. In *The Treasury of the Abhidharma* (*Abhidharmakośa*), Vasubandhu gives an elaborate explanation of the Buddha's "powers" (*prabhāva*), one of which is the power to "manifest" (*nirmāṇa*), "transform" (*pariṇāma*), and "continue" (*adhiṣṭhāna*) external objects.[66] In his discussion of the concept of manifestation, Vasubandhu raises the question of continuity. He says that the action of a manifestation normally has to mirror the action of the person who created it. In most situations, the manifestation can only speak when the person who created it is speaking. Otherwise it has to remain silent. The one exception to this rule is the manifestation of the Buddha. The Buddha has the power to create a manifestation and cause it to speak when the Buddha himself is silent. How does Vasubandhu explain the exception? By using the verb *adhi-sthā*. It is by an act of *adhiṣṭhāna* that the Buddha is able to set manifestations in motion to act in his place when he himself has ceased to act. If *adhiṣṭhāna* involves the power to set something in motion, how far does the power extend? Does *adhiṣṭhāna* continue after death, or is it only something that can continue during a person's life? Vasubandhu focuses on the Buddha's disciple Mahākāśyapa, but his explanation shows how one can use *adhiṣṭhāna* to think about the continuing activity of the Buddha.[67]

> Does the *adhiṣṭhāna* continue only as long as the person is alive or also after death? *Adhiṣṭhāna* also [continues] after death, because it is by Ārya Mahākāśyapa's *adhiṣṭhāna* that [his] skeleton continues to exist. [*Adhiṣṭhāna*] does not apply, however, to something that is not solid [such as Mahākāśyapa's flesh].[68]

Adhiṣṭhāna inheres in the bones that Mahākāśyapa left behind to wait for the appearance of the future Buddha.[69] In other words, it is like a relic that continues when the source of the relic is no longer present. Here the only limitation on the function of *adhiṣṭhāna* is that it has to reside in something like bone that is solid enough to retain its shape.

When the word *adhiṣṭhāna* is used to name a potential or power bestowed on an object, it is no longer possible to translate it simply as "continuation." But the other obvious alternatives present problems as well. In some contexts, *adhiṣṭhāna* comes very close to the word "vow" (*praṇidhāna*). In the description of Prabhūtaratna's vows in *The Lotus Sūtra*, the word *praṇidhāna* is used for a general statement of Prabhūtaratna's intentions and *adhiṣṭhāna* for the specific promise. But it is impossible to make such a clear distinction in every case. There are just as many places where *praṇidhāna* names the specific promise. There are also places where *adhiṣṭhāna* refers to someone's general "power" or "influence," rather than to a specific vow. In Haribhadra's commentary on the opening lines of *The Perfection of Wisdom in Eight Thousand Lines*, he asks how Ānanda can say, "Thus have I heard," when he did not actually hear all the words of the Buddha. The answer is this: "When teaching is made by the *adhiṣṭhāna* of the Tathāgata, it is like his teaching: It is heard from the Buddha himself, because of his power (*sāmarthya*), even when it is heard from someone else."[70] Here *adhiṣṭhāna* refers to the Buddha's continuing influence, an influence that can be felt directly or through the mediation of others. To capture all of these meanings in a single word is virtually impossible. It seems best to use a general phrase like Conze's "sustaining power" and remind oneself that the power sometimes has a strong element of continuity and often is focused in specific resolutions or vows.[71]

In most of the passages quoted so far, *adhiṣṭhāna* is a power that continues from the past into the future. It responds to the problem of continuity and grows out of speculation about the remnants of an absent saint. But there is also a class of examples where *adhiṣṭhāna* expresses an influence or power that takes place in the present. When the young pilgrim Sudhana meets the bodhisattva Maitreya at the end of the *Gaṇḍavyūha Sūtra*, Maitreya manifests the vision of a peaked dwelling, and in the peaked dwelling Sudhana sees a miraculous manifestation of Maitreya's career. It is "by the power of *adhiṣṭhāna*" that Maitreya creates the vision.[72] When Vimalakīrti empties his room to prepare for the visit of Mañjuśrī, he does it with *adhiṣṭhāna*.[73] When the goddess in *The Teaching of Vimalakīrti* transforms Śāriputra from a man to a woman in order to teach him a lesson about distinctions of gender, she does it with *adhiṣṭhāna*.[74] There is no reason to assume in any of these passages that *adhiṣṭhāna* comes from a past resolution (although there is nothing to rule it out). The word indicates simply the present power of the saint.

The most far-reaching examples of the Buddha's *adhiṣṭhāna* are ones where it is difficult to tell whether the power comes from past resolutions or from the Buddha's present action. It is common in the Perfection of Wisdom literature to find *adhiṣṭhāna* used almost as a synonym for words that refer to the Buddha's "power" or "grace." A good example is the following exchange between Śāriputra and the Buddha in *The Perfection of Wisdom in Eight Thousand Lines*:

> *Sariputra:* It is through the Buddha's might [*anubhāva*], sustaining power [*adhiṣṭhāna*] and grace [*parigraha*] that Bodhisattvas study this deep perfection of wisdom, and progressively train in Thusness?
>
> *The Lord:* So it is, Sariputra. They are known to the Tathagata, they are sustained and seen by the Tathagata, and the Tathagata beholds them with his Buddha-eye.[75]

The concept of *adhiṣṭhāna* can also be interwoven with the bodhisattva's vow on one side and the power of the Buddha on the other. When we first looked at the story of Sadāprarudita's "act of truth," we focused almost completely on the power of the bodhisattva vow. But if we look closely at the language of the passage, we find that the power of the bodhisattva's resolution is deeply enmeshed in the power of the Buddha.

> Sadaprarudita replied: "Do not trouble your mind about the mutilated condition of my body! I shall myself now make it whole again by the magical power of my enunciation of the Truth [*satyādhiṣṭhānena*]. As I am in truth irreversible, have been predicted to full enlightenment, and am known to the Tathagatas by my unconquerable resolution—may through this Truth, through this utterance of the Truth [*satya-vacanena*] this my body be again as it was before!" That very moment, instant and second, through the Buddha's might [*anubhāva*] and through the perfect purity of the bodhisattva 's resolution, the body of the Bodhisattva Sadaprarudita became again as it had been before.[76]

The passage sets three different concepts in such close proximity that they practically explode with meaning. There is the *adhiṣṭhāna* or "power" of the act of truth itself; there is the bodhisattva's "resolution" (which corresponds to "vow" in the sense of "wish"); and there is the "might" of the Buddha. The passage traces Sadāprarudita's miraculous transformation to each of these causes in turn. It is almost as if the author could not decide what really was the cause. But the confusion does not come from any lack of clarity. The event not only has many causes but the causes are all related, and they are related so closely that they are virtually identified. On one level, the act of truth works out of forces that inhere in the bodhisattva career itself, but not without support from the Buddha's might. Part of the transformation that takes place in Sadāprarudita's journey is the realization that he can rely on his own power, but his sense of self-reliance also reflects the sense that he has been nurtured by the power of others. From one perspective, his own *adhiṣṭhāna* is simply the recognition, acceptance, and actualization of the *adhiṣṭhāna* of the Buddha.

It is this combination of causal elements that brings the concept of *adhiṣṭhāna* so close to a theistic concept of grace. The *adhiṣṭhāna* of a Buddha or great bodhisattva surrounds people and nurtures them through the stages of the bodhisattva path. It also elicits a response of recognition and resolution. There is no indication in Sadāprarudita's story that the power of the Buddha is the lingering presence of a vanished saint. It is a lively force that nurtures and guides him in a difficult quest. But what finally distinguishes the concept of *adhiṣṭhāna* from the idea of divine power in a theistic system is the logic of "remainder." The concept of *adhiṣṭhāna*, like the concept of a vow or a manifestation, grows out of an image of the Buddha as a being who acts by leaving behind remnants of his power. It is a measure of the religious richness of the Mahāyāna that this principle could be transformed into an image of power so affirmative and so all-embracing that the absence of the Buddha almost disappears from view.

Chapter 5

The Synchronic Dimension of the Buddha's Absence

Susan Sontag has said that the force of a photographic image comes from its ability to turn the tables on reality—to turn reality into a shadow.[1] We found in chapter 3 that signs of the Buddha also turn the tables on reality, but in a different way. Like photographs, the Buddha's physical remnants assume the status of material realities. They are not just images of an absent reality but deposits (or, as Stanley Tambiah says, sedimentations) of the saint they signify. In some situations, they can even become more real or more present than the saint. Like the traces of a subatomic particle in a cloud chamber, they can make accessible a power that otherwise would be unapproachable, unfocused, or simply unavailable. But what makes the Buddha's traces distinctive is that they can also turn the tables on themselves. Part of the process of interpreting or "reading" a relic in a Buddhist context is to understand that it is self-reflective and self-critical—as if to say, "This is an object that has power and is worthy of veneration, but its greatest power comes from its ability to shift attention away from what it *is* to what it is *not*."

We have already confronted this type of interpretation when we considered the exchange between Tambiah and his Thai informants over the interpretation of amulets. When Tambiah asked the Thai businessman to explain why amulets brought him prosperity, the businessman said that they reminded him of a moral discipline, and the moral discipline itself was enough to bring good luck. The same process of interpretation was present in the scriptural account of the Buddha's death. In the *Mahāparinibbāna Sutta*, the Buddha advised monks not to venerate the remnants of his physical body but to focus on the discipline that would promote their own spiritual welfare. The responsibility of caring for the Buddha's physical remains fell instead to prominent members of the lay community. Monks and nuns were expected, ideally, to get on with the quest for nirvana and to leave the great acts of merit making to the laity. But the distinction between the veneration of physical objects and the pursuit of a moral ideal was not strictly limited to the distinction between the laity and the monks. Tambiah's Thai informants had a good grasp of the interpretive process that led from the physical object to the moral message that lay behind it. They understood that the signs of the saints made available not just an accumulation of power but an example and a message.

When I noted this process of interpretation for the first time, I referred to it as *synchronic* in order to stress the timeless quality of these interpretive judgments. From the synchronic point of view, even at the moment when the Buddha is sitting with a group of disciples and delivering his teaching, when he is as present in a physical sense as he can actually be, there is also a sense in which the Buddha is not there at all. What the disciples perceive as a physical presence is actually an absence. The absence may be depicted as an absence of speech (as in Bhāvaviveka's image of the silent Buddha), or it may be conceived as the absence of identity itself, but the absence is an essential part of the experience a person has of the Buddha, and it has to be confronted whenever someone wants to probe beneath the surface and develop a deeper awareness of what the Buddha is.

The doctrinal implications of the synchronic sense of absence are apparent in many ways throughout Buddhist literature. We have already encountered one example in the Buddha's famous exchange with Vakkali. The Buddha is reported to have said that it was not enough to see the "vile body" that was present to the senses. To see the Buddha properly one also had to "see" the Dharma. Out of this passage and others like it grew the doctrine of the two Bodies of the Buddha—the Form Body (*rūpa-kāya*) and Dharma Body (*dharma-kāya*)—the doctrine on which so much of the philosophical discussion of the Buddha is based.[2] The doctrine is a fundamental one in Buddhist thought and is found in all but the earliest scriptural accounts of the Buddha. What is most surprising about the doctrine, however, is not that it is so pervasive but that it is so difficult to pin down. In different contexts the doctrine can take very different forms. To "see Dharma" may sometimes be no more than to see a physical book. But to see Dharma inevitably presses beyond the physical object toward the level of personal understanding. When someone sees Dharma as a material object, the process of interpretation suggests the immaterial. When someone sees form, it suggests the formless. When someone externalizes and objectifies the Dharma as a doctrine, it suggests understanding. And when someone understands the Dharma in a way that is limited or distorted by a particular perspective, it suggests the ultimate, nonconceptual, and inclusive awareness of the Buddha. When this process of interpretation has run its course, it leaves a concept of the Dharma with many layers—a concept in which the layers themselves are deeply interfused. To understand the elements that motivate this process of interpretation, we need to find a way to separate the layers and identify the steps that a philosopher like Bhāvaviveka would go through in an attempt to confront the Dharma Body of the Buddha.

The Dharma Body

One of the most basic expressions of the distinction between the physical Buddha and the Dharma is the distinction between the relics of the Buddha's physical body and the texts that embody the Buddha's teaching. In *The Perfection of Wisdom in Eight Thousand Lines* we read:

> Suppose that there are two persons. One of the two, a son or daughter of good family, has written down this perfection of wisdom, made a copy of it; he would then put it up, and would honour, revere, worship, and adore it with heavenly flowers, incense, perfumes, wreaths, unguents, aromatic powders, strips of cloth, parasols, banners, bells, flags, with rows of lamps all round, and with manifold kinds of worship. The other would deposit in Stupas the relics of the Tathagata who has gone to Parinirvana; he would then take hold of them and preserve them; he would honor, worship and adore them with heavenly flowers, incense, etc., as before. Which one of the two, O Lord, would beget the greater merit?
>
> . . . Greater would be the merit of the devotee of the perfection of wisdom compared not only with that of a person who would build many kotis of Stupas made of the seven precious things, enshrining the relics of the Tathagata. It would be greater than the merit of one who would completely fill the entire Jambudvipa with such Stupas.[3]

This passage sets up the contrast between the Buddha's physical body and the Dharma as a distinction between two kinds of worship. A person has the option of building a shrine to worship the Buddha's relics or of making a copy of a text to worship the Buddha's teaching. It is tempting to read a social message into the passage and treat the distinction between the two kinds of worship as a distinction between a form of popular worship and an elite tradition of scribal wisdom. But the text is not drawing a contrast between worship and study, or even between those who favor tangible remnants of the Buddha over remnants that are more intellectual. It is simply drawing a contrast between the worship of one physical object and another. Worship of a relic enshrined in a stūpa would be effective, but, given a choice, the passage favors worship of the text itself.[4]

To get a picture of the ritual setting where this worship was carried out, we can turn again to the story of the melancholy young pilgrim Sadāprarudita. When Sadāprarudita reaches the goal of his journey, he sees his teacher, Dharmodgata, preaching in the marketplace of a city called Gandhavatī ("The Fragrant"). Next to Dharmodgata he sees a peaked dwelling where Dharmodgata has placed a book containing the Perfection of Wisdom. The book has been inscribed on gold tablets, and over the book hover thousands of gods scattering heavenly flowers, sandalwood powder, and gold dust. When Sadāprarudita asks the leader of the gods why he is offering such extravagant worship, the god explains that the book is the Perfection of Wisdom, the mother of bodhisattvas, and anyone who trains in the Perfection of Wisdom attains the omniscience of a Buddha. It is this causal association between the Perfection of Wisdom and the Buddha's omniscience that makes it possible for the physical text to serve as a ritual substitute for the Buddha and to gather around itself all of the devotional actions normally associated with the cult of the Buddha's relics. In fact, we find that the ritual substitution of a book or written phrase for a physical relic of the Buddha is quite common in Buddhist literature of this period. Gregory Schopen has shown that early Mahāyāna sūtras often describe the physical book as an object that makes a "spot of earth become a shrine" of the Buddha.[5] In later centuries it became common to enclose impressions of the Buddha's words inside stūpas in place of the remnants of the Buddha's physical body.[6] The pattern of association eventually became so deeply embedded in Mahāyāna tradition that shrines or temples often took on the appearance of libraries and the libraries often doubled as temples.

The relationship of contrast and substitution between the book as a physical expression of the Dharma and the physical form of the Buddha allowed a rich variety of symbolic and imaginative transpositions, not just in the act of worship but also in the literary expressions of the Buddha's teaching. The passage in *The Perfection of Wisdom in Eight Thousand Lines* that distinguishes between the worship of the book and the worship of relics starts by drawing a simple, one-dimensional contrast between the book and the physical relics of the Buddha. But as the passage develops, the distinction between the physical Buddha and the Dharma takes on more complexity of meaning. After distinguishing the book from the Buddha's physical relics, the text refers to the physical book itself as a relic (*śarīra*).[7] This makes possible a second distinction between the Dharma in its material form, as letters on a page, and the Dharma as an act of understanding. The sūtra says, "O Kauśika, the Tathāgata attains his body (*śarīra*) through the skill-in-means of the Perfection of Wisdom. This [body] is the location (*āśraya*) of omniscience. At this location omniscience comes into being, the Buddha relic (*śarīra*) comes into being, the Dharma relic (*śarīra*) comes into being, and the Saṃgha relic (*śarīra*) comes into being."[8] At first the words of the sūtra seem to outline a series of stages for someone to follow in meditating on the omniscience of a Buddha. But the causal sequence cannot be followed consistently. The word for the Buddha's "body" at the beginning of the passage is also the word for Buddha "relic" at the end. The text makes most sense if it is read as suggesting not a sequence of practice but the simultaneous transposition of images that might take place when someone meditates on the different meanings of the Perfection of Wisdom. Like Sadāprarudita when he walked into the marketplace in Gandhavatī, a person first encounters the Perfection of Wisdom in a particular location, a location that is identified in this passage with the body of the Buddha. This location arises out of the Perfection of Wisdom (as a form of understanding) and manifests itself in the Perfection of Wisdom (as a book). This location is worthy of worship in part because it is the site of the Dharma relic but also because it is associated with the Buddha's omniscience. As the text explains, this location is the place where the Buddha's omniscience is attained. By implication, it is also a place where the student or the worshiper can follow the Buddha's example and realize the Perfection of Wisdom for himself or herself.

The play on the word *śarīra* ("body" or, in the plural, "relics") in this passage illustrates why so much speculation about the Buddha was able to coalesce around the concept of the "body." When they are grouped together, the different Sanskrit words that express an aspect of the concept of the "body" allow an enormous range of conceptual possibilities. In addition to the word *śarīra*, which suggests a remnant or relic as well as a physical body, there is also a word for the Buddha's "personal being" (*ātma-bhāva*). At the beginning of *The Large Sūtra on the Perfection of Wisdom*, the Buddha's "personal being" is associated with a number of miraculous signs that indicate in advance the grandeur of the teaching that the Buddha is about to deliver. This body is said to be one "with which one can never be satiated" and one "that is consistent with the essential nature of all things."[9] Other texts refer to the Buddha's physical body with words that indicate "form" or "shape"—sometimes a shape that is quite palpable and sometimes a shape that is merely a "reflection" of another reality.[10] These meanings can all be subsumed and others added in the word *kāya*, the word that eventually came to dominate the doctrinal reflection on the concept of the Buddha Bodies. *Kāya* can mean not only the physical body, like *śarīra* and *ātma-bhāva*, but also "body" in the sense of "combination" or "collection." This further meaning makes it possible to speak of the Buddha's body as a "combination" of virtues or as a "collection" of teachings. When the different meanings of the word *kāya* are combined with the different meanings of the word *dharma*, it is possible to speak of the Buddha simultaneously as the physical entity that consists of the Dharma (a physical text), a combination or collection of the Dharma (the teaching), and a combination of *dharma*s (virtues or qualities) that are the Buddha's distinguishing characteristics.[11]

To distinguish the different ways one can speak of the Dharma as a "body," we can turn to the more systematic work of the commentators. The Perfection of Wisdom literature itself generated a long tradition of explanation, from massive, multivolume works such as Haribhadra's *Light on the Ornament of Realization* (*Abhisamayālaṃkārālokā*) to brief verse summaries like Dignāga's *Epitome of the Perfection of Wisdom* (*Prajñāpāramitāpiṇḍārtha*).[12] The commentators do their best to bring order out of the varied and sometimes inconsistent expressions in the sūtras themselves. Dignāga, for example, confronts the ambiguity in the scriptural concept of the Perfection of Wisdom by saying, "The Perfection of Wisdom is nondual knowledge; it is also the Tathāgata and [the goal] to be attained. The word ['Perfection of Wisdom'] also refers to the book and the path, since [the book and the path] have this [Perfection of Wisdom] as their meaning and their goal."[13] The verse gives not one but three definitions of the Perfection of Wisdom. Dignāga first identifies the Perfection of Wisdom with the Buddha's nondual awareness, then he says that this nondual awareness is the Tathāgata (which is another way of saying that the Perfection of Wisdom is the Buddha in the form of the Dharma Body). Then Dignāga identifies the Perfection of Wisdom not only with the book in which this understanding is expressed but also with the path that is used to attain it. In a passage based on Dignāga's verse, Haribhadra explains that nondual knowledge is the primary or literal (*mukhya*) meaning of the word "Perfection of Wisdom," and the book and path are secondary or metaphorical (*gauṇa*) meanings.[14] What makes the metaphorical usage possible is that the book and the path are "conducive to attaining" the Perfection of Wisdom in the primary sense: they are the means someone can use to become a Buddha.

The distinction between the Perfection of Wisdom as a book and the Perfection of Wisdom as a path reflects a traditional distinction in Abhidharma literature between the Dharma as teaching and the Dharma as understanding. In *The Treasury of the Abhidharma (Abhidharmakośa)*, Vasubandhu says, "The Master's true Dharma is twofold: it is scripture (*āgama*) and understanding (*adhigama*)."[15] In the commentary, Vasubandhu explains that the word "scripture" refers to the three parts of the Buddhist canon (Sūtras, Vinaya, and Abhidharma) and that the word "understanding" refers to the "auxiliaries of enlightenment" (*bodhipakṣya*). Earlier in the same text, Vasubandhu explained that the auxiliaries of enlightenment constitute the fourth Noble Truth, the path to the cessation of suffering,[16] so Vasubandhu evidently uses the term "auxiliaries of enlightenment" as another way of referring to the path to nirvana. He also explains that the Dharma as "understanding" (*adhigama*) is carried out by a "practitioner" (*pratipattṛ*). "Understanding," in other words, is another name for what Dignāga called the "path" (*pratipad*).

Vasubandhu approaches the same point from a somewhat different perspective elsewhere in the text when he explains the meaning of the three refuges.[17] He opens the discussion by asking, "What does someone take refuge in who takes refuge in the Buddha, Dharma, and Saṃgha?" To answer his own question, he says that refuge in the Dharma is directed toward the experience of nirvana, an experience that is "uniquely characterized by the pacification of suffering," thus identifying the Dharma not with the path to nirvana, as in the earlier passage, but with nirvana itself. If we put Dignāga's comments about the Perfection of Wisdom together with Vasubandhu's reflections on the nature of the Dharma, we have four possible ways to understand the meaning of Dharma. The Dharma can be thought of as nondual awareness, as a book or collection of teachings, as a path, or as the cessation of suffering.

These options seem to have gained a certain amount of currency in the literature of Vasubandhu's time. In a discussion of the three refuges at the beginning of the *Ratnagotravibhāga*, for example, the author says that there are two kinds of Dharma in which someone can take refuge: the Dharma as teaching (*deśanā*) and the Dharma as understanding (*adhigama*).[18] The distinction follows Vasubandhu almost to the letter. But Asaṅga's commentary on the text gives us something we did not get from Vasubandhu. Asaṅga groups the "path" and "cessation" together under the heading of Dharma as "understanding." He explains that understanding can come in two forms: either the experience of cessation that is the goal of the path or the practice of the path itself.[19] In other words, the understanding of the Dharma can correspond to either the third or the fourth of the four Noble Truths. Asaṅga goes on to say that the distinction between Dharma as path and Dharma as cessation corresponds to a distinction between means and end: the Dharma can either be used to attain the goal, or it can be identified with the goal itself. With the help of Asaṅga's explanatory comments, we can simplify the list of meanings for the word "Dharma" by grouping path and cessation together, thus reducing our list of four to a list of three: the Dharma as a book or collection of teachings, the Dharma as understanding (including both the Dharma as path and the Dharma as goal), and the Dharma as nondual awareness. The list can be simplified even further if we group understanding and nondual awareness together under a category of Dharma as a cognitive process or state.

Grouping the different definitions of Dharma together helps bring order to what would otherwise be a confusing series of explanatory options, but it also poses some odd problems. In Bhāvaviveka's account of the Buddha Bodies, he points out that an attempt to equate the Dharma with the Buddha's insight makes it difficult to explain why there should be two separate acts of refuge, one in the Buddha and one in the Dharma.[20] If the Buddha and the Dharma are identical to the Buddha's insight—whether this insight is viewed as the cessation of suffering or as an experience of nonduality—there is no reason for anyone to take separate refuge in the Dharma. Taking refuge in the Buddha would be enough. Bhāvaviveka responds to the problem by saying that the Dharma should be understood in two ways: as a means and as a result. He does not say any more about what he means, but the commentary on the *Ratnagotravibhāga* again makes it easy to reconstruct what he had in mind. If the Dharma can be either the cessation that comes at the end of the path or the path itself, the same term can refer to two different things, and the two different things can be the objects of two separate acts of refuge. Refuge in the Buddha can be directed toward the Dharma as goal, and refuge in the Dharma itself can be directed toward the Dharma as path.

The *Ratnagotravibhāga* actually handles the problem somewhat differently. Instead of distinguishing two separate meanings of the word "Dharma," as Bhāvaviveka does, the text argues that there is actually only *one* refuge, the refuge in the Buddha, and refuge in the Dharma and Saṃgha are merely conventional devices.[21] Whether one of these two strategies is more effective than the other is impossible to decide simply on the basis of the texts themselves, but it is worth knowing the nature of the philosophers' questions, even if the questions yield no clear answer. The quest for a deeper understanding of the concept of Dharma created a tension in the philosophers' minds. There was a strong impulse to unify the understanding of Buddha and Dharma under a single category, and there was an equally strong impulse to distinguish the Buddha and Dharma as different objects of devotion. The two impulses were held together by the ambiguity of the word "Dharma." What this word referred to in a particular context depended on the perspective from which the question was asked.

If we follow the argument of the *Ratnagotravibhāga* a step beyond the controversy about the act of refuge, we find that the text calls attention to another important level of meaning. In a passage that approaches the concept of the Dharma through the medium of the Dharma Body, the text says:

> The Dharma Body should be understood in two ways: as the completely pure Dharma Element and as the profound and extensive teaching that flows from that [Dharma Element].[22]

Here the text equates the Dharma Body with two categories: a body of teaching and the pure Dharma Element (*dharma-dhātu*). The identification of the Dharma with a body of teaching is already familiar from other contexts. Asaṅga's commentary on the verse adds a somewhat new perspective by distinguishing the "profound" teaching of the bodhisattva canon (*bodhisattva-piṭaka*) from the "extensive" teaching of other canonical literature, but the idea itself does not break new ground. This is not true, however, of the concept of the Dharma Element. Asaṅga's commentary makes it clear that "Dharma Element" is not just another name for the Buddha's awareness; he explains that instead it is "the object of nonconceptual knowledge."[23] It is not the Buddha's knowledge but rather the *reality* that the Buddha knows.

What does this new term add to our understanding of the word "Dharma"? First, on the most mechanical level, it adds the possibility of a new set of conceptual equivalents. If we look at *The Discrimination Between the Middle and the Extremes*, for example, we find that the term "Dharma Element" appears in a list of the synonyms for Emptiness:

> In brief, the synonyms of Emptiness are Thusness, the Reality Limit, Sign-less[ness], the Ultimate, and the Dharma Element.[24]

Vasubandhu's commentary gives a brief explanation of what the synonyms mean:

> [To say that Emptiness is] Thusness means that [Emptiness] is not different, in the sense that it always [remains] the same. [To say that Emptiness is] the Reality Limit means that it is not false, in the sense that it is not a false entity. [To say that Emptiness is] Signless[ness] means that it is the cessation of signs in the sense that it is the absence of all signs. [To say that Emptiness is] the Ultimate means that it is the object of the knowledge of the saints and thus is the

> object of the knowledge that is ultimate. [To say that Emptiness is] the Dharma Element means that it is the cause of the qualities of a saint, and all the attributes of a saint arise with this [Emptiness] as their basis. Here the word "element" means cause.[25]

Vasubandhu does not associate all of the terms explicitly with the object of the Buddha's awareness, but in cases where the term could go either way, as is true of the term "Ultimate" (*paramārtha*), he follows Asaṅga's lead and emphasizes the objective aspect of Emptiness.

Once the Dharma Body has been identified with the *object* of the Buddha's awareness, the possibilities of conceptual elaboration are almost limitless. Most of the fundamental texts in the Mahāyāna philosophical tradition set out to determine not simply *how* the Buddha knows but *what* the Buddha knows. Sometimes the content of the Buddha's cognition is spoken of as the "nature" or "identity" (*svabhāva*) of the categories of phenomenal existence (*dharmas*). This nature or identity can be referred to as the Reality or "thatness" (*tattva*) of a thing, it can be referred to as Thusness (*tathatā*), or it can be referred to simply as Dharma Nature or "*dharma*-ness" (*dharmatā*). In the tradition of the Perfection of Wisdom literature, the nature or identity (*svabhāva*) of things finally is that they have no nature (*niḥsvabhāva*), and this lack of nature constitutes their Emptiness (*śūnyatā*). Again in the terminology of the Perfection of Wisdom literature, the Emptiness of things can be referred to as their dependent arising (*pratītya-samutpāda*), and dependent arising is said to be identical to no-arising (*anutpāda*).[26] Because the Buddha can be considered a *dharma* like everything else, and the nature of all *dharmas* is Emptiness, it is possible to say that the nature of the Buddha (*buddhatva*) is also the nature of all things, a statement that can easily be transformed into the claim that all things have Buddha Nature.[27] In a verse that is widely quoted in Mahāyāna philosophical literature, the Buddha is said to be similar to all *dharmas* by virtue of the fact that all *dharmas* have the characteristic of no-arising (*anutpāda*).[28] Depending on the context or the purpose of a particular author or text, all of these equivalents of Emptiness can be identified with the Dharma Body of the Buddha, and because the Dharma Body *is* the Buddha, they can also be identified with the Buddha as an individual or with Buddhahood itself.

To think of the Dharma as the object of the Buddha's knowledge not only provides us with a new list of synonyms and a new list of conceptual equivalents but also with a new series of problems. If objects of knowledge are closely tied to the mind that knows them—so closely, in some situations, that there is no duality between them—is the Dharma an object that is constituted by the mind, or is it present in an unchanging way apart from the mind that knows it? This question and others like it test the limits of the concept of nonduality. If the Dharma Nature is pure and undifferentiated, it should allow no duality. And if it does not allow any duality, how can it be known at one moment and not at another? There is a fascinating passage in *The Descent to Laṅkā Sūtra* that raises precisely this question. The text explains that the word "Dharma" can have two meanings: It can refer to the Dharma Nature that is known individually (*pratyātma-dharmatā*) and to the Dharma Nature of ancient duration (*paurāṇa-sthiti-dharmatā*).[29]

> When I said this, O Mahāmati, I had in mind two kinds of Dharma. What are these two kinds of Dharma? I had in mind the Dharma Nature that is known individually and the Dharma Nature of ancient duration. Of these, what do I mean by the Dharma Nature that is known individually? It is the object of individual understanding that Tathāgatas have understood and I also have understood, without anything being lost or anything being added. It is devoid of words and concepts and free from the duality of syllables and understanding. What is the Dharma Nature of ancient duration? O Mahāmati, the ancient road of the Dharma Nature is like a mine of gold, silver, or pearls. This is the duration of the Dharma Element, O Mahāmati: whether Tathāgatas arise or Tathāgatas do not arise, the Dharma Nature of *dharmas*, the duration of the Dharma, the certainty of the Dharma endures.

It is almost as if we were hearing an echo of Bhāvaviveka's comment on the ambiguity involved in the act of refuge in the Dharma. The Dharma is one, but it can be approached in two ways. It can be the Dharma known at one moment rather than another, and it can be the Dharma that never changes. The distinction between these two aspects of the Dharma is one more reminder of the tension between unity and diversity in the speculative tradition of the Mahāyāna. To accommodate two contradictory options, the concept of the Dharma can be split, not into two Dharmas, but into Dharma viewed from two different points of view.

One of the most revealing ways to explore the implications of Dharma in its objective mode is to focus again on the metaphors concealed in the key technical terms. It is clear from Vasubandhu's commentary on the synonyms of Emptiness that the word for Dharma Element (*dharma-dhātu*), for example, gains a large part of its meaning from a metaphor of substance. The text defines the Dharma Element as the *cause* of the qualities of a saint. What kind of cause does the text have in mind? The verses that follow suggest that it is the *substance* out of which the qualities of sainthood are fashioned. The verses compare Emptiness to water, gold, and space and explain that, no matter how much these substances may appear to be transformed, their underlying nature remains unchanged:

> [Emptiness] is defiled and purified when it is stained and unstained. Its purity is thought to be similar to the purity of water, gold, and space.[30]

Water can be stained by mud and other kinds of impurities, but the impurities can always be washed away. A piece of gold can be buried in a dung heap, and the sky can be covered by smoke, but the defilements never affect their underlying substance.[31] All someone has to do is pull the gold out of the dung heap or wait for the wind to blow the smoke away and the natural purity of the gold or the sky is restored. These three substances not only can be defiled without losing their purity but they can be shaped or transformed in various ways without losing their original nature. Water may flow in different streams, but when the streams reach the ocean, they become a single mass of water.[32] Someone can change the shape of a piece of gold by molding it into a statue, but the statue is still gold.[33] Space can be limited or enclosed in a pot, but it is still space. To say that the Dharma is a Dharma *Element* (*dhātu*) is to say that it is a substance out of which things can be fashioned, and not just an ordinary substance, but a substance that retains its original nature no matter how much it appears to be changed.

The metaphor of substance often appears side by side in the literature with a metaphor of "foundation" or "place." There is a well-known verse, for example, in *The Mahāyāna Abhidharma Sūtra* that says:

> The primordial Element is the foundation (*samāśraya*) of all *dharmas*. Because it exists, all states of rebirth exist and also the attainment of nirvana.[34]

Here the Dharma Element is depicted as the foundation or container (*samāśraya*) of all the factors of existence. It is because all things are based on or contained in this primordial Element that they are able to evolve into the different forms they eventually assume. Bhāvaviveka quotes another version of the verse with the word "seed" substituted for the word *dharma*.[35] The modified version enhances the organic dimension of the metaphor, but it does not change the metaphor's underlying implication. In both versions, the Dharma Element functions as the ground on which or in which all the factors of existence (both positive and negative) reside and grow.

The word "foundation" (*samāśraya* or the related form *āśraya*) can also be used to indicate that the Dharma Element serves as the *place* where the experience of enlightenment occurs. This is part of the implication of the Yogācāra image of the attainment of the Dharma Body as a "change of standpoint" (*āśraya-parāvṛtti*).[36] The idea of place comes into play in the discussion of the Dharma Body as the "foundation" (*āśraya*) on which the other Bodies of the Buddha are based.[37] It is also reflected in a fascinating tradition of speculation about the possible meanings of the throne of Buddha's enlightenment (*bodhimaṇḍa*). In a literal sense, the throne is the diamond seat at Bodh Gayā where the Buddha comes to attain enlightenment. But the concept can be extended and generalized to include not only other places in other realms where enlightenment occurs but any spot where the Dharma is preached or made known.[38]

The image of the Dharma Element as the foundation or place for the act of enlightenment occurs in another common series of illustrations that treat enlightenment as a precious substance. *The Ornament of the Mahāyāna Sūtras* speaks of the experience of Buddhahood as a basket of jewels waiting to be uncovered and a mine waiting to be discovered.[39] A Buddha is someone who succeeds in removing the covering from the basket and digging through the layers of earth that conceal the mine. Here the key idea is not one of turning around or changing the point at which one stands but of uncovering the treasure that lies beneath one's feet. Exactly what the treasure is depends on which aspect of the Dharma the text chooses to stress. The jewels can be identified with the teachings (*dharmas*) that arise out of the Buddha's enlightenment or with the distinctive qualities (*dharmas*) that define the Buddha's experience. In either case, however, the riches of the Dharma are present, waiting to be revealed.

These spatial images of the act of enlightenment help us expand the concept of the Dharma in important directions, but they also help us go back and understand Bhāvaviveka's picture of reality in a way that was not possible earlier. In the first two chapters of this book, we found that Bhāvaviveka visualized reality as a mountain or a palace. If we now consider Dharma to be not just the perception of reality but reality itself, and if we understand Dharma as the foundation on which enlightenment is based, then the process of enlightenment can be visualized not only as a *change of place* and an *uncovering* of the true (and precious) ground but also as an *ascent* to a new vantage point. By changing place and discovering the ground that lies beneath one's feet, one also ascends to the top of the mountain of reality. The author of *The Ornament of the Mahāyāna Sūtras* makes the connection between these two images explicit by picturing the Buddha's change of standpoint as the ascent of a mountain:

> When the Tathāgata stands there [having completed the change of standpoint], he sees the world as if he were standing on the king of mountains. He has compassion on those who love peace, to say nothing of those who love continued existence.[40]

In his commentary on this passage, Sthiramati explains that to "stand there" means to have attained the pure Dharma Element through a change of standpoint.[41]

The spatial imagery in this verse, along with the spatial imagery associated with other aspects of the Dharma, suggests that Bhāvaviveka's image of reality connects on a deep level to some of the most basic conceptual patterns in the Mahāyāna. And these patterns are not confined to the understanding of reality. The concept of the Dharma bridges the gap between reality and awareness, as do other concepts associated with the content of the Buddha's enlightenment. We found when we were discussing Bhāvaviveka's concept of Emptiness that there was a natural identification of the object that the Buddha knows with the cognition by which the Buddha knows it: the Emptiness known is equivalent to the Emptiness that knows.[42] Whether we are talking about the Dharma or about Emptiness, reality and the perception of reality are capable of being exchanged and identified with each other, and both can be identified with the Buddha as Dharma Body. Bhāvaviveka's palace may be firmly rooted in the soil of external reality, but it too can be understood as a reflection of the being whose awareness most fully encompasses the structure of reality. To climb the structure is not only to command the correct vision of reality and gain the awareness of a Buddha; it is to know that the structure in essence *is* the Buddha—that the Buddha and reality are one.

All of this applies, of course, for the person who is bent on traveling in the footsteps of the Buddha, climbing the mountain that the Buddha climbed and standing at the place where the Buddha gained illumination, but what about the person who waits at the bottom of the mountain, for whom the Dharma is still not underfoot but overhead? For someone like this, the orientation of the spatial metaphor shifts from the ground to the atmosphere, and the preaching of the Dharma seems to come like rays from the sun or like a shower of rain.

> Enlightenment is like a great cloud with regard to the crop of benefits [that it produces] for the world.
> It is like the full moon because it is full of merit and knowledge.
> It is like the great sun because it sends out the light of knowledge.
> Just as the innumerable rays that are combined in the sphere of the sun,
> Always perform a single action, and illuminate the world,
> Innumerable Buddhas are combined in the pure Element.
> In what they need to do, they perform one action: they emit the light of knowledge.[43]

In the text from which these lines come, they are meant to confront another version of the old problem of unity and diversity: how can something like the Dharma, which is pure and undifferentiated (to say nothing of being empty), have a variety of effects? The image of the Dharma as the sun or a great rain cloud answers this question just as the image of the Dharma Element as water or gold answered a similar question about the Dharma's essence. The sun and the rain are one, but they affect different people in different ways.

These new images of the Dharma add a dimension, however, that was missing in the earlier comparisons. The sun and rain *actively* affect the things they fall upon. The sun warms and illuminates them, and the rain causes them to grow. Or, to be more precise, the sun and rain offer them the possibility of growth. Sometimes the seeds that they fall on lack the ability to grow:

> When the king of the gods sends rain, a seed that no longer can function as a seed because it is rotten does not produce a plant. Likewise, when Buddhas appear who are capable of fulfilling every wish, someone who is not fortunate does not receive the benefit of hearing the True Dharma.[44]

A rotten seed cannot use the nourishment of the rain, and someone whose mind is obscured by clouds of misdeeds cannot see the rays of the sun.

> All objects of knowledge are illuminated in a single moment by the cognitions of the Buddha, just as the world is illuminated by the rays emitted in a single act of illumination by the sun.

> The sins of sentient beings obscure the cognitions of the Buddha just as clouds and the like are thought to obscure the rays of the sun.[45]

The image of the Dharma as the sun can be combined in a fascinating way with the image of the enlightenment as a passage up a mountain. Those who climb highest on the mountain feel the warmth of the sun's rays before the sun reaches the people who still labor in the valleys.

> The Buddha pervades the world just as the sun pervades the sky, and [the Buddha] illuminates those who are ready to be taught, according to their merit, just as [the sun illuminates] the mountains.
>
> When the sun rises, it spreads out thousands of glorious rays and illuminates the whole world, but it shines first on the high mountains, then on the middle, and then on the low. Like the sun, the Buddha shines on groups of living beings in the appropriate order.[46]

These verses indicate that the Buddha's actions naturally are all-embracing[47] and that the Buddha does not distinguish between one person and another, but the Buddha's actions affect each person differently, depending on the moral readiness or preparation that shapes each person's response.

The metaphors of the sun and rain represent fascinating transformations of the spatial image of the Dharma, but they also blur the synchronicity of the Dharma in an important way. Until now we have been following the question we posed at the beginning of the chapter: what stages of thought would one go through to confront the Dharma Body of the Buddha at the deepest possible level? We have found that the investigation leads in two related directions: one can move from the Dharma as a physical book to the Dharma as a teaching and the Dharma as a state of nondual awareness, and one can pursue the Dharma by investigating the nature of reality itself. Ultimately, the Emptiness that is the *content* of the Buddha's awareness is not distinguishable from the *awareness* itself, but conceptual and metaphorical expressions of the Dharma picture it in these two distinguishable ways. When we talk about the effect of the Dharma on the people who receive it, however, the pure synchronicity of the Dharma begins to merge with factors that are inescapably diachronic. The Buddha may have (or be) no concept, and the Buddha may be the source of a pure, undifferentiated power, but that power gives the impression of being differentiated according to different situations and needs, and the differences vary in time and space.

The differences in the effect of the Dharma can come from two directions. They can arise from decisions that were made before the bodhisattva became a Buddha, or they can arise after the enlightenment from differences in the preparation of those who receive the Dharma. In practice, of course, it is not a question of choosing one option to the exclusion of the other. A full picture of the Buddha's activity has to contain an account of both. When the author of *The Ornament on the Mahāyāna Sūtras* compares the differences in the

Buddha's action to the streaks of color in a tie-dyed cloth, he gives just one part of the story.[48] The knots of the Buddha's previous vows may carry on into the future and create patterns when the cloth is dipped in the water of Emptiness, but the Buddha also has to be understood as the Emptiness into which the cloth is dipped, or (in another version of the same metaphor) as the rain that sprinkles every plant in the same way but is absorbed differently by each. The Buddha's actions are differentiated diachronically by vows and promises and synchronically by the needs and abilities of the people who receive them.

When the philosopher Śāntideva comments on the actions of the Buddha, he combines the diachronic and synchronic dimensions in a single formula. In the key verse that marks the transition in his argument from the definition of Emptiness to the definition of the Buddha, Śāntideva says, "*Because of someone who is ready to be taught* and *because of a vow*, the form of the Buddha is seen."[49] The person who is "ready to be taught" (*vineya*) is someone who has prepared to become a fit recipient of the Dharma. But what this person sees is also determined by the vows that brought a particular Buddha to enlightenment in a particular way.[50] Diachronic factors are woven together with synchronic factors in a single moment of interaction that allows a person to "see" the form of the Buddha. It is true that the Dharma should be confronted and perceived in the same way at all times and in all places, but the process that leads to enlightenment produces inescapable differences. The Dharma may remain forever unchanged, but the effects of the Dharma are enmeshed inevitably in the snares of time.

The Eternal Buddha

One of the most striking consequences of the combination of diachronic and synchronic modes of thinking in Mahāyāna literature is the concept of the eternal Buddha. Mahāyāna writers take great delight in challenging conventional images of the Buddha, either by giving them a new interpretation or by reevaluating their place on the path to liberation, but there is no more radical challenge to the traditional understanding of the Buddha than the idea that the Buddha lasts forever. To say that the Buddha is eternal (*nitya*) overthrows the basic doctrine that everything, including the personality of the Buddha himself, is impermanent (*anitya*). Yet this is exactly what the Mahāyāna sources seem to do, as in the Mahāyāna sūtras that describe the Buddha as having an "eternal body" or "an immeasurable span of life" (*aparimitāyus*).[51]

The problematic aspects of the doctrine of the eternal Buddha were not overlooked by the Mahāyāna authors themselves. Bhāvaviveka acknowledges its difficulty when he includes it in his outline of the objections raised by other Buddhists against the Mahāyāna. Bhāvaviveka tells us about an opponent who argues, "To teach that the Buddha is eternal contradicts the scriptural statement that everything is impermanent."[52] This seems to be the case, Bhāvaviveka says, because the teaching contradicts the doctrine of impermanence and because it violates the assumption that the peace of nirvana is a definitive cessation of suffering. If the Buddha continues to be active, the Buddha must continue to change, and if the Buddha continues to change, the quest for enlightenment does not lead to a state of peace.[53] But how seriously should these contradictions be taken? Is the doctrine of the eternal Buddha a radical break with previous tradition, or did it grow in some way out of very basic and traditional speculation about the nature and activity of the Buddha?

On the literal level, the answer to these questions is clear. There is no way to ignore the novelty of the formula itself. To say that the Buddha is eternal or has immeasurable life, as many Mahāyāna sūtras do, contradicts the letter of the doctrine of impermanence. But the Mahāyāna does not simply repeat the formulas without interpretation, and the interpretation shows not only great complexity but also strong lines of continuity between the Mahāyāna doctrine and more traditional conceptions of the Buddha. To answer these questions seriously, we have to look at the Mahāyāna sources themselves and see how they interpret the scriptural images of the Buddha's permanence.

One common Mahāyāna strategy for visualizing the Buddha's teaching career as extending beyond the normal span of thirty or forty years is to think of the parinirvana itself as a manifestation of the Buddha's powers of illusion. Interpreted in this way, the parinirvana can be understood as a device for teaching people who need to be encouraged by the image of a finite goal, rather than as an event that brings the Buddha's teaching career to an end. This model of the Buddha's career is found in a number of influential sūtras that date from the early period in the development of the Mahāyāna.[54] *The Lotus Sūtra*, for example, says:

> O sons of good family, a Tathāgata does what a Tathāgata has to do. Perfectly enlightened for so long, a Tathāgata has immeasurable life, he lasts forever. Without having entered parinirvana, a Tathāgata makes a show of parinirvana for the sake of those who are ready to be taught.[55]

This picture of the Buddha's career does not coincide well with more traditional accounts of the life of the Buddha Śākyamuni, but it does not require that *The Lotus Sūtra* abandon the literal interpretation of parinirvana as the end of the Buddha's career. This Buddha can still be located in the period that lies between enlightenment and the parinirvana. There may still be a time when this Buddha will *literally* attain parinirvana and not merely make a show of it. At that point this Buddha will be no different from the Buddha Prabhūtaratna, mentioned in chapter 4, whose vow made it possible for his form to appear after his parinirvana.[56] His actions will then have to take place through the lingering effects he leaves behind. For the present, however, this Buddha still functions as if he were in the midst of an active career.

What does it mean, then, to say that this Buddha has immeasurable life (*aparimitāyus*)? One possibility is that human beings, with their limited capacities, cannot conceive of the enormous measure of the Buddha's career. This is the option that seems to apply in the chapter on the measure of the Tathāgata's life in *The Sūtra of Golden Light*:

> The drops in all the oceans of water can be counted, but no one can count the life of Śākyamuni.
>
> As far as the Sumeru mountains are concerned, all their atoms can be counted, but no one can count the life of Śākyamuni.
>
> However many atoms there are on earth, it is possible to count them all but not to count the life of the Buddha.
>
> If anyone should wish to measure the sky, (it is possible,) but no one can count the life of Śākyamuni.[57]

Another option is to say that a Buddha's life is not subject to an artificial limit but can be manifested in any length to serve the needs of sentient beings.[58] In both cases, the theoretical limit of parinirvana is left in place. It is only from the point of view of ordinary beings, with their limited imagination, that the Buddha seems to last "forever."

There is a passage in the larger *Sukhāvatīvyūha Sūtra* that clearly seems to suggest the possibility of an "immeasurable life" (that is, one that the human imagination cannot fully encompass) within the limits of a conventional career:

> Ānanda asks: Has Dharmākara already attained enlightenment and parinirvana, has he not yet attained enlightenment, or has he attained enlightenment recently, and does he continue to maintain, promote, and teach the Dharma?
>
> The Lord answers: He is not a past or future Tathāgata. He has attained enlightenment, and he continues to maintain, promote, and teach the Dharma.[59]

By the way he frames the question, Ānanda allows three options. One is that Dharmākara, the bodhisattva who was to become the Buddha Amitābha, is still a bodhisattva and has not yet attained enlightenment. Another is that he has attained enlightenment and gone on to achieve parinirvana. A third is that he has attained enlightenment but not parinirvana and is still involved in an active teaching career. The Buddha chooses the third option. He does not seem to reject the idea of parinirvana entirely. Instead he locates the activity of the Buddha Amitābha in a period between enlightenment and parinirvana.

Bhāvaviveka's concept of the Buddha's "uninterrupted" or "eternal" activity is more radical than this, but it still does not conflict with the idea of parinirvana as a cessation of all activity. In his account of the Buddha's silence, Bhāvaviveka pictures enlightenment as the complete cessation of concepts. After the moment of enlightenment, the Buddha was in a perpetual state of concentration, without the concepts or discursive activity that would produce any action. But the force of previous vows and the needs of the people who were ready to be taught came together to produce the appearance of speech. This model effectively projects the radical cessation of the parinirvana back onto the moment of enlightenment itself. The possibility of any action flowing from the Buddha's own conceptual activity stops when the Buddha is enlightened, not just when he achieves parinirvana. But this cessation is no barrier to having the Buddha *appear* to act indefinitely through the agency of various manifestations. Once Bhāvaviveka has begun to think of the Buddha's actions as a series of illusory manifestations, the process can continue literally without end. The Buddha may have withdrawn from action in the most important sense and may remain forever in silence, but he continues to act forever through his manifestations.

With this illusory conception of the Buddha's action, Bhāvaviveka can think of the Buddha as eternal in two separate ways. The Buddha's manifestations continue to act *eternally*, as long as there is anyone in samsara who needs their help, and the Buddha can remain *eternally* fixed in nonconceptual concentration. In the language of the Buddha Bodies, Bhāvaviveka can say that the Form Body of the Buddha acts eternally for the welfare of others, while the Dharma Body remains eternally free from conceptual activity. In fact, these are precisely the two elements that Bhāvaviveka brings together in his verse on the concept of the eternal Buddha: "[The Buddha] is called eternal because [as the Dharma Body] he is completely free from concepts . . . , and because [as the Form Body] he always accomplishes what is good [for others]."[60] The commentary on the verse explains the last part of this formula as it once described the activity of the Manifestation Body: "[The Buddha] is eternal because he constantly accomplishes great vows and acts for the welfare of sentient beings as long as there is samsara."[61] The Buddha acts eternally through manifestations and yet remains eternally free from action.

It is not surprising, in view of all we have seen about the Mahāyāna theory of the Buddha, to find that the two elements in Bhāvaviveka's account of the eternal Buddha reflect the diachronic and synchronic aspects of the Buddha's absence. The career that created the Buddha came to an end at the moment of enlightenment, but its effects continue in a diachronic sense through the actions of the Buddha's manifestations. Meanwhile, the Buddha has become identified with the eternal Dharma, a Dharma that is pure, undifferentiated, and eternally unchanging. Bhāvaviveka is not the only philosopher who takes this two-pronged approach to the question of the eternal Buddha. The author of *The Ornament of the Mahāyāna Sūtras* makes the same point when he says that the Buddha is eternal in nature (the Dharma Body) and eternal in constancy and continuity (the Form Body).[62] In both cases the symmetry is clear.

The Mahāyāna concept of the eternal Buddha is a major transformation of traditional concepts of the Buddha's career, but it is constructed out of elements that would have been very much at home in earlier literature. There is an idea that the Buddha continued to influence disciples by setting in motion events that would linger after the cessation of the Buddha's active career, and there is an idea that the Buddha is eternally identified with the Dharma. The Mahāyāna applies these insights in radically new ways, but the ideas themselves are deeply embedded in traditional conceptions of the Buddha.

This chapter began with a simple question about the absence of the Buddha: In what way is the Buddha absent, not just in the present as opposed to the past but at all times, even when the form of the Buddha seems to be present? As we traced the answer to this question through Mahāyāna literature, we found a complex cluster of symbolic associations and speculative doctrines focused on the concept of the Dharma Body. To confront the Buddha's absence in the most timeless sense, a person must face the fact that the Buddha is not just a living, breathing, human form but also a book and a teaching. In addition, a person must confront the fact that the teaching is not just a series of syllables and words but is also a deep awareness, and one has to understand that the awareness itself is indistinguishable from the empty reality that it makes known. The stages in this process are defined differently in different expressions of the Mahāyāna tradition, but the process itself affects the way all Mahāyāna philosophers think through their insights into the nature of the Buddha.

We also found, however, that the synchronic aspect of the Buddha's nature could not be separated completely from matters of sequence and chronology. In its essence (in its Emptiness), the Dharma is timeless, but the impact of the Dharma cannot be separated from the long process of preparation that makes a Buddha capable of delivering it *this* way and not another, nor can it be separated from the process of study that makes a disciple of the Buddha capable of hearing it at *this* moment rather than another. The confrontation between a single person and the Dharma takes place at the point where time intersects with timelessness, where eons of proper preparation suddenly coalesce to reveal a state of affairs that has always been present. These two dimensions of the Buddha's nature intersect in philosophical accounts of the eternal Buddha, but their most powerful expression is in the mature Mahāyāna theory of the Buddha Bodies. The next step in this exploration of the philosophers' vision of the Buddha is to see how Bhāvaviveka combined diachronic and synchronic modes of understanding in his own distinctive transformation of the doctrine of the Buddha Bodies.

Chapter 6

Bhāvaviveka's Theory of the Buddha

The two dimensions of Buddhist speculation about the Buddha—the diachronic and the synchronic—impose important constraints on any attempts to explain what the Buddha was and is. As the last two chapters have shown, these constraints manifest themselves in a variety of ways throughout Buddhist literature, from the earliest scriptural accounts of the Buddha's activities to the most elaborate philosophical conceptions of the Buddha's nature. It is difficult, however, to find Indian Buddhist philosophers in the period of the classical commentators, from the fifth to the seventh centuries, who were willing to grapple in a systematic way and in their own independent style with the theoretical constraints that had been delivered to them by their tradition. In this respect, Bhāvaviveka's magnum opus, *The Verses on the Essence of the Middle Way* (*Madhyamakahṛdaya-kārikās*) with the commentary that is known as *The Flame of Reason* (*Tarkajvālā*), is a delightful rarity. In the final third of the third chapter, from verse 266 to verse 360, Bhāvaviveka develops a full-fledged theory of the Buddha. The most appealing aspect of the text, however, is the one that is also a source of frustration, at least to those who are unaccustomed to dealing with the complexity of Mahāyāna literature in this period. Bhāvaviveka does not just elaborate the formulaic accounts of the Buddha found in other literature. He puts his own original and distinctive imprint on traditional formulas. He struggles with the standard theories, tests them, criticizes them, and squeezes them for poetic meaning. In the process he gives us an account of the Buddha that is more personal, more difficult, and at the same time more representative of the deep dilemmas that Buddhist intellectuals faced in Bhāvaviveka's time than many of the more standard systems. The purpose of this chapter is to probe beneath the surface of Bhāvaviveka's words, to see how he worked with the metaphorical devices and the conceptual restraints that were available to him in his own tradition, and to see how he took the theory of the Buddha and made it his own.

The Ultimate Buddha: A Negative Version of the Two-Body Theory

When Bhāvaviveka presents his own theory of the Buddha he is usually content with a theory of only two Buddha Bodies, although he acknowledges and even borrows some aspects of the three-body theory that by his time was widely accepted in the philosophical circles of the Mahāyāna. Whether he clings to the two-body theory out of deference to the works of Nāgārjuna and the traditions of his school or for some other reason is not immediately clear. But this is definitely the point where any investigation of Bhāvaviveka's theory of the Buddha must begin.

In its most common form, the theory of two Buddha Bodies involves a distinction between the Form Body (*rūpa-kāya*) and the Dharma Body (*dharma-kāya*), a distinction that was popularized and given devotional form in many of the hymns of the early Mahāyāna. In Mātṛceṭa's *One Hundred and Fifty Verses* (*Śatapañcāśatka*), a hymn of praise to the Buddha, we read: "Even when you had attained nirvana, you showed the unbelieving world, 'My Dharma and Form Bodies are meant for others.' For when you handed over the Dharma Body completely to the virtuous and split the Form Body into parts, you attained parinirvana."[1] The same distinction is echoed in Nāgārjuna's *Jewel Garland (Ratnāvalī)*: "If the causes of the Buddha's Form Body are as immeasurable as the world, how can someone measure the causes of the Dharma Body? The Buddhas' Form Bodies arise from the collection of merit; and, to put the matter briefly, O king, the Dharma Body is born from the collection of insight."[2] These verses grow out of the old canonical distinction between the Buddha's "vile body" and the Buddha's teaching, but they can easily be extended to include other aspects of the Dharma as well, from the Dharma as book to the Dharma as knowledge and the Dharma as Emptiness.

Bhāvaviveka was well aware of the distinction between the Form Body and the Dharma Body and used it comfortably when he was commenting on the theories of other philosophers,[3] but he most often based his own account of the Buddha on the distinction between a Tathāgata Body and a Manifestation Body. A typical passage is the one we have already mined for information about Bhāvaviveka's concept of the previous vow:

> The Tathāgata Body (*tathāgata-kāya*) is free from concepts, but because of a promise to seek the welfare and happiness of others and because of a previous vow (*pūrva-praṇidhāna*), a Manifestation Body (*nirmāṇa-kāya*) arises from it that is capable of assisting everyone. On this basis, a teaching arises that consists of syllables, words, and sentences. [This teaching] reveals to the followers of the excellent vehicle the selflessness of *dharmas* and persons—[a doctrine that is] not shared by heretics, disciples, and solitary Buddhas—in order to complete the perfections. This [teaching] is called the Mahāyāna. The teaching arises in spoken form when the ultimate Buddha is present, so [we] consider the Teacher to be the agent of this teaching.[4]

Even through the veil of technical terminology that shrouds this passage, it is easy to see that Bhāvaviveka presupposes a model of two bodies. What he calls the Tathāgata Body corresponds to what in other contexts would be called the Dharma Body,[5] and his Manifestation Body corresponds to the Form Body. The term "ultimate Buddha" in the last line seems to be another way of referring to the Tathāgata (or Dharma) Body. Oddly enough, the most ambiguous word in the passage is "Teacher" in the last line. Normally the word "Teacher" would be used to refer simply to the Buddha himself. But here the Buddha appears in two forms. It is not immediately obvious whether the word refers to the Manifestation Body that delivers the teaching or to the Tathāgata Body that is its ultimate source. The connection between the Manifestation Body and the spoken teaching would seem to suggest that the Manifestation Body is the Teacher, but there are strong reasons to suspect that Bhāvaviveka considers the Teacher to be the Tathāgata Body itself.

Before we look more deeply into the meaning of Bhāvaviveka's names for the Buddha Bodies, however, we should stop to ask an even more basic question. If there was already a perfectly serviceable pair of terms to distinguish between the Buddha's two bodies, the Form Body and the Dharma Body, why would Bhāvaviveka muddy the waters by introducing new terminology? The first answer to this question is that the terminology is not really new. It is common in Mahāyāna sūtras to find questions about the Buddha's identity posed as questions about the Body of the Tathāgata. In a late chapter in *The Teaching of Vimalakīrti*, there is a long discussion of what it means to "see" the Buddha. Vimalakīrti uses a series of negative examples to rule out all the different ways a person can go astray by trying to "see" the Buddha in a literal sense; then he says that the Buddha should be seen as if there were nothing to see.[6] He summarizes his comments about the Buddha with a reference to the Tathāgata Body: "Such is the body of the Tathāgata. It is thus that he should be seen and not otherwise. He who sees him thus sees him correctly; he who sees him otherwise sees him wrongly." If the Dharma Body is the more common term for the Buddha's more profound or more elevated aspect, why not frame the passage as a search for the Dharma? The text could say that the Form Body is visible to the senses but the Dharma Body is not, and anyone who identifies the Buddha with the Form Body has missed the most important aspect of the Buddha's identity. It is easy to see, however, why the text does not follow this strategy. Vimalakīrti is not trying to distinguish one valid aspect of the Buddha from another but is asking what it means to see the *Buddha*, plain and simple. Rather than suggest that there are different forms of the Buddha, each of which needs to be treated in a different way, the text argues that there is *one* Buddha, and someone who wants to see this Buddha has to see that there is no Buddha to see. The term "Tathāgata Body" sidesteps the distinction between the Dharma Body and Form Body, but for a reason that is related to the strategy of the text itself: it underlines the unity of the Buddha in the face of a diversity of manifestations.

This concern for the unity of the Buddha is also implicit in Bhāvaviveka's reference to the Manifestation Body rather than the Form Body. It is not that he is indulging in an act of great idiosyncrasy by avoiding the traditional term. The Manifestation Body is associated with the Form Body in a wide variety of Mahāyāna literature.[7] But this substitution of terms has the effect of calling attention to the illusory quality of the Form Body. Of all the words that can be used to refer to the Form Body, "manifestation" (*nirmāṇa*) is the one that underlines most explicitly its illusory nature.[8] By contrasting the Buddha as Manifestation Body with the Buddha as Tathāgata Body, Bhāvaviveka stresses even further the actual oneness of the Buddha. It is not that the Buddha has two equally valid or real bodies, one associated with the Dharma and one with the Buddha's physical form. Bhāvaviveka's choice of words indicates that there is only a *Buddha* Body combined with a series of Illusory Bodies. It also explains why Bhāvaviveka uses the term "Teacher" in such an ambiguous way at the end of the passage. The term is normally used to refer only to the Buddha himself, without distinguishing different aspects in the Buddha's identity or different levels of reality. To use it here as a synonym for the Tathāgata Body is to suggest that the Tathāgata Body is the Buddha, period—a Buddha who is not to be confused with the illusory manifestations that are more directly accessible to the senses.

Then what did Bhāvaviveka understand the Tathāgata Body to be? He does not spend much time in this particular passage on a definition, but he does give enough clues to make his intention clear. One key term is the phrase "free from concepts [or discursive ideas]" (*niṣprapañca*). "Free from discursive ideas" is a qualifying phrase that can apply either to the object that the Buddha knows or to the act of knowing itself. Which of these two possibilities did Bhāvaviveka have in mind? In another passage on the Buddha Bodies in the commentary on verse 291 of chapter 3 in *The Verses on the Essence of the Middle Way*, he says that the Tathāgata Body "consists of knowledge" (*jñānātmaka*). This suggests that Bhāvaviveka identifies the Buddha with the state of awareness that constitutes his enlightenment. Another piece of evidence that supports the same interpretation is the term "ultimate Buddha" (*paramārtha-buddha*) at the end of this passage. The term could be used to mean "the Buddha considered from the ultimate point of view," in which case it would not distinguish decisively between the Buddha as an act of cognition and the Buddha as reality itself. But the term can also mean "the Buddha who is characterized by or identified with the ultimate." Bhāvaviveka takes great pains elsewhere in his commentaries to explain that the word "ultimate" (*paramārtha*) applies first to an act of cognition rather than to the object that a person knows.[9] If the primary meaning of the word "ultimate" in this passage is "ultimate awareness," as it is elsewhere in Bhāvaviveka's work, then the ultimate Buddha (or the Buddha-as-ultimate) is identical to the final state of the Buddha's understanding. It is identical, in other words, to enlightenment itself.

This definition of the ultimate was not unique to Bhāvaviveka. One of the best explanations of the meaning of the word in Madhyamaka literature comes from Jñānagarbha, a Mādhyamika who followed Bhāvaviveka by about two hundred years and identified himself with Bhāvaviveka's tradition of thought. Jñānagarbha explains that "ultimate" is one of a group of words that seem at first glance to refer to objects of cognition but that actually gain their meaning primarily from an act of cognition and only secondarily from the object defined by the cognition.[10] To illustrate this point, Jñānagarbha's commentator cites the word "measure." When someone uses the word "measure" to refer to a certain amount of material, like five bushels of rice or ten yards of cloth, the word seems to refer to the rice or cloth itself. But to call the rice a "bushel" or the cloth a "yard," someone first has to measure it. There may be rice before there is any measuring of the rice (about this Jñānagarbha and his commentator have nothing to say), but there is not a "bushel" of rice until the rice is actually measured. Jñānagarbha and his commentator argue that the word "ultimate" (*paramārtha*) is like the word "bushel." It seems at first to refer to the "object" (*artha*) that is "ultimate" (*parama*), but the object is not an "ultimate" object until it has been cognized and defined by an ultimate act of cognition. So they take the position that the word "ultimate" refers primarily to an act of cognition and only secondarily to the object that is cognized by the "ultimate cognition."

The distinction between the ultimate-as-object and the ultimate-as-cognition was important to Bhāvaviveka and Jñānagarbha as a step in the analytical process that determines the nature of Emptiness. To construct their argument, Bhāvaviveka and Jñānagarbha start with a distinction between two kinds of ultimate cognition: one that is subject to conceptual distinctions and another that is not.[11] The "conceptual ultimate" can be rationally scrutinized, and it can be distinguished as a particular point of view among others. Bhāvaviveka calls it the ultimate that is "accessible to discursive ideas" (*saprapañca*). Jñānagarbha calls it the "rational" (*nyāyānusāra*) ultimate.[12] In either case, this conceptual ultimate is a standpoint or form of understanding that allows distinctions. A person can adopt it and use it to construct a rational argument. What makes it ultimate is not that it transcends concepts but that there is no other rational standpoint, other than itself, from which it can be contradicted.[13] The second kind of ultimate cognition is one that results from applying the conceptual ultimate to itself. When the conceptual ultimate is examined ultimately (that is, from the standpoint of the conceptual ultimate), it is no more defensible as an independent category than any of the conventional categories themselves. This final erasing of the distinction between ultimate and conventional is what Jñānagarbha had in mind when he said, "[The Buddha] considers the relative and the ultimate to be identical in nature because there is no difference between them."[14] From the ultimate point of view, even the distinction between the ultimate and the conventional does not apply.

The distinction (and the absence of distinction) between conceptual and nonconceptual ultimates gives to Bhāvaviveka's account of the Buddha a feeling of levels within levels. Bhāvaviveka identifies the Tathāgata Body with the ultimate Buddha, and he associates it with an ultimate state of awareness, but ultimately the Tathāgata Body and the ultimate Buddha are not a state of awareness any more than they are anything else. Everything is equally empty. Bhāvaviveka makes this point with exquisite care in the definition of the Buddha that opens his discussion of Buddhahood in the third chapter of *The Verses on the Essence of the Middle Way*:

> The no-arising of cognition, which is called "Buddha" because it is the understanding of this [reality], is the primary [Buddha] because it is the understanding that is no-understanding and because it dispels the sleep of concepts.[15]

As we have already seen in chapter 2, the first part of the verse echoes a traditional definition of the Buddha ("[he] is called 'Buddha' because [he] understands this").[16] Behind the words of the English translation lies the simplest of tautologies: the Buddha is *buddha* ("the one who has understood") because he has attained *bodha* ("understanding"). In the second part of the verse, Bhāvaviveka takes this simple formula and begins to fill it with new meaning. The being who is called Buddha is identified with "the no-arising of cognition" (*anudayo dhiyaḥ*). This is also a traditional formula, but one with a distinctively Mahāyāna flavor. The phrase echoes the passage in *The Perfection of Wisdom in Eight Thousand Lines* where the Buddha is defined as no-arising.[17] To equate the Buddha-as-understanding with "the no-arising of cognition" begins to unravel the concept of understanding but not yet to contradict it. For that we have to turn to the third and fourth parts of the verse.

Bhāvaviveka begins the second half of the verse with the words "is the primary [Buddha] because it is the understanding that is no-understanding" (*abodhabodhato mukhyo*). Logically these words belong together. The *primary* or *literal* reason for calling the Buddha *buddha* is not that he has understanding but that he has the understanding that is no-understanding. But what does Bhāvaviveka mean by "primary" (*mukhya*)? Haribhadra is one person to whom we can turn for an answer. In his explanation of the term "Perfection of Wisdom," he distinguishes between "primary" (*mukhya*) and "secondary" (*gauṇa*) meanings.[18] He says that the word refers primarily to nondual awareness and only secondarily to a book or a path. Bhāvaviveka does not refer directly to a secondary meaning in his verse about the Buddha, but he does in the commentary. Rather than "secondary" (*gauṇa*), he calls the nonliteral meaning "metaphorical" (*upacāra*), but he has the same semantic distinction in mind.[19] The Buddha is *literally* someone who has no-understanding (*abodha*) and only *metaphorically* someone who has understanding (*bodha*). In the construction of the verse, the metaphorical definition gives way to a definition that is more consistent with the understanding that everything, including understanding itself, is empty of identity.[20]

After using the third part of the verse to invert the traditional definition, Bhāvaviveka comes back in the fourth part to another traditional formula. It is a formula that even his Buddhist opponents would not consider controversial: "[The understanding of reality is called 'Buddha'] . . . because it dispels the sleep of concepts." In an important passage in the subcommentary on *The Treasury of the Abhidharma (Abhidharmakośa)*, Yaśomitra explains that a Buddha is someone whose wisdom has blossomed (*vibuddha*) like a lotus and someone who has woken up (*prabuddha*) from the sleep of ignorance.[21] Bhāvaviveka has his own idea of the ignorance from which a Buddha wakes up—an idea that would not be acceptable to someone in Yaśomitra's school—but the formula itself would have been quite familiar. When it is combined with the formula that starts the verse, the effect of the Sanskrit, if not the English, is of a modern picture in an ancient frame. There is a traditional formula to start and one to finish, and in the middle stands Bhāvaviveka's own reversal of the categories of Buddhahood. It is as if he were saying, "You have heard that a Buddha is understanding. Well, a Buddha is just the opposite. The Buddha is no understanding. And why? Because he has awakened from a dream, just as you have heard!"

In the verse that follows, Bhāvaviveka pauses to give a more conventional account of the Buddha:

> Or [he is called "Buddha"] because he finishes [recognizing] the things that have to be recognized and so forth, because he understands equality, or because he opens the lotus-minds of fortunate people with manifestations.[22]

As he explains in the commentary, the three possibilities mentioned in the verse are drawn from different scriptural definitions of the Buddha. The first is based on a tradition that a Buddha is someone who has completed a practice oriented toward the four Noble Truths: a Buddha finishes recognizing suffering, removing the arising of suffering, realizing cessation, and practicing the path. The second possibility comes from a passage in *The Large Perfection of Wisdom Sūtra* that defines enlightenment as an understanding of "equality" (*samatā*). The third comes from a passage in *The Descent to Laṅkā Sūtra* where the enlightenment that occurs in this world is attributed to the Buddha's manifestation rather than to the Buddha himself.[23] In the commentary, Bhāvaviveka explains that these passages approach the Buddha from a relative point of view (*saṃvṛtyā*).

With this brief journey into conventional reality behind him, Bhāvaviveka returns to the main focus of the argument in this part of the text. The next twenty-three verses vary little in tone or method from the definition of the "Buddha" as the one who has no understanding. Bhāvaviveka gives a negative explanation of the terms "Sambuddha," "Sugata," and "Tathāgata," then rings the changes on the negative characteristics of the Buddha, from "immeasurable" and "incalculable" to "nonconceptual" and "subject to no characteristic."[24] This section of the text also contains a series of verses that describe the beings who approach the Buddha in this negative mode. To see a Buddha about whom so little can be said is an achievement that is little short of Buddhahood itself: it belongs only to the greatest of bodhisattvas.

> Like space, heroic beings see him without seeing. They live without concepts and without effort, and their eyes are clear.
>
> They pay homage to the Lord without any homage, reflection, or words. To them also we pay sincere homage.[25]

As the commentary explains, these heroic beings are the bodhisattvas of the tenth stage, bodhisattvas who are just on the verge of attaining Buddhahood themselves.

Bhāvaviveka is a logician (*tārkika*) and one who is quite confident of his own powers, but even logicians fare poorly in comparison to the great practitioners of the bodhisattva path.

> [The Buddha] is as inaccessible to logicians as heaven is to sinners, detachment is to those who are passionate, and the sun is to those who have been born blind.[26]

This verse is found in the same section of the text where Bhāvaviveka makes the tantalizing concession to his Brahmanical opponents of identifying the Buddha with the supreme Brahman (*paraṃ brahman*) of the Upaniṣads. He only does this, however, to rank the Hindu gods in the same category as a blind logician and to contrast the gods to the great bodhisattvas who have attained the tenth stage of the path.

> [Verse:] This is the supreme Brahman that even [gods] such as Brahmā do not grasp.
>
> [Commentary:] [Gods] such as Brahmā, Viṣṇu, and Śiva (*maheśvara*) are proud of the way they see reality, but they see [reality as] an object. They do not understand the supreme Brahman. The word *brahman* can refer either to the Lord of Creatures or to nirvana. Here it refers to nirvana. [Gods such as Brahmā] do not understand [the supreme Brahman], because it cannot be seen with knowledge that has an object.[27]

By this stage of the argument, Bhāvaviveka's negative account of the Buddha is almost at an end. The only thing left for him to do is identify who it is that he has been describing for the last twenty-five verses. We know from Bhāvaviveka's account of the Buddha in other texts that he identifies this being, the being who is the understanding that is no-understanding, who cannot be defined by any characteristics, and who can be worshipped only by the discipline of no-worship, as the Tathāgata Body. But Bhāvaviveka does not make the identification explicit until the last verse in this section of the text, and even then he does so in response to an odd and perhaps even troubling question: if the Buddha's understanding cannot be characterized or distinguished in any way, how do we know that it is characteristic of a Buddha? Bhāvaviveka's answer, as one might expect, has two parts:

> [We] consider [the Dharma Body] to be the Tathāgata's Body because it is not different in nature from [the Tathāgata] and because it is the reality that [the Tathāgata] has understood. And [we] do not [consider] it to be anyone else's [body] because [others] do not understand it.
>
> Ultimately [the Dharma Body] is not an object (*viṣaya*) of words or thought, but [conventionally] it is the nature (*svabhāva*) of the Tathāgata to have primary and secondary characteristics (*lakṣaṇa-anuvyañjana*) and these [characteristics] belong [only] to him. The [Dharma] Body is not different in nature from this Tathāgata, so [we] consider [it] to be the Body of the Tathāgata. What is its identity? Emptiness. As it is said:
>
> In Emptiness there is said to be no difference at all. Emptiness is identical [to the Buddha]. Whoever sees Emptiness sees the Buddha. [The Buddha] is not different from Emptiness.
>
> Or, speaking of [the Tathāgata as] a moment of insight, the Tathāgata does not grasp any combination of aggregates, powers, grounds of confidence, and special Buddha attributes, and he understands that the object grasped and the subject that does the grasping are equal in nature. [We] consider this [moment of insight] to be the Body only of the Tathāgata, not of anyone else. Why? Others, such as disciples (*śrāvaka*), do not understand this [equality] correctly.[28]

Ultimately the mode of understanding that Bhāvaviveka has just finished describing is identical to Emptiness, and Emptiness cannot differ from the essence of the Tathāgata any more than it can differ from the essence of anything else. It is only from the conventional point of view that one can identify this understanding as belonging to the Buddha and not to someone else.

The Conventional Buddha: A Positive Version of the Two-Body Theory

Bhāvaviveka introduces his discussion of the Buddha in verse 266 of the third chapter of *The Verses on the Essence of the Middle Way* with the claim that Madhyamaka philosophers should be ready to maintain their own position not only about reality but also about the Teacher who understands reality. You would think that this challenge would call forth a full-fledged, affirmative theory of the Buddha, with all of the miraculous powers and attributes that distinguish the Buddha from other beings. Instead, Bhāvaviveka begins his account of the Buddha in the verses we have just reviewed by giving a description of all the things that the Buddha is not. In style and tone, this opening definition of the Buddha simply extends the negative mode of analysis that characterized the preceding section of the text. Why does Bhāvaviveka start his account of the Buddha in such a negative way? This question forces us to look more closely at one of the more intriguing structural features of Bhāvaviveka's argument.

In chapter 2, we found that Bhāvaviveka's argument falls naturally into a three-part pattern. It begins with an assumption of distinctions, moves on to a stage in which distinctions do not apply, then reappropriates the distinctions that have been left behind. This reappropriation is chastened and informed by the analysis that takes place in the second part of the argument, but it still involves a positive evaluation of categories that earlier had been rejected. Bhāvaviveka's account of the Buddha in the third chapter of *The Verses on the Essence of the Middle Way*—extending from the definition of reality in verse 266, through the discussion of the bodhisattva path in verses 292–345, to the final description of the Buddha Bodies in verses 346–360—constitutes the third stage of Bhāvaviveka's analysis of reality. It is, in other words, a positive appropriation of the categories of reality. In this section of the chapter, Bhāvaviveka moves beyond the critical analysis of Emptiness into aspects of the figure of the Buddha that are appropriate for worship, practice, and devotion.

The fascinating thing about Bhāvaviveka's treatment of the Buddha, however, is that it too has a three-part structure, with the first two stages reversed. In the first part (verses 266–291), Bhāvaviveka starts out in a negative mode by telling us everything that the Buddha is *not*. In the second part (verses 292–345), he takes up the aspect of Buddhahood where the distinctions of ordinary practice can be most positively embraced—the path that leads bodhisattvas to the final achievement of Buddhahood. Finally, in the third part (verses 346–360), Bhāvaviveka returns and reappropriates the positive elements in the figure of the Buddha himself. Informed by the active image of the great practitioners of the path, the Buddha finally takes on all the majestic attributes of a bodhisattva but carries them to an even higher degree of perfection. It is this third part of Bhāvaviveka's analysis of the Buddha that gives us the first truly positive account of the Buddha's two Bodies in Bhāvaviveka's text.

In the first part of his analysis of the Buddha, Bhāvaviveka plays skillfully on the negative relationship between the Tathāgata Body and Emptiness. In the one verse where the topic of the Buddha's Form Body comes up, it is treated as little more than an illusion. But in the third stage of the argument, where the positive attributes of the Buddha are reappropriated, Bhāvaviveka reverses this relationship. He starts, as he did earlier, with a description of the Dharma Body, but he describes it in such a way that it is virtually indistinguishable from the Form Body. In fact, the distinction between the two is so attenuated that when he finally makes the transition to the Form Body, the transition comes almost as a surprise.

Bhāvaviveka achieves this effect by presenting the Dharma Body as if someone were perceiving it *conventionally*, through the lens of the Buddha's manifestations. The first few verses on the Dharma Body sound as if Bhāvaviveka were setting the reader down in the middle of the teaching scene pictured in the *Tathāgataguhya Sūtra*, but without the benefit of the philosopher's insight. The philosopher knows that the Buddha's teachings belong only to a manifestation and that the Tathāgata Body remains silent. But the ordinary listener who sits at the feet of the Buddha's manifestation—the one who, as the text says, "is ready to be taught" (*vineya*)—does not perceive the Tathāgata Body that lies behind the manifestation. For a disciple, the Manifestation Body is a representation of the Dharma Body itself. It is as if the Dharma Body and Manifestation Body were doubly indistinguishable. The naïve disciple who is not yet aware of the full implications of Emptiness sees only the conventional Buddha: for such a person, the Buddha is identical to the conventional image. To the philosopher who penetrates to the last stage in the analysis of the two truths, the two Buddhas are also indistinguishable, not because there is no ultimate Buddha, but because, in the end, there is no distinction between the ultimate and the conventional. For both kinds of disciples the circle is closed.

Bhāvaviveka begins his assimilation of the Manifestation Body into the Dharma Body in verse 346:

> [The bodhisattva] becomes a Buddha and opens the minds of fortunate beings with the pure, cleansing rays of teaching just as the sun [opens the blossoms in] a pond of lotuses.[29]

Bhāvaviveka does not call this Buddha a "manifestation." If he did, he would be calling attention to the fact that it is an illusion precisely at the moment when he wants to stress its reality. But in verse 268, which is the only verse in the chapter where he mentions the manifestations of the Buddha, Bhāvaviveka has said, "Manifestations open the lotus-minds of fortunate beings."[30] The connection here is hard to miss: the Buddha described in verse 346 is a Buddha seen (and heard) through the medium of the Buddha's manifestations. As the commentary on verse 268 also explained, this is a Buddha seen only from the perspective of relative truth (*saṃvṛtyā*). By now the difference between relative and ultimate truths would be so deeply engraved in the minds of Bhāvaviveka's readers that it would have become second nature, but this is not the time to make analytical distinctions between the two truths. Here at the culmination of the argument Bhāvaviveka is interested not in analysis but in praise. The image of the teaching that awakens a person's mind as the sun awakens the lotuses in a pond is followed by images of the teaching as the water that cools passions, the boat that saves people from the ocean of samsara, streams of jewels that bring help to the poor, a guide for those who are lost in the jungle of samsara, a spell for those who are bitten by the snake of the defilements, a drum to wake those who sleep in ignorance, a hero who frees beings from the prison of samsara, an ambrosia that brings satisfaction, and a lion's roar that drives away pride. The point in these verses is precisely the opposite of the analytical point in the earlier sections of the text, although it is no less philosophical. Bhāvaviveka is not distinguishing the true nature of the Tathāgata from false appearances but is rather showing how someone can see through the manifestations of the Buddha to a powerful and positive image of the Dharma itself.

It is only in verses 356–59 that Bhāvaviveka makes the transition from this account of the Buddha's Dharma to an account of the Buddha's Form:

> The [Buddha's] incomparable Form [Body] is surrounded by a fathom of light that has the appearance of a rainbow; its splendor consists of permanent,

radiant, and complete primary and secondary characteristics; its ornament is glory; it is charming to the mind and eyes; and it surpasses all things in beauty.

[With this form] and with a miraculous voice that has sixty attributes [the Buddha] captivates the minds of all beings.

With body and voice like a wishing jewel, [the Buddha] assumes the universal form of all the gods to help those who are ready to be taught.

The word that begins this string of verses shows that these verses are meant to describe the Form Body, but the distinction between the Form Body and the Dharma Body still seems to blur in the poet's phrases, since the Form Body has a voice, and the voice is what delivers the Dharma that Bhāvaviveka has already so lavishly described. Distinctions can blur for a variety of reasons. It is possible that a distinction is there but that we do not see it. It is also possible that there is a distinction but that we are looking for it in the wrong way. Or it is possible that the author has deliberately elided the distinction to make a poetic and doctrinal point. The last possibility is the one that seems to apply in these verses. Bhāvaviveka can make a clear distinction when he wants to. But here at the end of the text, the point is not to divide the image of the Buddha into sharp analytical categories. The point is to unify the concept of the Buddha, but this time from the conventional rather than the ultimate perspective. Ultimately the Buddha is called the Tathāgata Body, a body that is identical to the Buddha's ultimate awareness and identical to Emptiness itself, but conventionally, the Buddha appears as a salvific proclamation of the Dharma inextricably associated with the visible form of the Buddha's body. To strike these two claims together in a way that recognizes their differences and also acknowledges their unity is Bhāvaviveka's way of ringing the changes on the words, "Whoever sees the Dharma sees me; whoever sees me sees the Dharma."

The Three-Body Theory

In the commentary on the verses about the Buddha's body and voice, Bhāvaviveka explains that the Form Body can be divided into two further categories: the Enjoyment Body (*sambhoga-kāya*) and the Manifestation Body (*nirmāṇa-kāya*). As we saw in our discussion of Asaṅga's theory of the Dharma Body, these two bodies can be added to the category of the Dharma Body to make up a system of three Buddha Bodies. Through the influence and prestige of the works of Asaṅga and his school, this system eventually became the dominant one in Mahāyāna philosophical discussion of the Buddha. It has also dominated most popular studies of the topic in the West. Bhāvaviveka is at least one important example of an author, however, who was aware of the three-body theory and still chose not to make it an integral part of his own system. It is possible that he held back out of reverence for an older Mahāyāna system of two bodies (as in the works of Nāgārjuna), but it is more likely that he simply thought it unnecessary and perhaps even found that it broke the symmetry of the argument he wanted to make about the nature of the Buddha.

As we have already seen, the distinction between the Tathāgata Body and the Manifestation Body gave Bhāvaviveka a tool with enough dialectical sophistication to fashion a complex theory. With only these two categories, he could explore the relationship between illusion and reality as deeply as he wanted without needing a third. By casting the distinction between the two bodies as a distinction between the Tathāgata himself (or the Tathāgata Body) and the Tathāgata's manifestations, Bhāvaviveka could draw on a different set of scriptural associations and make a subtle series of points about the unity of the Dharma Body and the Form Body. But there still were moments in the commentary when the Manifestation Body was not enough to answer every question about the form of the Buddha. These were moments when it was not only appropriate but necessary for Bhāvaviveka to have access to the concept of the Enjoyment Body, not just to account for the position of his opponents but to clarify a position of his own.

In Mahāyāna literature, the concept of the Enjoyment Body is associated with a tradition that states that the Buddha's enlightenment occurs in a realm beyond this world and is only projected into this world by the appearance of a manifestation. This tradition appeared at least as early as *The Descent to Laṅkā Sūtra*, and it became part of the standard account of the Buddha in the works of Asaṅga. In the commentary on verse 268 (where he gives the conventional definition of the Buddha), Bhāvaviveka quotes a passage from the *The Descent to Laṅkā Sūtra* that says, "Buddhas are enlightened in the palace of Akaniṣṭha, which is delightful and free from all evil: it is only a manifestation that is enlightened here."[32] According to the cosmology outlined in chapter 3 of the *The Treasury of the Abhidharma*, the "palace of Akaniṣṭha" is the highest of seventeen levels in the Form Realm (*rūpa-dhātu*), the last five of which are occupied by the deities of "the Pure Abode" (*śuddāvāsika*).[33] In Bhāvaviveka's commentary on verse 291 (the verse that identifies the Buddha as the Tathāgata Body), he associates the enlightenment that takes place in Akaniṣṭha with the Form Body (*rūpa-kāya*), the Fruition Body (*vipāka-kāya*), and finally the Enjoyment Body (*sambhoga-kāya*): "According to Ārya Vajrasena, the Form Body that is located in Akaniṣṭha and based on the Dharma Body is the Fruition Body. According to Ārya Asaṅga, it is the Enjoyment Body. The location (*āśraya*) of attributes (*dharmas*), such as the powers, grounds of confidence, and special Buddha qualities, is the Dharma Body. The one that attains enlightenment in Jambudvīpa is the Manifestation Body."

This passage can be read simply as a concession to Bhāvaviveka's opponents rather than as a statement of Bhāvaviveka's own position, but there are other passages in the commentary on *The Verses on the Essence of the Middle Way* that indicate Bhāvaviveka also adopted this position as his own. At the beginning of the commentary on verse 291, before he makes any mention of Vajrasena or Asaṅga, Bhāvaviveka outlines his own theory of the Buddha

Bodies. In this passage, he says, "When [a bodhisattva] achieves enlightenment in the palace of Akaniṣṭha, [the bodhisattva] attains a Tathāgata Body that consists of knowledge." The idea that the Buddha's enlightenment occurs in Akaniṣṭha is woven most deeply into the structure of the argument, however, in the fourth chapter of the text, where Bhāvaviveka responds to the disciples' (*śrāvaka*) objections to certain aspects of the Mahāyāna doctrine of the Buddha. At the beginning of the chapter, the disciples pose an objection in the form of a syllogism: "The Teacher's body (*śarīra*) is not the place (*āśraya*) where nonconceptual cognition occurs because it is a body, like the body of a cowherd."[34] According to the commentary, the syllogism is meant to defend the position that the word "Buddha" refers to "the moment of cognition that follows the diamondlike concentration (*vajropama-samādhi*) and is attained by the sixteen moments of thought in the path of liberation (*vimukti-mārga*)."[35] The disciples are arguing that the "place" (*āśraya*) of enlightenment is not a body but a moment in the mental development of a saint. Bhāvaviveka recognizes that the Buddha (in the form of the Tathāgata Body) is a state of awareness, but he also insists that the Buddha has to be located in a body. In his response to the disciples' objection, he argues that this body is the Enjoyment Body in Akaniṣṭha: "Nonconceptual enlightenment is defined as perception that is free from the memory of [own-being and other-being], after own-being (*svabhāva*) and other-being (*para-bhāva*) have been understood. [We] also take the position [that] this is the Teacher. To argue that this [state of perception] does not have the manifestation (*nirmāṇa*) called 'Śākyamuni' as its location is to prove the obvious, because its location is the Enjoyment Body in Akaniṣṭha."

Why would he resort to such a theory here when the theory plays such a small role in the presentation of his own thought elsewhere in the text? It is difficult to give a convincing reply to this question without going more deeply into the history of the idea of the Enjoyment Body (and related concepts) than is presently possible. But the place of the Enjoyment Body (or of the idea that the Buddha attained enlightenment in the palace of Akaniṣṭha) in Bhāvaviveka's argument does allow at least a partial answer. His reply to the disciples' objection shows that he accepts their premise about purity of location: the locus of the Buddha's enlightenment has to be pure, just as the enlightenment itself is pure. This assumption is similar to the doctrine of the "extraordinary" or "supermundane" (*lokottara*) character of the Buddha, a doctrine that appeared in the literature of the Mahāsāṃghikas and then became an axiom of the Mahāyāna. The Mahāsāṃghikas began from a passage in the *Saṃyutta Nikāya* that spoke of the Buddha as "unstained by the world" (*anupalitto lokena*) and then constructed a doctrine of the Buddha as a being who transcends all worldly impurities.[36] According to the preface of the *Mahāvastu*, the Buddha utterly transcends the world and only manifests himself in this world to help others.[37] This is the position that has been referred to as a form of Buddhist Docetism because it seems so similar to the early Christian Docetic heresy that the incarnation of Christ was only an illusion.[38] It is only a small step from the apparent Docetism of the *Mahāvastu* to the formal doctrine that the Buddha attained enlightenment in the highest, most pure, most pleasing level of the Form Realm and only manifested that enlightenment to beings whose minds were oppressed by the categories of this mundane sphere.

Perhaps the most intriguing element in Bhāvaviveka's account of Akaniṣṭha, however, is not the appearance of yet another variant on the theme of illusion but his return to the language of location and place. The concept of the Dharma Body as the "location" (*āśraya*) of the attributes of the Buddha's awareness was found in the Abhidharma. The concept of place was echoed again in the work of Bhāvaviveka's own successor Jñānagarbha, when he defined the Dharma Body as the "location" of every inconceivable virtue, a location that was worthy of worship.[39] But there were barriers to speaking of the Tathāgata Body literally as a specific "place," as Bhāvaviveka suggests in verse 278:

> [The Buddha] does not provide a foundation [for thought] because he has no distinguishing mark. He cannot be conceptualized because he does not provide a foundation [for thought]. He is not subject to conceptual diversity because he cannot be conceptualized. He is not an object because he cannot be apprehended.[40]

It simply did not fit Bhāvaviveka's argument about the ineffable nature of the Tathāgata Body to speak of it literally as a place where virtues, attributes, and qualities reside.

For a "place" to worship, Bhāvaviveka turned instead to the Form Body, located either in the palace of Akaniṣṭha or in this world. As he said in the commentary on verse 268, "a 'Buddha' is someone to whom masses of bodhisattvas make offerings in the palace of Akaniṣṭha, in a region that arises from the most excellent and extraordinary roots of virtue." While the Buddha remains in Akaniṣṭha surrounded by a crowd of exalted bodhisattvas, other sentient beings worship the Buddha's manifestations in this world. Bhāvaviveka's conception of the Buddha allows its own dialectic of place, as in Hsüan-tsang's attempt to interpret the locations that were made sacred by the Buddha's former presence, but it is a dialectic that involves a number of different levels and phases. There is the contrast between the vision of the Buddha who is a physical form and can be seen with physical eyes and the Buddha who is no physical form and can be seen only with the seeing that is no-seeing. There is also the contrast between the form seen in this world and the form seen by accomplished bodhisattvas in the palace of Akaniṣṭha.

All of these concepts hold an answer to the pilgrim's question with which we began this inquiry into the implications of the image of the Buddha's empty throne. "Where do I look," the pilgrim says, "to find the Buddha?" Bhāvaviveka's answer is a complex one and involves equal elements of form and formlessness, seeing and no-seeing. The last step we need to take in tracing the philosopher's vision of the Buddha is to look more closely at what it means to "see" so that we can understand how the act of seeing itself shapes what the philosopher sees.

Part III

The Buddha Eye

The one who has the eye of knowledge, not some other [eye], is the one who sees. So an intelligent person concentrates on the quest for the knowledge of reality.

An intelligent person, even one who is blind, sees the three worlds without any obstruction. Such a person sees the things that he wants to see, whether they are far away, subtle, or concealed.

(The Verses on the Essence of the Middle Way)

Bhāvaviveka pictures the philosophers' quest for knowledge as a quest for vision. The practitioners of the bodhisattva path first climb the palace of reality in order to see all of reality spread out at their feet. They then pass through a stage in which they recognize that the palace is an illusion and can be truly seen only by an act of no-seeing. Finally, in the state of Buddhahood, they achieve the mastery over illusion and reality that allows them, through their own vision, to illuminate the minds of others.

An early example of an eye inscribed on the dome of a stūpa, detail of a brass image of the Budda Śākyamuni, The Asia Society, New York: Mr. and Mrs. John D. Rockfeller 3rd Collection.

CHAPTER 7

Buddhahood and the Language of the Senses

Hsüan-tsang's Encounter with the Pirates

One of the most striking episodes in Hsüan-tsang's travels occurred early in his visit to India, before he even had the chance to gaze on the tree that marked the site of the Buddha's enlightenment. After he had made his way down through the Northwest, where he had visited the cave of the Buddha's shadow and been granted a vision of the Buddha's form, he entered a region where the traces of the Buddha seemed to lie thick on the ground. The journey was not easy. India was generally a peaceful land during the time of Hsüan-tsang's visit, but his travels took him and his companions through mountains, forests, and border regions where the law was not the Law of the Buddha but the law of the jungle, and even Hsüan-tsang's sanctity was scant protection. Shortly after they had left the town of Rājapuri in the Punjab, Hsüan-tsang and his companions were forced to pass through a forest where they were attacked by a band of robbers and stripped of all their possessions.[1] They managed to escape with their lives only by throwing themselves into a swamp full of matted vines, swimming a river, and taking refuge with a farmer on the other side. As discouraging as experiences like this must have been, however, there were also moments that must have whetted Hsüan-tsang's appetite for the challenges that lay ahead. Not long after his narrow escape from the robbers, Hsüan-tsang visited Ayodhyā, where Asaṅga was said to have ascended to the palace of Tuṣita Heaven and received the cardinal texts of the Yogācāra tradition. For someone like Hsüan-tsang, whose journey in part was a search for texts, the site must have offered not only consolation but promise for the adventures still to come.

When he left Ayodhyā, Hsüan-tsang made the next stage of his journey down the Ganges by boat.[2] According to his biographer, Hui-li, the boat held more than eighty people, all traveling downriver toward the confluence of the Yamunā and the Ganges. Eighty people made a good-sized group and must have given Hsüan-tsang a sense of security that he would not have had when he and his small band of companions confronted the robbers outside Rājapuri, but even a crowd of this size was not enough to protect the boat from the pirates who preyed on river travelers. When the boat entered a stretch of river lined by dense forests of Aśoka trees, Hsüan-tsang and his companions saw ten boatloads of pirates slip into the water and row furiously in their direction. The sight of the pirates apparently threw many of the passengers into a state of panic. According to Hui-li, there were some who threw themselves into the river to escape. Others, like Hsüan-tsang, waited on the boat to cast themselves on the mercy of the pirates.

It seems that the pirates were devotees of the goddess Durgā. Hui-li tells us that they had a custom once a year to sacrifice "a man of fine character and handsome features" to the goddess to ensure her blessing. After they had searched the passengers and stripped them of all their valuables, their attention fell on the figure of Hsüan-tsang himself. Hsüan-tsang seemed to be just the man they needed. According to Hui-li, the pirates looked at one another and said, "The time for our sacrifice to the goddess is almost past, and we haven't yet been able to find anyone. Now this monk is pure and handsome in appearance. Wouldn't it be auspicious to use him for our sacrifice to her?" Hsüan-tsang overheard their conversation and said, "Truly I could not begrudge it if this despicable body of mine would serve for your sacrifice. However, my purpose in coming from afar was to worship the Bodhi tree and Buddhist images, to visit Vulture Peak, and to inquire about the Dharma of the Buddhist scriptures. Since I have not yet fulfilled my intention, I fear it might not be so auspicious if you, generous sirs, were to sacrifice me to your goddess."

Hsüan-tsang's protest apparently caused the pirates little hesitation; perhaps he was too good a victim to pass up. The leader of the pirates ordered his men to build an altar and prepare the sacrifice. As the pirates led Hsüan-tsang to the altar, he made one final request—that he be left in peace for a moment to compose his thoughts and prepare himself for death. The events that followed are important enough to quote in detail:

> The master then concentrated his mind (*chuan hsin*) on the palace in Tuṣita Heaven and reflected (*nien*) on Maitreya, vowing to be reborn there where he could pay homage to the bodhisattva and learn from him the *Yogācārabhūmi* while listening to the fine Dharma. After having gained complete wisdom, he would then be reborn into this world again where he would teach these same men, bringing them to practice good deeds and to abandon all evil acts and where he would propagate the Dharma widely for the benefit of all beings.

> Next the master paid homage to the Buddhas of the Ten Directions, and then he sat mindfully (*cheng-nien erh tso*), fixing his thoughts on Maitreya, free of any other [mental] object (*wu fu i yüan*). It seemed that in his mind (*yü hsin-hsiang chung*) he ascended Mount Sumeru, passed through the first, second, and third heavens, and then saw the palace in Tuṣita Heaven with Maitreya bodhisattva sitting on a dais made of marvelous gems and surrounded by heavenly beings. With that he became so enraptured, both mentally and physically, that he was no longer aware of being on the sacrificial altar and had forgotten all about the pirates.

Hsüan-tsang's biographer goes on to say that while Hsüan-tsang sat in this state of rapturous concentration, oblivious to all that was going on around him, a great storm arose from the four quarters of the heavens, overturning the pirates' boats and tearing up the trees. The pirates were suddenly filled with fear. They turned to the passengers and asked why a seemingly ordinary monk could bring such extraordinary natural forces to his defense. When the passengers told the pirates about Hsüan-tsang's journey and his reputation for holiness, the pirates threw themselves down and begged Hsüan-tsang for forgiveness. Hsüan-tsang rose from his meditation and responded to their expressions of repentance with a stirring sermon about the terrors of hell. The story ends with the pirates confessing their sins, taking the five precepts of Buddhist lay disciples, and restoring the stolen property to its rightful owners.

As is often the case in the biographies of saints, whether the saints are Buddhist or belong to another tradition, it is hard to separate fact from fiction. This episode in Hsüan-tsang's life reads like a Buddhist version of the story of Saint Catherine, a story that contains the same band of persecutors (soldiers instead of pirates), the same threat of imminent death (by torture on a wheel rather than sacrifice on an altar), and the same miraculous events that lead to the deliverance of the saint and the conversion of her persecutors. The miraculous aura that surrounds the story of Saint Catherine has struck some people as less than fully believable.[3] But no matter how skeptical one is about the miraculous events in the story of Hsüan-tsang's escape from the pirates, there is at least one element that not only has a ring of authenticity but that also tells us something important about Hsüan-tsang's personal piety. Embedded in the narrative is a model of meditation that transports Hsüan-tsang "in his mind" beyond this world into the presence of Maitreya in the palace of Tuṣita Heaven. We may question the authenticity of the story itself, but it is difficult to doubt the significance of such visual experiences in Hsüan-tsang's practice of the Dharma, not only because his biographer was so closely associated with Hsüan-tsang's circle of followers and knew its traditions well but because the vision of Maitreya is so consistent with other important elements in Hsüan-tsang's life.

The biographies tell us that Hsüan-tsang showed a similar devotion to Maitreya on his deathbed.[4] As he lay dying, surrounded by his disciples, he dedicated the merit he had gained from his life's work to ensure that those who were present around him would be reborn with Maitreya in Tuṣita Heaven. When one of his disciples asked him whether he thought that he would be reborn in Tuṣita himself, he answered, "Quite certain!" The moment of death among his friends and disciples in China summoned up the same aspiration that had guided Hsüan-tsang's visionary experience years before on the makeshift altar along the Ganges. This story also recalls the visual experiences that were so prominent at other crucial moments in Hsüan-tsang's travels. There were the events in the cave of the Buddha's shadow, where Hsüan-tsang's discipline and devotion brought him a vision of the Buddha's form, a vision that others thought had been permanently lost. There were also the events at the Bodhi tree, where Hsüan-tsang "gazed on" the site of the Buddha's enlightenment and threw himself down "with much grief and tears in his self-affliction."[5] The story does not tell us that Hsüan-tsang expressed the emotion of that moment by crying out or beating his breast. His eyes, the seat of his vision, filled with tears. And when Hsüan-tsang developed his portrait of Bhāvaviveka, he spoke of Bhāvaviveka's vision of Avalokiteśvara and his desire to wait in the Asuras' palace (rather than in the palace of Tuṣita Heaven) for a vision of Maitreya. The emotion of these moments is expressed as a function of the eyes and as an act of vision.

In a fine study of the meaning of meditation in the tradition of Hsüan-tsang's school, Alan Sponberg argues that the visualization process, so much a part of Hsüan-tsang's response to the approach of death, deserves recognition as a distinctive form of meditative practice. The process of concentrating on the figure of a great bodhisattva, excluding everything else from the mind and developing or being granted a vision of the bodhisattva in heaven, is not one that can be reduced to any of the other more familiar types of meditation. Unlike the predominant form of meditation in the Ch'an or Zen tradition, Hsüan-tsang's visualization was an absorption so deep that he lost all awareness of his surroundings, but it was not a process in which sensory experience came completely to a stop. If anything, it was a state of enhanced sensation. In his mind, Hsüan-tsang *saw* Maitreya in the palace with a vividness and intensity that replaced his sensation of the ordinary world. It was as if Hsüan-tsang had been transported from one plane of reality to another, anticipating in the experience of meditation a real journey that would take place after death. Hui-li makes it clear that Hsüan-tsang's concentration while on the pirates' altar was meant to prepare him for rebirth in Maitreya's presence, and the accounts of Hsüan-tsang's actual death in China, surrounded by a band of disciples rather than a band of pirates, repeat the same theme. Someone might perform the visualization at other moments in life, just as Bhāvaviveka fasted and chanted to receive a vision of Avalokiteśvara, but Hsüan-tsang used this visualization to shape his passage into the next life.

The repetition of Hsüan-tsang's visualization as a preparation for death makes it hard to overlook in any serious study of Hsüan-tsang's religiosity. Like Bhāvaviveka, he seems to have tempered the analytical quality of his experience with an element of fervent devotion. But there are indications in the choice of the terminology in Hui-li's retelling of the story that suggest we are on the edge of a phenomenon that is larger still. When Hsüan-tsang began the process of concentration that led to his vision of the palace in Tuṣita Heaven, Hui-li says that Hsüan-tsang "reflected" (*nien*) on the figure of Maitreya. This act of reflection is just the beginning of the meditation, but it is out of this reflection that the later experience grows. Hui-li does not indicate that there is anything unusual or significant about the term *nien* itself (although, by giving the Chinese word, Sponberg suggests that it is used in a technical sense). The story itself could be interpreted to mean that Hsüan-tsang did nothing more than select the figure of Maitreya out of a series of objects to give it special attention. But when the story is read against the Indian background, the Chinese word is like a hole scratched in a frosty windowpane. It opens up a whole new world of associations. The term *nien* translates the Sanskrit term *anusmṛti*. In the Indian context, *anusmṛti* can be used in a general sense to mean "recollection," "remembrance," or "calling to mind," but in Buddhist literature it conveys these meanings in a series of specific, ritually charged environments, from the three, four, five, six, or ten *anusmṛti*s of the Pali canon to the elaborate contemplation of the image of the Buddha that goes by the name of "Buddha-recollection" (*buddhānusmṛti*) in the Mahāyāna sūtras.[6]

Sometimes "recollection of the Buddha" takes the form of calling to mind a catalog of distinctive attributes, as in the following passage from the Chinese Āgamas:

> A *bhikṣu* correct in body and correct in mind sits crosslegged and focuses his thought in front of him. Without entertaining any other thought he earnestly calls to mind [*anusmṛ-*] the Buddha. He contemplates the image of the Tathāgata without taking his eyes off it. Not taking his eyes off it he then calls to mind the qualities of the Tathāgata—the Tathāgata's body made of *vajra*, endowed with the ten Powers [*bala*] and by virtue of the four assurances [*vaiśāradya*] intrepid in assemblies. . . .[7]

Sometimes "Buddha-recollection" involves a course of concentration and discipline that lasts as long as a week (although even an ordeal of this length does not always guarantee success):

> [A] bodhisattva, whether he is a householder or one who has gone forth [*pravrajita*], when he has gone alone to a secluded place and seated himself, after concentrating on the Tathāgata, Arhat, Samyaksaṃbuddha Amitāyus in accordance with what he has heard, then faultless in the mass of the precepts and undistracted in mindfulness [*smṛti*] should he concentrate for one day and night, for two, three, four, five, six, or seven days and nights. If he concentrates on the Tathāgata Amitāyus with undistracted thought for seven days and nights, then when seven days and nights have elapsed he shall see the Lord, the Tathāgata Amitāyus. If he does not see the Lord by day, then in a dream while sleeping the face of the Lord, the Tathāgata Amitāyus will appear.[8]

What is so striking about these two passages, especially after reading the story of Hsüan-tsang's contemplation of Maitreya, is their visual form. The recollection of the Buddha in all these cases involves a process of visualization. Sometimes it may be no more than a reminder of the Buddha's distinctive characteristics, designed to reassure monks when the prospects of spiritual progress seem particularly bleak. Sometimes it may be closer to the quest for a specific vision.[9] But in both cases it is an experience that is visual in form.

Focusing on the role of visualization and visual experience in Hsüan-tsang's travels opens a host of new possibilities for the interpretation of Hsüan-tsang's writings and the intellectual tradition they represent. It is impossible to take the story of Hsüan-tsang's visualization seriously and still defend the idea that meditation is or should be a single, monolithic phenomenon.[10] Hsüan-tsang's visualization is not Ch'an, and there is no way to assimilate one to the other without doing violence to both. The story also gives a way to attack the stereotype of the philosopher as someone who has transcended the concerns of everyday religious life. Hsüan-tsang had a reputation in China as one of the most accomplished philosophers of his age, but when the pirates led him to the altar and threatened his life, he did not concentrate on Emptiness as a reality free from concepts and cognitive marks. Instead, he visualized the splendor of Tuṣita Heaven and put himself in the hands of Maitreya. The most significant thing about the story, however, may be even more basic than this. The story shows that Hsüan-tsang's religion was, to a remarkable extent, a religion of the eyes. He was affected by other sensory experiences, of course, and he recognized their power, but at crucial moments in his life he came back to a devotion that was visual in form. He conceived of the Buddha and other objects of his devotion as visual objects and responded to them in a visual way.

This point may seem so obvious that it does not even need to be stated. The language of vision is so basic to the discussion of Buddhahood, so much a part of the Buddhist conceptual landscape, that it is almost invisible. The philosophers' accounts of the Dharma Body that occupied our attention in chapter 5 could have been understood as little more than an extended footnote on the scriptural statement, "Whoever sees the Dharma sees me; whoever sees me sees the Dharma." But when we read the sentence for the first time and considered its meaning, we focused on the distinction between the different Buddha Bodies. To focus first on the *seeing* itself would be like asking a sword to cut itself or the eye to see itself. And yet the sentence is built on a metaphor of seeing. The symbolic and metaphorical associations that inform Hsüan-tsang's understanding of the act of seeing also inform his understanding of the Buddha. By this I mean not just Hsüan-tsang's understanding of *the Buddha*, but Hsüan-tsang's *understanding* of the Buddha—the cognitive and emotive act of placing himself in relation (if I can substitute a spatial metaphor for Hsüan-tsang's own metaphor of vision) to the complex reality he knew as the Buddha. The challenge in Hsüan-tsang's story is to look at the notion of seeing and through it to discern Hsüan-tsang's understanding of the act of understanding itself.

Sponberg had this challenge in mind when he related Hsüan-tsang's vision of Maitreya to the vision (*kuan*) Hsüan-tsang cultivated as part of his study of Yogācāra "philosophy." The same Chinese word, *kuan*, can be used in both contexts. It can refer to the vision of a Buddha or great bodhisattva, like Hsüan-tsang's vision of Maitreya in heaven, or it can refer to the cultivation of insight in the study of philosophy.[11] In the philosophical context, the word *kuan* does not suggest the all-embracing sensory experience associated with a visualization of the Buddha. The philosophical form of vision has more to do with the discrimination of different levels of reality (or the discrimination of reality from error), and it has more to do with a gradual process of intellectual development than with a sudden vision of a bodhisattva in a heaven. But both uses of the word *kuan* share the same visual metaphor. Recollection and insight both have to do with the cultivation of some form of vision.

Bhāvaviveka and the Philosopher's Eyes

The association of philosophical insight with a metaphor of vision is present in Bhāvaviveka's philosophical tradition as well. The Sanskrit word *vipaśyanā* that lies behind the philosophical use of the Chinese *kuan* names the discriminating vision that comes after the calming of all mental distractions.[12] It follows but is intimately associated with the practice of "calming" (*śamatha*) meditation. In some contexts, *śamatha* and *vipaśyanā* represent the two poles of meditative practice, with a focusing and concentration of the mind followed by a precise analysis of the nature of reality. Bhāvaviveka uses somewhat different terms but makes the same point at the beginning of the third chapter of *The Verses on the Essence of the Middle Way*:

> No one sees [his or her] face [reflected] in muddy or turbulent water, and [no one sees] reality in a mind that is unconcentrated and covered with obstructions. . . .
>
> After concentrating the mind, one analyzes with wisdom.[13]

The association of analytical insight with vision is most obvious, however, in the word we translate "philosophy." To practice philosophy is to "see" (*darśana*) reality. The word *darśana* can also name the systems of philosophy that are generated out of this act of seeing, as in the title of the well-known philosophical compendium *Sarva-darśana-saṃgraha* ("The Compendium of All Philosophical Systems" or "The Compendium of All Modes of Seeing").[14] There is nothing intrinsic in the word, however, that limits it to the philosophical use. When the *Mahāparinibbāna Sutta* describes the four places of Buddhist pilgrimage as sites that one should "see and be moved by," the seeing is closer to the vision we express when we say that someone "takes the *darśan*" of a guru than it is to the cool discernment of philosophy.[15] Jan Gonda has pointed out that seeing a person in Vedic literature comes very close to touching him and that seeing has traditionally been prescribed in rituals as a way of gaining advantage from a great being or of participating in his or her nature.[16] The word for this powerful experience of communion, like the word for philosophy, is simply "seeing."

The metaphor of vision manifests itself in other ways as well. If philosophers intend to see reality, they have to have "eyes." But the eyes that see through the appearances that shroud the real nature of things are not the same as physical eyes. As we noticed in chapter 2, Bhāvaviveka starts the presentation of his own philosophy with the verses that serve as the epigraph for this part of the book, a description of the philosopher's eyes:

> The one who has the eye of knowledge, not some other [eye], is the one who sees. So an intelligent person concentrates on the quest for the knowledge of reality.
>
> An intelligent person, even one who is blind, sees the three worlds without any obstruction. Such a person sees the things that he wants to see, whether they are far away, subtle, or concealed.[17]

Bhāvaviveka then develops this image of the philosopher's eyes through the same three-part pattern that manifests itself in other aspects of his thought. In the second stage of the argument, the philosopher's eyes appear not as the eyes that see things more clearly but as the eyes that see nothing at all.

> Someone who gets rid of an eye disease and has eyes that are pure and clear does not see spots, hairs, flies, or a double image of the moon.
>
> Likewise, someone who gets rid of the eye disease of defilements and objects of cognition and has the clear eye of true knowledge does not see anything at all.[18]

Finally, in the third stage of the argument, Bhāvaviveka pictures the philosopher's eyes as the eyes of a bodhisattva. They are eyes that see the illusory nature of things but still respond to the suffering of others:

> [The bodhisattva] has climbed the mountain peak of wisdom and is free from grief, but looks with compassion on ordinary people who suffer and are burned by grief.
>
> Then, with an eye that is moist with compassion, [the bodhisattva] sees that [the wisdom-eyes of] ordinary people have been covered by an imaginary net created by the art of conceptual thought.[19]

Here the circle is completed as it was with the image of the Buddha's Dharma Body and the palace of reality. The bodhisattva sees the Emptiness of things but sees it in a way that still makes it possible to be involved in the world's suffering.

In his verse about the bodhisattva's eyes, Bhāvaviveka plays on the traditional distinction between the sage who has no grief and the ordinary people who are burned by grief.[20] But he modifies the image by adding the tears of compassion. The model he has in mind is a bodhisattva like Avalokiteśvara ("The Lord Who Looks Down"), who sees the world with the eyes of wisdom and compassion simultaneously. Even if we do not take literally Giuseppe Tucci's suggestion that Avalokiteśvara is the deification of the vision (*avalokana*) of the Buddha, Avalokiteśvara's sight still combines the insight that is expressed in *The Heart Sūtra*, where it says that he "looked down and saw the five aggregates as empty of own-being," with the compassionate oversight that is expressed in *The Lotus Sūtra*, where it says that Avalokiteśvara is someone who "sees all beings with mercy and love."[21] To add tears to the bodhisattva's eyes not only gives the image a Mahāyāna flavor but turns it from the passive vision of an ascetic to the vision of someone who is about to rise into action. Descriptions of Avalokiteśvara in texts like *The Lotus Sūtra* portray a being whose most important trait is the desire to help those who fall into danger. The sūtra says, "If they hear [him], see [him], and later recollect [him], he will effectively destroy all the suffering and grief of sentient beings."[22]

It is this active dimension of vision that seems most significant in Bhāvaviveka's understanding of the Buddha himself. The Buddha is by definition someone who has perfected the vision of reality: a Buddha is one who truly sees. But when a lesser person contemplates the Buddha, the Buddha's crucial characteristic is not his own *seeing*. It is his ability to *illuminate* the minds of others who have not yet seen. The idea that the eye shines and illuminates its object is an ancient notion in Indian tradition,[23] and the terminology for vision and illumination in the description of Buddhas and great bodhisattvas allows an easy transition from one idea to the other. The words *āloka* and *locana* can mean either illumination or vision, and *darśana* can mean either to see or to show. Bhāvaviveka seems to play directly on the meaning of these words only once in the account of his own philosophy, even though it is present in the background of all his descriptions of the Buddha. In the verse that follows the description of the bodhisattva who has climbed the mountain peak of wisdom and looks out on (*ālokya*) the people below, Bhāvaviveka describes the people themselves as blind (*alocana*) and lacking the intelligence to see (*āloka*), even though reality itself is as clear as the autumn sky.[24] The passage can also be read as suggesting that ordinary people labor in darkness (*alocana*), even though they are illuminated (*ālokya*) by the gaze of the bodhisattva. The clouds that obscure their vision exist only in the minds of the people themselves.[25] The added irony in the passage, of course, is that reality is truly seen by not seeing. The person who has no sight is like the person who does not have the Buddha Body because he has no understanding. It is precisely the Buddha's no-understanding that constitutes his true understanding.[26] If this person could really see what it means not to see, or really understand what it means not to understand, he would be enlightened.

The image of the Buddha as the source of illumination is also one of the key images in Bhāvaviveka's description of the Manifestation Body. In the two verses that give a conventional definition of the Buddha (verses 268 and 346), Bhāvaviveka pictures the Buddha as someone who opens the minds of other beings with the rays of his teaching the way the sun brings a pond of lotuses to flower. Again there is a change from passive to active. Bhāvaviveka takes the traditional image of the Buddha as the one whose mind has opened or whose wisdom has blossomed (*vibuddha*) like a lotus and transforms it into an action directed toward others. It is not just the Buddha who "blossoms" but also those who feel the warmth of his illuminating rays.[27] The change makes a useful point about the Buddha's role as a source of compassion, a virtue that is associated particularly with the Mahāyāna, but the change is not necessarily peculiar to this tradition. André Bareau has pointed out that the *Mahāparinirvāṇa Sūtra* of the Dharmaguptakas speaks of the Buddha as the "Eye of the World."[28] The name indicates not only that the Buddha knows the truth about the world but also that he makes it known to those who live in the world. The epithet "eye of the world" also serves as a name for the sun and stresses the role of the Buddha as the one who illuminates the minds of people who labor in the darkness of this world. All of these possibilities are suggested by Bhāvaviveka's image of the Buddha as the source of light and vision.

The imagery that associates the Buddha with light and especially with the light of the sun is far too extensive to consider here in any detail. It is so pervasive and so dominant in some levels of the Buddhist tradition that Max Müller and a few other like-minded scholars once argued that the Buddha legend was a solar myth.[29] Müller's theory is no longer in fashion, but the language of illumination in Bhāvaviveka's thought still has important parallels in the early scriptures. "The Sūtra on the Turning of the Wheel of the Law" (*dhammacakka-pavattana sutta*) uses a stock phrase to describe the Buddha's understanding of the four Noble Truths: "Monks, at the thought of this Noble Truth of suffering, concerning things that had not been learned before, there arose in me vision, insight, knowledge, wisdom, and illumination."[30] Here vision (*cakkhu*), illumination (*āloka*), and wisdom (*paññā*) are interidentified, metaphorically if not in reality. B. G. Gokhale has pointed out that the imagery of light and illumination is further enriched by the addition of fire, especially the flame of a lamp.[31] Like the gods, the Buddha is often associated with radiant light and particularly with the light that illuminates the minds of his disciples. Some of the most striking visual representations of the Buddha's power of illumination are the images of the Buddha as a pillar of fire.[32] Sometimes the pillar stands alone, sometimes it appears behind the Buddha's empty throne, but its importance as a focus of devotion is hard to deny. Bhāvaviveka no doubt had associations like these in mind when he called his two major works *The Lamp of Wisdom* and *The Flame of Reason*.

As he says early in the third chapter of the verses that accompany *The Flame of Reason*, "Wisdom is the lamp whose light cannot be obscured and the fire that [burns] the fuel of the defilements."[33]

Structural Similarities Between Different Kinds of Vision

The association of wisdom with fire and illumination certainly is not unique to Bhāvaviveka. If he only used the images of the eyes to embellish his argument, they would simply show his familiarity with the conventional images that Buddhist authors have long used to represent the Buddha. But the metaphors are not mere embellishments. They reflect something very deep and important about Bhāvaviveka's understanding of reality. To borrow a phrase from George Lakoff and Mark Johnson, they are not just metaphors for Bhāvaviveka to write with but metaphors for him to think with and, above all, to live with.[34] We have already seen one aspect of the significance of these metaphors when we noted that the images of the eyes followed the same three-part pattern that was found in other aspects of Bhāvaviveka's thought. This pattern gave a predictable structure to Bhāvaviveka's presentation of reality, but it also mapped a path and a cognitive discipline. The three-part pattern expresses a process of cognition through which a person can come, in a practical sense, to *know* the Buddha and eventually even *become* a Buddha. When Bhāvaviveka and other Madhyamaka authors speak of "seeing" the Buddha, it is this cognitive practice that they have in mind. Vision functions for them as a metaphor for the process of enlightenment itself.

To say that a metaphor is a tool to live with means in part that it can be used to organize and channel the practical choices a person makes to carry out even the most basic actions of everyday life. To illustrate the way metaphors control actions, Lakoff and Johnson use the example of the metaphor "argument is war." The metaphor appears in some of the most common phrases we use to describe the process of argument: We can speak of attacking or defending a position. We can speak of a person winning or gaining ground. And when the argument is over, we can ask one side to concede defeat, or we can demand that both sides reach a truce. It is not that the argument is literally an act of war but that the terminology of war can be used to express the actions involved in certain kinds of adversarial communication. Yet to picture an argument as a form of warfare is not just a neutral representation of one set of procedures by another but one that actually affects the way people act out the process of argument itself. If an argument is understood as defending or attacking territory, it is less likely that the participants will try to identify common ground, and if an argument has to have a winner and a loser, it limits the way the argument can be concluded. As Lakoff and Johnson say, we do not just talk about arguments as if they were war; we act out the metaphor when we argue. This is not the most complex metaphor,

metaphor, but it has a pervasive effect, and its effect often goes unacknowledged precisely because we take the metaphor so much for granted.

If this is true of the metaphor "argument is war," it is also true of the metaphor "knowing is seeing." To think of knowing as a form of seeing gives knowledge a vividness and liveliness that would be hard to convey with a bare syllogism, but the metaphor also structures and limits Bhāvaviveka's understanding of knowledge itself. It may seem obvious to think of knowing as seeing. It corresponds, after all, to one of the most basic functions of the body: we "know" most directly and clearly in many situations only through the eyes. But the metaphor involves limitations of at least two kinds: it ties different kinds of seeing together, and it distinguishes the knowledge that comes from seeing from the knowledge that comes from the other senses.

In Bhāvaviveka's work, seeing comes in different forms, but the use of the same word gives the impression that the different acts of seeing are counterparts of one another. What is said of one is often said of another, even though they may be very different kinds of experience. Because they are named by the same name, they are taken to represent analogous activities and often seem to occupy the same place in the system of Bhāvaviveka's thought.

If we look closely at the three-part pattern that governs Bhāvaviveka's account of the Buddha, we find that he uses the metaphor of vision like a thread to sew the different parts of the argument together, even though the type of vision changes radically from one part of the text to another. The vision that dominates large portions of the text is the negative vision of the philosopher who has learned to analyze the categories of existence and see nothing at all:

> Someone who gets rid of an eye disease and has eyes that are pure and clear does not see spots, hairs, flies, or a double image of the moon.
>
> Likewise, someone who gets rid of the eye disease of defilements and objects of cognition and has the clear eye of true knowledge does not see anything at all.[35]

This negative mode of vision is reflected in the final vision of Emptiness: "Emptiness is empty of any identity such as 'Emptiness,' so a wise person does not see Emptiness as 'Emptiness.'"[36] And when the Buddha is defined as the one who does not arise, has no form, does not change, and so forth,[37] the vision that is no vision is extended to the devotional vision of the great bodhisattvas:

> Like space, heroic beings see him without seeing. [These bodhisattvas] live without concepts and without effort, and their eyes are clear. They pay homage to the Lord without any homage, reflection, or words. To them also we pay sincere homage.[38]

These are the bodhisattvas after whom the philosophers and practitioners of the text hope to model themselves.

A few verses later Bhāvaviveka returns to the same image:

> [The Buddha] is invisible to a physical eye and invisible to a divine eye, and he cannot be seen by conceptual or nonconceptual cognition.[39]

The metaphor of vision also appears in the startling verse that equates the Buddha with the Supreme Brahman:

> [The Buddha] is the Supreme Brahman that even [gods] such as Brahmā do not grasp.[40]

In his commentary on this verse, Bhāvaviveka explains that "grasping" is a form of vision. Brahmā, Viṣṇu, and Śiva may take pride in their vision of reality, but their vision still suffers from the fault of objectification. They still think they are seeing *something*. But the Supreme Brahman (which Bhāvaviveka here equates with nirvana rather than with what he calls "the Lord of Creatures") cannot be seen by any cognition that has an object.

Then, in one of the most important transitions in the text, Bhāvaviveka moves to the practice of the bodhisattva path. On the surface the verse does not look too promising:

> If someone practices this and lives without any apprehension, what can [this practitioner's] mind desire, hate, or be ignorant of?

The awkwardness of the verse in English comes in part from the pronoun "this" that suspends in midair with no obvious referent. In fact, it refers back to the "Brahman" of the previous section. Bhāvaviveka is using the verse to play on the meaning of two doctrinal formulas that involve the term Brahman. To "practice this" is to engage in *brahma-caryā*, to engage in an ordinary religious discipline that leads to nirvana.[41] When Bhāvaviveka speaks of "living without any apprehension," he is also updating the practice of the four "states of Brahmā" (*brahma-vihāra*): friendliness, compassion, joy, and equanimity. The full visual significance of the verse only emerges in the commentary when Bhāvaviveka asks, "How does someone carry out this practice?" The answer is that the practice is carried out by the recollection (*anusmṛti*) of the Buddha. This is the same recollection that Hsüan-tsang used to visualize Maitreya in the palace of Tuṣita Heaven. Bhāvaviveka quickly explains that this recollection is characterized by no-recollection and no-reflection, but the significance of the point is hard to miss. When he asks himself what it means to see the Buddha, he refers to the recollection that Hsüan-tsang used at the moment of death.

What we have here is a series of steps that carry us from one domain of practice to another. While the subject matter changes, the metaphor remains the same. In the analytical section of the chapter, Bhāvaviveka was developing the vision of reality (*tattva-darśana*) in the philosophical sense. At the beginning of the third part of the chapter, he took up the vision of the

Buddha in a similar analytical mode. Here he marks the transition into the bodhisattva path with a reference to the practice of visualization. Does he also use a visual image to mark the transition from the bodhisattva path to the final description of the Buddha? The answer is yes, and in quite a striking way. He starts the last section of the chapter with a picture of the Buddha as a source of illumination:

> [The bodhisattva] becomes a Buddha and opens the minds of fortunate beings with the pure, cleansing rays of teaching just as the sun [opens the blossoms in] a pond of lotuses.[42]

It is almost as if the chapter were nothing more than a sustained reflection on what it means to see. One section has to do with an analysis of the nature of things, the next with an analysis of the Buddha himself, the next with the path that leads to Buddhahood, and the next with the illumination that comes from the Buddha as an external source of vision.

Each of these metaphors makes a useful point about the nature of vision, but the combination of different images tells more than any of the images individually. First, there is a clear similarity in structure between the vision of reality and the vision of the Buddha. The concept of the Buddha occupies the same position in Bhāvaviveka's metaphor as the concept of reality. This is a point we noted when we considered the different meanings of the word "Dharma," but here we have even more confirmation of Bhāvaviveka's desire to view the Buddha as the equivalent of reality itself. At the other end of the spectrum is the practice of recollection (*anusmṛti*). We have already noted that recollection has an element of visualization: it is used to invoke the presence of Buddhas or great bodhisattvas through visual meditation. Here the visual dimension of recollection is confirmed, but not because Bhāvaviveka says anything explicit about the technique of recollection. All he tells us directly about recollection is what it is not. But the recollection of the Buddha is homologous with the vision of the Buddha; it occupies a comparable position in the structure of Bhāvaviveka's thought. Even without being told directly, we know that he understands recollection as an act of seeing.

When these relationships are brought to the surface, they show that Bhāvaviveka is not just creating a series of isolated arguments or analyzing a series of unrelated concepts. He follows lines of continuity that draw different elements in his thought together into a coherent whole. The metaphors join concepts that might otherwise seem incompatible—concepts that are as far apart as the analysis of the identity of earth and the visual recollection of the Buddha—and they tie the concepts together into a system that is as much a system of imagination as it is of hard analysis. Even more important than this, however, is the suggestion that the text is linked to a series of practices outside the text itself, practices that we now only dimly perceive but that were part of the imaginative milieu in which Bhāvaviveka created the text. He does not tell us much about the actual conduct of recollection, and what he tells us is largely negative, but we know from the place it holds in his system that Bhāvaviveka thought it was an important means of access to the Buddha. We know so little about Indian Buddhist philosophers as religious practitioners that this is precious evidence, and it is evidence that confirms some of the most important aspects of Hsüan-tsang's image of Bhāvaviveka the devotee. There is no description here of the visualization of Avalokiteśvara, but it is no longer so difficult to believe that the person who gives recollection such a central place in his system also fasted and chanted so that he could receive a vision of the great bodhisattva.

If we want to pursue the connection between Bhāvaviveka's philosophical vision and the piety that informed his vision of the Buddha, we can push the metaphor of vision a step further. Bhāvaviveka seems to have left us a trace of his own personality in the verse that starts his final account of the Buddha. There is a great deal of uncertainty about the name we should use to designate the philosopher I have been calling Bhāvaviveka. There is evidence in the colophons to the Tibetan and Chinese translations of some of his works that he was known as Bhavya rather than Bhāvaviveka. In any case, the word *bhavya* appears twice in the third chapter of *The Verses on the Essence of the Middle Way*, both times in the same context.[43] Our philosopher describes the Buddha as someone who opens the minds of fortunate beings with his manifestations or with the rays of his teaching. The "fortunate beings" are *bhavya*—which may be the name of the philosopher himself.

Why would the philosopher write his own name into the text? What message could he be trying to convey? There are a number of possible explanations. We have already noticed that Bhāvaviveka attributed a vow (*dīkṣā*) to himself in a way that stressed his own humility and at the same time associated himself with the promise that distinguished the greatest bodhisattvas. The combination of self-abasement and self-exaltation is a common feature of literature on the bodhisattva path and reflects one of the most basic ambiguities in the concept of the bodhisattva. Even the first stirrings of the aspiration to Buddhahood are the beginning of the mind of enlightenment (*bodhicitta*), and the mind of enlightenment participates, no matter how remotely, in the grandeur of enlightenment itself. In Bhāvaviveka's verse, there could be a similar sense of irony. After a chapter filled with intense philosophical analysis, the last image the philosopher leaves of himself is the image of a lotus sitting in a pond and slowly opening to the warm rays of the Buddha's teaching. It is an image of humility, the image of a pious devotee. But the image also implies that the philosopher has been illuminated with the flash of insight that makes a system come clear. This is an experience of illumination that students (in Bhāvaviveka's time as well as ours) labor long and hard to acquire.

This image of the philosopher's illumination suggests a dimension in the experience of insight that is seldom emphasized in accounts of philosophical vision. Bhāvaviveka's final image of vision is one in which the vision is granted, not grasped. A bodhisattva can aspire to the moment when he or she will be able to illuminate others, but someone who is just beginning to progress on the path to enlightenment depends on the illumination that comes from others. This means, among other things, that tradition (*āgama*) retains authority and power even in the most rigorously rational of the Mahāyāna systems, but it also helps explain one of the most puzzling aspects of the terminology of vision in the early Mahāyāna sūtras. It is clear from the practice of recollection and from other visual phenomena in these sūtras that visualization played an active role in the religious world out of which the sūtras arose, but there is no obvious word for the act of visualization itself. Apart from "recollection," the most likely designation of the act of visualization is *samādhi*. But *samādhi* is a generic word for concentration and does not necessarily have a visual content. What seems to have held the Indian tradition back from naming the phenomenon directly was a certain reticence about the source of the experience itself. In the Maitreya chapter of the *Gaṇḍavyūha Sūtra*, where Maitreya manifests the story of his bodhisattva career to the pilgrim Sudhana by displaying a peaked dwelling, the verb "to see" is used throughout, but in its causative form with Maitreya as the subject. Sudhana is not the agent. He is simply one of the objects, the one whom Maitreya "causes to see" the manifestation. The logic of vision in this story is such that while Sudhana "sees," he only sees the vision that is granted to him by the power of Maitreya.[44]

It is tempting to ask whether the same logic applies to the philosopher's vision of reality—to ask, in other words, whether there is an element of grace or empowerment from a source outside the philosopher himself that makes analytical vision possible. The question does not, on the face of it, seem likely to yield a positive answer. The vision of reality is one that comes from exercising a person's own analytical powers; it is not in any obvious sense a gift from someone else. It is clear also that Bhāvaviveka's text was meant to serve, in part, as a manual for debate. It plots a line of attack for students to follow when they confront not only a string of external opponents but also the objections that come from their own instinctive fear of Emptiness. To carry out this process effectively, a student has to be independent and self-reliant. This part of the visualization process requires a firm, autonomous rationality. But there are two points where Bhāvaviveka's philosophical vision does seem to have a gratuitous if not a gracious quality.

The first of these has to do with the origin of the philosophical quest itself. Bhāvaviveka's method of investigation begins with the categories of the sūtras. He conceives of his philosophy as a rational process that is *subsequent to* and *consistent with* the categories of tradition (*āgama*).[45] This is why the arguments with other Buddhists in *The Verses on the Essence of the Middle Way* are framed as arguments about the interpretation of tradition. The "ultimate" (*paramārtha*) that is the object of the philosopher's quest is not only the "ultimate object" and the "ultimate knowledge" but the "ultimate meaning."[46] To explore the Buddha's ultimate awareness is not just a question of metaphysics and epistemology but also of interpretation. When Bhāvaviveka says that the Buddha illuminates the minds of fortunate beings (like himself) with the rays of his teaching, he means in part that the Buddha has provided the categories of analysis that set the philosophical process in motion. Without this prior tradition, there would be no Buddhist philosophy.

But the philosophical vision also seems to be gratuitous in another, less obvious sense. I just mentioned that Bhāvaviveka's final image of vision is of a vision that has been granted, not grasped. These are words that I have imposed on the text, not ones that Bhāvaviveka uses himself, but they correspond to a distinction of which Bhāvaviveka was well aware. The reason Brahmā and the other gods did not have the vision of Emptiness was that they grasped it as an object. If they could have given up the objectification not only of the object of vision but of vision itself, they would have had the true vision that is no-vision. This is not an experience of grace in the normal sense of the word, but it has a gratuitous quality: it requires a giving up rather than a grasping, a no-seeing rather than a seeing. There is a similarity of structure, if not of substance, that places this no-seeing in the same metaphorical world as the seeing of the Buddha. And the seeing of the Buddha is also an experience of being seen, an experience of seeing that also involves a sense that one is illumined by the Buddha's (absent) presence.

The Ranking of the Different Senses

The lines of similarity that tie different forms of vision together give us one way to think about the structure implicit in Bhāvaviveka's metaphor of vision, but it is not the only way. Vision is defined not just by what it includes but also by what it excludes. If philosophy is understood as seeing rather than hearing, it implies certain choices that affect the practice of philosophy itself. There is likely to be less stress, for example, on rote learning—on the memorization and recitation of what is heard—and more stress on direct scrutiny of an object (whatever that may mean in a particular philosophical context). The philosopher is more likely to say, "Don't just take my word for it, but come and see for yourself." By choosing to represent knowledge as vision rather than as hearing, Bhāvaviveka implies a choice about the relationship between the memorization and recitation of the sūtras and the analysis of the categories they contain, a choice that places the evidence of the sūtras (as knowledge gained through hearing) in a secondary or preliminary role in comparison to the knowledge that comes through direct analysis. To understand what Bhāvaviveka means by seeing the Buddha, we also have to consider what it is about vision itself that makes it so useful to express what Bhāvaviveka thinks of as knowledge. And we have to understand how this group of experiences—all named in some way by the term "vision"—is related to the experiences of the other senses.

It is not difficult to find images of the other senses in Bhāvaviveka's work. Some of them are even associated with the metaphor of vision itself. When Bhāvaviveka describes the Buddha in the verses that bring the chapter to a close, he starts with an image of illumination: the Buddha opens the minds of fortunate beings with the rays of his teaching. The following verses then make it clear that the dominant image is actually not one of light but of sound. In what is probably the most sustained example of synesthesia in the text, Bhāvaviveka describes the Buddha's verbal utterance of the Dharma as a sensory experience that engages all the senses:

> With the water of teaching, more cooling than the Himalayas, the moon, or sandalwood, he puts out the fire of the defilements in the minds of sentient beings.
>
> With the great boats of the three vehicles, he speedily saves beings from the ocean of existence with the waves of birth, transmigration, and suffering and the crocodiles of death.
>
> With the jewel-streams of his eloquent phrases, he completely dispels thirst and removes the world's beginningless poverty of good qualities.
>
> People wander in the forest of existence, and they have [only their] ignorance to show the way. He opens [their] wisdom-eye and leads [them] to nirvana.
>
> With the spells of knowledge, he truly cures the people who have been bitten by the snake of the defilements and are no longer conscious of their own welfare.
>
> He uses his teaching compassionately like the sound of a drum to awaken the living beings who have no one in this world to protect them and who have long slept the sleep of ignorance.
>
> He conquers the four Māras and frees those who have long been bound by the chains of thirst in the prison of samsara.
>
> With the lovely ambrosia of wisdom, he brings satisfaction to beings who are like a fire and cannot be satisfied by anything divine or human.[47]

Here the teaching is pictured not just as something that illuminates the mind but as something that quenches thirst, satisfies hunger, and transports a person to bodily safety.

The bodhisattvas in the tenth stage of the path, with their innumerable hands, heads, and mouths, offer worship to the Buddha in a form that engages another combination of senses. They offer sweet-smelling flowers as large as Mount Meru. They praise the Buddha with hymns. They offer parasols and canopies that sparkle with the light of jewels. As their last form of worship, they offer peaked dwellings where the Buddha can sit in splendor. Bhāvaviveka certainly was not blind to the appeal of the other senses, but it was the metaphor of vision that he returned to again and again in order to organize his thought. What was it about seeing that distinguished it for Bhāvaviveka from the activity of the other senses?

The easiest distinction to draw is the one between seeing and hearing. In the epistemological system that Bhāvaviveka inherited from the Buddhist logicians and the tradition of reflection on which their system was based, the knowledge that came from hearing was secondhand, indirect, and obscured even in the best of circumstances by a veil of conceptuality. To *see* something, however, was to know it directly, without anything between the eye and the object that could distort its meaning. The distinction between verbal knowledge and direct perceptual knowledge was elaborated with immense subtlety not only by the logicians who worked within the Yogācāra tradition but also by the followers of Bhāvaviveka himself. What concerns us here, however, is not the system but the instinct on which the system was built. In the work of Bhāvaviveka and the work of the Buddhist logicians, there is an intrinsic distrust of words. Words may be essential to convey certain types of meaning, but they are no substitute for direct perception. To see something is to know it more directly than to hear about it through words.

The distinction between the knowledge that comes from hearing and the knowledge that comes from direct perception can be pictured in the traditional example of a goldsmith. When a person takes a piece of gold to sell to a goldsmith and says that it contains a certain amount of gold, the goldsmith does not take the seller's word for it. The goldsmith weighs it and tests it to find out whether the words are correct. The Buddha advises his disciples to treat his teaching the same way the goldsmith treats someone's claims about gold. They should weigh it and test it to find out whether it is correct. This is not to say that words are completely unimportant or that the teaching of the Buddha is in any way less authoritative or less powerful for the fact that it has to be tested. But the testimony of the tradition is firmly in favor of the notion that hearing is just the beginning of a process of examination and practice. At best it can produce "the wisdom that consists of hearing" (*śrutamayī prajñā*).[48] It then has to be superseded by other forms of wisdom that offer more direct understanding.

What is curious about this model for the study of philosophy is that philosophy itself occupies an ambiguous position. From one point of view, philosophy, or the analysis of the nature of things, offers a more direct understanding of reality than a person can gain simply from hearing about it from a teacher. To analyze something is to develop "the wisdom that consists of thinking" (*cintāmayī prajñā*), the wisdom that follows and supersedes "the wisdom that consists of hearing." In this respect, philosophy is like seeing. It is the direct knowledge that supersedes the indirect knowledge that comes from hearing a teacher's words. But philosophy also has to be expressed in language. Philosophers spin arguments and construct syllogisms. Their words, as words, are just as far from the direct experience of reality as the first hearing of the Buddha's teaching is from enlightenment. The gap between logic and the direct experience of reality was one that the philosophers themselves recognized and crystallized in a tradition of verses about the blindness of logicians. Bhāvaviveka made the point this way:

> [The Buddha] is as inaccessible to logicians (*tārkika*) as heaven is to sinners, detachment is to those who are passionate, and the sun is to those who have been born blind.[49]

So philosophy can be treated in two ways. In the language of sensory metaphors, it can be speaking and hearing (as the logic of the logician is in Bhāvaviveka's verse), or it can be direct insight (as when it is pictured as the vision of reality).

Why is there such ambiguity? One explanation is that philosophy plays the awkward but essential role of joining two different areas of experience. For Bhāvaviveka, it functions as the bridge between the world of ordinary discourse and the direct vision of reality. It can have this function because it belongs, in a metaphorical sense, to both worlds. It is constructed out of the raw material of language, but it uses these words and concepts to scrutinize the nature of things, to look beneath the veil of appearances, and to see things as they are. Bhāvaviveka makes this point in a forceful way at the end of his analysis of Yogācāra philosophy, although it is not Bhāvaviveka but the Yogācāra philosopher himself who first raises the problem. The Yogācāra objector says:

> Reality is not known through inference because it is not an object of logical reasoning (*tarka*). So the Dharma Nature cannot be grasped by logical reasoning.[50]

Bhāvaviveka admits that reality cannot be an *object* of inference, but he argues that rational analysis is necessary to distinguish false knowledge from true knowledge and to prepare for nonconceptual insight.

> Here [we] use the flawless inference that follows tradition to turn back the flood of all diverse concepts.
>
> Buddhas see all objects of knowledge without seeing, just as they are, with a mind like space and with nonconceptual knowledge.
>
> Reality cannot be understood as an object of inference, but inference can rule out the opposite of the knowledge of reality.
>
> The differences between different traditions cause differences of opinion, and even when there is no difference in tradition, what can one do [to resolve disputes] but resort to rational investigation?
>
> [We] do not agree that an assertion by itself can rule out its opposite. And how can there be any nonconceptual knowledge without understanding its opposite?[51]

Bhāvaviveka makes the point even more concisely in *The Lamp of Wisdom*: "Inference that follows tradition negates all concepts and brings about nonconceptual insight. So the ultimate is not an object of inference, but [inference] has priority, because there is no other way of investigating what is true and false."[52]

What is at stake here is not just a dispute between schools but an evaluation of reason itself as a means of knowledge. The Yogācāra philosopher is arguing that ultimate reality can be known in the end only by direct perception (*pratyakṣa*), rather than by inference (*anumāna*). In the terminology of the Buddhist logicians, perception grasps the object as a bare particular (*svalakṣaṇa*) without being mediated through language. The distinction is one that Bhāvaviveka accepts on a metaphorical level. He agrees that to know reality directly is to see it without any concepts or words to obscure its meaning. But he associates this seeing with rational analysis rather than with perception. He says that inference brings about nonconceptual insight and that inference has priority over other forms of knowledge because there is no other way of distinguishing true cognition from false. This is an argument that seems to turn the normal ranking of the different means of knowledge upside down. It seems to give a privileged status to words, when all words are able to do is obscure the vision of reality. What is it about Bhāvaviveka's understanding of reality that makes this inversion possible?

Bhāvaviveka admits that words can only act on words and cannot give access to the direct experience of reality, but he argues that words can be used to negate the false implications of other words. Language can be used against language to clear away the veil that prevents someone from seeing reality clearly. Then can words grant vision itself? The answer is no, or at least it would be no if there were really any such thing as the direct vision of things. Bhāvaviveka's position about the priority of rational argument depends in the end on his critique of vision itself. Ultimately there is no such thing as a direct vision of things, any more than there is anything else. The logician may be blind (as Bhāvaviveka suggests in verse 286), but his blindness is as close to vision as no-understanding is to enlightenment. If the logicians understand that true vision is no-vision, their blindness is no different from sight. Rational argument can produce the vision of reality precisely because there is nothing to see and no seeing to see it.

The way Bhāvaviveka makes this argument more precise is to go back again to the doctrine of the two truths. The acquisition of knowledge is a transaction that takes place in the realm of conventional usage. On the conventional level, this knowledge is accessible to analysis and rational investigation. But when this same transaction is analyzed from the ultimate point of view, there is no acquisition and no knowledge. This does not make it impossible or even inappropriate for someone to plunge ahead on the conventional level to distinguish true knowledge from false. When the scriptures are ambiguous or are subject to different interpretations, there is no other way to resolve disputes than to resort to rational investigation. This, at least, is Bhāvaviveka's position, and it seems also to be the reason why he called the commentary on his greatest work *The Flame of Reason*, even when there were opponents like Candrakīrti waiting in the wings to say that he was scorching himself with the flame of his own reason.

The ambiguity of the relationship between vision and words also seems to explain the strange synesthesia that creeps into Bhāvaviveka's final description of the Buddha's teaching. He pictured the Buddha's words the way he understood his own investigation of the categories of reality: they were words that could bring a direct experience of liberation. Their first function was to illuminate the minds of others, but they were also like the snow of the Himalayas, the ambrosia that brings perfect satisfaction, the spell that cures snakebite, and the boats that save someone from a stormy ocean. They brought liberation that someone could taste and touch. These images of unmediated sensory experience were reflections in their own way of the experience of vision. They brought reality directly before the senses. But what made it possible for the Buddha's *words* to convey the taste of liberation was the realization that there were no words and no taste. They all arose like the vision of a palace in a dream.

Translation

Bhāvaviveka's Account of the Buddha in the Third Chapter of *The Verses on the Essence of the Middle Way* with the Commentary of *The Flame of Reason*

(Verses 266–360)

Introductory Note

This exploration of Bhāvaviveka's vision of the Buddha has been based on the longest sustained account of Bhāvaviveka's own philosophy, the third chapter of *The Verses on the Essence of the Middle Way* (*Madhyamakahṛdayakārikā*) with the commentary known as *The Flame of Reason* (*Tarkajvālā*). The chapter itself is entitled "The Quest for the Knowledge of Reality" (*Tattvajñānaiṣaṇā*). As we have already seen and as Bhāvaviveka himself does not fail to make clear, "reality" is another way of naming the Dharma Body of the Buddha. Without doing great injustice to Bhāvaviveka's thought, we can read the title of the chapter as another way of naming "The Quest for the Knowledge of the Buddha." The portion of the chapter that is translated here (verses 266–360) comprises his account of the theory of the Buddha and gives clear expression to his understanding of the experience of enlightenment that lies at the end of the philosophical quest.

Bhāvaviveka's account of the Buddha can be divided into three parts. The first part begins with a pair of definitions—a definition of reality and a definition of the Dharma Body—from the point of view of ultimate truth. The distinction between reality and the Buddha who knows reality, although important, is only a formality. As Bhāvaviveka says later in the chapter (in the commentary on verse 283), the reality that is known and the knowledge that knows it are ultimately indistinguishable. The second part of Bhāvaviveka's account of the Buddha takes up the stages of the bodhisattva path. The third part returns to the concept of the Buddha but from a conventional point of view and in a more affirmative mode.

The text consists of a series of verses with a commentary that is attributed to Bhāvaviveka himself. In most cases the commentary follows the verses quite closely. On rare occasions, Bhāvaviveka seems to allow himself the freedom to digress or expand on a point that has been introduced in a verse. My translation is based on the Sanskrit text of the verses edited by Yasunori Ejima in *The Development of Madhyamaka Philosophy in India: Studies on Bhāvaviveka* (Tokyo: 1981). Professor Ejima's edition was based on a handwritten copy of a single palm leaf manuscript that was made by Rahula Samkrtyayana in Źa-lu monastery in Tibet in the 1930s. With the help of Dr. Jiang Zhongxin of the Chinese Academy of Social Sciences, Ejima's edition has been compared with photographs of the original manuscript now on deposit in the Nationalities Library in Beijing. Corrections of Ejima's edition are listed at the end of the translation. Major emendations have also been explained in the notes to the translation.

For the text of the commentary, we are forced to rely on the eleventh-century Tibetan translation made by Dīpaṃkaraśrījñāna (Atiśa) in collaboration with Tshul-khrims Rgyal-ba. My translation of the commentary is based on the edition found in the *sDe-dge Tibetan Tripiṭaka bsTan-ḥgyur Preserved at the Faculty of Letters, University of Tokyo (Dbu ma)*, number 3856, volume 3, pages 20–165, folios *Dza* 40b–329b (Tokyo: 1977). In some cases the reading of the Derge edition is inferior to the reading of the Peking edition. When I have chosen the reading of another edition or when I have found it necessary to emend the text, I have listed these changes in another list of corrections, emendations, and textual variants found at the end of the translation. Again, when the changes are particularly significant or involve an element of controversy, I have also discussed them in the notes.

Anyone who has worked with modern translations of Indian Buddhist texts, especially texts that are philosophical in nature, knows that the style and terminology of translation vary widely from one translator to another. In keeping with the spirit of the Madhyamaka authors themselves, I have attempted to tread a middle way between extremes. This translation is meant to be useful to someone who has some prior knowledge of Mahāyāna Buddhist thought but who is not necessarily a specialist in the languages of the Indian tradition. It is meant, in other words, to be a translation, not just a series of notes for specialists in the field. In terminology, I have not tried to devise a new system but to follow the example of the translators who are best known to students and readers of Indian Mahāyāna literature. For the topics discussed by Bhāvaviveka in this section of the text, I have relied most heavily on Edward Conze's translations of the Perfection of Wisdom literature and on the discussion of Buddhist technical terms in Franklin Edgerton's *Buddhist Hybrid Sanskrit Dictionary* (New Haven: Yale University Press, 1953; reprint edition, Delhi: Motilal Banarsidass, 1970–1972). It would be impossible to mention or comment on every important Buddhist concept in the notes to the translation. That would require nothing short of an encyclopedia of Mahāyāna Buddhist thought. But I have tried to expand on points of controversy, either in Bhāvaviveka's own thought or in the interpretation of Bhāvaviveka's work, and to give the reader what is necessary to reconstruct the basic elements of Bhāvaviveka's imaginative world. I have concentrated particularly on the way in which Bhāvaviveka develops themes in different layers of his own writing in order to construct a complex image of the Buddha he sought to know.

Tracing the images and themes in Bhāvaviveka's writing makes one aware of Bhāvaviveka's skill as a writer. Bhāvaviveka was a philosopher through and through, but he also wrote verses with great rhetorical power. I have not tried to recast Bhāvaviveka's verses into English verse. It has seemed enough to reach, as far as the language will allow, for clarity of expression. I have, however, set the verses off from the prose of the commentary. When the rhetorical effect of a verse seems to strengthen or underline a particular aspect of Bhāvaviveka's thought, I have attempted to comment on it in the notes.

1. The Ultimate Buddha

Objection: Is it not a form of philosophical nihilism[1] to reject your opponent's position in this way[2] without holding a position of your own?

To respond, we now establish positions about reality (*tattva*) and the Teacher who understands this [reality] that are accepted in our own doctrinal system.

I. The Definition of Reality

266. No object of knowledge exists at all, so [the Buddhas] who know reality say[3] that the reality that has no equal is [the object] about which not even a nonconceptual cognition arises.

No [object of knowledge] that is listed in the five categories—past, future, present, indeterminate, and uncompounded—**exists at all, so [the Buddhas] who know reality,** or are omniscient, **say that the reality,** or ultimate, **that has no equal,** or is independent, nonconceptual, peaceful, without characteristic, not diverse, not arising, not ceasing, not a real thing, not created, and not expressible,[4] is the object **about which not even a nonconceptual cognition,** or [a cognition] that does not apprehend [any object],[5] **arises.**

II. The Definition of the Buddha

267. The no-arising of cognition, which is called "Buddha" because it is the understanding of this [reality], is the primary [Buddha] because it is the understanding that is no-understanding and because it dispels the sleep of concepts.[6]

The no-arising of cognition, which is called "Buddha" because it is the understanding of this kind of reality, **is the primary [Buddha] because it is the understanding that is no-understanding**—that is, because it does not apprehend any object of knowledge—**and because it dispels the sleep of concepts.** "Understanding" is a metaphor[7] for no-understanding.

Objection: Using "understanding" as a metaphor for no-understanding is like using "fire" as a metaphor for water.[8]

Reply: It is not this kind of metaphor because there is no [understanding] other than this [no-understanding], just as there is no "self" (*ātman*) when consciousness (*vijñāna*) is called "self."[9]

Objection: Then what does [the Buddha] do when he understands this?

Reply: He understands with the true understanding that does not apprehend [any object of knowledge], and, being free from the false concepts that are like sleep, he, as it were, dispels sleep.

> 268. Or [he is called "Buddha"] because he finishes [recognizing] the things that have to be recognized and so forth, because he understands equality, or because he opens the lotus-minds of fortunate people with manifestations.[10]

"He is called 'Buddha'" should be added [from the previous verse]. He is called "Buddha" **because he** uses the method of the three states (*vihāra*)[11] in a relative sense (*saṃvṛtyā*) to **finish [recognizing] the things that have to be recognized and so forth.** [A Buddha] finishes recognizing suffering, removing arising, realizing cessation, and practicing the path. Someone who has understood the four Noble Truths in this way is called "Buddha." As it is said:

> I have persevered in recognizing what needs to be recognized, removing what needs to be removed, realizing what needs to be realized, and practicing what needs to be practiced, so I am a Buddha.[12]

According to the Mahāyāna, the **understanding of equality** (*samatā*)[13] is called "Buddha." As it is said in *The Large Perfection of Wisdom Sūtra*:

> The knowledge of suffering does not lead to parinirvana, nor does suffering. The knowledge of arising does not lead to parinirvana, nor does arising. The knowledge of cessation does not lead to parinirvana, nor does cessation. The knowledge of the path does not lead to parinirvana, nor does the path. I say that the equality of the four Noble Truths is purification. Equality is Thusness.

Quotations such as this are definitive.

A "Buddha" is also someone to whom offerings are made by vast numbers of bodhisattvas who are capable of attaining Buddhahood at will. [These offerings are made] above the trichiliocosm in the palace called Akaniṣṭha, in a region (*maṇḍala*) that arises from the most excellent and extraordinary roots of virtue. [Such a Buddha] is crowned with the crown of sovereignty in the unexcelled, perfect Dharma by innumerable Buddhas from every direction. With innumerable virtuous practices, accumulated for three countless eons, [this Buddha] has completely overcome the darkness of defilements. He is like a wishing jewel and a wishing tree with varieties of powers. He understands the equality of all *dharmas* in a single moment of spontaneous insight,[14] without concepts, without obstructions (*āvaraṇa*), and without error. He understands the reality that is nondual, independent, nonconceptual, tranquil, not diverse, and not apprehended.[15] **He is called "Buddha" because,** while he remains there [in the palace of Akaniṣṭha], **with manifestations** (*nirmāṇa*) that (1) finish living in the palace of Tuṣita [Heaven], (2) migrate and enter the womb, (3) stay in the womb, (4) are born, (5) enjoy childhood, (6) are married, (7) go forth, (8) practice austerities and approach the seat of enlightenment, (9) subdue Māra, (10) attain perfect enlightenment, (11) turn the wheel of the Dharma, and (12) display parinirvana in hundreds of *koṭis* of continents,[16] he **opens the lotus-minds of fortunate people.** [These fortunate people] are sentient beings who, by accumulating great roots of virtue such as faith (*śraddhā*) in other lives, have worshiped [Buddhas] and brought the cause [of their illumination] to maturity. As it is said [in *The Descent to Laṅkā Sūtra*]:

> Buddhas are enlightened in the palace of Akaniṣṭha, which is delightful and free from all evil. It is only a manifestation that is enlightened here.[17]

And in *The Perfection of Wisdom in One Hundred Thousand Lines*:

> A bodhisattva has the wisdom-power to be born in the world of the great gods, dwell there, and attain enlightenment. The distinctive characteristic of wisdom is to approach the throne of enlightenment.

These quotations are conclusive.

We now explain what it means to call the Buddha "Sambuddha" and so forth.

> 269–270. Without apprehending [equality as an object], [the Buddha] understands the equality of different *dharmas*, because [*dharmas*] are equal in the sense that they do not arise or cease. Or [the Buddha] understands the equality of self and other. Therefore [the Buddha] is called Sambuddha among gods and human beings because [the Buddha] understands equality without understanding equality.[18]

Dharmas have many different characteristics, such as hardness, wetness, buoyancy, and motion, but these characteristics are not real. [The Buddha] understands that [their] only characteristic is **equality** (*samatā*). **[*Dharmas*] do not arise or cease.**[19] [*Dharmas*] are equal in the sense that they do not arise or cease—that is, they do not arise from themselves, from something else, from both, from no cause, from something that already exists, or from something that does not yet exist. [The Buddha] also [understands] **the equality of self and other.** [The Buddha] does not have any concept of subject and object and does not distinguish between subject and object. **[The Buddha] understands** [these two kinds of] **equality without apprehending [equality as an object]. Therefore [the Buddha] is called Sambuddha among gods and human beings because [the Buddha] understands equality without understanding equality.**

271. *Dharmas* cannot be subtracted or added. So [the Buddha] is [called] Tathāgata because [the Buddha] has understood (or gone) in this way, according to the Dharma Nature.[20]

The original nature of ***dharmas*** is such that they are neither perishable nor immutable, so they **cannot be subtracted or added.**[21] Tathāgatas may arise or not arise, but the Dharma Nature (*dharmatā*) remains the same.[22] **So [the Buddha]** is called **Tathāgata because [the Buddha] has understood** (*gata*) **in this way** (*tathā*), **according to the Dharma Nature,** without subtracting or adding any [*dharma*]. Or a Tathāgata is someone who has "gone in this way" and is called "Tathāgata" because he has "gone to" an understanding of equality[23] without deviating from the Dharma Nature.

To explain another synonym of this [word "Buddha"], we say:

272. [The Buddha is called] Sugata because, without understanding, he has understood what needs to be understood. [The Buddha has understood it] thoroughly, completely, and without falling into extremes.[24]

The word **thoroughly** shows that [what the Buddha has understood] does not have to be [understood] again, like a fever that has been thoroughly cured. The word **completely** shows that [the Buddha's understanding] is complete, like a pot that has been completely filled. **Without falling into extremes** shows that [the Buddha's understanding] is beautiful, like a beautiful shape. The word *gata* can be interpreted as "understood" and as "gone." If it is [interpreted as] "understood," **[the Buddha is called] Sugata because, without understanding, he has understood** all the conditioned *dharmas* (*skandhas*, *āyatanas*, and *dhātus*) **thoroughly and without falling into extremes.** If it is [interpreted as] "gone," **[the Buddha is called] Sugata because, without going, [the Buddha] has gone to** the supreme state of the Dharma Body by **thoroughly**, or properly, practicing the path, extinguishing **completely** even the slightest karma and defilements, and uprooting [them] **without falling into any extremes**—that is, [without falling] into the realms of rebirth.

273. [The Buddha] is immeasurable because he understands the immeasurable. [The Buddha] is incalculable because he cannot be grasped. [The Buddha] is unthinkable because he cannot be an object of thought. [The Buddha] is incomparable because he cannot be compared.[25]

The subject (*dharmin*) of this [verse] is the Buddha who was defined earlier as a single moment of insight into the equality of all *dharmas*.[26] **Immeasurable** is the property (*dharma*). **Because he understands the immeasurable** is the reason (*hetu*). [To say that the Buddha understands the immeasurable] means that he understands the limitless, immeasurable Dharma Element (*dharma-dhātu*). The example (*dṛṣṭānta*), "like space," is given later [in verse 280]. **[The Buddha] is incalculable because he cannot be grasped.** [The Buddha] cannot be grasped because he is not an object. If an object can be grasped, it can be calculated, but he is not accessible to the wisdom (*prajñā*) that is defined as the analysis (*pravicaya*) of all *dharmas*,[27] because his nature is Thusness. **[The Buddha] is unthinkable because he is not an object of** [the] **thought** that consists of the six forms of consciousness.[28] He is not a *dharma* that constitutes one of the sense media (*dharmāyatana*), and he is not [another kind of] *dharma*.[29] He is not a non-*dharma*. And he cannot be referred to in either of these two ways. **[The Buddha] is incomparable because he cannot be compared**—that is, there is nothing else like him and nothing to which he can be compared.

> 274ab. [The Buddha] is indefinable because it is utterly impossible to specify that he is one thing rather than another.

He **is indefinable because it is utterly impossible to specify that he is one thing rather than another.**[30] If things have color and shape, they can be specified as being one thing rather than another, but he has no color or shape, so he cannot be defined in any way as blue, yellow, red, white, long, short, high, low, and so forth.[31]

> 274cd. [The Buddha] cannot be displayed because there is no way to display him. [The Buddha] is happy because there is nothing to harm him.

[The Buddha] cannot be displayed because there is no way to display him. A way to display him would be to show that he arises, remains, or ceases, or is a man, woman, or neither man nor woman, and so forth. For [the Buddha] there is no way to do this, so he cannot be displayed. **[The Buddha] is happy because there is nothing to harm him.** He is free from all the harm of birth, old age, and death.

> 275. [The Buddha] is called eternal for two reasons. He is eternally free from appearance and thus is completely free from concepts, and he eternally accomplishes what is good.

[The Buddha] is called **eternal** because **he is eternally free from appearance and thus is completely free from concepts.** The smallest unit of matter has no appearance when it is divided into atoms, and atoms [have no appearance] when they are divided into separate parts.[32] Mind and mental phenomena last only for a moment, and [moments] disappear into their beginning, middle, and ending parts. In the Dharma Element, none of these things exists, so what can give rise to concepts? And if concepts do not arise, they also do not cease. This is [one reason] why [the Buddha] is called eternal. [The Buddha] is also called eternal **because he eternally accomplishes what is good** for sentient beings. As it says in the sūtras, sentient beings are as limitless as space, karma and defilements are limitless, and samsara is limitless. [The Buddha] is called eternal because he constantly accomplishes great vows and acts for the welfare of sentient beings as long as there is samsara.

> 276. [The Buddha who has these characteristics] is peaceful because he is empty of identity. He has no distinguishing mark[33] because he has no identity, because he does not serve as a distinguishing mark [for anyone else], and because he has no [concept of any] distinguishing mark.

"The Buddha who has these characteristics" should be supplied. [The Buddha] **is peaceful because he is empty of identity** (*svabhāva*). For [someone] who thinks that [the Buddha] has an identity, [the Buddha] must be [subject to] an unbroken chain of actions, such as birth and death, going and coming, and speaking, and must be capable of determination like [other] things that possess a certain action. But if [the Buddha] is empty of identity, he is free from all action. Therefore, if [being empty of identity implies that the Buddha] has no action, being empty of identity implies that [the Buddha] is peaceful. **[The Buddha] has no distinguishing mark because he has no identity.** If [the Buddha] has no identity, it is impossible for marks such as existence (*bhāva*) and nonexistence (*abhāva*) to apply. Furthermore, **he has no distinguishing mark because he does not serve as a distinguising mark [for anyone else] and because he has no [concept of any] distinguishing mark.** That is, he does not serve as a distinguishing mark for anyone else and does not conceive of any distinguishing mark himself.

> 277. Because he has no distinguishing mark, he has no appearance, and because he has no appearance, [he has no distinguishing mark]. For liberated [practitioners] who want to see [him], he has no distinguishing mark and no appearance.[34]

It is precisely **because he has no distinguishing mark** that **he has no appearance**. He does not appear to have such distinguishing marks as eternal, noneternal, existing, or not existing. **And because he has no appearance, [he has no distinguishing mark]. Liberated** practitioners (*yogin*) **who want to see** him see him without any distinguishing mark or appearance. As it is said in passages such as the following:

> A bodhisattva who is only one birth [away from enlightenment] does not see the Tathāgata as form. [The bodhisattva] does not see [him] as having any distinguishing mark. [The bodhisattva] does not see [him] as having any quality.

[The bodhisattva] does not see [him] as a *dharma*. [The bodhisattva] does not see [him] as a non-*dharma*.

278. [The Buddha] does not provide a foundation [for thought] because he has no distinguishing mark. He cannot be conceptualized because he does not provide a foundation [for thought]. He is not subject to conceptual diversity because he cannot be conceptualized. He is not an object because he cannot be apprehended.

The Buddha **does not provide a foundation [for thought]**[35] **because he has no distinguishing mark**. For the Buddha cannot be grasped as having any marks, such as offering resistance, experiencing, grasping a distinguishing mark, creating, or forming an impression.[36] **He cannot be conceptualized because he does not provide a foundation [for thought].** He cannot be conceptualized because it is impossible to conceptualize something that does not provide a foundation [for thought]. **He is not subject to conceptual diversity because he cannot be conceptualized.** For if something can be conceptualized, a word can be applied to it in accordance with the concept, and it is then subject to conceptual diversity. But if it cannot be conceptualized, it is not subject to conceptual diversity. **He is not an object because he cannot be apprehended** as an object. It is because he cannot be conceptualized that one does not apprehend [him] as an object.

For reasons that have already been stated, the Buddha who was defined earlier also:

279. Does not arise, does not have any form, and does not change.
[The Buddha] is luminous, equal and not equal, unlimited, nonconceptual, and without characteristic.

To say [that the Buddha] **does not arise** means that no cognition arises when nothing has the absolute identity of an object.[37] **Does not have any form** (*ākāra*) means that [the Buddha] has no color or shape.[38] **Does not change** means that he has brought all action to an end.[39] **Luminous** means that he is free from the darkness of obstructions to liberation and omniscience. **Equal** means that he is similar to all *dharmas* in that his nature is Emptiness. **Not equal** means that he is not the same as others, such as disciples and solitary Buddhas. **Unlimited** means that he grasps the Dharma Element. **Nonconceptual** means that he is defined as a perceptual cognition, so he is free from the concepts that [come from] imagination and memory.[40] **Without characteristic** means that he does not have the characteristics of the [gross] elements or the derivatives of the elements.[41] These positions (*pakṣa*) should be taken with the reasons (*hetu*) stated in preceding [verses].

280ab. Like space, heroic beings see him without seeing.

Like space should be taken as the similar example (*sādhārmya-dṛṣṭānta*) for all the subjects (*dharmin*) and properties (*dharma*) stated earlier.[42] This [verse] explains that **heroic beings** (*mahātman*), namely the bodhisattvas who have achieved the tenth stage [of the bodhisattva path][43] and accumulated an immeasurable store of merit and knowledge, **see this** kind of Buddha **without seeing.**

These bodhisattvas are worthy of praise.

> 280cd–281. [These bodhisattvas] live without concepts and without effort, and their eyes are clear. They pay homage to the Lord without any homage, reflection, or words. To them also [we] pay sincere homage.

When they have practiced the four meditations (*dhyāna*), which constitute the divine states (*divya-vihāra*), and the four immeasurables (*apramāṇa*), which constitute the brahman states (*brahma-vihāra*), and **live without concepts** in Emptiness, signlessness, and wishlessness, which constitute the holy states (*ārya-vihāra*), their actions arise **without effort,** or spontaneously, **and their eyes are clear.** These [states] were mentioned earlier.[44] **Homage** (*namaskāra*) is the act of physically holding together the palms of the hands and so forth. **Reflection** (*manaskāra*) is a mental activity connected with that [physical act]. **Words** are words of praise and so forth. By skill-in-means (*upāya-kauśalya*), [the bodhisattvas] perform these three actions and others in a relative sense (*saṃvṛtyā*). But ultimately there is no agent and no one to perform the action. In this way [without any ultimate form of action], **they pay homage to the Lord** (*nātha*), or Teacher (*śāstṛ*), who has just been described. **To them also** we **pay sincere**[45] **homage**. The word **also** indicates that when we pay respectful homage to the bodhisattvas who have cultivated nonconceptual understanding and can become fully enlightened at will, it goes without saying that we pay respectful homage to the omniscient, perfectly enlightened Buddha who alone is the Lord of the world.

Objection: If [the Buddha] is like this, how can someone refer to him with words like "Buddha" and "Sugata"?

Reply:

> 282. Words such as "Buddha" are used metaphorically[46] in a way that corresponds to [the Buddha's] progress, but ultimately [the Buddha] is considered indescribable because he cannot be conceptualized in any way.

[We] have already explained that [the Buddha] understands by no-understanding and so forth,[47] so [the Buddha] cannot be referred to [literally] with words such as "Buddha." But, from the relative point of view, **[the word] "Buddha" [is] used metaphorically** because [the Buddha] understands all *dharmas*. The word "Sugata" is used because he has gone to what has to be gone to. The word "Tathāgata" is used because he has gone in a certain way. The word "Bhagavān" is used because he has accumulated the wealth of an immeasurable store of merit. The word "Arhant" is used because he is worthy of honor. The word "Svayambhū" is used because his knowledge does not rely on anyone else. The word "Jina" is used because he has conquered the four Māras. The word "Muni" is used because he is silent in body, speech, and mind.[48] [These words are used] **in a way that corresponds to [the Buddha's] progress** (*pratipatti*) in moral conduct (*śīla*), concentration (*samādhi*), wisdom (*prajñā*), and insight (*jñāna*). **But ultimately,** or in reality (*tattvataḥ*), **[the Buddha] is considered indescribable because he cannot be conceptualized in any way.**

When an object can be conceptualized, it can be described metaphorically as having a certain feature. But because [the Buddha] cannot be conceived as an object:

> 283ab. Here speech comes to an end. It[49] is not accessible to thought.

[The Buddha] is not an object (*viṣaya*) of the six forms of consciousness (*vijñāna*) that are characterized by the discriminative cognition of things. The word **it** refers to both reality (*tattva*) and knowledge (*jñāna*). Because the object that is grasped and the subject that grasps it are the same, there is no difference between reality and knowledge.

> 283cd. Ideas come to an end, and knowledge becomes silent.

This [verse] means that [the Buddha] cannot be conceived by the mind and is not an object of logical reasoning (*tarka*).

> 284. This is the Dharma Body of the Buddhas who have an endless store of merit and know countless objects of cognition, and it is the happy cessation of conceptual diversity.[50]

Buddhas have accumulated **a store of merit** for three countless eons **and** truly **know countless objects of cognition,** whether they are past, present, future, indeterminate, or unconditioned. Since no *dharma*s have absolute identity, the no-arising of a single moment of cognition[51] is called "Buddha." **This is the Dharma Body of the Buddhas** because it is the locus (*āśraya*) of the Buddha-qualities that begin with the powers, the grounds of confidence, and the special qualities.[52] **It is the cessation of conceptual diversity** because it is the cessation of any use of words. It is **happy** because it is fearless in its own right and removes fear in others. As is said in the *Tathāgatajñānamudrā Sūtra*:[53]

> Truth is the Body of the Tathāgata. It utterly surpasses sight. It is not a body, is not created, is not born, does not cease, is not produced by a combination [of causes], does not arise, does not remain, is not established, has no end, has no limit, is happy, and is utterly quiet.

This can be established through reason (*yukti*).

> 285. [The Buddha] is invisible to a physical eye and invisible to a divine eye, and he cannot be seen by conceptual or nonconceptual cognition.

Some think that the Tathāgata is invisible because he is far away or hidden. Others think that the Tathāgata is visible when he is near. For their sake [we] explain that **[the Buddha] is invisible to a physical eye** because he is not located in any place. This is because a physical eye with no impediment can see things that are hidden or far away. He **is invisible to a divine eye** because he does not even have a subtle form. A divine eye sees the extremely subtle form of the aggregates between lives.[54] **Conceptual cognition** is inferential (*anumāna*) cognition because [inference] has to do with concepts [that come] from imagination and memory.[55] **Nonconceptual cognition** is perceptual (*pratyakṣa*) cognition because it grasps particulars (*vastu-mātra*). It is impossible to see him even with this [perceptual] cognition, so [the verse] means that [the Buddha] is not the object of any cognition at all.

Therefore:

> 286. [The Buddha] is as inaccessible to logicians as heaven is to sinners, detachment is to those who are passionate, and the sun is to those who have been born blind.[56]

The prefix (*sva*) in the word **heaven** (*svarga*) refers to a concern for possessions (*ātmīya-grāha*). Heaven is [called heaven] because it is free from that [concern]. It is the dwelling place of gods. [Heaven] is the result of virtuous karma, so sinners cannot do anything to accomplish it, much less gain access to it. **Passion** (*raṇa*) is the cause of all the faults of samsara. [Those who are passionate possess] these passions.[57] **Detachment** (*araṇā*)[58] is a form of meditation (*dhyāna*) that those [who are passionate] need to develop, but **those who are passionate** are incapable of developing it. **Those who have been born blind** have not seen, do not see, and never will see **the sun**. To them it is not an object of knowledge. Similarly, logicians (*tārkika*)—whether they are Buddhist or not—cannot use mental effort to see the Dharma Body through inference (*anumāna*).[59] [The Dharma Body] is not accessible to them.

Why do they not see [the Dharma Body]? Because:

> 287ab. [The Dharma Body] is not something that exists, it is not something that is absent, it is not something that both exists and is absent, it is not something different from these two, and yet it is not different [from these four options].

[The Dharma Body] does **not exist** as one of the aggregates[60] because it is not the object of a cognition of existence. **It is not something that is absent,** like a rabbit's horn,[61] because it is not the object of a cognition of absence.

It is not something that both exists and is absent because nothing is grasped by a cognition of both [existence and absence]. **It is not something different from these two** because nothing is characterized as being different from what exists and [is absent]. **It is not different [from these four options]** because it is possible to say that it exists and so forth in a relative sense. How does it exist? As a combination of the powers, grounds of confidence, and special qualities of a Buddha. How is it absent? As a complex combination of causes and conditions that has no identity. How is it something that both exists and is absent? When it is spoken of in both these two ways.

Objection: Non-Buddhists (*tīrthika*) think that the Supreme Self (*paramātman*) also is nonconceptual, eternal, and unchanging.[62] How does the Dharma Body differ from this [Supreme Self]?

Reply: These [non-Buddhists] say that the Supreme Self is subtle because it possesses the attribute of being subtle, great because it possesses the attribute of being great, unique because it possesses the attribute of being unique, and pervasive because it possesses the attribute of being pervasive.[63] But the Dharma Body:

287cd. is not subtle, great, or unique, and is neither far nor near.

This is because it has no attributes and is not located in any place.

Even though the Person (*puruṣa*) is nonconceptual, those who hold the doctrine of the Person (*puruṣa-vādin*) consider it to be the cause of the origin of the world.[64] Those who hold the doctrine of Primal Matter (*pradhāna-vādin*) consider Primal Matter to be the cause of the manifestation of the world. To show that the Dharma Body does not have the same characteristics as these, we say:

288ab. Nothing is born or manifested from it in any way.

If [the Dharma Body] does not exist, it cannot cause [the origin of the world] and cannot bring about [its] manifestation.

They also think that a liberated self transcends the world and dwells in liberation called "the transcendent"[65] and that when someone sees the person that goes beyond darkness, he or she is dissolved into it. But [the Dharma Body] cannot be seen or apprehended.

288cd. In it nothing remains or is dissolved.

In reality, a perfectly developed path to liberation has no appearance (*ābhāsa*), and because it is impossible to apprehend self and other, nothing remains and nothing is dissolved.

Those who hold the doctrine of Brahmā say that Brahmā is the highest [being] in the world and the ancestor of [all other] beings. To show that [the Dharma Body] is more exalted than this [Brahmā], we say:

289ab. It is the Supreme Brahman that even [gods] such as Brahmā do not grasp.

Brahmā, Viṣṇu, Maheśvara, and so forth take pride in their vision of reality (*tattva-darśana*), but their vision has an object. They do not understand the Supreme Brahman. The word *Brahman* can refer to the Lord of Creatures (*prajāpati*) or to nirvana.[66] Here it refers to nirvana. These [gods such as Brahmā] cannot understand it because it cannot be seen with knowledge that has an object (*sālambana*).

Those who declare infallible such statements as "There is no Dharma higher than the truth"[67] are conditioned (*saṃskṛta*) and subject to conceptual diversity (*saprapañca*). To show that this [statement] is not the only truth, we say:

289cd. The Sage who spoke the truth said that this [Dharma Body] is the ultimate truth.

The unconditioned (*anabhisaṃskṛta*) is not false, so it **is the** only **ultimate truth**. In *The Diamond [Sūtra]* and other [sūtras], **the Sage who spoke the truth**[68] said, "When something is conditioned, it is false. When something is unconditioned, it is not false."

Great Brahmā has an exalted position because he rules over thousands. Others, such as Śiva,[69] have a high position because they are worshiped by their own followers. But this [Dharma Body]

290. is worshiped by sages and saints such as Ārya Avalokiteśvara and Ārya Maitreya with the discipline of no-worship.

Many sages, such as Avalokiteśvara, Maitreya, Samantabhadra, and Mañjuśrī, who have mastered the tenth stage by fulfilling the perfections, have been purified by the practice (*bhāvanā*) of no-apprehension (*anupalambha*)[70] and understand that one does not apprehend anything as having any identity, worship this [Dharma Body] by **the discipline of no-worship.** That is, [they worship] by [acts of] homage (*namaskāra*), praise, and contemplation with empty and illusory body, speech, and mind. This is because they worship [the Dharma Body] as not being an object of worship.

Objection: If [the Dharma Body] is free from conceptual diversity, nonconceptual, and all-pervasive, how does someone know that it is the Tathāgata's Body and not the body of someone else?

Reply:

291. [We] consider [the Dharma Body] to be the Tathāgata's Body because it is not different in nature from [the Tathāgata] and because it is the reality that [the Tathāgata] has understood. And [we] do not [consider] it to be anyone else's [body] because [others] do not understand it.

Ultimately [the Dharma Body] is not an object (*viṣaya*) of words or thought, but [conventionally] it is the nature (*svabhāva*) of the Tathāgata to have primary and secondary characteristics (*lakṣaṇa-anuvyañjana*)[71] and these [characteristics] belong [only] to him. The [Dharma] Body **is not different in nature from** this Tathāgata, so **[we] consider [it] to be the Tathāgata's Body.** What is its identity? Emptiness. As it is said:

> In Emptiness there is said to be no difference at all. Emptiness is identical [to the Buddha]. Whoever sees Emptiness sees the Buddha. [The Buddha] is not different from Emptiness.

Or, speaking of [the Tathāgata as] a moment of insight, the Tathāgata does not grasp any combination of aggregates, powers, grounds of confidence, and special Buddha attributes, and he understands that the object grasped and the subject that does the grasping are equal in nature. **[We] consider** this [moment of insight] **to be** only the **Tathāgata's body,** not anyone else's.[72] Why? Others, such as disciples (*śrāvaka*), do not understand this [equality] correctly.

The Master distinguishes the three Bodies in his own treatise by saying:[73]

> When [a bodhisattva] achieves enlightenment in the palace of Akaniṣṭha, [the bodhisattva attains] a Tathāgata Body that consists of knowledge (*jñānātmaka*). [This Body] comes from an immeasurable store of merit and knowledge accumulated for countless hundreds of thousands of *nayutas* of *koṭis* of eons; it is nonconceptual, like a many-faceted wishing jewel; it is free from all conceptual diversity; it has removed both kinds of obstructions (*āvaraṇa*); and it spontaneously creates a Form Body that continues for the benefit of all. From the nonconceptual Tathāgata Body, through the power of a previous vow (*pūrva-praṇidhāna*) that has been nurtured (*paribhāvita*) by a mode of conduct (*śīla*) that brings benefit to others, there arises a Manifestation Body that benefits all. In hundreds of *koṭis* of continents, it displays the actions of a Buddha: it reaches the end of its stay in the palace of Tuṣita, transmigrates and enters the womb, stays in the womb, is born, enjoys childhood, is married, goes forth, practices austerities and approaches the seat of enlightenment, subdues Māra, attains perfect enlightenment, turns the wheel of the Dharma, attains parinirvana, and so forth.[74] Based on this (*tadāśritya*)[75] a voice arises that is called "Mahāyāna" by those who follow the excellent vehicle. [This voice] is characterized by a succession of syllables, roots, and words, has sixty qualities,[76] and delights the minds of sentient beings. The three bodies—knowledge (*jñāna*), form (*rūpa*), and speech (*vāc*)—come from the three restraints (*saṃvara*). They are said to be transformations of body, speech, and mind.

It also says in *The Diamond Sūtra*:

> Those who saw me by my form and those who followed me by my voice have acted incorrectly. Those people will not see me.
>
> Through the Dharma one should see the Buddha, for the Dharma Bodies are the guides. The Dharma Nature cannot be discerned, and it is not capable of being discerned.[77]

This [sūtra] also explains the three Bodies according to the distinction between relative and ultimate [truth]. Here [in *The Diamond Sūtra*] knowledge (*jñāna*) is considered the Dharma Body.

But in *The Great Perfection of Wisdom* [*Sūtra*] it says, "Someone seeks to see the Tathāgata as the Dharma Body, Form Body, and Knowledge Body." Here the Dharma Body is considered to be the twelvefold teaching.[78]

Objection: Then there would be no second refuge.[79]

Reply: This is not true, because the Dharma is both a means (*sādhana*) and a result (*phala*).

According to Ārya Vajrasena, the Form Body located in Akaniṣṭha and based on the Dharma Body is the Transformation Body (*vipāka-kāya*).[80]

According to Ārya Asaṅga, this is the Enjoyment Body (*sambhoga-kāya*).[81] The basis (*āśraya*) of attributes such as the powers, grounds of confidence, and special Buddha attributes, is the Dharma Body. The one that attains enlightenment in Jambudvīpa is the Manifestation Body (*nirmāṇa-kāya*).

Thus, the Dharma, Form, and Manifestation Bodies belong to the Sugata and no one else. Disciples and so forth seem to have Liberation Bodies (*vimukti-kāya*), but the Dharma Body is different from these.

2. The Bodhisattva Path[1]

I. The Practice of the Six Perfections[2]

To show that a practitioner (*yogin*) who carries out the Brahman practice[3] sees the Dharma Body, [we] say:

> 292. When [a practitioner] practices this [Brahman practice] and lives [in the Brahman states] without any apprehension, what can [this practitioner's] mind desire, hate, or be ignorant of?

When a practitioner (*yogin*) seeks to know this[4] and, by thought and practice,[5] **practices** [it] in the form of no-apprehension **and lives** [in it] without concepts and **without apprehension,** there is no basis (*āśraya*) here where [this practitioner] can rest, so **what can [this practitioner's] mind desire, hate, or be ignorant of?** Desire, hatred, and ignorance do not arise if they have no basis.

Question: How does [a practitioner] carry out this practice?

Reply: [A practitioner] carries out this practice by recollection (*anusmṛti*) of the Buddha.[6] But this recollection is no-recollection, and it is no-reflection (*amanasikāra*). As it says in *The Perfection of Wisdom*, "Recollection of the Buddha is no-recollection, and it is no-reflection." It says in the *Anantamukhanirhāradhāraṇī*, "One practices recollection of the Buddha, but not according to form, major and minor characteristics, qualities, *dharmas*, or no-*dharmas*."[7] In "The Tathāgata Chapter"[8] it says, "To see the Tathāgata is to see Emptiness, signlessness, wishlessness, no-arising, no-cessation, no-birth, no thing, and no-effort." And it says in the *Akṣayamatinirdeśa Sūtra*, "What is Buddha-recollection? It is not the discrimination of form and characteristics. It is not the discrimination of birth, caste, and time. It is not the discrimination of past virtues. It is not the discrimination of pride in one's later insight. It is not the discrimination of one's present state. And it is not an occasion for hindrances. It does not raise up any distinguishing marks. It lays to rest all concepts and conceptual thought."

When [a bodhisattva] practices this:

293. How can [the bodhisattva] suffer any of the pain that comes from losing something that is desired or [gaining] something that is not desired? [Such a bodhisattva] is as unstained by the conditions of this world as a lotus is [unstained] by water.

[A bodhisattva] does not grasp things as desired or not desired, so **the** feeling of **pain that comes from losing something that is desired or** gaining **something that is not desired** does not arise for this [bodhisattva]. Even though [a bodhisattva] dwells in the world, **[the bodhisattva] is not stained by the** eight **conditions of this world** (*loka-dharma*)—namely, gain, loss, fame, ignominy, pleasure, pain, praise, and blame—because [the bodhisattva] is not attached to them, **just as a lotus is** born in water but is not stained **by** the impurities of the **water.**

Nirvana-without-foundation (*apratiṣṭhita-nirvāṇa*) has already been mentioned,[9] but it should be mentioned again here.

294a. [A bodhisattva] does not leave samsara,

Because [a bodhisattva] has not removed defilements.

294b. But [a bodhisattva] is free from the harm of samsara.

Because [a bodhisattva] does not create harmful (*akuśala*) *dharma*s and has overcome defilements.

294c. [A bodhisattva] does not attain nirvana,

Because [a bodhisattva] is concerned about sentient beings.

294d. But it is as if [a bodhisattva] were located in nirvana.

Because [a bodhisattva] is capable of acting for others and for [the bodhisattva's own] self.

295a. [A bodhisattva] is not burned by the fire of defilements.

Because [a bodhisattva] has avoided defiled practices.

295b. Even though [a bodhisattva] is defiled, [the bodhisattva is defiled] in the way that space is [defiled].

[A bodhisattva] has some defilements to serve as the seed of samsara, but [the bodhisattva] is not stained by them.

> 295c. [A bodhisattva] has no mind and has no no-mind.

Active (*pravṛtti*) consciousness has ceased, and resulting (*vipāka*) consciousness continues. Why? Because:

> 295d. [A bodhisattva] has reached the attainment [of cessation].

[A bodhisattva] has reached the attainment of cessation (*nirodha-samāpatti*) by practicing meditation (*dhyāna*) and by skillfulness of body and mind.[10]

When [a bodhisattva] has attained extraordinary (*lokottara*) attainment (*samāpatti*) and resides in nirvana-without-foundation but does not attain enlightenment,

> 296. [The bodhisattva] has climbed the mountain peak of wisdom and is free from grief but looks with compassion on ordinary people who suffer and are burned by grief.[11]

Extraordinary (*lokottara*) **wisdom** (*prajñā*) is like a **mountain peak** because it is great and lofty. To **climb** that peak is to live properly with [the wisdom that consists of] hearing, thinking, and practice. **Free from grief** means that [the bodhisattva] understands that *dharmas* are illusory and thus [the bodhisattva] has no grief. **With compassion** means that the continuum of [the bodhisattva's] mind is fixed in compassion. **Looks on ordinary people who suffer and are burned by grief** means that [the bodhisattva] sees ordinary people whose minds are burned by the grief that comes from losing one's parents and so forth and who continually experience the suffering that comes from impermanence.

> 297. Then, with an eye that is moist with compassion, [the bodhisattva] sees that [the wisdom-eyes of] ordinary people have been covered by an imaginary net created by the art of conceptual thought.[12]
>
> 298. They have been wounded by the arrows of birth, old age, sickness, and death, and they have become sick. They are weak, miserable, and unfortunate, and they have no protector and no final refuge.
>
> 299. Trying to extinguish suffering, they have fallen into a river of suffering. With deluded minds they have continued to increase the cause of suffering.
>
> 300. The ambrosia of reality, the happy cessation of conceptual diversity, is as clear as the autumn sky. [The ordinary people] whose cognition functions in such a way that they do not see [this reality] have no [wisdom-]eye.[13]

These [verses] present the subject matter and the purpose of the [seven verses] that follow. When a bodhisattva resides in nirvana-without-foundation and sees ordinary people with a wisdom-eye that is moist with compassion, [the bodhisattva] possesses the qualities that begin with the torment of compassion (verses 301–302); [the bodhisattva] sends forth rivers [that come from the mountain] of the perfections (verse 303); [the bodhisattva] removes the suffering of others (verse 304); [the bodhisattva] acts like a wishing tree (verse 305); whether [the bodhisattva] is born in a good or bad realm, [that realm] becomes a place that is beneficial and pleasant for others (verse 306), and when [the bodhisattva] is born there, [the bodhisattva] attracts a following that is patient and pure;[14] and [the bodhisattva] is like the sea and is filled from many directions by rivers of merit (verse 307).

Then, when **[the bodhisattva]** looks on ordinary people **with a** wisdom-**eye moist with compassion,** in what state does [the bodhisattva] see these ordinary people? [The bodhisattva] **sees** them as being **covered by an imaginary net created by the art of conceptual thought** and so forth. This is the construction [of the verses]. The art of conceptual thought (*vikalpa-śilpa*) comes from mental cognition (*mano-vijñāna*). [The wisdom-eyes of ordinary people] are surrounded and covered by the imaginary net created by the art of conceptual thought. The net consists of [concepts of] existence, absence, and so forth, and the many ways of apprehending the conditioned *dharma*s (*skandha*s, *āyatana*s, and *dhātu*s) as a foundation.

But they are not just covered by this imaginary net. What else [do they experience]? **They are wounded and sick from the pain of birth, old age, sickness, and death.** Birth is the arising of the aggregates. Old age is [their] transformation. Sickness is [their] becoming ill. Death is [their] destruction. These [four things] are **arrows** that are unpleasant to the mind. Because [ordinary people] are **wounded** by these [arrows], [they] are constantly **sick** and unhappy.[15] Furthermore, **they are weak, miserable, and unfortunate, and they have no protector and no final refuge.** They are weak because they do not know how to get out of the house of rebirth. They are miserable because they are poor in good qualities (*kuśala-dharma*). They are unfortunate because they come to a bad end. They have no protector because they lack the ten qualities that offer protection, beginning with faith (*śraddhā*) and moral conduct (*śīla*).[16] They have no final refuge because they do not know the way to go forth.

Furthermore, **trying to extinguish suffering, they have fallen into a river of suffering. With deluded minds they have continued to increase the cause of suffering.** [Ordinary people] are like someone who is swept away by a stream and seizes on a river to be saved, only to be swept away more forcefully than before.[17] Ordinary people have sunk in a river of suffering because of previous actions. Trying to extinguish this suffering, they have fallen into a river of suffering: they create even greater hindrances and by these actions seize onto actions that turn into a vast river of samsara.[18] With minds deluded by ignorance they have continued in the stream of samsara to increase the causes of suffering—that is, they hold onto the mental habit of considering this [world] to be real because of passion, rebirth, the false view of the self, and rites and observances. [A bodhisattva] sees [ordinary people] this way.

These [three verses] have explained that [ordinary people] continue in the stream of samsara. To explain that they have lost the means of liberation, we say: **The ambrosia of reality, the happy cessation of conceptual diversity, is as clear as the autumn sky. [The ordinary people] whose cognition functions in such a way that they do not see [this reality] have no [wisdom-]eye.** Ultimate reality is as satisfying as ambrosia. It is the cessation of all the difficulties of birth and so forth, the cessation of all verbal and conceptual diversity, and [is] as clear as the autumn sky. Those [ordinary people] whose cognition functions in such a way that they do not see this [reality] have no eye because they lack the wisdom-eye. [A bodhisattva] sees ordinary people injured in this way by suffering and many defilements. This is the construction [of the verse].

What are the virtues (*guṇa*) of a bodhisattva who sees ordinary people this way and does such things as send forth the rivers of the perfections?

> 301. An accomplished [bodhisattva], who is tormented by compassion and dedicated to the welfare of these [ordinary people], has a mind as hard as a diamond and is the greatest of beings.
>
> 302. [The bodhisattva] practices the discipline of generosity, moral conduct, patience, fortitude, meditation, and wisdom, after [practicing the two kinds of] wisdom and [the six kinds of] recollection, at an appropriate time and in a way that is appropriate to [the bodhisattva's] abilities.

Tormented by compassion means that [the bodhisattva's] mind is tormented by the power of compassion. **Dedicated to the welfare of these** means that [the bodhisattva] is strongly dedicated[19] to the welfare of ordinary people. **Has a mind as hard as a diamond** means that [the bodhisattva's] aspiration to enlightenment (*bodhicitta*) cannot be cut even by a diamond.[20] **The greatest of beings** means that [the bodhisattva] surpasses disciples and so forth just by generating the aspiration [to enlightenment]. **Accomplished** (*kṛtin*)[21] means that [the bodhisattva] has been well trained in the bodhisattva practices that begin with superior moral conduct.[22]

[The bodhisattva] **practices the discipline of generosity, moral conduct, patience, fortitude, meditation, and wisdom.** These six perfections, together with compassion, summarize the whole Mahāyāna. As is said by the great Master Nāgārjuna:

> Generosity, moral conduct, patience, fortitude, meditation, and wisdom, together with compassion, are the Mahāyāna that is praised by Buddhas and bodhisattvas.
>
> Generosity is to give up one's possessions. Moral conduct is to act for the sake of others. Patience is called the antidote to anger. Fortitude is strength in virtues.

Meditation is undefiled concentration. Wisdom is determination of the truth.

From generosity comes enjoyment, from moral conduct pleasure, from patience beauty, from fortitude radiance, from meditation peace, and from wisdom liberation. Compassion accomplishes everything.

From these seven virtues, in which all the perfections are included, one attains Buddhahood, which is the object of inconceivable knowledge.[23]

After [practicing the two kinds of] wisdom and [the six kinds of] recollection at an appropriate time and in a way that is appropriate to [the bodhisattva's] abilities means that [the bodhisattva] practices generosity and so forth after practicing relative (*sāṃvṛta*) and ultimate (*paramārtha*) wisdom (*prajñā*)[24] and six kinds of recollection (*anusmṛti*),[25] at the time that is appropriate for discipline and with effort that is appropriate to [the bodhisattva's] abilities. As it says in *The Questions of Subāhu Sūtra* (*Subāhuparipṛcchā Sūtra*):

> If someone cannot practice generosity, sacrifice, renunciation, and so forth [all at once], they should be practiced individually. They should be practiced repeatedly, one step at a time, with the idea of controlling passion, removing avarice, renouncing the fear of giving, being committed to the practice of generosity, making effort in the discipline of sacrifice, and being strong in augmenting renunciation. A similar point can be made about the other five perfections.[26]

Someone who wants to take up the six perfections and practice them in a superior way should take up the superior practice of saving and liberating[27] all sentient beings. To explain this, we say:

> 303. To help all sentient beings, [the bodhisattva] sends forth rivers with the lovely water of pure merit from the mountain of generosity and so forth.

To help all sentient beings, [the bodhisattva] sends forth the **rivers** of the six perfections **from the mountain of generosity,** moral conduct, **and so forth.** As **water,** these [rivers] have **merit** that is **pure** because it is free from passion, hatred, and ignorance, and **lovely** because it removes sin.

After that, when [the bodhisattva] has greatly increased the desire for generosity:

> 304. [The bodhisattva] always removes all the suffering of poverty and begging by [sacrificing] everything, whether it is part of [the bodhisattva's] body or not, to all those in need.

With a sense of identification with **all those in need, [the bodhisattva] always,** sincerely, of [the bodhisattva's] own accord, without animosity toward anyone else, and without remorse, **removes,** without exception, **all the suffering** or sadness, that comes **from poverty and begging**, or going hungry and having to ask [for help], **by [sacrificing] everything**, such as clothing, food, jewelry, sons, daughters, head, hands, and feet,[28] **whether it is part of [the bodhisattva's] body or not.** By the practice of sacrifice (*tyāga*), great sacrifice, and extreme sacrifice, [the bodhisattva] fulfills the perfection [of generosity].

When this [perfection] has been fulfilled:

> 305. [The bodhisattva] constantly delights and fulfills the hopes of those who are in need, and [the bodhisattva] always serves as a wishing tree, rich with inexhaustible fruit.

[The bodhisattva] constantly delights and fulfills the hopes of those who are in need, and [the bodhisattva] always serves the needs of [other] beings like **a wishing tree, rich with inexhaustible fruit** that comes from the ripening of the perfections. Here **those who are in need** are those who lack wealth. **Hope** is a synonym for aspiration, wishing, longing, and so forth. **Constantly delights and fulfills** means to fulfill constantly by delighting. This means that [a bodhisattva] is rich and worthy of respect because [a bodhisattva] has the inexhaustible fruit that comes from the ripening of the perfections and acts like a wishing tree for the benefit of [other] beings.

When [a bodhisattva] has developed this generous mode of conduct, [the bodhisattva] takes up faultless moral conduct (*śīla*).

> 306. When [a bodhisattva] is born in a good realm, [the bodhisattva] brings happiness and benefit to others. Or [when the bodhisattva is born] intentionally in another [realm], it is because that [also] brings happiness and benefit to others.

[A bodhisattva] who is pure in conduct is born only in good realms and does not fall into bad realms. But if [the bodhisattva] is born **intentionally in another**, bad realm, [the bodhisattva] is born in a place that **brings happiness and benefit to others.** It is not to bring happiness and benefit to [the bodhisattva's own] self.

When [the bodhisattva] is born in these [realms]:

> 307. In each realm [the bodhisattva] has a group of followers that is devoted, pure, patient, and limitless,[29] and [the bodhisattva] is filled like the ocean by the many-mouthed rivers of merit.

In those realms, [the bodhisattva] **has a group of followers that is devoted, pure, patient, and limitless,** and [the bodhisattva's] accumulation of merit and knowledge is **filled by the many-mouthed streams** of the six perfections—generosity, moral conduct, patience, fortitude, meditation, and wisdom—**just as the ocean** is filled by rivers with many mouths. This is [the end of] the discussion of the perfections.

II. The Irreversible Stage: The Ten Masteries[30]

To explain the masteries (*vaśitā*), we say:

308. When [a bodhisattva's] mind is skillful and undistracted and [the bodhisattva] naturally understands and discriminates objects of cognition, [the bodhisattva] remains as many eons as [the bodhisattva] wants.

A **mind that is skillful and undistracted** is clever and attentive. [A person who has this kind of mind] resides in one aspect of tranquillity (*śamathāṅga*). A mind that **naturally understands and discriminates objects of cognition** comes from practicing the cognitive ability to analyze (*pravicaya*) and discriminate the conditioned *dharmas* (*skandhas*, *dhātus*, and *āyatanas*) for many hundreds of thousands of lives. [A person who has this kind of mind] has [another] aspect of tranquillity. When [a bodhisattva] has these [two aspects of tranquillity], [the bodhisattva] **remains as many eons as [the bodhisattva] wants** by the power of meditation (*dhyāna*), concentration (*samādhi*), and attainment (*samāpatti*). This means that [the bodhisattva] has mastery over life (*āyuḥ-vaśitā*) because [the bodhisattva] extends (*adhiṣṭhāna*) the life span for immeasurable eons.[31]

309ab. [The bodhisattva] has the understanding that comes from attaining innumerable, immeasurable concentrations.

This means that the bodhisattva has mastery over mind (*ceto-vaśitā*) because [the bodhisattva] enters profound awareness (*nidhyapti-jñāna*) in **innumerable concentrations** (*samādhi*).

309cd. [The bodhisattva] decorates endless world systems with ornaments.

[The bodhisattva] has mastery over personal belongings (*pariṣkāra-vaśitā*) because [the bodhisattva] displays the sustaining power (*adhiṣṭhāna*) to **decorate** all **world systems** with many magical arrays (*vyūha*).

310ab. [The bodhisattva] displays the ripening of karma by the application of artistic skill and action.

[The bodhisattva] has mastery over karma (*karma-vaśitā*) because [the bodhisattva] **manifests artistic skill,** or art, **and action** in any way [the bodhisattva] likes and because [the bodhisattva] displays sustaining power (*adhiṣṭhāna*) over the time for **the ripening of karma.**

310cd. [The bodhisattva] is born any way [the bodhisattva] wishes because of a desire to benefit ordinary people.

Because of a desire to benefit ordinary people means that [the bodhisattva] wants to do what is beneficial for ordinary people. **[The bodhisattva]** has mastery over birth (*upapatti-vaśitā*) because [the bodhisattva] **is born** in all world systems.

311ab. [The bodhisattva] displays world systems filled with Buddha Bodies.

[The bodhisattva] has mastery over aspiration (*adhimukti-vaśitā*) because [the bodhisattva] **displays** all **world systems filled with Buddhas.**

311cd. [The bodhisattva] displays perfect enlightenment at any time and in any Buddha-field [the bodhisattva] wishes.

[The bodhisattva] has mastery over vows (*praṇidhāna-vaśitā*) because [the bodhisattva] **displays** the **enlightenment** of Buddha manifestations **at any time and in any field [the bodhisattva] wishes.**[32]

312ab. With the eye of knowledge, [the bodhisattva] sees the nature of every object of cognition.

[The bodhisattva] has mastery over knowledge (*jñāna-vaśitā*) because [the bodhisattva] displays perfect enlightenment with regard to all attributes (*dharmas*)[33] in all forms.[34]

312cd. [The bodhisattva] has understood the distinctions between attributes, and [the bodhisattva] has received a name and so forth.

[The bodhisattva] has mastery over attributes (*dharma-vaśitā*) because [the bodhisattva] displays the mode of entry (*mukha*) into an infinite number of attributes (*dharmas*).

In addition, [the bodhisattva] has mastery over power (*ṛddhi-vaśitā*) because [the bodhisattva] displays innumerable manifestations (*nirmāṇa*) in a single moment in all world systems.[35]

313ab. By yawning with power, [the bodhisattva] shakes innumerable worlds.

To shake is to agitate. **[The bodhisattva] shakes** Buddha-fields consisting of innumerable continents and so forth.[36] To **yawn with power** is to act playfully.[37] [The bodhisattva] can do this because [the bodhisattva] has properly practiced the [four] bases of power.[38] This is the meaning of this half of the verse.

313cd. At the same time or at different times [the bodhisattva] emits fire and water from his body.

At the same time [the bodhisattva] emits fire upward **and water** downward, or fire downward and water upward. **Or at different times** [the bodhisattva] burns like a mass of fire and emits showers of water like a great cloud.

> 314ab. [The bodhisattva] spreads radiance in every direction.

The radiance that comes from [the bodhisattva's] body pervades every direction even more completely than [the radiance of] the sun and the moon.

> 314cd. To shock the gods, [the bodhisattva] manifests hells and so forth.[39]

So that all the gods and so forth will feel remorse, **[the bodhisattva]** intentionally **manifests hells and so forth.** In what way? So that gods and human beings who have become infatuated by their attachment to various desires will feel remorse, [the bodhisattva] manifests cruel hells, the world of Yama, and so forth. [The hells contain] six regions.[40] There is a pit of coals (*kukūla*) with great wreaths of roaring fire. There is mud made of excrement (*kuṇapa*).[41] There is [a road made of knives] guarded by Yama's cruel hosts, with angry faces and fearful voices and with knives, wheels, and saws in their hands. There is a forest of swords (*asipattravana*) with terrifying barking dogs. There are Śalmalī trees (*ayaḥśalmalīvana*) with flocks of iron-beaked ravens. And there is the river Vaitaraṇī from which comes the sound of people who are weeping as they are boiled in [molten] copper that is *yojanas* across.

Similarly:

> 315. [The bodhisattva] manifests assemblies of Buddhas who are like relatives of the world and sparkle with the jewels of immeasurable, extraordinary, inconceivable virtues.

With power, **[the bodhisattva] manifests [Buddhas] who sparkle with the jewels of extraordinary, inconceivable virtues,** consisting of the forces, convictions, and infallible penetrations.[42] [These Buddhas are] **like relatives of the world,** adorned with the primary and secondary characteristics [of a Buddha]. And [their] **assemblies** [are] made up of monks, nuns, laymen, and laywomen.

> 316. At will [the bodhisattva] turns great mountains into gold, jewels, beryl, pearls, diamonds, and sapphires, and [the bodhisattva] makes fire cold.

At will [the bodhisattva] turns great mountains into gold and so forth. At will **[the bodhisattva] makes** a blazing **fire** as **cold** as snow.

> 317. With a great body, [the bodhisattva] comes and goes anywhere, even through [things that are made of] diamond and so forth, without any hindrance, miraculously, and instantaneously.

With a great body, [the bodhisattva] manifests himself **coming and going,** even through the Vindhya Mountains[43] and so forth, **without any hindrance,** quickly, **miraculously,** and in any direction.

> 318. [The bodhisattva] manifests endless world systems entering into [the bodhisattva's] own body or into an atom without any harm to sentient beings.

[The bodhisattva] puts **endless world systems into [the bodhisattva's] own body or** puts these world systems **into an atom.** And [the bodhisattva] manifests this **without** causing fear or **harm** to any of the gods, human beings, or animals who live in these world systems.

> 319. At will [the bodhisattva] shrinks world systems to the size of an atom and expands atoms to the size of a world system. [The bodhisattva] also turns them upside down.

At will [the bodhisattva] shrinks world systems and makes them **the size of an atom.** If [the bodhisattva] wants to expand these [atoms], [the bodhisattva] makes these atoms as large as innumerable world systems. [The bodhisattva] turns the top portion of a world system into the bottom and turns the bottom portion into the top.

> 320. Equipped with the [appropriate] size, splendor, color, voice, and behavior, [the bodhisattva] enters the assemblies of [gods] such as Brahmā to teach those who are ready to be taught.

Equipped with the size, splendor, color, voice, and behavior of Brahmā and so forth,[44] **[the bodhisattva] enters the assemblies of [gods] such as Brahmā.** Why? [The bodhisattva] wants **to teach** the fortunate beings[45] **who are ready to be taught.**

> 321. [The bodhisattva] appears and disappears so that no one knows where [the bodhisattva] is. Moved by compassion, [the bodhisattva] overwhelms the power of others.

To **appear** is to make the body visible. To **disappear** is to conceal it or become invisible. [The bodhisattva] does both of these things. **No one,** not even Brahmā and so forth, **knows where [the bodhisattva]** comes from or where [the bodhisattva] goes. **[The bodhisattva] overwhelms the power of others.** [The bodhisattva] is moved by compassion, so [the bodhisattva] does this to break their pride, not to compete with them.

> 322. At will [the bodhisattva] takes control of the going, standing, and speaking of beings.[46] To those who lack insight, [the bodhisattva] gives confidence and pleasure.[47]

[The bodhisattva][48] **takes control of beings** in these ways according to [the level of] their aspiration. **[The bodhisattva] gives confidence**, memory, and intelligence, **and** physical **pleasure to those who** lack them.

323. [The bodhisattva] sends out rays to soothe those who suffer in hell, and [the bodhisattva] leads them to the same condition as the Lords of the Gods and so forth.

To completely **soothe** the suffering of the sentient beings **who suffer** the pain of heat **in** the eight hot **hells**[49]—Avīci, Saṃjīva, Kālasūtra, Tāpana, Mahātāpana, Saṃghāta, Raurava, and Mahāraurava—and cold in the cold hells—Utpala,[50] Kumuda, Padma, Mahāpadma, and so forth—[the bodhisattva] releases cool and warm rays. If the inhabitants of hell are merely touched by these rays, they die and are reborn **in the same condition as the Lords of the Gods,** the Yāmas, and the Tuṣitas.[51]

324. [The bodhisattva] fills every direction with manifestations created for everyone who is ready to be taught, and [the bodhisattva] creates extraordinary pleasure with the jewel-shower of teaching.

[The bodhisattva] fills every direction with manifestations, such as disciples, solitary Buddhas, Śatakratu, Brahmā, Lokapāla, Maheśvara, and Nārāyaṇa. These [manifestations] are created **for everyone who is ready to be taught. With the jewel-shower of teaching** that comes from these manifestations, **[the bodhisattva] creates extraordinary pleasure.**

325. [At will, the bodhisattva] sustains innumerable past, present, and future bodies, the completion of Buddha-fields, and the destruction and creation of innumerable world systems.

[The bodhisattva] sustains (*adhitiṣṭhati*) **innumerable past, present, and future bodies.** [The bodhisattva] sustains (*adhitiṣṭhati*) impure fields as pure. [The bodhisattva] sustains immeasurable Buddha-fields as if they were destroyed and created, even though the time [for their destruction and creation] has not yet come. [The bodhisattva] sustains those that have been destroyed as if they were created. [The bodhisattva] sustains those that have been created as if they were destroyed.

326. Also at will, [the bodhisattva sustains] a Buddha-field in [the bodhisattva's] own body, [the bodhisattva's] own body in that [Buddha-field], and a Buddha Body in [the bodhisattva's] own field.

[The bodhisattva] sustains (*adhitiṣṭhati*) [the bodhisattva's] body as a Buddha-field. [The bodhisattva] sustains that Buddha-field as [the bodhisattva's] own body. [The bodhisattva] sustains the Buddha-field as the Body of the Tathāgata.

327–328. From the rays of light and the pores [of the bodhisattva's body], from musical instruments,[52] from the sky, or from manifestations comes a sound that fills the world. [The sound] is delightful to hear, penetrating, clear, deep, broad, and as charming as [the sound of] a cuckoo.

From the pores and the rays of light of [the bodhisattva's] own body, from drums that are beaten or unbeaten, **from the sky, or from** the **manifestations** that have just been mentioned **comes a sound.** This sound is **delightful to hear, penetrating, clear, and as charming as [the sound of] a cuckoo.** None can understand its meaning, it resounds with a great sound, and its sound is pervasive.

What does it do? For ordinary people:

329. [With this voice, the bodhisattva] speaks the Dharma to teach those who are ready to be taught. [The Dharma] is peaceful and has only the taste of quietude, but because of the convictions and faculties [of the listeners, the bodhisattva teaches it] in many ways.

[While ordinary people have different] **convictions and faculties,** such as faith,[53] **[the Dharma] has only the taste of quietude and is peaceful.** [A bodhisattva] speaks the Dharma **in many ways** to remove fear and to bring fortunate beings to maturity.

This is [the end of] the discussion of the mastery of power. [Power] is well explained in the seventeenth chapter [of *The Root Verses on the Middle Way*].[54] Anyone who wants to consider the ten masteries in detail should consult the long and detailed explanation in *The Jewel-Cloud Sūtra* (*Ratnamegha Sūtra*).[55]

III. The Stage That Is One Birth Away from Enlightenment: The Superknowledges[56]

Now [we] explain the superknowledges:

330–331. [The bodhisattva] knows where, how, how long, and which of many sentient beings have minds that are defiled, unwholesome, pure, pleasurable, painful, lower, middle, higher, or truly superior.

Defiled[57] means to be affected by primary and secondary defilements.[58] **Unwholesome** means to have tendencies such as passion, hatred, ignorance, pride, and false views. **Pure** is to have removed the tendencies toward the defilements. To be free from the three kinds of suffering is to have **pleasure,** or to experience birth at the [right] time[59] is to have pleasure. The opposite [of pleasure] is **pain.** The nature of these two [states] is [respectively] to have no pain and to have no pleasure. **Lower** means extremely low and also other [levels of inferiority].[60] **Middle** means higher than that. **Higher** is supreme, excellent, and superior. To be located in the three vehicles is **truly superior.** To take delight in rebirth is not truly superior. The bodhisattva knows **where, how, how long, and which of many sentient beings** are born with **minds** that are classified as being small, broad, great, or immeasurable. [The bodhisattva] knows how they are classified by what they contain and where they are located, and [the bodhisattva] knows this in a moment. This is a description of the superknowledge of knowing the minds of others.

There are two kinds of clairvoyance (*divya-cakṣus*).[61] One has death and rebirth as its object; the other has form (*rūpa*) as its object. Here [in the following verse] it is the pure physical eye (*māṃsa-cakṣus*) that has unhindered access to subtle, concealed, and distant things and is said to have form as its object. To describe the knowledge that comes from this [type of clairvoyance], we say:

> 332. [The bodhisattva] has the clairvoyance to see all forms everywhere, including subtle things among the gods and manifestations as well as gross things among the opposite.

Gods do not have the clairvoyance of a bodhisattva, but a bodhisattva does have the clairvoyance of the gods.[62] [A bodhisattva] is able to see form in the realm of the gods. The **manifestations** are those that belong to Tathāgatas and Arhants. **Subtle things** means atoms and so forth. **The opposite** is the opposite of gods and [manifestations]. [The opposite of the gods] is the realm of human beings, Asuras, the inhabitants of hell, hungry ghosts, and so forth. The opposite of manifestations is something that arises from causes and conditions. **Gross**[63] means Mount Meru and so forth. With clairvoyance [a bodhisattva] sees **all forms,** without exception, **everywhere,** [in every] realm. This is a description of the clairvoyance that has form as its object.

> 333. [The bodhisattva] has the clairaudience to hear the words spoken by gods, magical arrays,[64] saints, and manifestations, as well as those [spoken] by human beings, [words that are spoken] far away and also the opposite.

[By] gods means [the words spoken] by gods. **Saints** means the words [spoken] by disciples and so forth. **Magical arrays** means the words [spoken] by the magical array (*vyūha*) that arises from the body of the Buddha Vairocana who resides in the palace of Akaniṣṭha. This is described in the *Gaṇḍavyūha* [*Sūtra*].[65] **The words [spoken] by a manifestation** are the words [spoken] by a fully enlightened Buddha in Jambudvīpa and so forth. **Spoken** means spoken in the form of particular words, which consist of syllables and so forth. **Human beings** are born in the four continents. **Far away** is something that exceeds the range of normal hearing. **The opposite** is what is unspoken as well as what is near. With clairaudience [a bodhisattva] hears all these things. This is a description of the superknowledge of clairaudience.

334. [The bodhisattva] remembers [the bodhisattva's] own and others' previous lives everywhere, with the distinctions of names, clans, and so forth, and [the bodhisattva] causes others to remember.

[The bodhisattva] remembers, from one life to many thousands of lives, that [the bodhisattva] has had a certain name, a certain caste (*jāti*), a certain clan (*gotra*), a certain length of life, certain food, an experience of certain kinds of pleasure and pain, and so forth.[66] **[The bodhisattva] also causes others to remember** similar things. This is a description of the superknowledge of remembering previous lives.

335. Everywhere [the bodhisattva] knows the death, transmigration, and rebirth of all the beings who are located in different realms as a result of various good and bad actions.

Gods, Asuras, human beings, inhabitants of hell, animals, and hungry ghosts experience the results of many different kinds of good and bad actions and die, or reside in a bad state. They transmigrate, or reside in an intermediate state. They are born, or enter a state of rebirth, and assume bodies in this world and above.[67] [The bodhisattva] sees their **death, transmigration, and rebirth,** so he is said to have the superknowledge of clairvoyance.

Those who say that there is an intermediate state think that there is subtle form in the intermediate state.[68] According to them, [the existence of the intermediate state] is established by the earlier explanation [in verse 332] of the superknowledge that sees form. For those who say that there is no intermediate state, this [verse 335] is a description of the physical eye that sees form, as in the earlier [verse 332]. Now [in this superknowledge, the bodhisattva] sees death, transmigration, and rebirth with the mind, just as [the bodhisattva] knows the minds of others. It says in scripture that these two [types of vision] together are called the superknowledge of clairvoyance.[69] [However,] in the account of the five eyes, the two [that is, the physical eye and clairvoyance] are distinguished:[70] the one that has form as its object is the physical eye, and the one that has death, transmigration, and rebirth as its object is clairvoyance.

Next comes a description of the superknowledge of power:

336. [The bodhisattva] teaches those who are ready to be taught by manifesting [life in] Tuṣita, transmigration, entry into the womb, enlightenment, and so forth.

When [the bodhisattva] has finished practicing the bases of power[71]—namely, the concentrations of mind, energy, zeal, and investigation—and resides in the concentration of the hero's march[72] in the tenth stage, [the bodhisattva] creates manifestations in world systems equal in number to the sands of the Ganges. [The bodhisattva does this] **to teach the beings who are [ready to be] taught** by the sight of a Buddha. To the fortunate beings who are ready to be taught, [the bodhisattva] **manifests** [the acts of] **life in** the **Tuṣita** dwelling, **transmigration,** birth, displaying skill,[73] being married, going forth, engaging in asceticism, subduing Māra, enlightenment, turning the wheel of the Dharma, attaining parinirvana, and maintaining the Dharma.

For those who want to worship Tathāgatas:

> 337–338. Without moving from [the bodhisattva's] own field, [the bodhisattva] intentionally manifests bodies in as many Buddha-fields as there are grains of dust in innumerable world systems, and each body has an equally vast number of hands, heads, and tongues.[74]

Without moving from [the bodhisattva's] own field, in as many Buddha-fields as there are atoms **in innumerable world** systems, **[the bodhisattva] intentionally manifests** the manifestation **bodies** of an equally vast number of sentient beings as teaching devices. And in each of these [sentient beings, the bodhisattva] manifests **an equally vast number of hands and heads,** and in each of the heads [the bodhisattva manifests] an equally vast number of **tongues.**[75]

Held in these hands are:

> 339. Multicolored clusters of fragrant flowers as numerous as the sands of the Ganges, as big as Mount Meru, and emitting rich, fine, sweet fragrances. With these [flowers],[76]

Emitting fragrances means that their fragrances fill every direction. To have **rich, fine, sweet fragrances** is to have many fine, sweet fragrances.[77] Their size is the size of Mount Meru. Their number is the number of the sands of the Ganges. They are clusters of fragrances as well as clusters of flowers.

> 340. Intending to bring benefit to the world, [the bodhisattva] worships the perfectly enlightened and awakened Buddhas with [eyes] moist with devotion and praises them continually with hymns.

Someone who understands reality is **perfectly enlightened** (*sambuddha*), and someone who has dispelled the sleep of ignorance is **awakened** (*buddha*). [The bodhisattva] **worships** [these Buddhas] because [the bodhisattva] wants to generate the vow (*praṇidhāna*) that is the means **of bringing benefit to the world. With** great **devotion, [the bodhisattva] worships** [the Buddhas] with manifested bodies **and,** with the tongues of these [manifested bodies], [the bodhisattva] continually **praises them with hymns** about [their] supreme virtues.

In addition:

> 341. [The bodhisattva worships the Buddhas] with immeasurable jeweled parasols and canopies, decorated with networks of pearls, and sparkling with jewel-rays like sprouts and teeth.

Parasols, canopies, and flags made of jewels such as sapphires are **decorated with networks of pearls.** They surpass ordinary measure. The jewels seem to sparkle with rays, and the rays that [come] from these [jewels] are like sprouts and teeth.

[What follows is] the praise that consists of peaked dwellings:[78]

342. [The bodhisattva worships the Buddhas with peaked dwellings] that have pleasant upper rooms and radiant pillars. [These dwellings are] hung with garlands of pearls, constructed with a mass of different jewels, and [decorated] with paintings.

Something that has **pleasant upper rooms and radiant pillars** is pleasant because of its upper rooms and radiant pillars. **Hung with garlands of pearls** means [that the peaked dwelling is] customarily hung with garlands of pearls. To be **constructed with a mass [of different jewels]** is to be constructed or built with a mass of different kinds of jewels. [The peaked dwellings] also are ornamented with beautiful golden stairways, benches, and so forth.[79]

343. These peaked dwellings shine with hundreds of lamps, with the light of radiant jewels. They are as high as the clouds and fill every direction with light.

A **peaked dwelling** is a particular dwelling place. Its **lamps** are **the light of radiant jewels.** It shines or glows with **hundreds** of these [lamps] continuously burning. **As high as the clouds** means high enough to touch the sky. These peaked dwellings **fill every direction with** the many-colored **light** of different kinds of jewels. With these [peaked dwellings], the bodhisattva offers worship. To whom? To the perfectly enlightened Buddhas.

344. The accomplished [bodhisattva] listens continuously to [the Tathāgatas'] many-faceted teaching and teaches it to others without dropping or adding as much as a word or syllable.

An **accomplished [bodhisattva]** is one who is well trained.[80] All Tathāgatas teach in many ways. [The bodhisattva] **listens continuously and teaches others** what [the bodhisattva] has heard **without dropping or adding as much as a syllable.**[81]

345. [The bodhisattva] is exalted by the accumulation of merit and knowledge for innumerable countless eons, has completed the perfections, and is a supreme person.

The one who **is exalted by** the strength of **the accumulation of merit and knowledge for innumerable countless eons has completed the** ten **perfections** as described [earlier], **and is a supreme person.**

What does [this supreme person] do?

3. The Conventional Buddha

I. The Dharma Body

346. [The bodhisattva] becomes a Buddha and opens the minds of fortunate beings with the pure, cleansing rays of teaching, just as the sun [opens the blossoms in] a pond of lotuses.

After completing the perfections, **[the bodhisattva]** attains enlightenment at will. Then, on the mountain peak of omniscience, whenever [the bodhisattva] wishes, [the bodhisattva] **becomes a Buddha and,** in accordance with [the bodhisattva's] vow (*praṇidhāna*), **opens** [the minds of] those who are ready to be taught **with the** thousand **rays of teaching, just as the sun [opens the blossoms in] a pond of lotuses.** [The rays are] **pure** in nature and capable of dispelling ignorance in the minds of those who are ready to be taught. [The teaching] consists of the sūtrāntas and so forth.

Similarly:

347. With the water of teaching, more cooling than the Himalayas, the moon, or sandalwood, [the Buddha] puts out the fire of the defilements in the minds of sentient beings.

Heat that has been extinguished by snow and the like will spring up again if the right conditions are present. But when the heat of **the fire of the defilements** has been extinguished by the water of the Buddha's teaching, it does not spring up at all. This is the distinctive characteristic of a saint (*ārya*).

From the first arising of the aspiration [to enlightenment] (*prathama-cittotpāda*), [bodhisattvas] vow that, having saved themselves, they will save sentient beings who have not been saved.[1] This vow is [now] fulfilled. Having saved himself from the ocean of transmigration:

> 348. With the great boats of the three vehicles, [the Buddha] speedily saves beings from the ocean of existence where the waves are birth, transmigration, and suffering and the crocodiles are death.[2]

The ocean of existence is surrounded by **waves** that consist of the manifold **suffering of rebirth and transmigration,** and it also [is surrounded] by the **crocodiles of death. With the great boats of the** disciple, solitary Buddha, and great **vehicles, [the Buddha] speedily saves** all **beings from** sinking [in this ocean], and he takes them to the island of liberation where there is no bondage.

> 349. With the jewel-streams of his eloquent phrases, [the Buddha] completely dispels thirst and removes the world's beginningless poverty of good qualities.[3]

People are extremely poor in good qualities and are overcome by thirst. **With the** many **jewels of eloquent phrases,** which are [eloquent because they are] consistent with the Buddha's insight, **[the Buddha]** cuts off **thirst** for existence and **removes poverty** by undertaking the accumulation of a wealth of virtuous qualities such as faith.

He teaches like a great master of the way.

> 350. People wander in the forest of existence, and they have [only their] ignorance to show the way. [The Buddha] opens [their] wisdom-eye and leads [them] to nirvana.[4]

Because of their actions, **people wander** by themselves **in the forest of existence,** and they do not know the way because it is concealed by ignorance. He shows them the way. **[The Buddha] opens [their] wisdom-eye and leads them to** the city of **nirvana.**

[The next verse] compares [the Buddha] to the medicine that belongs to someone who knows how to cure a person who has been poisoned.

> 351. With the spells of knowledge, [the Buddha] truly cures the people who have been bitten by the snake of the defilements and are no longer conscious of their own welfare.[5]

Ordinary people **have been bitten by** the fangs of **the snake of the defilements,** such as passion, **and are no longer conscious,** or are ignorant, **of** what will bring about **their own welfare.** The **knowledge** of Emptiness, signlessness, and wishlessness is a **spell** or a medicine. **With these** [forms of knowledge] **he cures** them.

[The next verse] compares [the Buddha] to someone who sounds a musical instrument to awaken [sentient beings].

352. [The Buddha] uses his teaching compassionately, like the sound of a drum, to awaken the living beings who have no one in this world to protect them and have long slept the sleep of ignorance.[6]

Ordinary people have no protector to awaken them, and from time immemorial they have been overwhelmed by the sleep of ignorance in the houses of samsara. **[The Buddha]** has compassion on them and **uses his teaching** of the true Dharma **like the sound of a** beaten **drum to awaken [them].**

Having already saved himself:

353. [The Buddha] conquers the four Māras and frees those who have long been bound by the chains of thirst in the prison of samsara.[7]

He frees from the bonds of thirst beings whose minds **have long been bound in samsara by chains** that consist of the six kinds **of thirst**. How? **He conquers the Māra** of the aggregates with diamondlike concentration.[8] With Emptiness he conquers [the Māras that consist of] the defilements and death. With friendliness (*maitrī*) he conquers the Māra that is one of the gods.

With the ambrosia of wisdom[9] alone he brings satisfaction.

354. With the lovely ambrosia of wisdom, he brings satisfaction to beings who, like a fire, cannot be satisfied by anything divine or human.

When more fuel is added to a raging fire, it burns brighter rather than being quenched. Likewise, the more sentient beings experience objects such as form that are divine and human, the more their thirst increases. But with a taste of **the ambrosia** of his **wisdom, he brings** them **satisfaction.**

[The next verse] compares [the Buddha] to a lion.

355. In assemblies he sounds the lion's roar of Emptiness and drives away the untamed[10] heretics' pride in their own wisdom as if [he were a lion driving away] the passion of wild, rutting elephants.

Heretics who have great, false pride and cannot be tamed by other sentient beings are [like] rutting elephants. They are [as it were] in a state of passion[11] because they are proud of their knowledge, even though they are ignorant. To drive this [passion] away, [the Buddha teaches] Emptiness in assemblies of many people like a great lion's roar. This roar drives away the heretics' passion for knowledge as if it were the rut of elephants. [This roar] is an expression of the Dharma Body, which is identical to the knowledge of a perfectly enlightened Buddha.

II. The Form Body

The following [verses] describe the [Form] Body that is defined as the Enjoyment and Manifestation [Bodies].

> 356–357. The [Buddha's] incomparable Form [Body] is surrounded by a fathom of light that has the appearance of a rainbow; its splendor (*śrī*) consists of permanent, radiant, and complete primary and secondary characteristics; its ornament is glory (*lakṣmī*); it is charming to the mind and the eyes; and it surpasses all things in beauty.

The Form Body of the Lord is produced by the expansion of innumerable good practices. It **is surrounded by a fathom of light** that is inscribed with wreaths of different colors **like a rainbow.** It has **the splendor** (*śrī*) **of primary and secondary characteristics.** These [primary and secondary characteristics] are **permanent** in the sense that they do not move from the appropriate place, and they are **radiant** in brilliance (*tejas*). **It is ornamented with** its own **glory** (*lakṣmī*). **It charms the mind and eyes. This** incomparable Body **surpasses all** other **things in beauty.** It arises from the power of the Dharma Body and from a previous vow (*praṇidhāna*).

[The next verse] describes [the voice] that arises from the Form Bodies.

> 358. [With this form] and with a miraculous voice that has sixty attributes, [the Buddha] captivates the minds of all beings.

[The Buddha's voice] is **miraculous** (*saprātihārya*) in the sense that it is capable of power (*ṛddhi*), proclamation (*ādeśanā*), and delivery of teaching (*anuśāsanī*).[12] Its power (*ṛddhi*) is pervasive, gentle, and profound. Its proclamation (*ādeśanā*) consists of explaining how long men and women will live and explaining that sentient beings, because of their good or bad actions, have been or will be born in the six realms and, after being reborn for a certain period of time, will achieve liberation. It is also well known for the infinitely miraculous delivery of teaching (*anuśāsanī*). It teaches that the Dharma is one thing and not another, that one thing is to be practiced and not another, that certain factors, such as desire, lead to rebirth and other [factors], such as the bases of mindfulness (*smṛty-upasthāna*),[13] are conducive to enlightenment.

A voice that has sixty attributes is a voice with the following sixty attributes:[14] affectionate, gentle, beautiful, charming, pure, stainless, luminous, attractive, good to listen to, invulnerable, melodious, disciplined, not harsh, not severe, well disciplined, pleasing to the ear, delightful to the body, satisfying to the mind, satisfying to the heart, generating joy and bliss, not burning, acknowledgeable, recognizable, transparent, amiable, lovable, authoritative, informative, reasonable, coherent, not redundant, energetic as a lion's roar, like an elephant's trumpeting, like the sound of thunder, like the voice of the

Lord of Nāgas, like the sound of the Kiṃnaras singing, like the sound of a stormy ocean,[15] like the sound of a cuckoo's song, like the sound of Brahmā's cry, like the sound of a pheasant's call, sweet as the voice of the Lord of Gods, like the sound of a drum, not haughty, not humble, grammatically sound, free from error, unfailing, undaunted, irrepressible, joyful, comprehensive, beneficial,[16] charming, fulfilling all sounds, satisfying all the senses of living beings, irreproachable, unchangeable, unwavering, known in all assemblies, endowed with the best of forms. These sixty attributes are described in the *Guhyādhipatinirdeśa Sūtra.*[17]

359. With body and voice like a wishing jewel, [the Buddha] assumes the universal form of all the gods to help those who are ready to be taught.

The body that has just been described is **like a wishing jewel** that fulfills the aspirations, wishes, and intentions of living beings. **With this [body] and with the voice** that has also just been described, **[the Buddha]** manifests many divine forms to teach all beings. He does this through the vow to accomplish the welfare of all sentient beings, with the form that is appropriate to each of the people who are ready to be taught and with the purpose of bringing these [people] to maturity.

360. This, which has just been described, is the beginning of the majesty—the innumerable, immeasurable, astonishing mine of virtues—attained by a sage who follows this path.

This (*iti*) marks the end of the chapter. **Which has just been described** (*evam*) refers to the virtues described [in the preceding verses]. **The beginning** (*ādi*) shows that only a few virtues have been mentioned here and many others could be mentioned. [The virtues] are **innumerable** in the sense that there are greater than a hundred, a thousand, and so forth. They are **immeasurable** because of the greatness of their power. They are **astonishing** because they amaze the mind. Their **mine** (*ākara*) is their location. And what is this [astonishing mine of virtues]? **Majesty** (*māhātmya*) or greatness. [This majesty] is the Buddhahood attained by the gradual realization of the [bodhisattva] stages (*bhūmi*) and so forth. Who [attains this majesty]? **A sage** who wisely distinguishes the relative (*saṃvṛti*) and the ultimate (*paramārtha*). What kind of [sage is this]? Someone who has attained [Buddhahood] by **following** and staying on **the** great **path,** or the Mahāyāna, that has been described in the words "not relinquishing the aspiration to enlightenment, taking the vow of an ascetic, and seeking the knowledge of reality."[18]

The majesty of [a Buddha's] innumerable, immeasurable, and astonishing virtues is described in many sūtras. There are ten infinitely varied Buddha *dharmas*:[19] (1) The infinitely varied Form Bodies of the Lords are pure. (2) [Buddhas] completely understand all *dharmas* because their eyes are pure and there is nothing to impede their infinitely varied vision of all beings.

(3) They have pure, infinitely varied ears that perceive the voices of all beings without obstruction. (4) They have attained an infinitely varied sense of smell that is a perfect Buddha sense organ. (5) They have an infinitely varied tongue whose sound penetrates the realms of all sentient beings. (6) They have infinitely varied bodily action: they manifest Tathāgata Bodies that are consistent with the minds of all sentient beings. (7) The action of their minds is infinitely varied: without deviating from the Dharma Body, [their minds] penetrate without any obstruction in the past, present, and future, and they are pure. (8) Buddhas also manifest miracles of transformation, such as the birth of a Buddha and so forth, and their unimpeded state of liberation is infinitely varied. (9) In accordance with their pure intention, they possess as spotless magical arrays all infinitely varied, pure world systems. (10) Having created [manifestations] in Buddha-fields that are free from impurity, they carry out the act of teaching. [These manifestations possess] the diverse practices of a bodhisattva, are magically created by a vow, fulfill the attributes of insight, are fully enlightened, fulfill all Buddha attributes, and are infinitely varied.

Similarly, there are three hundred special Buddha attributes described in the *Tathāgatadaśabhūmika Sūtra*:[20] [Buddhas] achieve the ten Buddha-knowledges in a single moment. There are ten ways in which they do not exceed the time of a Buddha. Buddhas have ten inconceivable locations. They have ten knowledges that are accomplished by the sustaining power of the infinite comprehensions. They have ten great and extensive qualities that are unapproachable by those who are confused. They have ten majesties. They have ten great purities. Buddhas have ten actions. They have ten lineages of the knowledge-ocean. Buddhas have ten guides. Buddhas have ten limitless entrances into the teaching. Buddhas have ten essential *dharmas*. Buddhas have ten places where there is no attachment. The Buddhas have ten ornaments. The Buddhas have ten masteries over the gods. The Buddhas have ten perfect actions. The Buddhas have ten forms of skill-in-means. The Buddhas have ten intentions. The Buddhas have ten powers. They have ten attributes of sovereignty over the Dharma. The Tathāgatas have ten dwellings. They have ten complete understandings of all *dharmas*. They have ten locations of omniscience. They have ten pure recollections of the Tathāgata. They have the ten attributes that comprise quick vision of the Tathāgata. The Buddhas have ten concentrations. They have ten Tathāgata states. The Buddhas have ten liberations. These are described in the *Tathāgatadaśabhūmika Sūtra*. These [virtues] are not shared by disciples, solitary Buddhas, and so forth.

The majesty of the Tathāgata is described in the *Dhāraṇīśvararājā*, *Ratnamegha*, and *Daśabhūmika Sūtras*. Anyone who wishes to understand it in detail should consult those sūtras.

[Here ends] the third chapter, [entitled] "The Quest for the Knowledge of Reality," of *The Flame of Reason*, the commentary on *The [Verses on the] Essence of the Middle Way*.

Corrections, Alternative Readings, and Emendations of the Text

I. Sanskrit Text

Verse Number	*Ejima's Reading*	*Translator's Reading*
275	nirābhāsāt tadātmanā	nirābhāsatadātmanā
280	mahātmānam	mahātmānaḥ
283	cittasyāyam	cittasyedam
305	manoramāḥ	manoramaḥ
306	tad anyatra	tadanyatra
327	stūpebhyo	tūryebhyo
347	manaḥ kleśāgni	manaḥkleśāgni
348	janmāvṛto duḥkha	janmāvarttaduḥkha
350	avidyādharmadeśikaṃ	avidyāmārgadeśikaṃ
355	durdanta	durdānta

Corrections, Alternative Readings, and Emendations of the Text

II. Tibetan Text

Folio and Line Number	*Reading in Derge Edition*	*Translator's Reading*
122a/3	rtog pa med pa ñid kyis	rtogs pa med pa ñid kyis (P)
122a/3	rtog pa med pa ñid rtog pa'o	rtogs pa med pa ñid rtogs pa'o (P)
122a/3	'o na rtog pa	'o na rtogs pa (P)
122a/6	gtsug lag	gtsug lag khaṅ (P)
124a/1	rtog pa med pa'i tshul gyis	rtogs pa med pa'i tshul gyis (P)
124a/7	chos ma yin pas ma yin la	chos ma yin pa yaṅ ma yin la (P)
125a/5	mtshan ma med pa ñid du	mtshan ma ñid du
125b/5	ji skad bstan pa'i skabs kyis	ji skad bstan pa'i skabs kyi
129b/6	spaṅs pa / sa thams cad	spaṅs pas thams cad (P)
130a/3	'gro ba rnams kyi	'gro ba rnams kyis
131b/3	ji lta źe na	ji ltar źe na (P)
132b/4	ma choṅs pa	choṅs pa
134b/3	brtag	dag
134b/4	brtag	dag
135a/4	sṅon	mṅon
137b/7	khyad	khyab (P)
138b/6	lha yin no	lha'i'o (P)
143a/6	pha rol pa daṅ bcas pa	rol pa daṅ bcas pa (P)

NOTES

Notes to Introduction

1. There has been broad and thus far inconclusive discussion of the correct form of this philosopher's name. As David Seyfort Ruegg has pointed out, the forms "Bhāvaviveka" and "Bhavya" (among others) are both retrievable or reconstructable from Indian, Tibetan, and Chinese sources. See Ruegg, "On the Authorship of Some Works Ascribed to Bhāvaviveka/Bhavya," in *Earliest Buddhism and Madhyamaka*: 59–71, edited by David Seyfort Ruegg and Lambert Schmithausen (Leiden: E. J. Brill, 1990) and *The Literature of the Madhyamaka School of Buddhist Philosophy in India* (Wiesbaden: Otto Harrassowitz, 1981). On the background of this controversy see also Christian Lindtner, "Adversaria Buddhica," *WZKS* 26 (1982), pp. 167–94. In this book I have chosen to use "Bhāvaviveka," the form of the name that is most recognizable in North American scholarship, but I eagerly await Christian Lindtner's further exploration of the priority of the name "Bhavya."
2. The latest arguments about the authenticity of Bhāvaviveka's works are summarized by David Seyfort Ruegg in "On the Authorship of Some Works Ascribed to Bhāvaviveka/Bhavya" and in *The Literature of the Madhyamaka School of Buddhist Philosophy in India*. In this book I have attempted to strike a balance between competing claims by basing my reconstruction of Bhāvaviveka's thought—in substance, imagery, and form—on the evidence of *The Verses on the Essence of the Middle Way* (*Madhyamakahṛdayakārikās*) with elaboration from Bhāvaviveka's commentary on Nāgārjuna's *Root Verses on the Middle Way* (*Mūlamadhyamakakārikās*) and from the commentary on the *Madhyamakahṛdayakārikās* called *The Flame of Reason* (*Tarkajvālā*). My approach is similar to the one that Ruegg attributes to the Tibetan scholar lCaṅ skya Rol pa'i rdo rje (1717–1786)—to focus on Bhāvaviveka's two major works as the most reliable sources for the study of Bhāvaviveka's position and to treat *The Flame of Reason*, at least provisionally, as an accurate expansion of the sense of Bhāvaviveka's verses. Scholars who are familiar with the controversies over the authenticity of Bhāvaviveka's works can explore the congruence between *The Flame of Reason* and *The Verses on the Essence of the Middle Way* at the end of this book, where the sections of these works that deal with Bhāvaviveka's image of the Buddha are translated in their entirety. On Bhāvaviveka's role in the history of Indian doxography, see Olle Qvarnström, *Hindu Philosophy in Buddhist Perspective: The Vedāntaviniścaya Chapter of Bhavya's Madhyamakahṛdayakārikā*, Lund Studies in African and Asian Religions, vol. 4 (Lund: Plus Ultra, 1989).
3. Steven Collins, *Selfless Persons: Imagery and Thought in Theravāda Buddhism* (Cambridge: Cambridge University Press, 1982), p. 264.
4. Jonathan Z. Smith, *To Take Place: Toward Theory in Ritual* (Chicago: University of Chicago Press, 1987), p. xi.
5. See Richard Rorty, *Philosophy and the Mirror of Nature* (Princeton: Princeton University Press, 1979; 2nd printing, with corrections, 1980), where Rorty traces his own position to Wittgenstein, Heidegger, and Dewey. See also Jacques Derrida, *Margins of Philosophy*, trans. Alan Bass (Chicago: University of Chicago Press, 1982), where Derrida traces his position to Nietzsche.

6. As in the *Republic* 540a-c, in *Platonis Opera*, ed. Ioannes Burnet, vol. 4 (Oxford: Oxford University Press, 1902; reprint ed., 1978).
7. *MMK* XXV.19 and XXII.16.
8. Louis de La Vallée Poussin, "Nihilism (Buddhist)" in *The Encyclopedia of Religion and Ethics*, ed. James Hastings (New York: Scribner's, 1917).
9. See, for example, K. E. Kirk's classic study of the beatific vision as a goal in Christian theology, *The Vision of God: The Christian Doctrine of the Summum Bonum* (2nd ed., London: Longmans, Green, 1932).

Notes to Chapter 1

1. The story is told in Samuel Beal, trans., *Si-Yu-Ki*: *Buddhist Records of the Western World* (London: Trubner, 1884; reprint ed., Delhi: Munshiram Manoharlal, 1969), vol. 2, pp. 223–27. Beal's interpretation was substantially supplemented and revised by the commentary of Thomas Watters in *On Yuan Chwang's Travels in India* (London: Royal Asiatic Society, 1905), vol. 2, pp. 214–24.
2. The term "celestial bodhisattva" refers to those beings who have proceeded so far along the path to enlightenment and accumulated such powers of merit and wisdom that they are capable of intervening miraculously in this world to save other beings. While the worship of the bodhisattva Maitreya is not confined to the Mahāyāna, the elaborate cult of celestial bodhisattvas is considered to be one of the more important and distinctive features of the Mahāyāna. In Bhāvaviveka's mind these celestial bodhisattvas were associated with the tenth and last stage (*bhūmi*) of the bodhisattva path and were comparable in status (though superior in wisdom) to the gods Śiva, Viṣṇu, and Brahmā. See *MHK* III.290 with its commentary for Bhāvaviveka's statement of this comparison.
3. In the fifth chapter of the *MHK*, Bhāvaviveka uses the term *yogācāra* as a name for the school of Asaṅga and Vasubandhu, but the practice of yoga is certainly not confined to the Yogācāra school. Bhāvaviveka commonly uses the word *yogin* as a general term to refer to a practitioner of the path to Buddhahood.
4. In the first verse of the 5th chapter of the *MHK*, Bhāvaviveka says, "Other [Mahāyāna teachers] who [think they] are wise and who are arrogant about their own interpretation say that the Yogācāras clearly give the best presentation of the ambrosia of reality" (*anye pracakṣate dhīrāḥ svanītāv abhimāninaḥ / tattvāmṛtāvatāro hi yogācāraiḥ sudeśitaḥ*).
5. At least this is the way Watters interprets Hsüan-tsang's account of Bhāvaviveka's message to Dharmapāla.
6. Hsüan-tsang gives his own account of the legend in *Records*, vol. 1, p. 226.
7. For a more detailed account of Hsüan-tsang's devotional attitude toward Maitreya see the stories that begin chapter seven in this book.
8. Vajrapāṇi is mentioned frequently in early Mahāyāna literature as a spirit (*yakṣa*) in the entourage of certain Buddhas or bodhisattvas. See, for example, *The Sūtra of Golden Light*, trans. R. E. Emmerick (London: Pali Text Society, 1979), pp. 33, 37, 66. In later Tantric literature he takes on the more exalted status of a bodhisattva, as David Snellgrove has noted in *Indo-Tibetan Buddhism* (Boston: Shambhala, 1987), vol. 1, pp. 134–41. Étienne Lamotte has discussed the evolution of Vajrapāṇi's role in Indian Buddhism in "Vajrapāṇi en Inde," in *Mélanges de Sinologie offerts à Monsieur Paul Demiéville*, pp. 113–59, Bibliothèque de l'Institut des Hautes Études Chinoises, vol. 20 (Paris: Presses Universitaires de France, 1966).
9. On the traditions involved in the attainment of such suspended animation, see Paul Griffiths, *On Being Mindless: Buddhist Meditation and the Mind-Body Problem* (La Salle, Ill.: Open Court, 1986).

10. *Records*, vol. 2, pp. 142–44; Watters, vol. 2, pp. 144–46. Another version appears in the *Divyāvadāna*, ed. P. L. Vaidya (Darbhanga: Mithila Institute, 1959), p. 37. For a Central Asian variant of the story of Mahākāśyapa, see Ronald Emmerick, ed., *The Book of Zambasta* (London: Oxford University Press, 1968), pp. 331–35.
11. *Records*, vol. 2, pp. 304–6.
12. *Records*, vol. 2, pp. 156–58.
13. *Records*, vol. 2, pp. 148–49; Watters, vol. 2, p. 148.
14. Wendy Doniger O'Flaherty, *Dreams, Illusions, and Other Realities* (Chicago: Chicago University Press, 1984).
15. *Laṅkāvatāra Sūtra*, ed. Bunyiu Nanjio, Bibliotheca Otaniensis, vol. 1 (Kyoto: Otani University Press, 1923). Wendy Doniger O'Flaherty comments on this story in *Dreams, Illusions, and Other Realities*, pp. 271–74.
16. *Records*, vol., 2, pp. 156–58.
17. *MHK* III.12. The verse is echoed from time to time in later literature. See, for example, Haribhadra's *Ālokā*, p. 169; and *Madhyamakaratnapradīpa* I.6 in Christian Lindtner, "Atiśa's Introduction to the Two Truths, and Its Sources," *JIP* 9 (1981), p. 172.
18. Heinrich Gerhard Franz has shown that early prototypes of the Indian temple tower were represented in Buddhist reliefs from the region of Mathurā as early as the Kuṣāṇa period. See "The Origins of the Tower-Temple in India," in *South Asian Archaeology 1981*, ed. Bridget Allchin (Cambridge: Cambridge University Press, 1981), pp. 280–84. Franz also discusses a relief from the Amarāvatī school in the Musée Guimet that shows a multistoried temple structure.
19. *MHK* III.253–54.
20. Willem B. Bollee has discussed the architectural form of the peaked dwelling in "Le *kūṭāgāra* ou de la maison des hommes au manoir dans l'Inde orientale et l'Asie du Sud-Est," *Bulletin d'études indiennes* 4 (1986), pp. 189–214. See also Ananda K. Coomaraswamy, "Indian Architectural Terms," *JAOS* 48 (1928), pp. 250–75; and K. de Vreese, "Skt. Kūṭāgāra," in *India Antiqua* (Leiden: Brill, 1947), pp. 323–25. In *MHK* III.342–43 Bhāvaviveka describes these peaked dwellings as having "beautiful balconies, pillars that glow with jewels, golden stairways, hundreds of lamps, and towers so high that they fill every direction with their light"—a description that comes closer to the literary models discussed here than to the examples mentioned by Bollee.
21. P. L. Vaidya, ed., *Aṣṭasāhasrikā Prajñāpāramitā* (Darbhanga: Mithila Institute, 1960), chs. 30–32; trans. Edward Conze, *The Perfection of Wisdom in Eight Thousand Lines and Its Verse Summary* (Bolinas, Calif.: Four Seasons Foundation, 1973). Lewis Lancaster has commented on the story in "The Story of a Buddhist Hero," *The Tsing Hua Journal of Chinese Studies*, N.S. 10 (1974), pp. 83–89.
22. On the significance of the substitution of the physical text of a sūtra for the Buddha (in the form of the Dharma Body), see chapter 5 in this book.
23. This is particularly common in stories about the "prediction" (*vyākaraṇa*) of a bodhisattva's future enlightenment. See, for example, the story of Megha and Dīpaṃkara in *Mahāvastu*, ed. Émil Senart (Paris: Société Asiatiques, 1890–1897) vol. 1, pp. 231–39, where Megha makes an offering of flowers and the flowers rise magically over the head of the Buddha. The same actions occur in the prediction of the future enlightenment of the Goddess of the Ganges in chapter 19 of *The Perfection of Wisdom in Eight Thousand Lines* (*Aṣṭasāhasrikā Prajñāpāramitā*).
24. The tears of compassion appear in verse III.296 and the tears of devotion in verse III.340.
25. P. L. Vaidya, ed., *Gaṇḍavyūha Sūtra*, Buddhist Sanskrit Texts, no. 5 (Darbhanga: Mithila Institute, 1960), pp. 368–418. The sūtra has been translated by Thomas Cleary, *The Flower Ornament Scripture*, vol. 3 (Boston: Shambhala, 1987). Luis O. Gómez comments on the story in "The Bodhisattva as Wonder-worker," in *Prajñā-*

pāramitā and Related Systems: Studies in Honor of Edward Conze, ed. Lewis Lancaster, Berkeley Buddhist Studies Series 1 (Berkeley: Berkeley Buddhist Studies Series, 1977), pp. 221–61. On the significance of the monument of Barabuḍur itself, see Luis O. Gómez and Hiram W. Woodward, Jr., eds., *Barabuḍur: History and Significance of a Buddhist Monument,* Berkeley Buddhist Studies Series 2 (Berkeley: Asian Humanities Press, 1981).

26. Bhāvaviveka mentions the *Gaṇḍavyūha Sūtra* and the "magical arrays" (*vyūha*) that arise from the body of Vairocana in his commentary on *MHK* III.333.
27. *Bodhisattvajñānādhiṣṭhānābhinirhārād āgataḥ* (Vaidya ed., p. 416).

Notes to Chapter 2

1. This point has been made forcefully by Jacques Derrida in "White Mythology: Metaphor in the Text of Philosophy," *Margins of Philosophy,* trans. Alan Bass (Chicago: University of Chicago Press, 1982).
2. "On Truth and Falsity in Their Ultramoral Sense," in *The Complete Works of Nietzsche,* ed. Oscar Levy (1909–1911; reprint ed., New York: Russell and Russell, 1964), vol. 2, p. 180; quoted by Derrida in *Margins of Philosophy,* p. 217.
3. *MHK* V.8–9: *atrocyate pramāṇaṃ naḥ sarvaṃ tāthāgataṃ vacaḥ / āptopadeśaprāmāṇyād bhadro hi pratipadyate // nāgamāntarasaṃdigdhaviparyastamatiḥ paraḥ / tasmāt tatpratipattyarthaṃ tanmṛgyo yuktimannayaḥ.*
4. Haribhadra explains that the word "progress" (*pratipatti*) means to proceed (*vartana*) through the discipline of no-apprehension (*anupalambha-yogena*) in a way that is unique to the Mahāyāna (*Ālokā,* p. 32).
5. As in *MMK* XXIV.18: "Dependent arising is what we call Emptiness. It is a dependent designation, and it alone is the middle path (*madhyamā pratipad*)."
6. Bhāvaviveka often uses the words *naya* or *nīti* in this way to refer to a distinctive approach or mode of understanding. See, for example, *MHK* III.44, 62, 114, 128, 272; IV.1, 15, 60; V.46, 88, 99. The word *naya* also plays an important role in the Jaina discussion of philosophical diversity. Umāsvāti, for example, defines the word *naya* by saying, "*Nayas* lead to, that is, they allow one to obtain, cause, enable, bring about, illuminate, grasp, and manifest, the [list of] categories that begin with the soul (*jīvādīn padārthān nayanti prāpnuvanti kārayanti sādhayanti nirvartayanti nirbhāsayanti upalambhayanti vyañjayanti nayāḥ*)." My translation of Umāsvāti is adapted from Kendall Wayne Folkert, "Two Jaina Approaches to Non-Jainas: Patterns and Implications" (Ph.D. dissertation: Harvard University, 1975), p. 26. The term *naya* is also used in the same sense in the Perfection of Wisdom Sūtras. See Edward Conze, *Materials for a Dictionary of the Prajñāpāramitā Literature* (Tokyo: Suzuki Research Foundation, 1973), s. v. *naya.*
7. It would be impossible to enumerate all the cognitive terms that involve an element of motion. Any attempt at a list would have to include not only words such as *pratipatti, pratipad,* and *pratīti* that express a sense of progress but also words such as *adhigati* and *abhisamaya* that express achievement of the goal. In some applications of the metaphor of motion, the goal has to be achieved without stopping in a particular place. See the discussion of "nirvana-without-foundation" (*apratiṣṭhita-nirvāṇa*) in *MHK* III.294.
8. The Sanskrit for this phrase and the phrases from Śaṅkara's commentary are quoted from J. L. Shastri, ed., *Brahmasūtra-śaṅkarabhāṣyam* (Delhi: Motilal Banarsidass, 1980).
9. The exact nature of the preparation suggested by the term "now" (*atha*) in the first line of the *Brahmasūtras* was a subject of considerable controversy. For one view of the question see the discussion of Śaṅkara's commentary that follows.
10. George Thibaut, trans., *The Vedānta Sūtras of Bādarāyaṇa with the Commentary of*

Śaṅkara, Sacred Books of the East, vols. 34 and 38 (Oxford: Clarendon Press, 1890–1896; reprint ed., New York: Dover Publications, 1962), vol. 1, p. 3.

11. Wendy Doniger O'Flaherty, *Dreams, Illusion, and Other Realities*, p. 128.
12. As Jonathan Culler points out in his criticism of Stanley Fish's theory of the reader in *On Deconstruction: Theory and Criticism After Structuralism* (Ithaca, N.Y.: Cornell University Press, 1982), pp. 64–83.
13. Wilhelm Halbfass has pointed out that the translation of *darśana* as "philosophy" presents a number of problems. See "Observations on Darśana," *WZKS* 23 (1979), pp. 195–203; and "Darśana, Anvīkṣikī, Philosophie," in *Indien und Europa. Perspektiven ihrer Geistigen Begegnung* (Basel: Schwabe & Coag, 1981), pp. 296–327; translated as *India and Europe: An Essay in Understanding* (Albany: State University of New York Press, 1988), pp. 263–86. I discuss some of these problems in Part Three of this book.
14. *MHK* III.1–2.
15. *MHK* III.251–52.
16. *MHK* III.296–97.
17. *Mahābhārata* XII.17.19: *prajñāprāsādam āruhya naśocyāñ śocato janān / jagatīsthān ivādristho mandabuddhīn avekṣate.*
18. Translation quoted from John Ross Carter and Mahinda Palihawadana, *The Dhammapada* (New York: Oxford University Press, 1987), p. 116. Carter and Palihawadana note that the palace of wisdom can be equated with the "divine eye" (*dibba-cakkhu*).
19. On the identification of the palace or temple with the cosmic mountain in Indian temple architecture, see Stella Kramrisch, *The Hindu Temple* (Calcutta: 1949; reprint ed., Delhi: Motilal Banarsidass, 1976), vol. 1, pp. 161–76.
20. *MHK* III.1–6.
21. Bhāvaviveka uses a series of Sanskrit synonyms, *dhī*, *mati*, and *buddhi*, rather than a single word. I have translated all of them as "intelligence."
22. The Sanskrit verses are found in Akira Yuyama, ed., *Prajñā-pāramitā-ratna-guṇa-saṃcaya-gāthā* (Cambridge: Cambridge University Press, 1976), p. 35. Gregory Schopen has made the excellent suggestion that *puṇya* ("merit") in Yuyama's edition should be emended to *paṇya* ("payment") to correspond to the Tibetan *rñan pa*. Richard Gombrich has described a similar "eye ceremony" in modern Śrī Laṅkā. See "The Consecration of a Buddhist Image," *JAS* 26 (1966), pp. 23–36. The ceremony has ancient precedent. Buddhaghosa mentions it in the fifth century C.E. and claims that it was performed in the lifetime of the emperor Aśoka.
23. *MHK* III.7. See Shotaro Iida, *Reason and Emptiness: A Study in Logic and Mysticism* (Tokyo: Hokuseido Press, 1980), p. 61.
24. The term is *dharma-pravicaya*, as in *Abhidharmakośabhāṣyam of Vasubandhu*, ed. Prahlad Pradhan, rev. Aruna Haldar, Tibetan Sanskrit Works Series, vol. 8 (Patna: Jayaswal Research Institute, 1975), p. 2.
25. The stages in the bodhisattva path are explained in detail in the translation of Bhāvaviveka's text at the end of this book.
26. *MHK* III.14–16.
27. Śaṅkara lists distinction (*viveka*) as the first of four prerequisites (*sādhana-catuṣṭaya*) for the knowledge of Brahman in his commentary on *Brahmasūtra* I.1.1. The other three are detachment (*virāga*), the combination of calmness and equanimity (*śama-dama*), and the desire for liberation (*mumukṣutva*).
28. For a discussion of the Yogācāra position in *The Distinction Between the Middle and the Extremes* (*Madhyāntavibhāga*), along with Bhāvaviveka's response, see the introduction to my "Bhāvaviveka's Critique."
29. *MMK* XXIV.8–10.
30. I have discussed some aspects of this controversy in "Bhāvaviveka and the Early Mādhyamika Theories of Language," *PEW* 28 (1978), pp. 323–37. For an outline of the divisions in the Indian Madhyamaka tradition and a summary of the available

literature, see David Seyfort Ruegg, *The Literature of the Madhyamaka School of Philosophy in India* (Wiesbaden: Otto Harrassowitz, 1981).

31. *MHK* III.21–22, 25–26.
32. It is difficult to summarize the distinction between conventional and ultimate knowledge without appearing to take sides in the complex disputes that divided the Madhyamaka school in India and later in Tibet. Tsoṅ-kha-pa (an influential Tibetan philosopher who lived in the fourteenth century) interpreted Bhāvaviveka's arguments against some of his Mahāyāna opponents to mean that someone could *search for and find* the "intrinsic identity" (*raṅ gi mtshan ñid*) of a thing conventionally. In the account Bhāvaviveka gives of his own position in chapter 3 of *MHK*, he reserves the word *analysis* (*vicāra*) for the ultimate (*paramārtha*) investigation of the "identity" (*svabhāva*) of things. In the works of Bhāvaviveka's successor Jñānagarbha, the term "no-analysis" (*avicāra*) is used as one of the defining characteristics of conventional (or relative) truth. The key to this whole discussion is to determine what the individual philosophers mean by "analysis" (or its substitutes) and how far the analysis can be extended to the realm of conventional truth. I discuss this issue in the notes to my *Jñānagarbha's Commentary on the Distinction Between the Two Truths* (Albany: State University of New York Press, 1987). For an analysis of Tsoṅ-kha-pa's interpretation, see Robert A. F. Thurman, *Tsong Khapa's Speech of Gold in the Essence of True Eloquence* (Princeton: Princeton University Press, 1984). There is a fine discussion of more recent Tibetan interpretation in Donald S. Lopez, Jr., *A Study of Svatantrika* (Ithaca, New York: Snow Lion Publications, 1987).
33. The Buddhist logician Devendrabuddhi used this argument against a later group of Mādhyamikas. For references to this and other examples of the same argument, see my *Jñānagarbha's Commentary*, pp. 86–87.
34. *Jñānagarbha's Commentary*, p. 88.
35. *MMK* XXIV.14.
36. *MHK* III.45–46.
37. *MHK* III.129. Bhāvaviveka attributes this classification of the unconditioned *dharmas* to the Vaibhāṣikas. See Iida, *Reason and Emptiness*, pp. 220–21.
38. *MHK* III.215–23.
39. *MHK* III.247–50.
40. *Majjhima-Nikāya*, ed. V. Trenckner (London: Pali Text Society, 1888), vol. 1, pp. 190–91.
41. *MHK* III.242, 244–46, 251–58.
42. *MHK* III.263.
43. On the life of Śāntideva, see J. W. de Jong, "La légende de Śāntideva," *IIJ* 16 (1975), pp. 161–82.
44. Śāntideva, *Śikṣāsamuccaya*, ed. P. L. Vaidya, Buddhist Sanskrit Texts, no. 11 (Darbhanga: Mithila Institute, 1961); *Bodhicaryāvatāra of Śāntideva with the Commentary of Prajñākaramati*, ed. P. L. Vaidya, Buddhist Sanskrit Texts, no. 12 (Darbhanga: Mithila Institute, 1960).
45. *Yadā na bhāvo nābhāvo mateḥ saṃtiṣṭhate puraḥ / tadānya-gatyabhāvena nirālambā praśāmyati.* Sanskrit text found in *BCA* (Vaidya ed., p. 199).
46. *BCA* IX.36–38 (Vaidya ed., pp. 199–200). The commentator Prajñākaramati gives a useful explanation of the comparison between the form of the Buddha (*buddhabimba*) and the wishing jewel or wishing tree: "The Buddha form becomes visible just as [a wishing jewel or wishing tree] fulfills the desires of ordinary people. They [act] in accordance with [people's] capacities." What a person sees depends on a person's abilities. The Tibetan translator translates the word "form" (*bimba*) as "body" (*sku*). It is possible that Śāntideva meant to suggest that ordinary people see the Buddha as merely a "reflection" of enlightenment, as in the sūtra quoted by Candrakīrti in the *Prasannapadā*: "The Tathāgata is a reflection (*pratibimba*) of a pure, beneficial *dharma*" (p. 449).
47. The phrase is found in *MHK* III.360.

48. *Yatra dhīḥ notpadyate tad atulyaṃ tattvaṃ*. The words echo a line in the *Akṣayamatinirdeśa Sūtra: yatra jñānasyāpi apracāraḥ kaḥ punar vādo 'kṣarāṇām*. For further references see my *Jñānagarbha's Commentary*, p. 74.
49. *MHK* III.267.
50. *MHK* III.269–70, 272.
51. *MHK* III.291.
52. *MHK* III.346. The metaphor is a reminder of the received etymology of the word "Buddha." As Bhāvaviveka explains in verse 267, a Buddha is considered to be someone who has "woken up" (*prabuddha*) from the dream of ignorance. A Buddha can also be thought of as someone whose mind has "opened" (*vibuddha*) like a flower. Here the image is transformed into the active mode. A Buddha is not just someone whose mind has opened but someone who has the ability to open the minds of others.
53. Such as the hymns attributed to Nāgārjuna and Mātṛceṭa. See Christian Lindtner, *Nagarjuniana: Studies in the Writings and Philosophy of Nāgārjuna*, Indiske Studier 4 (Copenhagen: Akademisk Forlag, 1982); Christian Lindtner, "Mātṛceṭa's Praṇidhānasaptati," *Asiatische Studien* 38 (1984), pp. 100–28; and D. R. Shackleton Bailey, ed. and trans., *The Śatapañcāśatka of Mātṛceṭa* (Cambridge: Cambridge University Press, 1951).
54. *MHK* III.336–45.
55. *MHK* III.281 and 340.
56. Bhāvaviveka gives a prototype of the analytical question in *MHK* III.21–22, translated earlier.
57. See note 32.
58. *MMK* XXIV.18. Compare also *Acintyastava* 40: "Dependent arising is what you call Emptiness. The true Dharma is also like that, and so is the Tathāgata." The Sanskrit is found in Lindtner, *Nagarjuniana*, p. 152.
59. Exactly how this reengagement happens and how "real" it is becomes a topic of some concern in Mahāyāna treatments of the Buddha. See the discussion of the Buddha's Manifestation Body (*nirmāṇa-kāya*) in chapter 6.
60. In his commentary on *MMK* XVIII.5d ("conceptual diversity is stopped by Emptiness"), for example, Bhāvaviveka supplies the term "understanding" (*adhigama*) to produce a sentence that reads: "Conceptual diversity is stopped by the understanding of Emptiness." (He also reads "by Emptiness," *śūnyatayā*, rather than "in Emptiness," *śūnyatāyām*, which is found in the *textus receptus*.) I discuss the verse in "A Question of Nihilism: Bhāvaviveka's Response to the Fundamental Problems of Mādhyamika Philosophy" (Ph.D. dissertation, Harvard University, 1980), p. 216.
61. The term I am translating "philosophical nihilism" is *vitaṇḍā*. *Vitaṇḍā* is defined in *Nyāya-sūtra* I.2.3 as a form of disputation "that fails to establish a counter position" (*pratipakṣa-sthāpanā-hīno vitaṇḍā*). This was a charge to which the Madhyamaka critique was particularly vulnerable. See the note on *vitaṇḍā* in the introduction to *MHK* III.266 later in this book.
62. As in T. R. V. Murti, *The Central Philosophy of Buddhism* (London: George Allen & Unwin, 1960).
63. See, for example, Jacques Derrida, "Différance" in *Margins of Philosophy*, pp. 1–27; and "A Hegelianism Without Reserve," in *Writing and Difference*, trans. Alan Bass (Chicago: University of Chicago Press, 1978). Vincent Descombes gives a clear account of the issues at stake in Derrida's work in *Modern French Philosophy* (Cambridge: Cambridge University Press, 1980), chaps. 1 and 5.
64. The double vision is sometimes illustrated by the example of a jewel in the palm of the hand. It is possible to look at the jewel and simultaneously see both the jewel and the hand on which it rests. The image of the jewel in the hand is found in the title of one of Bhāvaviveka's lesser works, *The Jewel in the Hand* (*Karatalaratna), trans. Louis de La Vallée Poussin, *MCB* 2 (1932–1933), pp. 68–146.
65. The contrast between the Hegelian *Aufhebung* and Derrida's *différance* is discussed in Derrida's *Margins of Philosophy*, pp. 19–20.

66. Nishida Kitarō, "The Logic of the Place of Nothingness and the Religious Worldview," in *Last Writings: Nothingness and the Religious Worldview*, trans. David A. Dilworth (Honolulu: University of Hawaii Press, 1987), p. 70.
67. Nishida acknowledges his own indebtedness to D. T. Suzuki for calling his attention to the passages in the *Diamond Sūtra* that illustrate his point. As is often the case, Nishida does not set the concept of dialectic completely aside but juxtaposes it with concepts that make of it something it is not. He speaks of the "paradox" that is expressed through the "dialectic" of "is" and "is not." This is a dialectic in which there is no resolution, or a dialectic that is no dialectic.
68. As in *MMK* XXIV.1, 20.
69. Translation adapted from Lindtner, *Nagarjuniana*, pp. 154–55.
70. *MHK* III.289–90.
71. Daniel H. H. Ingalls has pointed out that Śaṅkara also knew how to use mutually contradictory and irreducible perspectives to good effect in his own teaching about Brahman. See "Śaṅkara on the Question 'Whose Is Avidyā?'" *PEW* 3 (1953), pp. 69–72.
72. Wayne C. Booth, *A Rhetoric of Irony* (Chicago: University of Chicago Press, 1974).
73. The story is told in *The Complete Works of Chuang Tzu*, trans. Burton Watson (New York: Columbia University Press, 1968), p. 49.
74. He makes this point in the commentary on *MHK* III.257.
75. In the commentary on *MHK* III.267.
76. Bhāvaviveka was aware that this pattern of analysis also made the concept of metaphor (*upacāra*) unstable, as in *MHK* VIII.35 and the commentary on *MHK* III.245–46.
77. In the commentary on *MHK* III.296.

Notes to Chapter 3

1. I use the word "landscape" rather than "geography" and speak of "sacred landscape" rather than "sacred geography" to indicate that I am talking not just about natural features of the land such as mountains and rivers but land as it is shaped by contact with human beings. John Brinckerhoff Jackson makes the cultural dimension the key in his own definition of "landscape" as "a composition of manmade or man-modified spaces to serve as infrastructure or background for our collective existence," in *Discovering the Vernacular Landscape* (New Haven: Yale University Press, 1984), p. 8. André Bareau has pointed out that most Buddhist sites were sacralized by association with traces of the Buddha. In some instances the cult of the Buddha also takes over natural sites whose sacrality predated the appearance of the Buddha. It is likely, as Bareau notes, that the four primary places of pilgrimage listed in the *Mahāparinibbāna Sutta* were associated with trees or groves that were sacred before the appearance of the Buddha. See André Bareau, "Le parinirvāṇa du Buddha et la naissance de la religion bouddhique," *BEFEO* 61 (1974), pp. 293–99.
2. Alfred Foucher, *La vie du Bouddha* (Paris: Payot, 1949), p. 18.
3. Foucher, pp. 108–9.
4. In works such as Edward J. Thomas, *The Life of the Buddha as Legend and History*, 3rd ed. rev. (London: Routledge & Kegan Paul, 1949) and the more specialized studies of Ernst Waldschmidt and André Bareau (see bibliography).
5. *Sutta-nipāta*, ed. Dines Andersen and Helmer Smith (London: Pali Text Society, 1965), p. 80; translation quoted from K. R. Norman, trans. *The Group of Discourses (Sutta-nipāta)*, vol. 1 (London: Pali Text Society, 1984), p. 76.
6. *Majjhima Nikāya*, vol. 1, pp. 487–88.
7. As in the beginning of the fourth chapter of *The Flame of Reason* where Bhāvaviveka

frames the dispute between the Mahāyāna and the Nikāya Buddhist (whom Bhāvaviveka refers to as a disciple: *śrāvaka*) about the nature of the Buddha as a dispute about the "place" (*āśraya*) where enlightenment is located.

8. Kees W. Bolle makes a similar point in "Speaking of a Place," in *Myths and Symbols: Studies in Honor of Mircea Eliade,* ed. Joseph M. Kitagawa and Charles H. Long (Chicago: University of Chicago Press, 1969), pp. 127–39. Bolle argues that Indian religion is incomprehensible without understanding the symbolic significance of specific locations. Sacred places give to the religions of India what Bolle calls "topographical religiosity."
9. Foucher, p. 19.
10. *Dīgha Nikāya* XVI.5.8. Parallel passages in other versions of the sūtra say only that faithful men and women should "recollect" (**anusmaraṇīya*) the four places. See Ernst Waldschmidt, ed., *Mahāparinirvāṇa Sūtra,* vol. 3, Abhandlung der Deutschen Akademie der Wissenschaften zu Berlin: Klasse für Sprachen, Literatur, und Kunst, 1950, no. 3 (Berlin: Akademie-Verlag, 1951), pp. 388–89.
11. James Legge, trans., *A Record of Buddhistic Kingdoms* (1886; reprint ed., New York: Paragon Book Reprint Corp. and Dover Publications, 1965), p. 68.
12. Étienne Lamotte, *Le traité de la grande vertu de sagesse de Nāgārjuna (Mahāprajñāpāramitāśāstra),* vol. 1 (1949; reprint ed., Louvain: Institut Orientaliste, 1966), pp. 176–79.
13. Beal, *Records,* vol. 2, pp. 1–13.
14. Legge, pp. 56–57. The story has obvious importance in lending the Buddha's authority to the creation of Buddha-images. It is repeated widely in Buddhist literature. See Padmanabh S. Jaini, "On the Buddha Image," in *Studies in Pali and Buddhism,* ed. A. K. Narain (Delhi: B. R. Publishing, 1979), pp. 183–88. Hsüan-tsang associates the story first with King Udayana of Kauśāmbī and only secondarily with Śrāvastī (Beal, *Records,* vol. 1, pp. 235; vol. 2, p. 4).
15. The cycle of stories associated with Sārnāth is found in *Records,* vol. 2, pp. 44–61 and in Thomas Watters, *On Yuan Chwang's Travels in India* (London: Royal Asiatic Society, 1904–1905), vol. 2, pp. 46–59.
16. *Vinaya* II.160–62.
17. *Jātaka* no. 12.
18. Watters points out that there is considerable inconsistency in the story about the prediction of Maitreya's enlightenment. The stūpa is described as being near Vārāṇasī, but the prediction is said to have taken place when the Buddha was staying at Rājagṛha.
19. *Records,* vol. 1, pp. 60–61.
20. *Records,* vol. 1, pp. 96–99.
21. *Records,* vol. 2, p. 49.
22. The largest redistribution of relics was associated with the reign of Aśoka, for example, *Records,* vol. 2, pp. 66–68. For a discussion of this aspect of Aśoka's career, see John Strong, *The Legend of King Aśoka: A Study and Translation of the Aśokāvadāna* (Princeton: Princeton University Press, 1983), pp. 109–19.
23. Here I use the word "relic" or "relics" not only to represent *śarīrāni* ("bones") or *dhātu* ("element" or "constituent") that are constituents of the Buddha's physical body, but also to mean objects that become holy by connection with the Buddha's form. John Strong suggests this expanded usage when he points out that relics are "not only the bodies, bones, or ashes of saints . . . , but also objects that they once owned and, by extension, things that were once in physical contact with them." See "Relics," in Mircea Eliade, ed., *The Encyclopedia of Religion,* vol. 12 (New York: Macmillan, 1987), pp. 275–76. When the word "relic" is applied not only to the physical remnants of the Buddha's body, but to objects that become holy by association, it comes close to the meaning of the word *caitya* (Pali *cetiya*), which could be translated by a more general term such as "holy object."

24. The word used in this classification of such "holy objects" is *caitya* (Pali *cetiya*) as in *Kaliṅgabodhi Jātaka* (*Jātaka* IV.228). A similar classification occurs in *The Questions of King Milinda* (*Milindapañho*), ed. V. Trenckner (London: Williams and Norgate, 1880), p. 341. This system of classification is discussed by Richard Gombrich in *Precept and Practice: Traditional Buddhism in the Rural Highlands of Ceylon* (Oxford: Clarendon Press, 1971), p. 105 and by Stanley Jeyaraja Tambiah, *The Buddhist Saints of the Forest and the Cult of Amulets* (Cambridge: Cambridge University Press, 1984), pp. 200–205.
25. Raoul Birnbaum, in "Thoughts on T'ang Buddhist Mountain Traditions and Their Context," *T'ang Studies* (1984), pp. 5–23, has pointed out that the journey breaks the boundaries of the standard typology of pilgrimage.
26. T. H. Barrett, "Exploratory Observations on Some Weeping Pilgrims," in *The Buddhist Forum, Volume 1, Seminar Papers 1987–1988*, ed. Tadeusz Skorupski (London: School of Oriental and African Studies, University of London, 1990), pp. 99–110.
27. Samuel Beal, trans., *The Life of Hiuen-tsiang* (London: Kegan Paul, Trench, Trübner, 1911), p. 105.
28. Stephen Owen comments on the melancholy tone of T'ang poetry in *Remembrances: The Experience of the Past in Classical Chinese Literature* (Cambridge: Harvard University Press, 1986).
29. Susan Huntington has argued persuasively that the so-called aniconic images in which the Buddha appears to be represented by a symbol, such as a pair of footprints or the tree of enlightenment, are not meant to be images of the Buddha per se but images of shrines where the focus of devotion is an object or place made sacred by the Buddha's former presence. See Susan L. Huntington, *The Art of Ancient India: Buddhist, Hindu, Jain* (New York: Weatherhill, 1985).
30. Edward Conze, trans., *The Perfection of Wisdom in Eight Thousand Lines and Its Verse Summary* (Bolinas, Calif.: Four Seasons Foundation, 1973), chaps. 30–32.
31. Conze, *Eight Thousand Lines*, p. 278.
32. The film is an episode in the series *The Long Search*, first transmitted by the British Broadcasting Corporation in 1977.
33. The episode is found in *Records*, vol. 1, pp. 93–94, and *Life*, pp. 60–63. An earlier account of the cave appears in Fa-hsien (trans. Legge), p. 39.
34. *Life*, p. 62.
35. Tambiah, *Buddhist Saints*, pp. 4–5. Tambiah adapts his analysis of signs from Arthur W. Burks, "Icon, Index, and Symbol," *Philosophy and Phenomenological Research* 9 (1949), pp. 673–89.
36. Tambiah, *Buddhist Saints*, pp. 199–200.
37. M. M. Bakhtin, *The Dialogic Imagination* (Austin: University of Texas Press, 1981), p. 84.
38. Keith Basso, "'Stalking with Stories': Names, Places, and Moral Narratives Among the Western Apache," in Stuart Plattner, ed., *Text, Play, and Story: The Construction and Reconstruction of Self and Society*, Proceedings of the American Ethnological Society, 1983, pp. 45–46.
39. It was able to have this impact not only because of its connection with the historical Buddha but also because of the place it occupied in Indian Buddhist cosmology. Hsüan-tsang repeats a tradition that the Buddha's "diamond throne" (*vajrāsana*) is the center of the trichiliomegachiliocosm (*trisāhasra-mahāsāhasralokadhātu*) and explains that all the Buddhas of the present era will attain enlightenment on the same site (*Records*, vol. 2, p. 116). Étienne Lamotte has commented on the history of this tradition in *The Teaching of Vimalakīrti*, trans. Sara Boin (London: Pali Text Society, 1976), pp. 94–96.
40. Michel Foucault, *The Order of Things*, a translation of *Les mots et les choses* (New York: Vintage Books, 1973), pp. xvii-xviii.
41. Foucault, *The Order of Things*, p. xviii.
42. Translation adapted from Lamotte, *The Teaching of Vimalakīrti*, pp. 118–19.

43. Keiji Nishitani, *Religion and Nothingness*, trans. Jan Van Bragt (Berkeley: University of California Press, 1982), p. 16.
44. *Religion and Nothingness*, p. 17.
45. *Religion and Nothingness*, p. 138.
46. The translation is adapted from my *Jñānagarbha's Commentary*, p. 101.
47. These epithets all have traditional parallels. Two of Nāgārjuna's hymns speak of the Buddha as "incomparable" and "inconceivable." The term "guide" (*nāyaka*) appears in the *Diamond Sutra* (Edward Conze, trans., *Buddhist Wisdom Books* [New York: Harper & Row, 1972], p. 63). The Tibetan term I translate as "worthy of worship" (*phyag gnas*) is obscure. It seems to refer to "a place for worship" by analogy with *phyag 'os* (*pūjya* or *vandya*). The *Diamond Sūtra* again provides a parallel: "Moreover, Subhuti, the spot of earth where this Sutra will be revealed, that spot of earth will be worthy of worship (*pūjanīya*) by the whole world with its Gods, men and Asuras, worthy of being saluted respectfully (*vandanīya*), worthy of being honoured by circumambulation" (*Buddhist Wisdom Books*, p. 56). This passage is discussed by Gregory Schopen in "The Phrase '*sa pṛthivīpradeśaś caityabhūto bhavet*' in the *Vajracchedikā*: Notes on the Cult of the Book in Mahāyāna," *IIJ* 17 (1975), pp. 157–81.
48. The Sanskrit of the passage is quoted by Candrakīrti in *Prasannapadā*, p. 539. A somewhat different version, which mentions the Buddha's "constant concentration," appears in the *Bodhicaryāvatārapañjikā* of Prajñākaramati: "Between the night in which the Tathāgata was enlightened and [the night] in which he attained parinirvana, he did not utter a single syllable. Why? The Lord was in constant concentration. Those who needed to be taught by syllables, sounds, and words heard a voice coming from the Tathāgata's mouth, from the point between his eyes, from the protuberance on his head" (*BCA*, p. 199).
49. Another Mahāyāna scriptural source for this radical conception of the Buddha's silence is *The Laṅkāvatāra Sūtra*, ed. Bunyiu Nanjio, Bibliotheca Otaniensis, vol. 1 (Kyoto: Otani University Press, 1923), pp. 142–43. A more common view is that the Buddha taught by uttering only a single syllable, as in *The Teaching of Vimalakīrti* (trans. Lamotte, pp. 11–13). The more radical doctrine that the Buddha said nothing at all is found largely in Mahāyāna philosophical literature. According to some commentators, however, it is not unknown even outside the Mahāyāna. Vasumitra and Vinītadeva report a Mahāsaṃghika position that "the Buddha never says a word because he remains in constant concentration, but beings jump for joy at the thought that he is speaking." The position is quoted in André Bareau, *Les sectes bouddhiques du petit véhicule* (Paris: École Française d'Extrême Orient, 1955), p. 60. In the fourth chapter of *The Flame of Reason*, as part of a critique of the position of the disciples (*śrāvaka*s), Bhāvaviveka treats the doctrine as a distinctive feature of the Mahāyāna.
50. *Niraupamyastava*, Sanskrit text edited by Giuseppe Tucci, "Two Hymns of the Catuḥ-stava of Nāgārjuna," *JRAS* (1932), p. 314.
51. The argument is found in the section on relative truth in my *Jñānagarbha's Commentary*, pp. 75–78.
52. For an example of some of the problems that accompanied this position in Tibetan Madhyamaka exegesis, see Donald S. Lopez, Jr., *A Study of Svātantrika* (Ithaca: Snow Lion, 1987), pp. 215–17.
53. The Sanskrit of this and the following quotations is found in the *Abhidharmakośa* (ed. Pradhan, rev. Haldar), p. 216.
54. *Triṃśikā* 26, 28–30. Sanskrit text edited by Sylvain Lévi, *Vijñaptimātratāsiddhi: Deux traités de Vasubandhu* (Paris: Bibliothèque de l'École des Hautes Études, 1925), p. 14.
55. Commentary on *MHK* V.4.
56. See Sthiramati on *Triṃśikā* 2: "Here [consciousness] is the *ālaya* because it is the place where the seeds of all defiled *dharmas* [are located]. *Ālaya* and 'place' (*sthāna*) are synonyms" (Sanskrit in Lévi, ed., *Vijñaptimātratāsiddhi*, p. 18).

57. For a more complete discussion of the "change of standpoint," see Lambert Schmithausen, *Der Nirvāṇa-Abschnitt in der Viniścayasaṃgrahaṇī der Yogācārabhūmiḥ* (Vienna: Österreichische Akademie der Wissenschaften, 1969), pp. 90–104; and *Ālayavijñāna: On the Origin and the Early Development of a Central Concept in Yogācāra Philosophy*, 2 vols., Studia Philologica Buddhica 4 (Tokyo: International Institute for Buddhist Studies, 1987).
58. *Madhyāntavibhāga* I.1: *abhūtaparikalpo 'sti dvayan tatra na vidyate / śūnyatā vidyate tv atra tasyām api sa vidyate.* Sanskrit quoted from Gadjin M. Nagao, ed., *Madhyāntavibhāga-bhāṣya* (Tokyo: Suzuki Research Foundation, 1964), p. 17.
59. *Evaṃ yad yatra nāsti tat tena śūnyam iti yathābhūtaṃ samanupaśyati yat punar atrāvaśiṣṭaṃ bhavati tat sad ihāstīti yathābhūtaṃ prajānātīty aviparītaṃ śūnyatālakṣaṇam udbhāvitaṃ bhavati* (Nagao ed., p. 17).
60. As David Seyfort Ruegg shows clearly in *La théorie du tathāgatagarbha et du gotra* (Paris: École Française d'Extrême Orient, 1969), pp. 319–25.
61. I. B. Horner, trans., *The Collection of the Middle Length Sayings (Majjhima Nikāya)*, vol. 3 (London: Pali Text Society, 1959; reprint ed., 1977), pp. 147–52.
62. *Yaṃ hi kho tattha na hoti tena taṃ suññaṃ samanupassati; yaṃ pana tattha avasiṭṭhaṃ hoti taṃ santaṃ idam atthīti pajānāti.*
63. For a review of literature on this problem see J. W. de Jong, "The Problem of the Absolute in the Madhyamaka School," *JIP* 2 (1972), pp. 1–6. Bhāvaviveka is one of the most important sources for identifying the actual points of controversy between the Yogācāra and Madhyamaka schools, as I have shown in my "Bhāvaviveka's Critique."

Notes to Chapter 4

1. Paul Demiéville expressed the point succinctly when he said, "The question of the body or bodies of the Buddha arises, in both a logical and a traditional sense, on the occasion of the parinirvana. When the Buddha was extinguished, did the community lose everything, including its reason for existence, or if it continued, how could it maintain continuity? Metaphysical nothingness can constitute a philosophy, but it cannot create a Church." (*Hōbōgirin: Dictionnaire encyclopédique du bouddhisme d'après les sources chinoises et japonaises* [Tokyo: Maison franco-japonaise, 1929–1930], s.v. *busshin*, translation mine). Paul Mus has criticized Demiéville for thinking of the question purely in doctrinal terms. He argues instead that intellectual attitudes toward the Buddha grew out of a process of "magical transposition" that made it possible for relics, texts, images, and monuments to stand for the Buddha and make present his power. See Paul Mus, *Barabudur: Esquisse d'une histoire du bouddhisme fondée sur la critique archéologique des textes* (Hanoi, 1935), vol. 2, p. 704. The question is still a lively topic of discussion, as is shown by Gregory Schopen's recent articles on the references to relics in Buddhist inscriptions.
2. As time went on, philosophers became somewhat less reticent about discussing devotional questions. Works such as Śāntideva's *Introduction to the Bodhi[sattva] Practice (Bodhi[sattva]caryāvatāra)* and Atiśa's *Lamp for the Path to Enlightenment (Bodhipathapradīpa)* weave devotional and philosophical questions together even more intimately than do the works of Bhāvaviveka.
3. *MMK* XXV.24.
4. Quoted from Bhāvaviveka's commentary on *MMK* XXV.24, in *The Lamp of Wisdom (Prajñāpradīpa)*. Tibetan trans. in *sDe-dge Tibetan Tripiṭaka bsTan-ḥgyur Preserved at the Faculty of Letters, University of Tokyo (Dbu ma)* (Tokyo, 1977–1979), vol. 2, no. 3853, pp. 120–21 (folios *Tsha* 240b-241a).
5. *MMK* XVIII.6.
6. This sentence appears in the commentary on *MHK* III.291. The full explanation is found in the translation that appears at the end of this book.

7. This is suggested by Bhāvaviveka's identification of the Tathāgata Body with what he calls the ultimate Buddha. In the commentary on *MHK* III.291, he makes the point explicit by defining the Tathāgata Body as the body that "consists of knowledge" (*jñānātmaka*).
8. *Imasmiṃ sati idaṃ hoti, imass' uppādā idaṃ upajjati. . . . Imasmim asati idaṃ na hoti, imassa nirodhā idaṃ nirujjhati.* The formula is found in the *Majjhima Nikāya*, vol. 1, pp. 262–64 and elsewhere in the Pali *suttas*. The translation is quoted from David Kalupahana, *Buddhist Philosophy: A Historical Analysis* (Honolulu: University Press of Hawaii, 1976), pp. 28–29.
9. In stating the conceptual requirements of the bodhisattva path, I have in mind the three-part summary of the bodhisattva's goal quoted at the beginning of Haribhadra's *Sphuṭārthā*: "As long as they do not fulfill their vows (*praṇidhāna-samāpti*), mature sentient beings (*sattva-paripāka*), and purify their Buddha-field (*buddha-kṣetra-pariśuddhi*), they do not perfectly realize the limit of reality (*bhūta-koṭi*)." See Samdhong Rimpoche, ed., *Ācāryaharibhadraviracitā Abhisamayālaṃkāravṛttiḥ Sphuṭārthā*, Bibliotheca Indo-Tibetica 2 (Sārnāth: Center for Higher Tibetan Studies, 1977), p. 5. These three elements do not necessarily occur together in all such literature. Lamotte cites a similar formula, however, in an appendix to *The Teaching of Vimalakīrti*: "Purifying the Buddha-fields is no other than purifying one's own mind and, by reaction, those of others. To obtain this result, the Bodhisattva should not only assemble all the bodhisattva virtues (*guṇa*) but also formulate the great vows (*mahāpraṇidhāna*). It is also said that he secures an immense buddhakṣetra through his vows (*apramāṇa-buddhakṣetrapraṇidhānaparigṛhīta*)" (p. 282).
10. *Mppś*, p. 406.
11. *BCA* IX.37–38.
12. *Madhyamakāvatāra* XII. 6–7. Tibetan translation edited by Louis de La Vallée Poussin, Bibliotheca Buddhica 9 (1907–1912; reprint ed., Osnabrück: Biblio Verlag, 1970), p. 360. Candrakīrti's introduction to these two verses states the problem of action about as concisely as it is possible to state it: "Someone who has no mind and no mental phenomena and is free from concepts cannot act. How then can [the Buddha] be the cause of actions such as you have described?"
13. *Buddha-bhūmi-sūtra and Buddha-bhūmi-vyākhyānā of Śīlabhadra*, ed. Nishio Kyōo (Tokyo: Kokusho Kankōkai, 1982), p. 70.
14. *MSA* IX.35: "Just as the knots in a piece of cloth cause it to be colored with different colors, the vows cause [the Buddha's] liberation to be colored with different kinds of knowledge." The Sanskrit text is found in S. Bagchi, ed., *Mahāyānasūtrālaṃkāra*, Buddhist Sanskrit Texts, no. 13 (Darbhanga: Mithila Institute, 1970), p. 42.
15. *MHK* I.4: *parārthodayadīkṣayā*. The Sanskrit text of chapter 1 is found in V. V. Gokhale and S. S. Bahulkar, "Madhyamakahṛdayakārikā Tarkajvālā, chapter 1," in *Miscellanea Buddhica*, ed. Christian Lindtner, Indiske Studier 5 (Copenhagen: Akademisk Forlag, 1985), pp. 76–108.
16. *MHK* I.20.
17. *MHK* III.301.
18. Śāntideva injects a similar sense of irony into the opening chapters of the *Bodhicaryāvatāra*, as I have noted in my "Gratitude to an Empty Savior: A Study of the Concept of Gratitude in Mahāyāna Buddhist Philosophy," *HR* 25 (1985), pp. 68–72.
19. Franklin Edgerton, *Buddhist Hybrid Sanskrit Dictionary* (New Haven: Yale University Press, 1953; reprint ed., Delhi: Motilal Banarsidass, 1970), s.v. *praṇidadhāti*.
20. *BCA* I.15–16c. The same distinction is found in Haribhadra's *Ālokā*, pp. 16 and 24.
21. The Sanskrit text is found in Giuseppe Tucci, ed., *Minor Buddhist Texts II*, Serie Orientale Roma 9 (Rome: Istituto Italiano per il Medio ed Estremo Oriente, 1958), pp. 192–93.
22. Helmut Eimer has edited the verse portion of the text in *Bodhipathapradīpa*, Asiatische Forschungen 59 (Wiesbaden: Otto Harrassowitz, 1978). The detailed explanation of the ritual is found in *Bodhipathapradīpapañjikā*, in *sDe-dge Tibetan*

Tripiṭaka bsTan-ḥgyur Preserved at the Faculty of Letters, University of Tokyo (Dbu ma) (Tokyo, 1977–1979), vol. 16, no. 3948, p. 125 (folio *Khi* 249a).

23. Translation quoted from *A Lamp for the Path and Commentary by Atīśa*, trans. Richard Sherburne, S. J. (London: Allen & Unwin, 1983), p. 43.
24. Stephan Beyer, *The Cult of Tārā: Magic and Ritual in Tibet* (Berkeley: University of California Press, 1978), pp. 29–33.
25. The *Ugradattaparipṛcchā* is cited in Śāntideva's *Śikṣāsamuccaya* (Vaidya ed., p. 152); also the *Vinaya-viniścaya-upāli-paripṛcchā*, ed. and trans. Pierre Python, O.P. (Paris: Adrien-Maisonneuve, 1973), p. 107. The *Śikṣāsamuccaya* contains a fine description of The Three Groups as they were known to Śāntideva: "[Verse:] 'One should always, devoutly keep the observance (*vidhi*) of good conduct (*bhadracaryā*) beginning with praise (*vandana*).' [Text:] For the *Ugradattaparipṛcchā* says that someone who is pure and has put on pure clothes should perform The Three Groups three times during the day and three times at night. Here the so-called confession of sins, rejoicing in the merit [of others], and invocation (*adhyeṣaṇa*) of Buddhas constitute The Three Groups, because they [lead to] the accumulation of merit. Here [in The Three Groups] praise [of the Buddhas] is included in the confession of sins. This is because confession is preceded by homage to the Buddhas in the *Upāli-paripṛcchā* [*Sūtra*]. Petitionary prayer (*yācana*) and invocation (*adhyeṣaṇa*) have the same meaning. Worship (*pūjā*), however, is not mentioned because it lacks power and thus is impermanent. Mental and spoken [worship] are not mentioned because they are well known in other sūtras. The fact that these three are mentioned shows their importance. Here [in the verse] praise means to say 'I do homage to all the Buddhas'" (Vaidya ed., p. 152). The passage goes on to describe the confession of sins and the act of worship (*pūjā*) in more detail, then it takes up the ten great vows (*praṇidhāna*) in the *Daśabhūmika Sūtra* and closes the chapter with a brief discussion of the transfer of merit (*pariṇāmanā*). For further discussion of The Three Groups, see Pierre Python, "Le rituel du culte mahāyānique et le traité tibétain *'phags pa Phuṅ po gsum pa* (sanscrit: *Ārya-Triskandhaka*)," *Asiatische Studien* 35 (1981), pp. 169–83.
26. The list of seven does not seem to have had a standard form. For some of the variants, see Christian Lindtner, "Mātṛceṭa's *Praṇidhānasaptati*," p. 105; and *Vinaya-viniścaya-upāli-paripṛcchā* (Python ed.), p. 98.
27. I suspect that this could be said of much more Mahāyāna literature than is generally recognized.
28. *Ratnāvalī* V.65. The translation is quoted from Nāgārjuna and the Seventh Dalai Lama, *The Precious Garland and the Song of the Four Mindfulnesses*, trans. Jeffrey Hopkins and Lati Rinpoche (London: Allen & Unwin, 1975), p. 87. The Tibetan text of the verse can be found in *Nāgārjuna's Ratnāvalī*, ed. Michael Hahn (Bonn: Indica et Tibetica, 1982), p. 155.
29. The vows play this role in *Ratnāvalī* V.65ff. and in another influential text known as "The Vow of the Practice of Samantabhadra" (*Samantabhadracaryāpraṇidhāna*). This text appears in the last chapter of the *Gaṇḍavyūha Sūtra* (Vaidya ed., pp. 420–36) and was widely distributed as a text in its own right. See, for example, Jes Peter Asmussen, ed. and trans., *The Khotanese Bhadracaryādeśanā*. Historisk-filosofiske Meddelelser Det Kongelige Danske Videnskabernes Selskab 39, no. 2 (Copenhagen, 1961). Recitation of the text played a key role in Atiśa's ceremony for the generation of the mind of enlightenment.
30. *Ratnāvalī* IV.90: "The bodhisattva vow and the transfer of merit are not mentioned in the disciple vehicle" (Hahn ed., p. 126).
31. Gombrich, *Precept and Practice*, pp. 217–26.
32. Conze trans., p. 286. The "act of truth," of course, is not just an ancient tradition. Gandhi used it to significant effect in the *satyagraha* campaigns that he referred to as his "experiments with truth."

33. This is a comparison I have explored in my "Gratitude to an Empty Savior," p. 65. Yuichi Kajiyama has suggested that it would be better to think of the vow as a flower rather than a stone. This variation adds further levels of meaning and resonates more deeply with traditional Buddhist images of the Buddha. See, for example, Étienne Lamotte, "Lotus et Buddha supramondain," *BEFEO* 69 (1981), pp. 31–44.
34. As in the story of Śāriputra and the goddess in *The Teaching of Vimalakīrti*, where the actions of the goddess are attributed to the power of a previous vow (Lamotte trans., p. 172).
35. Such as the list of the ten "great vows" in the first chapter of the *Daśabhūmika Sūtra*, ed. P. L. Vaidya, Buddhist Sanskrit Texts, no. 7 (Darbhanga: Mithila Institute, 1967), pp. 9–10. These are quoted and discussed at the end of the chapter on "The Observance of Good Conduct" (*bhadracaryāvidhi*) in Śāntideva's *Śikṣāsamuccaya*.
36. *Sukhāvatīvyūha* (*vistaramātṛkā*), ed. P. L. Vaidya. In *Mahāyāna-sūtra-saṃgraha*, Buddhist Sanskrit Texts, no. 17, part 1 (Darbhanga: Mithila Institute, 1961), pp. 221–53.
37. *Saddharmapuṇḍarīka Sūtra*, ed. P. L. Vaidya, Buddhist Sanskrit Texts, no. 6 (Darbhanga: Mithila Institute, 1960), pp. 149–50.
38. The word is *vigraha*, which can mean "individual form or shape" or simply "body."
39. It seems clear from the context that the "body" is revealed (*udghāṭita*), not the stūpa.
40. Vaidya ed., p. 150.
41. *Bahukalpakoṭīnayutaśatasahasraparinirvṛtaṃ tathā bhāṣamāṇaṃ dṛṣṭvā* (Vaidya ed., p. 153). It is painfully obvious in passages like this how much we need a verb to go with the noun "parinirvana." Literally Prabhūtaratna has been "parinirvanized."
42. Unlike the sections in chapter 15 where the Buddha speaks of his nirvana as being an "expedient device."
43. *MMK* XXIV.14.
44. On the use of the term *nirmāṇa* in non-Buddhist literature see Gopinath Kaviraj, "Nirmāṇakāya," *The Princess of Wales Saraswati Bhavana Studies* 1 (1922), pp. 47–58.
45. Nāgārjuna's *Vigrahavyāvartanī*, ed. E. H. Johnston and A. Kunst, *MCB* 9 (1948–1951), pp. 99–152. The objection is raised in the commentary on verse 2, and the reply is given in the commentary on verses 22–23. The work has been translated by Kamaleswar Bhattacharya, "The Dialectical Method of Nāgārjuna," *JIP* 1 (1971), pp. 217–261.
46. Lamotte, *The Teaching of Vimalakīrti*, p. 153.
47. *Dīgha Nikāya* II.209–12.
48. Brahmā's manifestations are similar to Nāgārjuna's "magical creations." The Pali word used to express Brahmā's act of "manifestation" is *abhinimminitvā*, a derivative of the same root that produces the Sanskrit words *nirmita* and *nirmāṇa*. The story is echoed in Mahāyāna form in *RGV* IV.53–4: "Without moving from Brahmā's place, Brahmā effortlessly manifests [his own] appearance everywhere in the dwelling of the gods. Similarly, the Buddha effortlessly appears to fortunate beings with manifestations (*nirmāṇa*) in all realms, without moving from the Dharma Body." In his translation of the *Dīgha Nikāya*, T. W. Rhys Davids suggests that the Pali story of Brahmā's manifestations was a model for the understanding of the Buddha in Mahāyāna and proto-Mahāyāna literature.
49. *Dīgha Nikāya* I.77. The translation is adapted from T. W. Rhys Davids, trans., *Dialogues of the Buddha* (1899; reprint ed., London: Pali Text Society, 1977), vol. 1, pp. 87–88.
50. Translation adapted from *Dialogues of the Buddha*, vol. 1, pp. 88–89.
51. *Paṭisambhidāmagga*, ed. Arnold C. Taylor (London: Pali Text Society, 1905–1907), vol. 2, pp. 205–14.
52. *Kośa* VII.48. The same division is observed, with somewhat different terminology, in *The Bodhisattva Stages* (*Bodhisattvabhūmi*), a work that is attributed to Asaṅga. See *Bodhisattvabhūmi*, ed. Nalinaksha Dutt, Tibetan Sanskrit Works Series, vol. 7

(Patna: Jayaswal Research Institute, 1966), p. 40. In this text, the power of "movement" is called the power of "transformation" (*pariṇāma*).

53. *MHK* III.324–29.
54. *MHK* III.336–43.
55. *Paṭisambhidāmagga*, vol. 2, p. 207.
56. The story is told in *Visuddhimagga of Buddhaghosācariya*, ed. Henry Clarke Warren, Harvard Oriental Series, vol. 41 (Cambridge: Harvard University Press, 1950), pp. 326–27.
57. The verse is found in *Niddesa I: Mahāniddesa*, ed. L. de La Vallée Poussin and E. J. Thomas (London: Pali Text Society, 1916–1917), vol. 2, p. 505.
58. The verse is found in *The Thera- and Therīgāthā*, ed. Hermann Oldenberg (London: Pali Text Society, 1883), p. 59.
59. *The Atthasālinī*, ed. Edward Müller (London: Pali Text Society, 1897), p. 16.
60. See chapter 3.
61. *MHK* III.325–26.
62. *DBh*, p. 62 and *BBh*, p. 64.
63. This is a summary of the meanings listed in V. S. Apte's *Sanskrit-English Dictionary*, 2 vols. (Poona: Prasad Prakashan, 1957).
64. The second half of *Gītā* IV.6 reads: *prakṛtiṃ svām adhiṣṭhāya saṃbhavāmy ātmamāyayā*. Śaṅkara glosses *adhiṣṭhāya* as *vaśīkṛtya* ("take control of"). See *The Bhagavadgītā with the Commentary of Śrī Śaṅkarācārya*, ed. Dinkar Vishnu Gokhale, 2nd ed. (Poona: Oriental Book Agency, 1950), p. 65.
65. *Kiñcic ca nirmāṇam adhitiṣṭhati yad uparate 'pi bodhisattve tathāgate vā 'nuvartata eva* (*BBh*, p. 45).
66. It is introduced in the commentary on VII.34 and taken up in detail in VII.48ff. The subcommentator Yaśomitra makes the distinction between these three aspects clear when he defines manifestation (*nirmāṇa*) as "generating an external object that has not existed before," and sustaining (*adhiṣṭhāna*) as "maintaining for a long time." See *Abhidharmakośa and Bhāṣya of Acharya Vasubandhu with Sphuṭārthā Commentary of Ācārya Yaśomitra*, ed. Swami Dwarikadas Shastri (Varanasi: Bauddha Bharati, 1970–1973), vol. 4, p. 1097.
67. Vasubandhu takes up the question of *adhiṣṭhāna* as a way of responding to a question about the uniqueness of the Buddha's *nirmāṇas*. In verse VII.51 he argues that the *nirmāṇas* of ordinary saints can only speak when the saints themselves are speaking, but the Buddha is capable of using *adhiṣṭhāna* so that the *nirmāṇa* can continue to speak when the Buddha himself is silent. The question in verse 52 is whether this *adhiṣṭhāna* can continue after death.
68. In the translation I have combined verse VII.52a and its commentary. In verse 52b, Vasubandhu reports the opinion of "others" who argued that Mahākāśyapa's *adhiṣṭhāna* was not sufficient to sustain the existence of his bones and who said instead that the bones had to be sustained by the power of deities.
69. On the legend of Mahākāśyapa, see chapter 1.
70. *Yatas Tathāgatādhiṣṭhāna-deśanāyāṃ taddeśanāvat tat-sāmarthyenānyataḥ śravaṇe 'pi Bhagavata eva sakāśāc-chravaṇam* (*Ālokā*, p. 6).
71. "Sustaining power" is the term that Conze uses most frequently for *adhiṣṭhāna* in his translations of the Perfection of Wisdom literature. See Edward Conze, *Materials for a Dictionary of the Prajñāpāramitā Literature* (Tokyo: Suzuki Research Foundation, 1973), s.v. *adhiṣṭhāna*.
72. *Gaṇḍavyūha Sūtra*, p. 408.
73. *The Teaching of Vimalakīrti*, p. 116.
74. *The Teaching of Vimalakīrti*, p. 170.
75. Conze trans., p. 159. The term *parigraha* carries a sense of physical sustenance or "upholding" and can be used to refer to both the Buddha's "sustenance" and the "sustenance" of a teacher. At the beginning of chapter 10, those who are capable of hearing the Perfection of Wisdom are those who have been "sustained by precep-

tors" (*kalyāṇamitra-parigṛhīta*). In his commentary on the passage, Haribhadra explains that they are "sustained" in the sense that they are "supported by *adhiṣṭhāna*" (*Ālokā*, p. 460).

76. Conze trans., p. 286.

Notes to Chapter 5

1. Susan Sontag, *On Photography* (New York: Dell Publishing, 1977), p. 180.
2. The distinction between the Form Body and the Dharma Body is not found explicitly in the earliest strata of the Pali canon, although it is suggested by a number of important canonical passages. For a discussion of the development of the concept in canonical literature, see Louis de La Vallée Poussin, "Studies in Buddhist Dogma: The Three Bodies of a Buddha (*trikāya*)," *JRAS* (1906), pp. 943–77; Gadjin Nagao, "On the Theory of the Buddha-body (*Buddha-kāya*)," *The Eastern Buddhist*, N.S. 6 (1973), pp. 25–53; and Frank Reynolds, "The Several Bodies of Buddha: Reflections on a Neglected Aspect of Theravada Tradition," *HR* 6 (1977), pp. 374–89.
3. Conze trans., pp. 105–8.
4. Comparisons between different kinds of worship are common in Buddhist literature and are not limited to texts that support worship of the Perfection of Wisdom. The *Āryāvalokana Sūtra*, quoted in Śāntideva's *Śikṣāsamuccaya* (Vaidya ed., p. 156), contains a similar passage that promotes the worship of stūpas: "Someone who honors a stūpa at the end of this *kalpa*, in this horrible time, gains more merit than someone who honors hundreds of thousands of *nayuta*s of *koṭi*s of Buddhas for a similar number of *kalpas*." Another sūtra promotes worship of the Buddha in paintings and books: "O Mañjuśrī, a son or daughter of good family might give food with a thousand flavors and pleasant clothes every day to solitary Buddhas as numerous as the sands in the whole world system and continue to give these things for *kalpas* as numerous as the sands of the Ganges. But another son or daughter of good family, O Mañjuśrī, who sees the Buddha painted in a painting or represented in a book (*pustakakarmakṛta*) would gain infinitely more merit. How much more so someone who made a gesture of folded hands, offered flowers, or offered incense, perfume, or a lamp. He would gain infinitely more merit still" (*Śraddhābalādhānāvatāramudrā Sūtra*, quoted in Śāntideva's *Śikṣāsamuccaya*, Vaidya ed., p. 165).
5. Gregory Schopen, "The Phrase '*sa pṛthivīpradeśaś caityabhūto bhavet*' in the *Vajracchedikā*: Notes on the Cult of the Book in Mahāyāna," *IIJ* 17 (1975), pp. 147–81.
6. Archaeological evidence for the substitution of scriptural phrases for relics in stūpas is common from the time of Bhāvaviveka on. See W. Zwalf, ed., *Buddhism Art and Faith* (London: British Museum Publications, 1985), pp. 108–9. There is scriptural evidence for this substitution in the *Ārya-pratītyasamutpāda-nāma-mahāyāna Sūtra*. The sūtra transforms a common phrase about the merit that comes from erecting a stūpa with a relic (*śarīra*) of the Tathāgata into a statement about a stūpa containing a verse about the Dharma Element. The sūtra equates the Dharma Element (*dhātu*) with dependent arising (*pratītya-samutpāda*), which is a common summary of the Buddha's teaching. The substitution gains force from ambiguity in the meaning of the word "element" (*dhātu*): *dhātu* can also mean "relic." For a discussion of this sūtra, see Gregory Schopen and Richard Salomon, "The Indravarman (Avaca) Casket Inscription Reconsidered: Further Evidence for Canonical Passages in Buddhist Inscriptions," *JIABS* 7 (1984), pp. 117–18.
7. The text mentions a Buddha relic, a Dharma relic, and a Saṃgha relic. In his commentary on this passage, Haribhadra explains that the Buddha relic consists of the various Buddha Bodies, the Dharma relic consists of the sūtras, and the Saṃgha relic consists of the congregation of bodhisattvas (*Ālokā*, p. 211).
8. *Aṣṭasāhasrikā Prajñāpāramitā* (Vaidya ed.), p. 29.

9. Edward Conze, trans., *The Large Sutra on Perfect Wisdom* (Berkeley: University of California Press, 1975), pp. 37–44. See also Lamotte, *Mppś*, pp. 518–19. The term *āsecanakātmabhāva* is reflected in Mātṛceṭa's description of the Buddha's form: "Because it never satiates the beholder (*āsecanakabhāvād*) and because of its mild aspect your body gives fresh delight as often as it is seen" (*Śatāpañcāśatka*, ed. D. R. Shackleton Bailey, pp. 73, 162).
10. See, for example, the word *vigraha* ("form" or "body") in chapter 4, note 38 and the word *bimba* ("form" or "reflection") in chapter 2, note 46.
11. The meanings of the word *dharma* (Pali, *dhamma*) have been widely studied. For a review of the literature, see John Ross Carter, *Dhamma: Western Academic and Sinhalese Buddhist Interpretations—A Study of a Religious Concept* (Tokyo: Hokuseido Press, 1978). Andrew Rawlinson comments on the general ambiguity in the Sanskrit words for "body" in "The Position of the *Aṣṭasāhasrikā Prajñāpāramitā* in the Development of Early Mahāyāna," in *Prajñāpāramitā and Related Systems: Studies in Honor of Edward Conze*, ed. Lewis Lancaster, Berkeley Buddhist Studies Series 1 (Berkeley: Berkeley Buddhist Studies Series, 1977), p. 30.
12. Edward Conze gives an account of this commentarial tradition in *The Perfection of Wisdom Literature*, 2nd ed. (Tokyo: Reiyukai, 1978).
13. *Prajñāpāramitā jñānam advayaṃ sā tathāgataḥ / sādhyā tādarthyayogena tācchabdyaṃ granthamārgayoḥ*. The Sanskrit text is found in Giuseppe Tucci, "Minor Sanskrit Texts on the Prajñā-pāramitā: 1. The Prajñā-pāramitā-piṇḍārtha of Diṅnāga," *JRAS* (1947), p. 56. The word *artha* should be taken in two senses, as the "meaning" of the book and the "goal" of the path.
14. *Mukhyā buddho bhagavān māyopamaṃ jñānam advayam. tatprāptyanukūlatvena tu padavākyasamūho grantho darśanādilakṣaṇo mārgaś ca gauṇī prajñāpāramitā* (*Ālokā*, p. 23).
15. *Kośa* VIII.39ab: *saddharmo dvividhaḥ śāstur āgamādhigamātmakaḥ*.
16. In the commentary on VI.66cd, Vasubandhu says, "The path is referred to as 'the auxiliaries of enlightenment.'" The reason for this identification is explained in detail in Lamotte, *Mppś*, pp. 1119ff.
17. *Kośa* IV.32. On Vasubandhu's explanation of refuge in the Buddha, see chapter 3 in this book.
18. *RGV* I.20–21.
19. *Adhigamadharmo hetuphalabhedena dvividhaḥ / yaduta mārgasatyaṃ nirodhasatyaṃ ca / yena yad adhigamyata iti kṛtvā* (Johnston ed., pp. 18–19).
20. See the commentary that follows *MHK* III.292.
21. *RGV* I.21: "The ultimate refuge of the world is the Buddha alone. This is because the Buddha is the Dharma Body and the Saṃgha has this [Dharma Body] as its final goal." The first half of the verse uses the word "Buddhahood" or "Buddha Nature" (*buddhatva*) rather than "Buddha," but the commentary explains that "Buddhahood" refers to the Tathāgatas, the Arhants, the perfectly enlightened Buddhas.
22. *RGV* I.145.
23. *Suviśuddhaś ca dharmadhātur avikalpajñānagocaraviṣayaḥ* (emend Johnston's *dharmadhātor* to *dharmadhātur*).
24. *MV* I.14: *tathatā bhūtakoṭiś cānimittaṃ paramārthatā / dharmadhātuś ca paryāyāḥ śūnyatāyāḥ samāsataḥ*.
25. Commentary on the preceding verse.
26. As in the dedicatory verse of Nāgārjuna's *MMK* (*Prasannapadā*, p. 3) and *MMK* XXIV.18. The identification of the Buddha with no-arising (*anutpāda*) appears in Bhāvaviveka's definition in *MHK* III.267. For scriptural references, see the notes on this verse in the translation at the end of this book.
27. For an Indian expression of this common Mahāyāna claim, see *MMK* XXII.16: "The nature (*svabhāva*) of the Tathāgata is the nature of the world; the Tathāgata has no nature (*niḥsvabhāva*), and the world has no nature." See also *MSA* IX.4: "All *dharmas* are the Buddha Nature (*buddhatva*), and there is no *dharma* at all."

28. *Anutpādadharmaḥ satataṃ tathāgataḥ sarve ca dharmāḥ sugatena sādṛśāḥ* (*Prasannapadā*, p. 449). The verse is quoted by Bhāvaviveka in the commentary on *MHK* III.239. Sthiramati quotes it in the commentary on *MSA* IX.4. For other references see Lindtner, "Atiśa's Introduction," pp. 176, 204.
29. *Laṅkāvatāra Sūtra* (Nanjio ed.), p. 143. Read *vartma* for *vanme.*
30. Verse I.16. Compare also *RGV* I.30, which substitutes the image of a jewel (*ratna*) for the image of gold. The Dharma Element as "cause" (*hetu*) is explained in the commentary on *RGV* I.149–152.
31. There is a discussion of a jewel buried in mud in the commentary on *RGV* I.68. In addition to being defiled by clouds or smoke, as in Asaṅga's commentary on *RGV* I.155, space can appear to be limited by a pot or a piece of cloth, as in *MSA* IX.15.
32. *MSA* IX.82–85.
33. *RGV* I.152cd: "Because it is like a reflection, the manifestation [of the Buddha] is like a gold image."
34. *Anādikāliko dhātuḥ sarvabījasamāśrayaḥ / tasmin sati gatiḥ sarvā nirvānādhigamo 'pi vā.* The verse is quoted in Sthiramati's commentary on the *Triṃśikā* (Levi ed., p. 37) and in Asaṅga's commentary on *RGV* I.149–152.
35. He quotes the verse as part of his critique of Yogācāra thought in both *The Lamp of Wisdom* and *The Flame of Reason.* See my "Bhāvaviveka's Critique," p. 55.
36. See chapter 3, note 57.
37. As in *MSA* IX.60 and *MS* (Lamotte ed., p. 83).
38. Lamotte comments on the different meanings of the *bodhimaṇḍa* in *The Teaching of Vimalakīrti,* pp. 94–96. Some of the speculation flows from an ambiguity in the meaning of the word *maṇḍa.* The word can be interpreted either as the "place" where enlightenment occurs or as the "essence" of enlightenment itself. See, for example, Haribhadra's explanation of the term *bodhimaṇḍa*: "The *bodhimaṇḍa* on which [the Buddha] sat is a spot of earth that is so named because the essence (*maṇḍa*) or core (*sāra*) of enlightenment is present there" (*Ālokā*, p. 206). The discussion of the *bodhimaṇḍa* was broadened by some authors to include discussion of the Buddha's enlightenment in Akaniṣṭha Heaven, an enlightenment that was then manifested here in this world. For a more detailed discussion of this tradition, see the commentary on the Buddha's Enjoyment Body in chapter 6.
39. *MSA* IX.2 and 5.
40. *MSA* IX.13. Compare Bhāvaviveka's description of the bodhisattva in *MHK* III.294–296.
41. *Sūtrālaṃkāravṛttibhāṣya* (*Mdo sde rgyan gyi 'grel bśad*), in *sDe-dge Tibetan Tripiṭaka bsTan-ḥgyur Preserved at the Faculty of Letters, University of Tokyo (Sems-tsam)* (Tokyo: 1979–1981), vol. 3, no. 4034, p. 56 (folio *Mi* 114b).
42. See chapter 2, note 60.
43. *MSA* IX.27cd-29. Bhāvaviveka elaborates this image of the Dharma Body in his closing account of the Buddha in *MHK* III.346ff.
44. *AA* VIII.10 as explained in Haribhadra's commentary (*Sphuṭārthā*, p. 84).
45. *MSA* IX.33–34.
46. *RGV* IV.44–45.
47. See also *MSA* IX.18–21 and Asaṅga's commentary on *RGV* I.25.
48. This illustration was discussed in the section on the Buddha's previous vows in chapter 4.
49. *BCA* IX.36. The verse is discussed in chapter 2.
50. Bhāvaviveka sometimes uses the two-part formula and sometimes expands it to three. In his commentary on *MMK* XXV.24, he says that people hear the Tathāgata's voice as a result of three factors. There are the inclinations, faculties, and dispositions of the listeners themselves; there are the previous vows of the bodhisattva who became the Buddha; and there are "the roots of virtue" that the listeners accumulated when they were influenced by the Buddha (or the bodhisattva who was to become the Buddha) in previous lives. The last element in this three-part formula

deals neatly with the question of whether someone has to earn the Dharma or whether it can be granted by the power of the Buddha. Truly to hear the Dharma takes the right moral preparation, but this preparation depends as much on the influence of the bodhisattva working through the people who hear it as it does on their own action. For the reference to the Tibetan text, see chapter 4, note 4.

51. *Suvarṇaprabhāsa Sūtra*, ed. S. Bagchi, Buddhist Sanskrit Texts Series, no. 8 (Darbhanga: Mithila Institute, 1967), chap. 2; English translation by R. E. Emmerick, *The Sūtra of Golden Light*, Sacred Books of the Buddhists, vol. 27 (London: Pali Text Society, 1970; reprint ed., 1979).
52. *sDe-dge Tibetan Tripiṭaka bsTan-ḥgyur Preserved at the Faculty of Letters, University of Tokyo (Dbu ma)*, vol. 3, no. 3856, p. 78 (folio *Dza* 156a).
53. Bhāvaviveka adds this to the same list of objections that contained the objection about the Buddha's permanence: "To say that the Buddha has not attained nirvana contradicts the third seal of the Dharma by saying that there is no peace."
54. Such as *The Lotus Sūtra* and *The Sūtra of Golden Light*. See *Saddharmapuṇḍarīka Sūtra* (Vaidya ed.), chap. 15; and *Suvarṇaprabhāsa Sūtra*, chap. 2.
55. *Saddharmapuṇḍarīka Sūtra* (Vaidya ed., p. 190).
56. See chapter 4, note 37.
57. Translation quoted from Emmerick, *The Sūtra of Golden Light*, p. 5.
58. This is the conclusion that the author of the *Mahāprajñāpāramitāśāstra* comes to in his discussion of the term "eternal" (*Mppś*, pp. 2335–41).
59. Vaidya ed., p. 233.
60. *MHK* III.275.
61. The language is also shared by *AA* VIII.33: "[The body] by which he brings various benefits to living beings without interruption as long as there is samsara is the Manifestation Body of the Sage."
62. *MSA* IX.66cd.

Notes to Chapter 6

1. *Parārthāv eva me dharmarūpakāyāv iti tvayā / duṣkuhasyāsya lokasya nirvāṇe 'pi vidarśitam // tathā hi satsu saṃkrāmya dharmakāyam aśeṣataḥ / tilaśo rūpakāyaṃ ca bhittvāsi parinirvṛtaḥ.* Translation adapted from D. R. Shackleton Bailey, ed. and trans., *The Śatapañcāśatka of Mātṛceṭa*, p. 179.
2. *Ratnāvalī* III.10 and 12. The Tibetan text is edited by Michael Hahn, *Nāgārjuna's Ratnāvalī*, pp. 73–74.
3. As in the commentary on *MHK* III.291.
4. See chapter 4, note 4.
5. In this respect his terminology is close to the terminology of *The Teaching of Vimalakīrti*, where it says: "Friends (*sakhi*), the body of the Tathāgata (*tathāgata-kāya*) is the body of the Law (*dharmakāya*)" (Lamotte trans., pp. 38–39). Other parallels with *The Teaching of Vimalakīrti* are noted below.
6. Lamotte trans., pp. 238ff.
7. As in the doctrine of three Buddha Bodies discussed later.
8. In the commentary on III.291, Bhāvaviveka mentions Vajrasena's use of the term Fruition Body (*vipāka-kāya*) to refer to an aspect of the Form Body. In the theory of the Sarvāstivādins, the Fruition Body is equated with the Birth Body (*janma-kāya*). For an account of the Sarvāstivādin theory, see *Vijñaptimātratāsiddhi: Le Siddhi de Hiuan-tsang*, ed. and trans. Louis de La Vallée Poussin (Paris: Librairie Orientaliste Paul Geuthner, 1928–1929), pp. 766–73.
9. "In the word *paramārtha*, the word *artha* means an object of knowledge (*jñeya*). It refers to an object that someone investigates and understands. The word *parama* means supreme. The compound *paramārtha* [as a *karmadhāraya* compound] can

mean ultimate object, in the sense that it is both ultimate and an object. Or [as a *tatpuruṣa* compound] it can mean the object of the ultimate, in the sense that it is the object of nonconceptual knowledge, which is the ultimate. Or [as a *bahuvrīhi* compound] it can mean [the cognition] that is consistent with the ultimate object. [Such a cognition] is consistent with the ultimate object because it is the insight (*prajñā*) that is consistent with the ultimate object and possesses the ultimate object. When we say 'ultimately' (*paramārthena*), it is this [third] *paramārtha* that we mean." The Tibetan of the passage is found in Iida's *Reason and Emptiness*, pp. 82–83. The translation is mine. It is quoted with further explanation in my *Jñānagarbha's Commentary*, pp. 71–72.

10. *Jñānagarbha's Commentary*, p. 71.
11. Bhāvaviveka explains this distinction early in the third chapter of *The Flame of Reason*: "The ultimate is of two kinds: The first is effortless, transcendent, free from impurity, and free from discursive ideas. The second is accessible to effort, consistent with the prerequisites of merit and knowledge, pure, referred to as 'ordinary knowledge,' and accessible to discursive ideas." The Tibetan text is found in Iida's *Reason and Emptiness*, p. 86. The translation is mine.
12. *Jñānagarbha's Commentary*, p. 71.
13. I am adapting this particular comment about the conceptual ultimate from Jñānagarbha's account of the "expressible ultimate." Jñānagarbha uses "reason" (*nyāya*) more explicitly as a defining characteristic of the ultimate, although it is not a characteristic with which Bhāvaviveka would disagree.
14. *Jñānagarbha's Commentary*, p. 87.
15. *MHK* III.267.
16. This definition of the Buddha is found in Nāgārjuna's *Acintyastava* 41: *tadbodhād buddha ucyate* (Lindtner, *Nagarjuniana*, p. 154).
17. Conze trans., p. 291. This formula is echoed in turn several centuries later by Haribhadra in his definition of the Buddha's Essential Body as the "essence" that is identical to no-arising.
18. *Ālokā*, p. 23.
19. Bhāvaviveka is using a distinction that is common in Indian theories of meaning. See K. Kunjunni Raja, *Indian Theories of Meaning* (Madras: Adyar Library and Research Centre, 1963), chap. 6.
20. Bhāvaviveka's commentary is actually a bit more complicated than this. He mentions an opponent who complains about the idea that a word can be used to refer to its own opposite: "Using 'understanding' as a metaphor for no-understanding is like using 'fire' as a metaphor for water." Bhāvaviveka replies, "It is not this kind of metaphor because there is no [understanding] other than this [no-understanding], just as [there is no self] when consciousness is called 'self.'"
21. *Buddher vikasanād buddhaḥ, vibuddha ity arthaḥ / vibuddhaṃ padmiti yathā / atha vā avidyānidrādvayāpagamād buddhaḥ, prabuddha ity arthaḥ* (Dwarikadas Shastri, ed., *Abhidharmakośa & Bhāṣya of Acharya Vasubandhu with Sphuṭārthā Commentary of Ācārya Yaśomitra* [Varanasi: Bauddha Bharati, 1970], p. 5). There seem to be at least two mistakes in the printing: *vikasanād* should be read as *vikāsanād* and *padmiti* as *padmīti*.
22. *MHK* III.268.
23. *Laṅkāvatāra Sūtra* (Nanjio ed.), p. 269.
24. *MHK* III.273–79.
25. *MHK* III.280–81.
26. *MHK* III.286.
27. *MHK* III.288.
28. *MHK* III.291.
29. *MHK* III.346.
30. The words in the two verses are almost identical, although they occur in a different order: *nirmāṇair vāpi bhavyānāṃ buddhyambujavibodhanāt.*

31. *MHK* III.356–59.
32. *Laṅkāvatāra Sūtra* X.38ab, 39cd: *akaniṣṭhabhavane divye sarvapāpavivarjite / tatra budhyanti saṃbuddhā nirmitas tv iha budhyate* (Nanjio ed., p. 269). Compare also verses II.50, 93–94; X.774. Tibetan tradition preserves an important variant reading for the second *pāda* of the verse. In Se-ra rJe-btsun-pa's scholastic manual (*yig-cha*) used to study the doctrine of the Perfection of Wisdom in the Sera Je monastery, the verse is quoted as *gtsaṅ ma'i gnas lha spaṅs pa yi // 'og min gnas ni ñams dga' ba*. This suggests a reading of **śuddhāvāsavivarjite* ("free from [the deities of] the Pure Abode") instead of *sarvapāpavivarjite* ("free from all evil"). This variant has important bearing on the placement of the Buddha's Akaniṣṭha in the structure of Buddhist cosmology (see the following note). Akaniṣṭha is treated as the seat of enlightenment (*bodhi-maṇḍa*) in the commentary on Atiśa's *Bodhipathapradīpa*, vs. 8 (Sherburne trans., p. 34), and it is mentioned by Candrakīrti in *Madhyamakāvatāra* XII.1, 5 (La Vallée Poussin ed., pp. 355, 359).
33. *Kośa* III.2, 71–72 and VI.38. The number seventeen is the number adopted by the *Kośa* itself. The commentary on III.2 indicates that the number of levels in the Form Realm was the subject of some disagreement between schools. There is a Tibetan scholastic tradition (see the reference to the Sera Je *yig-cha* in the previous note) that distinguishes between the Akaniṣṭha where the Buddha attains enlightenment and the Akaniṣṭha of "the gods of the Pure Abode." This position was based on the variant reading **śuddhāvāsavivarjite* ("free from [the gods of] the Pure Abode") for the second *pāda* of the quotation from the *Laṅkāvatāra Sūtra* just noted. Apparently this variant entered the tradition after the time of Bhāvaviveka.
34. *MHK* IV.2: *nirvikalpadhiyaḥ śāstuḥ śarīraṃ nāśrayaḥ kila / śarīratvāc charīraṃ hi yathā gopasya neṣyate.*
35. Bhāvaviveka has abbreviated a more complex outline of the path in the Abhidharma tradition. See *Kośa* VI.44–45 and the discussion by Étienne Lamotte, *Histoire du bouddhisme indien: des origines à l'ère Śaka* (Louvain: Institut Orientaliste, 1958; reprint ed., 1967), pp. 683–84.
36. The doctrine is outlined by Lamotte, *Histoire*, pp. 690–93.
37. Translated by Lamotte, *Histoire*, p. 691.
38. Notably by Lamotte (*Histoire*, p. 690) and M. Anesaki, "Docetism (Buddhist)," *Encyclopedia of Religion and Ethics*, ed. James Hastings (Edinburgh: Clark, 1911), vol. 4, pp. 835–40. It is important to be aware that "illusion" does not mean the same thing in the Mahāyāna that it might mean to the theologians of the early Christian Church. In a system where everything finally is an illusion, illusion takes on its own sense of reality.
39. *Jñānagarbha's Commentary*, p. 101.
40. *MHK* III.278.

Notes to Chapter 7

1. The story is found in *Life*, pp. 72–74.
2. The story of Hsüan-tsang's encounter with the pirates is told in *Life*, pp. 86–90. It is retold by Arthur Waley in *The Real Tripitaka* (London: Allen & Unwin, 1952), pp. 38–41. I am much indebted to the Alan Sponberg's analysis of the story in "Meditation in Fa-hsiang Buddhism," in *Traditions of Meditation in Chinese Buddhism*, ed. Peter N. Gregory (Honolulu: University of Hawaii Press, 1986), pp. 15–43. Unless otherwise noted, translations from Hui-li's account of the story are taken from Sponberg's article.
3. Donald Attwater, *The Penguin Dictionary of Saints* (Hammondsworth, Middlesex: Penguin Books, 1965), pp. 209–10.

4. Sponberg, pp. 22–23. This is also a common theme in other accounts of Hsüan-tsang's life, as Paul Demiéville shows in "La *Yogācārabhūmi* de Saṅgharakṣa," *BEFEO* 44 (1954), pp. 387–95. See also Waley, *The Real Tripitaka*, pp. 127–30.
5. This episode has been discussed in chapter 2.
6. For a survey of the canonical sources on the practice of "recollection" (*anusmṛti*), see Lamotte, *Mppś*, pp. 1329–1429. In the *Mppś* itself, "recollection" is treated as an antidote to fear, especially for monks in remote places who practice meditation on the nine "horrors" (*aśubhasaṃjñā*) and fall prey to unproductive anxieties and fears. Sacrifice to the goddess does not have a place in the list of nine, but surely Hsüan-tsang would have had good reason to engage in "recollection" to calm himself when he faced death at the hands of pirates.
7. The list is extended to include the Buddha's face, the perfection of his moral qualities, various aspects of the Buddha's Body, and so on. See Paul M. Harrison, "Buddhānusmṛti in the Pratyutpanna-buddha-saṃmukhāvasthita-samādhi-sūtra," *JIP* 6 (1978), pp. 35–57.
8. Translation quoted from Harrison, p. 43.
9. As Stephan Beyer has noted in "Notes on the Vision Quest in Early Mahāyāna," in *Prajñāpāramitā and Related Systems*, ed. Lewis Lancaster, Berkeley Buddhist Studies Series 1 (Berkeley: Berkeley Buddhist Studies Series, 1977), pp. 329–40.
10. Sponberg makes this point quite forcefully in the article already cited.
11. The word *kuan* appears frequently in the first meaning in the titles of a series of sūtras that deal with the "visualization" of Buddhas and bodhisattvas. See Alexander Coburn Soper, *Literary Evidence for Early Buddhist Art in China* (Ascona: Artibus Asiae Publishers, 1959), pp. 141–50; also, Julian F. Pas, "The *Kuan-wu-liang-shou Fo-ching*: Its Origin and Literary Criticism," in *Buddhist Thought and Asian Civilization*, ed. Leslie S. Kawamura and Keith Scott (Emeryville, Calif.: Dharma Publishing, 1977), pp. 194–218, and "The Meaning of Nien-fo in the Three Pure Land Sutras," *Studies in Religion* 7 (1978), pp. 403–13.
12. Sponberg points out that *kuan* in its philosophical meaning can also represent the Sanskrit *abhisamaya*, a word that indicates understanding but that does not have the sense of vision. *Vipaśyanā*, however, is the more likely equivalent (Sponberg, p. 30, note 28). The element of discrimination in *vipaśyanā* is expressed by the prefix *vi-*. Sometimes this is a useful and true discrimination, as in the phrase "distinction between the two truths" (*satya-dvaya-vibhāga*) or "distinction between middle and extremes" (*madhyānta-vibhāga*). Sometimes it is a false distinction, as in the word commonly used for conceptuality (*vikalpa*). When the prefix *vi-* is combined with the verb to see (*paśyanā*), it suggests a visual process of discernment.
13. *MHK* III.15, 21ab.
14. *Sarva-darśana-saṃgraha of Sāyaṇa Mādhava*, ed. V. S. Abhyankar, 3rd ed. (Poona: Bhandarkar Oriental Research Institute, 1978).
15. As Gregory Schopen argues in "Burial '*Ad Sanctos*' and the Physical Presence of the Buddha in Early Indian Buddhism," *Religion* 17 (1987), pp. 193–225. Diana L. Eck gives a very useful account of the mechanics of *darśan* in *Darśan: Seeing the Divine Image in India* (Chambersburg, Penn.: Anima Publications, 1981).
16. Jan Gonda, *Eye and Gaze in the Veda*, Verhandelingen der Koninklijke Nederlandse Akademie van Wetenschappen, Afd. Letterkunde, vol. 75, no. 1 (Amsterdam: North-Holland Publishing, 1969), pp. 19, 55. Sudhir Kakar has commented on the power of these moments of visual communion in a more modern context: "This was *darshan*, 'viewing,' in its most intense form. There were tears of emotion running down the cheek of the middle-aged man sitting next to me, merging with drops of saliva dribbling out of the corner of his mouth, and I had the distinct feeling that my neighbors were visually feasting on Maharajji's face" (*Shamans, Mystics, and Doctors* [Boston: Beacon Press, 1982], p. 131).
17. *MHK* III.1–2.

18. *MHK* III.251–52.
19. *MHK* III.296–97.
20. See chapter 2.
21. Giuseppe Tucci, "À propos Avalokiteśvara," *MCB* 9 (1948–1951), pp. 173–219; Edward Conze, trans., *Buddhist Wisdom Books* (New York: Harper & Row, 1972), pp. 77–78; *Saddharmapuṇḍarīka Sūtra* (Vaidya ed.), p. 256.
22. *Śravaṇo atha darśano 'pi ca anupūrvaṃ ca tathā anusmṛtiḥ / bhavatīha amogha prāṇināṃ sarvaduḥkhabhavaśokanāśakaḥ* (Vaidya ed., p. 253).
23. Gonda has pointed out passages in the *Śatapatha-brāhmaṇa* that speak of the eye as "shining" (*dīpyate*) and "luminous" (*bhāti*). For the reference to these and similar notions elsewhere in the Veda, see *Eye and Gaze*, p. 5.
24. *MHK* III.300.
25. The *Ratnagotravibhāga* contains a passage that makes effective use of the image of clouds: "You [O Buddha] are like the sun [seen] through a hole in the clouds. The saints whose eyes are pure intelligence see you, but those whose intelligence is incomplete do not [see you] completely": *chidrābhre nabhasīva bhāskara iha tvaṃ śuddhabuddhīkṣaṇair āryair apy avalokyase na sakalaḥ prādeśikībuddhibhiḥ*. The Sanskrit is found in *RGV*, p. 77.
26. See chapter 2.
27. The image of the Buddha's "awakening" rays can be used for a serious doctrinal purpose, as in Haribhadra's definition of the nirvana achieved by those who do not follow the Mahāyāna: "They think that nirvana is like the blowing out of a lamp. With rebirth in the triple world ruled out, they are born immediately after the moment of death in lotus buds in pure Buddha-fields, concentrated in a pure realm. Then they are awakened by the rays of sunlight from Buddhas such as Amitābha to remove undefiled darkness. When the *bodhicitta* has been generated, in a state of liberation, they go to such places as hell, gradually acquire the prerequisites of enlightenment and become the teachers of the world. This is known from scripture. Because the defilements that are the cause of rebirth cease, the effect, which is rebirth in the three realms, also ceases. But this does not rule out birth in the pure realm. Therefore . . ., as is correctly explained in the *Satyakasatyakī* chapter of *The Lotus Sūtra*, 'O Śāriputra, in the future you will be a perfectly enlightened Buddha.' Also, 'There is one vehicle; there is no second'" (*Ālokā*, p. 133).
28. André Bareau, "The Superhuman Personality of the Buddha and Its Symbolism in the *Mahāparinirvāṇasūtra* of the Dharmaguptaka," in *Myths and Symbols: Studies in Honor of Mircea Eliade*, ed. Joseph M. Kitagawa and Charles H. Long (Chicago: University of Chicago Press, 1969), pp. 9–21.
29. See Richard M. Dorson, "The Eclipse of Solar Mythology," in *Myth: A Symposium*, ed. Thomas M. Sebeok (Philadelphia: American Folklore Society, 1955), pp. 15–38.
30. Translation adapted from *The Book of the Kindred Sayings* (*Saṃyutta-Nikāya*), trans. F. L. Woodward (London: Pali Text Society, 1930; reprint ed., 1965), Part Five, p. 358.
31. "'Āloko Udapādi': The Imagery of Illumination in Early Buddhist Literaure," unpublished paper delivered at the annual conference of the International Association of Buddhist Studies, Berkeley, 1987.
32. For an example of the pillar of fire at Amarāvatī, see Douglas Barrett, *Sculptures from Amaravati in the British Museum* (London: Trustees of the British Museum, 1954), Figure 35.
33. *MHK* III.10. The titles of Bhāvaviveka's other works also suggest vision and illumination. The "Jewel in the Hand Treatise," which exists only in Chinese, contains an image that is used to suggest clarity of vision. One is meant to see the two truths simultaneously just as one would see a clear jewel in the palm of one's hand. A related image is present in the title of the disputed work "The Jewel Lamp of Madhyamaka" (*Madhyamaka-ratna-pradīpa*). The only work ascribed to Bhāvaviveka that

does not contain a visual metaphor is "The Condensed Meaning of the Madhyamaka" (*Madhyamārtha-saṃgraha*).

34. George Lakoff and Mark Johnson, *Metaphors We Live By* (Chicago: University of Chicago Press, 1980).
35. *MHK* III.251–52. These verses were discussed in chapter 2.
36. *MHK* III.263.
37. *MHK* III.279.
38. *MHK* III.280–81.
39. *MHK* III.285.
40. *MHK* III.289ab.
41. Nāgārjuna explains the term *brahmacaryā* as a general pursuit of the ascetic life. It is probably no accident that Nāgārjuna associates *brahmacaryā* with vision, as Bhāvaviveka is about to do in the commentary on this verse: "If these [four Noble Truths] do not exist, there can be no results of the ascetic life, because one attains the results of asceticism by seeing the [four Noble] Truths. And without the results of asceticism, there can be no religious practice (*brahmacaryā*)." The Sanskrit of this passage is found in Johnston and Kunst, eds., "The *Vigrahavyāvartanī* of Nāgārjuna," *MCB* 9 (1948–1951), pp. 140–41.
42. *MHK* III.346.
43. For references to the discussion of Bhāvaviveka's (or Bhavya's) name see, note 1 to the Introduction. The word *bhavya* occurs in *MHK* III.268 and 346.
44. In other sūtras vision (*darśana*) is often something that is "given" by the Buddha. See, for example, the *Aparimitāyur-jñāna Sūtra*: "If someone copies or arranges to have copied the Aparimitāyuḥ Sūtra, ninety-nine *koṭis* of Buddhas will give him direct *darśana* at the moment of death." The Sanskrit text is found in Max Walleser, ed., *Aparimitāyur-jñāna-nāma-mahāyāna-sūtram*, Sitzungsberichte der Heidelberger Akademie der Wissenschaften: Philosophisch-historische Klasse, vol. 12 (Heidelberg, 1916), p. 23.
45. Both of these meanings are suggested by Bhāvaviveka's description of reason as *āgamānuvidhāyin* ("following tradition") at the end of his argument against the Yogācāra in *Prajñāpradīpa* XXV ("Bhāvaviveka's Critique," p. 73) and again in *MHK* V.105: "Here [the Buddha] uses faultless inference that follows tradition to turn back the flood of diverse concepts" (*ihānumānān nirdoṣād āgamānuvidhāyinaḥ / kalpitāśeṣavividhavikalpāpāṃ nirākṛteḥ*).
46. I comment on the different meanings of the word *artha* ("the meaning of meaning") in *Jñānagarbha's Commentary*, p. 109.
47. *MHK* III. 347–54.
48. There is a useful account of the three kinds of wisdom, "the wisdom that consists of hearing" (*śrutamayī prajñā*), "the wisdom that consists of thinking" (*cintāmayī prajñā*), and "the wisdom that consists of repeated practice" (*bhāvanāmayī prajñā*) in *Bhāvanākrama I* of Kamalaśīla, ed. Giuseppe Tucci, *Minor Buddhist Texts*, Part II, Serie Orientale Roma 9 (Rome: Istituto Italiano per il Medio ed Estremo Oriente, 1958).
49. *MHK* III.286.
50. *MHK* V.104: *tattvasyātarkagocarāt tadbodho nānumānataḥ / nātas tarkeṇa dharmāṇāṃ gṛhyeta dharmateti cet*. The same objection is found in chapter 25 of *The Lamp of Wisdom* ("Bhāvaviveka's Critique," p. 73).
51. *MHK* V.105–109: *ihānumānān nirdoṣād āgamānuvidhāyinaḥ / kalpitāśeṣavividhavikalpāpāṃ nirākṛteḥ // sakalajñeyayāthātmyam ākāśasamacetasā / jñānena nirvikalpena buddhāḥ paśyanty adarśanāt // ato 'numānaviṣayaṃ na tattvaṃ pratipadyate / tattvajñānavipakṣo yas tasya tena nirākriyā / āgamāntarabhedena bhedāyātāsu buddhiṣu / abhede 'py āgamasyānyaḥ kaḥ parīkṣākṣamo vidhiḥ // pratijñāmātrakā neṣṭā pratipakṣanirākriyā / aniṣiddhe vipakṣe ca nirvikalpā matiḥ kutaḥ*.
52. "Bhāvaviveka's Critique," pp. 73–74.

Notes to Translation

NOTES TO SECTION 1

1. The form of philosophical nihilism Bhāvaviveka is concerned about is called "cavil" (*vitaṇḍā*), defined in *Nyāya-sūtra* I.2.3 as a form of "sophistry" (*jalpa*) that refutes an opponent's position but fails to maintain a counterposition (*sa pratipakṣa-sthāpanā-hīno vitaṇḍā*). For a discussion of *vitaṇḍā* in the Nyāya tradition, see Mahāmahopādhyāya Bhīmācārya Jhalakīkar, *Nyāyakośa or Dictionary of Technical Terms of Indian Philosophy*, rev. ed. Mahāmahopādhyāya Vāsudev Shāstrī Abhyankar (Poona: Bhandarkar Oriental Research Institute, 1978), pp. 751–52. Kamaleswar Bhattacharya has argued that Mādhyamikas cannot be guilty of *vitaṇḍā* because they have no counterposition to establish. "Mādhyamika et Vaitaṇḍika," *Journal Asiatique* 263 (1975), pp. 99–102. This comment by Bhāvaviveka shows, however, that he took the charge quite seriously.
2. The Peking version of the Tibetan translation contains an explanation of the phrase "in this way" (*'di skad ces*) to relate this section of the text to earlier verses: "Is it not a form of philosophical nihilism (*vitaṇḍā*) to reject your opponent's position *by saying that even [the cognition of] an absence is false and [that the negation of existence is like the negation of] the self and pleasure*?" The claim that "even [the cognition of] an absence false" is discussed in verses 259–61. "Self and pleasure" appear in the explanation of the argument in verse 265.
3. The translation follows the Tibetan version of the verse and commentary, both of which read *gsuṅ* ("say"), rather than the Sanskrit version of the verse, which reads *viduḥ* ("know"). "Say" is consistent with the reference to the Buddha as teacher in the introduction to the verse.
4. The defining characteristics of reality (*tattva*) appear in a number of different forms in Madhyamaka literature. The list quoted here is similar to the one that appears in *MHK* I.1–2: "[Reality] is not accessible to logic (*apratarkya*), not known discursively (*avijñeya*), not a receptacle (*anālaya*), without characteristic (*alakṣaṇa*), not defined (*anirūpya*), understood directly (*svasaṃvedya*), without beginning or end (*anādinidhāna*), happy (*śiva*), nonconceptual (*nirvikalpa*), without image (*nirābhāsa*), without distinguishing mark (*nirnimitta*), not capable of being displayed (*nirañjana*), neither dual nor nondual, calm (*śānta*), and free from the functioning of cognition (*dhīpracāravivarjita*)." A shorter version of the same list is found in *MHK* III.245–46. Similar lists are found in earlier Madhyamaka works, such as *MMK* XVIII.9: "Independent, peaceful, nondiscursive, nonconceptual, and not diverse—this is the definition of reality."
5. Bhāvaviveka's identification of nonconceptual (*nirvikalpa*) cognition (*dhī*) with a cognition that is free from the apprehension (*upalabdhi*) of objects is a common element in his analysis of the Buddha's awareness. The commentary on III.267, for example, explains that the Buddha's understanding (*bodha*) is no-understanding (*abodha*) because it does not apprehend [reality] as an object." Compare also III.270, 278, and 292. The classic reference to non-apprehension as a part of the path to Buddhahood occurs in *Madhyāntavibhāga* I.6: "Based on apprehension, non-apprehension arises; based on non-apprehension, non-apprehension arises" (*upalabdhiṃ samāśritya nopalabdhiḥ prajāyate / nopalabdhiṃ samāśritya nopalabdhiḥ prajāyate*). Bhāvaviveka quotes the verse as *MHK* V.4 and discusses it at length in the commentary.
6. After defining reality as the object (*viṣaya*) that a Buddha knows, Bhāvaviveka defines the Buddha as the knowledge that knows this reality. In verse 266 he explains that reality is the object *about which no cognition arises*. Verse 267 says that the knowledge of reality (the knowledge that constitutes a Buddha) is *the no-arising of any cognition*. To situate the definition in the context of more traditional definitions

of the Buddha, Bhāvaviveka starts the verse with a formula, "one is called Buddha because one understands this (*tadbodhād ucyate buddho*)," echoing Nāgārjuna's *Hymn to the Inconceivable* (*Acintyastava*) 41 (Lindtner, *Nagarjuniana*, p. 154). The second quarter of the verse then explains that this Buddha (the one who is called Buddha because he understands this) is "the no-arising of cognition" (*anudayo dhiyaḥ*). The third quarter of the verse explains that this no-arising of cognition is the primary (*mukhya*) Buddha because the understanding that constitutes the Buddha is actually no-understanding. The last quarter of the verse then returns to the more traditional image with which the verse started and says that the understanding that is no-understanding makes it possible for the Buddha to dispel *saṃkṣaya*) the sleep of concepts. By "understanding" (*bodha*) the nature of reality (through no-understanding), a Buddha "wakes up" (*prabodha*) from sleep.

The word "primary" (*mukhya*) in the third quarter of the verse can be understood in either an ontological or a linguistic sense. From an ontological point of view, the no-arising of cognition is the most fundamental Buddha, the Buddha viewed from the ultimate perspective. Linguistically, the term "no-arising" is one that can be taken literally (*mukhya*) as a pure negation, as opposed to the positive designations that need to be read metaphorically (*aupacārika*). Bhāvaviveka uses the distinction between the primary (*mukhya*) and metaphorical (*aupacārika*) meanings frequently in his work, as in *MHK* VIII.35. For a general discussion of this distinction in Indian literature, see K. Kunjunni Raja, *Indian Theories of Meaning* (Madras: Adyar Library and Research Centre, 1963), chap. 6.

The Tibetan translation of the verse differs in three significant ways from the translation proposed here. The Tibetan translators interpret the word "no-arising" (*anudaya*) as a *bahuvrīhi* compound meaning "the one in whom there is no arising." They omit the word "called" (*ucyate*). And they reverse the order of the last two quarters of the verse. The result is a translation that reads: "The one in whom no cognition arises, because he understands this, is the primary Buddha, because he dispels (*saṅs*) the sleep of concepts and because he has expanded (*rgyas*) with no-understanding." The Tibetan translation is not inconsistent with the rest of Bhāvaviveka's thought when it interprets "no-arising" as "the one in whom there is no arising," although this translation tends to obscure the radical quality of Bhāvaviveka's negation. The Tibetan translation omits the word "called" for metrical reasons in the verse and restores it in the commentary. The reversal of the last two quarters of the verse is an artificial attempt to support the double etymology of the Tibetan word for Buddha (*saṅs rgyas*) in which the Buddha is said to dispel (*saṅs*) sleep and expand (*rgyas*) in wisdom. It is clear from the structure of the Sanskrit that the first and last quarters of the verse are, as it were, the metaphorical (*aupacārika*) frame within which Bhāvaviveka places his own account of the Buddha's literal (*mukhya*) meaning. For more on the explanation of the word "Buddha," see chapter 6, note 21.

Bhāvaviveka's definition of the Buddha as the "no-arising of cognition" (*anudayo dhiyaḥ*) appears in a number of other places in his work. See, for example, *MHK* IV.18: "Since no object of cognition exists, the no-arising of cognition with regard to that [nonexistent object] is perfect enlightenment. This is because [enlightenment] is consistent with the nature of the object" (*jñeyasya sarvathā 'siddher yas tatrānudayo dhiyaḥ / so 'yaṃ bodhyabhisambodhau jñeyatattvāviparyayāt*). For a similar definition in *The Lamp of Wisdom (Prajñāpradīpa)*, see my "Bhāvaviveka's Critique," p. 73. Bhāvaviveka distinguishes between the primary (*mukhya*) Buddha and the Manifestation Buddha in *MHK* IV.29cd: "If someone thinks that this [disciple's] liberation is like the Buddha's because it is the removal of defiled ignorance, this is wrong because [this liberation] does not belong to either the primary or the Manifestation Buddha" (*kliṣṭāvidyāprahāṇāc cet tanmuktir buddhavan matā / tad asat tadasadbhāvān mukhyanirmāṇabuddhayoḥ*). In the commentary that follows, Bhāvaviveka identifies the primary Buddha as the Dharma Body, as in verse III.284.

7. A similar point about metaphor (*upacāra*) is made in the introduction to *MHK* III.257: "[I] have already explained that, because seeing is completely unestablished, no-seeing is referred to metaphorically as seeing," *Sde-dge Tibetan Tripiṭaka bsTan-ḥgyur Preserved at the Faculty of Letters, University of Tokyo (Dbu ma)*, (Tokyo, 1977–1979), vol. 3, no. 3856, folios *Dza* 118b/7–119a/1.
8. Bhāvaviveka presents this objection as a question: "Would it not be the case that using 'understanding' as a metaphor for no-understanding is like using 'fire' as a metaphor for water?"
9. At the beginning of the eighteenth chapter of *The Lamp of Wisdom*, the chapter on "The Investigation of the Self," Bhāvaviveka explains that the word "self" (*ātman*) can be used conventionally to refer to consciousness (*vijñāna*). The chapter is translated in my "A Question of Nihilism: Bhāvaviveka's Response to the Fundamental Problems of Mādhyamika Philosophy" (Ph.D. dissertation: Harvard University, 1980), p. 199.
10. In verse 268, Bhāvaviveka pauses in his presentation of the ultimate Buddha to define the Buddha from the conventional perspective. This step is an important part of his logical method. Bhāvaviveka's approach to the logic of a Madhyamaka argument requires that he identify the subject (*dharmin*) from the conventional point of view, then analyze it from the ultimate point of view. He does this with the topics of analysis in many of the chapters of *The Lamp of Wisdom*, most notably the self (*ātman*) in chapter 18 (as mentioned in the previous note). Here he does it with the concept of the Buddha.

    Bhāvaviveka's three conventional definitions of the Buddha are also found in the commentary on *MMK* XXIV.5cd: "A Buddha is someone who understands the [four Noble] Truths or who causes them to be understood . . . , who understands that all *dharmas* are equal in their nonexistence . . . , or who is enlightened himself and enlightens those who are ready to be taught." In the commentary on *MHK* III.273, Bhāvaviveka explains that the second of these definitions, the Mahāyāna conception of the Buddha as "a single moment of insight into the equality of all *dharmas*," is the one that should be taken as the subject (*dharmin*) for the analysis in the following verses.

    The word that is translated here as "fortunate people" (*bhavya*) may be a reference to Bhāvaviveka himself. Bhāvaviveka's use of the word *bhavya* is discussed in chapter 7 of this book. The term is used in a similar way in *AA* VIII.10 and *RGV* IV.54, 55. For Bhāvaviveka's own explanation of the term, see the commentary that follows.
11. For a more complete account of the three "states" (*vihāra*), see the commentary on *MHK* III.280cd below.
12. *Abhijñātam abhijñeyaṃ bhāvanīyaṃ ca bhāvitam / prahātavyaṃ [ca] prahīṇaṃ ca tena buddho nirucyate.* The verse is quoted in the *Ratnapradīpa* and again in Śāntarakṣita's *Tattvasaṃgraha*. See Christian Lindtner, "Materials for the Study of Bhavya," in Eivind Kahrs, ed., *Kalyāṇamitrarāgaṇam: Essays in Honour of Nils Simonsson* (Oslo: Norwegian University Press, 1986), p. 188.
13. In the commentary on this verse and on *MHK* III.273, Bhāvaviveka expands this phrase to read "a single moment of insight into the equality of all *dharmas*." This conventional Mahāyāna conception of the Buddha's enlightenment serves as the subject (*dharmin*) of the verses in this section of the text.
14. Bhāvaviveka frequently refers to enlightenment as a single moment of insight (*ekakṣaṇajñāna*). See, for example, the commentary on *MHK* I.6 and the commentary on III.273. The *locus classicus* for the concept is chapter 7 of the *Abhisamayālaṃkāra* (*Ālokā*, pp. 908–11).
15. This is an abbreviated version of the definition of reality found in the commentary on verse 266.
16. Bhāvaviveka's list of the twelve acts of a Buddha is close but not identical to the list found in *DBh* (Vaidya ed., p. 10). For the numbering of the twelve acts I have followed Lamotte's version in *MS* (trans., pp. 267–68). For a more detailed account,

see Nicolas Poppe, *The Twelve Deeds of the Buddha*, Asiatische Forschungen, vol. 23 (Wiesbaden: Otto Harrassowitz, 1967).

17. *Akaniṣṭhabhavane divye sarvapāpavivarjite / tatra budhyanti saṁbuddhā nirmitas tv iha budhyate. Laṅkāvatāra* X.38ab, 39cd (Nanjio ed., p. 269). The Tibetan word *dgyes pa*, "pleasant" or "delightful," presupposes a Sanskrit original such as *śubha* rather than the *divya* ("divine") of the *Laṅkā*. The dGe-lugs-pa scholastic tradition preserves an interesting variant reading for the second quarter of the verse. The Sera Je *Yig-cha* on the *Abhisamayālaṃkāra* reads: *gtsaṅ ma'i gnas lṅa spaṅs pa yi // 'og min gnas ni ñams dga' ba*. This suggests a reading of *śuddhāvāsavivarjite*, instead of *sarvapāpavivarjite*. (See Se-ra rJe-btsun-pa, *Bstan bcos mṅon par rtogs pa'i rgyan 'grel ba daṅ bcas pa'i rnam bśad rnam pa gñis kyi dka' ba'i gnad gsal bar byed pa legs bśad skal bzaṅ klu dbaṅ gi rol mtsho zhes bya ba las skabs brgyad pa'i spyi don*, modern blockprint [Bylakuppe: Se-ra Je Monastery, n.d.].) In this Tibetan context, the verse is interpreted as meaning that the Akaniṣṭha where a Buddha is enlightened is not the Akaniṣṭha at the top of the Form Realm but another Akaniṣṭha that is accessible only to bodhisattvas. On Akaniṣṭha in the *Laṅkāvatāra*, see also *Laṅkāvatāra*, II.50; II.93–94; X.774.
18. These two verses follows the pattern Bhāvaviveka has already established in his definition of the Buddha in verse 267. There the Buddha was someone who "understands" (*bodha*) with no-understanding (*abodha*). Here the Sambuddha is someone who has an understanding of equality (*sambodha*) with no-understanding of equality (*asambodha*). In the commentary on verse 266, Bhāvaviveka explained that the understanding that is no-understanding is an understanding that does not apprehend reality as an object. Here he explains that the Buddha's understanding of equality is the understanding that does not apprehend (*anālambya*) equality. Equality itself can be understood in two ways: as the equality of *dharmas* (*dharma-samatā*) and as the equality of persons (*sattva-samatā*), as in *Mppś* pp. 325–27. Bhāvaviveka starts the verse with the traditional formula for the understanding of equality, then says that the Buddha can only understand this equality in a way that is free from understanding equality, or free from the grasping of equality as an object.
19. This phrase can also be read in a causative sense: "because [the Buddha] equally does not cause [*dharmas*] to arise or cease." Compare Nāgārjuna's *Hymn to the Transcendent* (*Lokātītastava*) 25: *na tvayotpāditaṃ kiṃcin na ca kiṃcin nirodhitam* (Lindtner, *Nagarjuniana*, p. 136).
20. This verse explains the meaning of Tathāgata, or thus (*tathā*) gone (*gata*). As Bhāvaviveka says in the commentary, the Sanskrit root *gam-* in the word *gata* can mean either to understand or to go. In either case, the Buddha goes in a way that is consistent with the way the Dharma Nature (*dharmatā*) goes—that is, without going.
21. On the meaning of the phrase "neither subtracted nor added" (*aprakṣepān nirutkṣepād*), compare *AA* V.21 and *RGV* I.154.
22. The sentence echoes the *Laṅkāvatāra Sūtra*: "Tathāgatas may arise or not arise, but the Dharma Nature of *dharmas* remains" (Nanjio ed., p. 143). For other examples of this formula, see Jikido Takasaki, "Dharmatā, Dharmadhātu, Dharmakāya and Buddhadhātu: The Structure of the Ultimate Value in Mahāyāna Buddhism," *Indogaku Bukkyōgaku Kenkyū* 14 (1966), pp. 903–19.
23. Literally, "Equality with respect to no-identity" (*niḥsvabhāva-samatā*).
24. The same three items appear in *Ālokā*, p. 184: "The Teacher's perfection (*sampad*) is twofold. This [twofold perfection] is expressed by the word Sugata. By practicing the extraordinary path, a Sugata has gone to (or achieved) the beautiful (*śobhana*) perfection of knowledge and removal, like a beautiful form. Or a Sugata has gone to (or achieved) [the perfection of knowledge and removal] thoroughly (*suṣṭhu*), without turning back, like a fever that has been thoroughly cured. Or a Sugata has gone to (or achieved) [the perfection of knowledge and removal] completely (*niḥśeṣam*), like a pot that has been completely filled."
25. Compare Nāgārjuna's *Hymn to the Inconceivable* 1 (Lindtner, *Nagarjuniana*, p. 141).

26. In the commentary on verse 268.
27. Wisdom (*prajñā*) is defined as "the analysis of *dharmas*" (*dharmapravicaya*) in the commentary on *Kośa* I.2 and elsewhere in the Abhidharma literature.
28. The six forms of consciousness are associated with sight, hearing, smell, taste, touch, and the mind. See *Kośa* I.16.
29. The word *dharmāyatana* is applied in *Kośa* I.15 to the aggregates (*skandha*) of feeling (*vedanā*), ideas (*saṃjñā*), and volition (*saṃskāra*), the *dharma* called *avijñapti*, and the three unconditioned *dharmas*.
30. Compare *MHK* VIII.94: "He is expressed through the superimposition of concepts, but in reality he is inexpressible (*avācya*). Moreover, because he is completely inexpressible, he is called indefinable (*nirañjana*)."
31. Compare the commentary on *Kośa* I.10a: "There are two kinds of form (*rūpa*): color (*varṇa*) and shape (*saṃsthāna*). Of these two, there are four colors beginning with blue. Other [colors] are divisions of these. There are eight shapes beginning with long. . . ."
32. This argument about the division of atoms is found as part of the critique of external objects in Dignāga's *Investigation of Objects* (*Ālambanaparīkṣā*), ed. F. Tola and C. Dragonetti, *JIP* 10 (1982), pp. 105–34. Bhāvaviveka discusses the argument in more detail in *MHK* V.31–39.
33. La Vallée Poussin defines "distinguishing marks" (*nimitta*) as "the particular conditions or modes of being of a thing" (*vastuno 'vasthāviśeṣa*) in a note to his translation of *Kośa* I.14cd.
34. This verse contains several textual problems. In the first quarter, the Sanskrit reads *animitto nirābhāsān* ("he has no distinguishing mark because he has no appearance"). The Tibetan of the verse and commentary reverse the relationship between the two terms and say: "He has no appearance because he has no distinguishing mark." Ejima's emendation (*animitto nirābhāsān nirābhāso 'nimittataḥ*) comes closer to the text presupposed by the commentary than the existing text of the Sanskrit. In the second quarter, the Sanskrit says only "because he has no appearance" (*nirābhāsatayāpi*). The Tibetan says, "Because he has no appearance, he has no distinguishing mark." In both cases I have followed the Tibetan. In the last quarter the Sanskrit text reads "compassionate" (*kṛpātmanām*). The Tibetan of the verse and the commentary suggests the reading "liberated" (*muktātmanām*). In this case, I have translated the verse to fit the Tibetan. It is possible that Bhāvaviveka is playing on the meaning of the word *muktātman* in the Vedānta tradition. In *MHK* VIII.23, Bhāvaviveka says that Vedāntins think of the self (*ātman*) as having two forms, one that is bound and one that is liberated. That verse seems to end, as this verse does, with the word *muktātman*. Unfortunately, the Sanskrit version of the verse has been lost.
35. The term "no foundation" (*apratiṣṭha*) is not widely used in Madhyamaka literature, but it is found frequently in the sūtras and is related to a series of other concepts that do figure in the philosophical tradition. See, for example, the discussion of nirvana-without-foundation (*apratiṣṭhita-nirvāṇa*) found in verses 292ff. A useful example of the term in a philosophical context is in the commentary on *BCA* IX.106ab: "If [a cognition] occurs after the object, from what does the cognition come?" The commentary quotes a passage from the *Ratnakūṭa*: "What can the mind become attached to, hate, or be ignorant of? Is it past, future, or present? The past is gone. The future has not yet arrived. And the present does not last. The mind, O Kāśyapa, does not grasp [anything] internally, externally, or apart from these two. For the mind, O Kāśyapa, has no foundation (*apratiṣṭha*)" (Vaidya ed., p. 245). For another scriptural parallel, see *Laṅkāvatāra* X. 631: "Just as a bird moves in the sky as it wishes, so does he move on the surface of the earth without any foundation (*apratiṣṭha*) and without being apprehended (*anālambya*)."
36. These five distinguishing marks characterize the five aggregates. Matter (*rūpa*) is

defined as "offering resistance" (*rūpaṇa*) in the commentary on *Kośa* I. 13. Feeling (*vedanā*) is defined as "experiencing" (*anubhava*) in *Kośa* I.14c. Ideas (*saṃjñā*) are defined as "grasping distinguishing marks" (*nimittodgrahaṇa*) in *Kośa* I.14d. Conditioning states (*saṃskāra*) are defined as "creating" (*abhisaṃskāra*) other events, in the commentary on *Kośa* I.15ab. In *Kośa* I.16, consciousness is defined as "forming a specific impression" (*prativijñapti*).

37. Literally, "no cognition arises of something that does not have the absolute identity of an object." What it means to say that something "does not have an absolute identity (*svabhāvāpariniṣpatti*)" is discussed in *MHK* III.257: "[A wise person] does not see things as having any real identity (*satsvabhāva*) because they have no absolute identity (*svabhāvāpariniṣpati*), like a magic elephant."
38. As discussed in the commentary on *MHK* III.274ab.
39. As discussed in the commentary on *MHK* III.276.
40. Literally, "the concepts (*vikalpa*) [that come] from imagination (*kalpanā*) and memory (*anusmṛti*) do not reach him."
41. Bhāvaviveka discusses the gross elements (*mahābhūta*)—earth, water, fire and air—and the derivatives of the gross elements (*bhautika*) in *MHK* III.26–65. On the gross elements (*mahābhūta*), see *Kośa* I.12. On the derivatives of the gross elements (*bhautika*), see *Kośa* I.35.
42. Bhāvaviveka has set up verses 273–79 as formal syllogisms with a subject (*dharmin*) and a series of reasons (*hetu*). The phrase "like space" (*vyomavat*) in this verse constitutes the example (*dṛṣṭānta*).
43. Bhāvaviveka gives an account of the tenth stage (*bhūmi*) of the path in verses 330–45.
44. The states (*vihāra*) were mentioned in the commentary on verse 268.
45. In the commentary on *MHK* I.3, Bhāvaviveka explains *bhāvataḥ* ("sincerely" or "with feeling") as *āśayataḥ* ("heartily" or "earnestly").
46. Jacques May explains that the word here translated as "metaphorically" (*samāropāt*) can have both an ontological and a linguistic function. It can refer to the process of superimposing a name on an object or of superimposing the wrong identity on an object. See *Candrakīrti Prasannapadā Madhyamakavṛtti* (Paris: Adrien Maisonneuve, 1959), p. 187. Bhāvaviveka discusses the ontological superimposition of the imagined identity of a snake on a real identity of a rope in his analysis of the Yogācāra concept of imagined nature ("Bhāvaviveka's Critique," p. 50). It is clear here, however, that he has the linguistic function in mind. As Renou points out in *Terminologie grammaticale du sanskrit* (s.v. *adhyāruh-*), *samāropa* (or the related word *adhyāropa*) functions in its linguistic mode as a type of metaphor (*upacāra*). Bhāvaviveka has already discussed the metaphorical function of terms such as "Buddha" in his commentary on verse 267. He mentions the same point again in IV.20ab and commentary: "Why is [the Buddha] called peaceful (*śānta*), empty (*śūnya*), non-dual (*advaya*), and so forth? By superimposing concepts (*kalpanāṃ samāropya*), [the Buddha] is called 'peaceful' and so forth. Terms such as 'pure' (*śuddha*), 'inherently luminous' (*prakṛti-prabhāsvara*), and 'the one who alleviates poverty and sickness' are applied as a result of a person's own concepts (*svavikalpena*), as in the case of a wishing-jewel."
47. He is referring to the explanation of the terms that refer to the Buddha in verse 267.
48. A comparable set of explanations is found in *BBh*, p. 64.
49. The manuscript reads *idam* (neuter) rather than *ayam* (masculine). It is possible that Bhāvaviveka has deliberately changed the form of the pronoun used to refer to the Buddha from masculine to neuter to underline the point he makes in the commentary: the Buddha as cognition (*jñāna*) can also be identified with reality (*tattva*). He returns to the masculine form of the pronoun in the next verse.
50. Bhāvaviveka uses the phrase "happy cessation of conceptual diversity" (*prapañcopaśamaḥ śivaḥ*) to describe reality in several places in his text. It appears, for example, at the end the chapter on the Vedānta (*MHK* VIII.104) and in Bhāvaviveka's

description of the "ambrosia of reality" (*tattvāmṛta*) in verse 300. "Cessation of conceptual diversity" (*prapañcopaśama*) appears separately in *MHK* III.138, and "happy" (*śiva*) appears in *MHK* I.1. Bhāvaviveka's source is *MMK* XXV.24.

51. This important formula combines Bhāvaviveka's definition of the Buddha as the no-arising of cognition (see verse 267) with the definition of enlightenment as a single moment of cognition (see the commentary on verse 268).
52. The ten powers (*bala*), the four bases of self-confidence (*vaiśāradya*), and the eighty special qualities (*āveṇika-buddha-dharma*) are frequently listed as qualities (*guṇa*) of the Buddha.
53. *Tathāgatajñānamudrāsamādhi Sūtra* (*Ārya-tathāgata-jñāna-mudrā-samādhi-nāma-mahāyāna-sūtra*), in *The Tibetan Tripitaka: Peking Edition*, ed. Daisetz T. Suzuki (Tokyo-Kyoto: Tibetan Tripitaka Research Institute, 1956–1961), no. 799, vol. 32, pp. 60–72 (folios *Thu* 250b-276a).
54. On the problem of interpreting Bhāvaviveka's understanding of the "divine eye" or clairvoyance (*divya-cakṣus*), see verses 332 and 334.
55. This definition of inference (*anumāna*) as a means of valid knowledge reappears in the commentary on verse 279.
56. Compare *Laṅkāvatāra* II.122 and Bhāvaviveka's *Ratnapradīpa* (Lindtner, "Atiśa," p. 169).
57. This sentence (*ñon moṅs pa rnams so*) says only that the passion defined in the previous sentence occurs in the plural. Its function is probably to indicate that "those who are passionate" possess more than one passion.
58. *Kośa* VII.35–36 explains that the "passionless concentration" (*araṇā-samādhi*) is the ability of an arhant to prevent others from generating some defilement (*kleśa*). The arhant projects an aura that prevents others from becoming passionate, hateful, or ignorant in his presence. Haribhadra distinguishes the *araṇā-samādhi* of a Buddha from that of an arhant by a matter of degree: "What is the difference between the *araṇā-samādhi* of disciples and so forth and the *araṇā-samādhi* of a Tathāgata? The *araṇā-samādhi* of disciples and so forth avoids the arising of defilements among human beings by saying, 'May no one generate defilements from seeing me.' The Tathāgatas' *araṇā-samādhi*, however, uproots the whole continuum of defilements among people in [whole] villages, and so forth" (*Ālokā*, p. 917).
59. To understand Bhāvaviveka's attitude toward "reason" (*tarka*), this statement has to be read alongside Bhāvaviveka's other statements about the the use of inference to rule out false conceptions of reality. He makes his point in favor of inference at the end of his argument against the Yogācāra philosophy. See my "Bhāvaviveka's Critique," pp. 73–74 and *MHK* V.105–109. I have discussed both of these passages in chapter 7.
60. Literally, "as form and so forth."
61. A rabbit's horn cannot be absent because it does not exist at all.
62. Bhāvaviveka is referring to the Vedānta position that he explores in more detail in *MHK* VIII.
63. Bhāvaviveka discusses these characteristics of the Vedānta conception of Brahman in more detail in *MHK* VIII. On "subtle" (*aṇiya*), see *MHK* VIII.7, 8; "great" (*mahā*), *MHK* VIII.2, 54; "unique" (*eka*), *MHK* VIII.11–13, 16, 73–78, 103; and "pervasive" (*sarvagata* or *sarvaga*), *MHK* VIII.16, 59, 90.
64. Here Bhāvaviveka takes up the positions of the Yoga and Sāṃkhya schools.
65. In the Tibetan translation, the name for this liberation (*mokṣa* or *apavarga*) is *'jig rten 'dus pa*, a phrase that corresponds to the Sanskrit *loka-saṃgraha* ("world-summation"). This does not seem to be a common technical phrase in the commentarial literature on the *Yogasūtras*, where one would expect to find the names of liberation in the Yoga tradition. It is possible that Bhāvaviveka is using the term *saṃgraha* in the sense of "totality" or "complete summation," in which case it could refer to a moment in which the world is brought to a definitive conclusion. It also is possible that *'dus pa* ("summation") is a copyist's error for *'das pa* ("passing beyond").

66. As in the compound *brahma-nirvāṇa* in *Bhagavad Gītā* II.72.
67. *Na hi satyāt paro dharmaḥ.*
68. *Satyavādin*, a common epithet of the Buddha. Compare *MHK* I.3 *avitathavādin*.
69. The text refers only to *īśvara* (God) rather than to *maheśvara* (Śiva), but we can assume that the word *mahā* is carried over from the name of *mahābrahmā*.
70. Bhāvaviveka gives a provocative definition of the practice of no-apprehension (*anupalambha-bhāvanā*) in *MHK* IV.21 and the accompanying commentary: "What is the discipline of no-apprehension? [It is the negation of the eightfold path:] no seeing, no ideas, no speech, no action, no livelihood, no effort, no mindfulness, and no concentration" (*adarśanam asaṃkalpo vāgavyāhṛtir akriyā / anājīvo 'samārambho 'saṃpramoṣo 'sthitis tathā*).
71. In the standard accounts of the Buddha there are thirty-two primary characteristics (*lakṣaṇa*) and eighty secondary characteristics (*anuvyañjana*).
72. Here Bhāvaviveka is coming at the phrase *svabhāvāsaṃbhedāt* ("not different in identity") from a slightly different angle. In his first explanation, he said that the Dharma Body had the same identity (*svabhāva*) as the Tathāgata himself because both were identical to Emptiness. Here he treats the Tathāgata not as an individual but as a moment of insight and says that the Dharma Body and the Tathāgata are identical because they are both an understanding of the same identity (*svabhāva*), namely "equal identity" (*sama-svabhāva*).
73. This quotation from the "Master" (*ācārya*) gives the impression of being a digest of important terms and formulas from the long discussion of Buddhahood in Bhāvaviveka's commentary on *MMK* XXV.24 (translated in my "A Question of Nihilism," pp. 317–24), but the quotation is not taken verbatim from that source. To compound the uncertainty over its origin, the quotation appears again with a number of curious variants in the *Madhyamakaratnapradīpa*, *Sde-dge Tibetan Tripiṭaka bsTan-ḥgyur Preserved at the Faculty of Letters, University of Tokyo (Dbu ma)* (Tokyo, 1977–1979), vol. 2, no. 3854, p. 143 (folios *Tsha* 285b/3–286a/3).
74. On the twelve acts of the Buddha, see the commentary on verse 268.
75. The text itself is does not specify what "this" is. It is possible that it is the Manifestation Body discussed at the end of the previous sentence. But it is more likely that the word refers back to the Tathāgata Body that began the previous sentence. The two sentences would then have parallel structures: "From the Tathāgata Body arises a Manifestation Body . . . and based upon that [Tathāgata Body] arises a voice. . . ." This is the pattern followed in Asaṅga's discussion of the relationship between the Dharma Body and the two Bodies that proceed from it: the Enjoyment Body and the Manifestation Body. Asaṅga says that both the Enjoyment Body and the Manifestation Body are "based on" (*āśritya*) the Dharma Body. See Bhāvaviveka's discussion of Asaṅga later in the text.
76. On the sixty qualities (*svarāṅgas*) see verse 358.
77. *Ye māṃ rūpeṇa adrākṣur ye māṃ ghoṣeṇa anvayuḥ / mithyāprahāṇaprasṛtā na māṃ drakṣyanti te janāḥ // dharmato buddhā draṣṭavyā dharmakāyā hi nāyakāḥ / dharmatā cāpy avijñeyā na sā śakyā vijānitum* (*Vajracchedikā*, ed. Edward Conze [Rome: Istituto Italiano per il Medio ed Estremo Oriente, 1957], pp. 56–57). The passage is translated by Edward Conze, *Buddhist Wisdom Books* (New York: Harper & Row, 1972), p. 63.
78. "The twelvefold Dharma teaching" (*dvādaśadharmapravacana*) is listed in *MV* 1266–78.
79. If the Buddha's Dharma Body is the same as the teaching, then to take refuge in the Buddha would be the same as taking refuge in the Dharma, and there would be no need for separate refuge in the Dharma. This problem is discussed in the *Kośa* and in the *RGV*. For references, see chapter 5 in this book.
80. Compare *DBh: evaṃ kṣetrakāyaṃ karmavipākakāyaṃ . . . ātmakāyam adhitiṣṭhati* (Vaidya ed., p. 45), where the Transformation Body is discussed as part of a description of different bodies manifested in the eighth *bhūmi*. Compare also *Laṅkāvatāra*

II.49: *kena nirmāṇikā buddhāḥ kena buddhā vipākajāḥ / tathatā jñānabuddhā vai kathaṃ kena vadāhi me.* Vajrasena is discussed by Paul Demiéville in "Les versions chinoises du Milindapañha," *BEFEO* 24 (1924), p. 60. Demiéville speculates that Vajrasena may have lived in the second century C.F. According to Chinese tradition Vajrasena held the view that the Buddha is pure Thusness, without form or sound, and the teaching arises from the consciousness of the disciples.

81. Asaṅga's position is outlined in *MS*, vol. 1, p. 83, vol. 2, pp. 266–67.

NOTES TO SECTION 2

1. Bhāvaviveka divides the bodhisattva path into four parts, as is common in other important Mahāyāna works on the path. In *Mppś* (pp. 1795–1798, and 2374), for example, we find that the path is divided into (1) the first arising of the mind [of enlightenment] (*prathamacittotpādika*) or first setting out on the [great] vehicle (*prathamayānasaṃprasthita*), (2) the practice of the six perfections (*ṣaṭpāramitā-caryāpratipanna*), (3) the irreversible stage (*avinivartanīya*), and (4) the stage that is limited to one birth (*ekajātipratibaddha*). These four parts can be correlated with the other standard division of the bodhisattva path into "stages" (*bhūmi*). Haribhadra (*Ālokā*, p. 831), for example, explains that the first of these four parts corresponds to "the stage for the practice of conviction" (*adhimukticaryā-bhūmi*), the second to bodhisattva stages one through seven, the third to bodhisattva stages eight and nine, and the fourth to bodhisattva stage ten. Bhāvaviveka has already covered "the stage for the practice of conviction" in chapters 1 and 2, the chapters he calls "Not Relinquishing the Mind of Enlightenment" (*bodhicittāparityāga*) and "Taking the Vow of an Ascetic" (*munivratasamāśraya*). Here in verse 292 he takes up the second part of the path (corresponding to the first through seventh bodhisattva stages) and focuses particularly on the practice of the six perfections. In his discussion of the third part (corresponding to the eighth and ninth bodhisattva stages) he concentrates on the ten masteries (*vaśitā*). In his discussion of the fourth part (corresponding to the tenth stage), he concentrates on the superknowledges (*abhijñā*). More will be said about the individual parts in the notes that follow. For further commentary on the bodhisattva path as a whole, see *Mppś*, pp. 1783–88 and pp. 2373–81.
2. In the commentary that follows verse 300, Bhāvaviveka explains that the introductory verses of this section of the text (verses 292–300) are the stage upon which the practice of the six perfections (in verses 301–7) is built. The introductory verses explain that a bodhisattva dwells in nirvana-without-foundation (*apratiṣṭhita-nirvāṇa*) and looks on people with a wisdom-eye that is moist with compassion. Verses 301–7 then explain how the ordinary virtues such as generosity (*dāna*) and moral conduct (*śīla*) are brought to perfection. Nirvana-without-foundation is first mentioned in the introduction to verse 294.
3. In the term "Brahman-practice" (*brahma-abhyāsa*), Bhāvaviveka is playing on the meaning of the terms "Brahman-practice" (*brahma-caryā*) and "Brahman-state" (*brahma-vihāra*) to describe the practice of the bodhisattva path. To add a further dimension to the play on the word "Brahman," he has also equated the Dharma Body with the Brahman that consists of nirvana (*brahma-nirvāṇa*) in the commentary on verse 289ab. On the term *brahmacaryā* in Madhyamaka literature, see Nāgārjuna's *Vigrahavyāvartanī*, vs. 54 (ed. Johnston and Kunst, p. 140). The *brahma-vihāras* are discussed briefly in 280cd.
4. "Seeks to know this" is an allusion to the title of the chapter, "The Quest for the Knowledge of Reality." The word "this" should be taken as a reference to Brahman and the Dharma Body.
5. "Thought" (*cintā*) and "practice" (*bhāvanā*) represent the last two of the three types of wisdom: the wisdom that consists of hearing (*śrutamayī-prajñā*), the wisdom that

consists of thought (*cintāmayī-prajñā*), and the wisdom that consists of repeated practice (*bhāvanāmayī-prajñā*). The three types of wisdom are discussed in *Kośa* VI.5.

6. For an example of the role of the recollection of the Buddha (*buddhānusmṛti*) in Mahāyāna literature, see Paul M. Harrison, "Buddhānusmṛti in the Pratyutpanna-buddha-saṃmukhāvasthita-samādhi-sūtra," *JIP* 6 (1978), pp. 35–57.
7. Bhāvaviveka is summarizing the definition of the recollection of the Buddha in the tenth chapter of the *Anantamukhanirhāradhāraṇī*: "Someone who has practiced this [recollection of the Buddha realizes that the Buddha is] not form, not no-form, not the major characteristics, not no-major characteristics, not the minor characteristics, not no-minor characteristics," and so forth. See Hisao Inagaki, *The Anantamukhanirhāra-Dhāraṇī Sūtra and Jñānagarbha's Commentary* (Kyoto: Nagata Bunshodo, 1987), pp. 153–54. The four scriptural quotations that appear here as illustrations of the concept of Buddha-recollection are quoted verbatim in the *Madhyamakaratnapradīpa, Sde-dge Tibetan Tripiṭaka bsTan-ḥgyur Preserved at the Faculty of Letters, University of Tokyo (Dbu ma)* (Tokyo, 1977–1979), vol. 2, no. 3854, p. 143 (folios *Tsha* 285a/4–285b/2).
8. *De bźhin gśegs pa'i le'u* (*tathāgata-parivarta*).
9. In *MHK* I.20–21, Bhāvaviveka introduced the concept of nirvana-without-foundation by saying, "They see the faults [of samsara], so they do not dwell in ordinary existence; and they are compassionate, so they do not [dwell] in nirvana. They dwell in ordinary existence because they have consecrated themselves for others. They do not grasp samsara and nirvana as different or the same, so those who are wise do not dwell anywhere, yet they dwell everywhere in ordinary existence." For a thorough discussion of this important concept in Mahāyāna literature, see Lamotte, *The Teaching of Vimalakīrti*, p. 45.
10. Bhāvaviveka mentions "the attainment of cessation" (*nirodha-samāpatti*) briefly in his commentary on *MHK* V.4. "[The store-consciousness (*ālaya-vijñāna*)] is called store-consciousness because, as a foundation, it is the cause of all active consciousness (*pravṛtti-vijñāna*) and is associated with mental phenomena (*caitta*) such as desire and conviction. . . . When conditions such as the eye, form, light, space, and mental activity coincide, the six forms of active consciousness arise from it. . . . [However,] there is no reason for there to be any cognition of objects when a someone is unconscious or when someone is in the attainment of unconsciousness (*asaṃjñi-samāpatti*), the attainment of cessation (*nirodha-samāpatti*), sleep, intoxication, or a fainting spell." For a thorough discussion of "the attainment of cessation" in Buddhist literature, see Paul J. Griffiths, *On Being Mindless: Buddhist Meditation and the Mind-Body Problem* (La Salle, Ill.: Open Court, 1986).
11. The verse and commentary identify the peak as Mount Meru. On the traditional antecedents of this verse, see chapter 2 in this book.
12. Bhāvaviveka uses a similar image in *MHK* I.8ab: "[A bodhisattva] sees that the wisdom-eye of the whole world is covered (*lokam ālokya sakalaṃ prajñālokatiraskṛtam*)." The similarity between these two verses suggests that III.297 contains a tacit contrast between the eyes of the bodhisattva and the eyes of ordinary people (*loka*). The eyes of the bodhisattva are open, while the eyes of ordinary people remain "covered" (*saṃvṛta*) by the illusions of ordinary existence. The image occurs frequently in Madhyamaka literature, especially in passages that give an etymology of relative (*saṃvṛti*) truth. See, for example, *Prasannapadā*, p. 30, and *Bodhicaryāvatārapañjikā* (Vaidya ed.), p. 174. The specific word for wisdom-eye varies somewhat with different contexts and different authors. In *Prasannapadā*, pp. 172–73, for example, Candrakīrti says that the entire world (*sarva-loka*) has its wisdom-eye (*mati-nayana*) obstructed (*upahata*) by the eye-disease of ignorance (*avidyā-timira*). In the passage just mentioned from the *Bodhicaryāvatārapañjikā*, Prajñākaramati says that the wisdom-eye (*buddhi-locana*) is covered (*āvṛta*) by the eye disease of ignorance.
13. In some places in his work, Bhāvaviveka uses the phrase "introduction of the ambrosia of reality" (*tattvāmṛtāvatāra*) as a description of his philosophical quest. In *MHK*

I.4 he says, "With [my] mind fixed on great enlightenment and with dedication to the welfare of others, [I] say as much as [I am] able in order to introduce the ambrosia of reality." In I.14, he speaks of "the ambrosia of understanding reality as an object" (*tattvārthādhigamāmṛta*). In III.354, it is the lovely ambrosia of the Buddha's wisdom that brings satisfaction to sentient beings. These sentient beings are the beings who, in II.2, could not be satisfied by knowledge of the True Law. The word *avatāra* ("introduction") is understood by the Tibetan translators as "leading into." In the Tibetan version of *MHK* I.4, for example, *avatāra* is translated as *bdud rtsir gzud pa* ("lead into the ambrosia"). But Bhāvaviveka also seems to be playing on the more conventional meaning of *avatāra* as "descent," as if the "descent" of the ambrosia of the Buddha's wisdom were the Buddhist counterpart of the "descent" of the deity in the Hindu concept of the "incarnation" (*avatāra*) of God. In verse 354, for example, the ambrosia of wisdom descends from the Buddha on the mountain of omniscience like the tears that flow from the eyes of the bodhisattva on the mountain of wisdom in verses 296–97.

Ambrosia is mentioned in earlier Madhyamaka literature in the phrase "ambrosia of teaching" (*śāsanāmṛta*) as, for example, in Nāgārjuna's *Acintyastava* 56; *Ratnāvalī* I.62, II.9; *MMK* XVIII.11; and in Mātṛceṭa's *Śatapañcāśatka* 24 and 72. Lamotte gives an extended note on "ambrosia" in *The Teaching of Vimalakīrti*, pp. 307–14, in which he observes that the "ambrosia" in Buddhist literature is not churned up from the deep, as it is in Hindu mythology, but descends from above.

On "the happy cessation of conceptual diversity" (*prapañcopaśama śiva*), see the note on *MHK* III.284.

Bhāvaviveka has already said that a person needs to avoid the "functioning" or "activity" of cognition (*dhī-pracāra*) in order to see reality (*tattva*) correctly. In *MHK* III.266, he defined reality as "[the object] about which not even a nonconceptual cognition (*dhī*) arises." This definition was consistent with the definition of reality in I.2 as "free from the functioning of cognition" (*dhī-pracāra-vivarjitam*). In III.10–11 he also spoke of "functioning without functioning" (*apracāra-pracāra*) in the clear sky of reality. The source of this terminology is a passage from the *Akṣayamatinirdeśa Sūtra* that is frequently quoted in Madhyamaka sources: "[Ultimate truth] is that toward which not even knowledge functions, let alone words" (*yatra jñānasyāpy apracāraḥ kaḥ punar vādo 'kṣarāṇām*). See *Prasannapadā*, p. 374 and *Jñānagarbha's Commentary*, p. 74. On the absence of the wisdom-eye, see the note on verse 297.

14. "Patient and pure" (*sran thub pa dag*): on the problems involved in the interpretation of this phrase, see the note on verse 307.
15. The commentary is consistent with the Tibetan translation of the verse, but it is not entirely consistent with the Sanskrit. First, it changes the Sanskrit order of "birth, death, old age, and sickness" to the more logical order "birth, old age, sickness, and death." Second, it omits the word "grief" (*śoka*). If we only had the Sanskrit, we would translate the verse: "They have been wounded by the arrows of birth, death, old age, sickness, and grief and have become sick."
16. The "ten qualities that offer protection" are not easy to identify. Clearly they are not the seven "treasures" (*sapta-dhana*), even though this is the only list of qualities in the *Mahāvyutpatti* that begins with "faith" (*śraddhā*) and "moral conduct" (*śīla*). In the commentary on *MHK* I.9, Bhāvaviveka explains the word "no protector" (*anātha*) with almost the same phrase: "To have no protector means to lack the ten qualities, beginning with faith, that offer protection." The reading of *mgon med* ("no protection") has to be emended to *mgon byed* ("offer protection"), but the earlier passage may be more accurate in omitting "moral conduct." If so, the "ten qualities that begin with faith" could be the five "faculties" (*indriya*: *MV* 976–81) plus the five "strengths" (*bala*: *MV* 982–87), each of which begins with "faith" (*śraddhā*). Another option is to follow Gokhale's suggestion of the "ten qualities" (*daśadharma*: *MV* 902–12), but this list of ten qualities does not include faith.

17. Bhāvaviveka seems to be saying that the person is swept away more forcefully by the "river" (*chu bo*) than he is by the "stream" (*'bab chu*). But the word translated as "seize" (*ma choṅs pa*) actually means "not seize." It is possible that Bhāvaviveka means that a person who is swept away by a stream does not have anything in the stream to hold on to to be saved and is swept away more forcefully than before. But it seems more likely that the negative particle has been introduced in a mistaken attempt to clarify the meaning of an otherwise obscure phrase in the Tibetan. Bhāvaviveka's intention is made more clear in the next two sentences.
18. Here Bhāvaviveka explains why he used the peculiar image of seizing onto a river in the previous sentence. Here people seize (*upādāna*) actions (*karma*) that flow or turn into (*saṃsaranti*) a river of samsara. It is odd to think of grasping a river, but it is the act of "grasping" in the flow of samsara that augments the flow of samsara itself.
19. The word "dedicated" (*dīkṣita*) plays an important part in Bhāvaviveka's presentation of the bodhisattva's vow. In his discussion of the sage's vow in his first chapter, he calls the vow *dīkṣā* ("ritual dedication") rather than *praṇidhāna* (the normal word for bodhisattva vow).
20. The Tibetan translates *vajra-śaila* ("diamond-stone" or "diamond-mountain") in the verse as "diamond-jewel" (*rdo rje rin chen*). The translation of the commentary makes it *rdo rje'i ri bo* ("diamond-mountain"). In view of the common comparison between the aspiration to enlightenment (*bodhicitta*) and a diamond-jewel (*vajraratna*), the translation of the verse is more likely the correct one. For an example of this comparison, see Prajñākaramati's *Pañjikā* on *BCA* I.17.
21. Here the word "accomplished" (*kṛtin*) is translated *legs bslabs* ("well trained"). In *MHK* I.30, it is translated *mkhas pa* ("wise") and glossed in the commentary as *kalyāṇamitra* ("preceptor" or "spiritual friend"). In both cases it refers to a bodhisattva who has made substantial progress on the path to liberation and is able to use that progress to help others.
22. Superior moral conduct (*adhiśīla*) is the first of three categories used to classify the practices (*śikṣā*) of the bodhisattva path. The other two are superior thought (*adhicitta*) and superior wisdom (*adhiprajñā*). The three categories are discussed in *MS*, chaps. 6–8 (pp. 212–58).
23. Nāgārjuna's *Ratnāvalī* IV.80abc and V.36–39.
24. Relative and ultimate wisdom are discussed in *MHK* III.7–13.
25. The six "recollections" (*anusmṛti*)—of the Buddha, the Dharma, the Saṃgha, moral conduct (*śīla*), sacrifice (*tyāga*), and divinities (*devatā*)—are discussed by Lamotte in *Mppś*, pp. 1329–1333.
26. Bhāvaviveka's quotation does not directly corrrespond to the text of the *Subāhuparipṛcchā Sūtra* in the Tibetan canon. The parallel passage is found in *Subāhuparipṛcchā Sūtra* (*Ārya-subāhu-paripṛcchā-nāma-mahāyāna-sūtra*) in *The Tibetan Tripitaka: Peking Edition*, ed. Daisetz T. Suzuki, no. 760 (26) (Tokyo-Kyoto: Tibetan Tripitaka Research Insititute, 1956–1961), vol. 24, p. 56, folios *Zi* 156b/7–157a/2.
27. In the commentary on *MHK* I.6, Bhāvaviveka explains that "great love" (*mahāmaitrī*) has four aspects: saving (*uttāraṇa*) all beings, liberating (*mocana*) them, enlightening them, and leading them to parinirvana. "Saving" is discussed separately in verses 7–8 and "liberating" in verses 9–11.
28. Compare *Nārāyaṇaparipṛcchā Sūtra* (quoted in Śāntideva's *Śikṣāsamuccaya*, Vaidya ed., p. 16): "O son of good family, the bodhisattva, the great being, should generate the following thought: 'I have sacrificed and given away my own body to all beings, how much more so external things. If anyone needs something for any reason, I will offer it as a benefit. I will give a hand to those who need a hand. I will give a foot to those who need a foot. I will give an eye to those who need an eye. Flesh to those who need flesh. Blood to those who need blood. Marrow to those who need marrow. Limbs great and small to those who need limbs great and small. I will sacrifice [my]

head to those who need a head, to say nothing of external things such as wealth, grain, gold, silver, jewels, ornaments, horses, elephants.'"

29. The first half of the verse presents difficult problems. We have three separate versions to use in deciphering its meaning. Ejima's Sanskrit reads *bhakta-śuddhopa-dhānantaparivāro*, which seems to mean "devoted, pure, bearing, limitless entourage." In the commentary on verses 297–300, there is a brief summary of the verse that seems to say, "He receives an entourage and possesses those who are patient" (*'khor gcugs śiṅ sran thub pa dag daṅ ldan zhiṅ*). The verse and commentary here have some of the same elements. The phrase *'khor gcugs* appears in the Tibetan of verse 307 and appears as *'khor yid gcugs* in the commentary. *Sran thub pa* ("patient") corresponds to *bzod* in the verse and commentary. It is not easy, however, to match this Tibetan version with the Sanskrit. The only possible counterpart of *bhakta* ("devoted") is *yid gcugs pa* (or *gcugs*). This is the word that I translated earlier as "receive." *Śuddha* ("pure") probably is represented by the *dag* in the commentary on verse 300 and the *brtag* in this verse and commentary. The copyist at some stage seems not to have recognized it as a separate word. The word *upadhā* then seems to correspond to *bzod* and *sran thub pa* ("patient"). It can, of course, mean to "bear." *Ananta* ("limitless") corresponds to *mtha' yas pa*. And *parivāra* ("entourage") corresponds to *'khor*. As a temporary expedient, I am translating the string of adjectives modifying *parivāra* by what seems to be the most reasonable combination of Sanskrit and Tibetan available, but this does not by any means solve all the textual problems.

30. Here Bhāvaviveka takes up the third part of his analysis of the bodhisattva path, the part in which the bodhisattva is irreversible (*avinivartanīya*). This part corresponds to the eighth and ninth of the ten bodhisattva stages (*bhūmi*). (For a discussion of the structure of the path as a whole, see the notes that precede verse 292.) The analysis of this part of the path focuses on the ten bodhisattva masteries (*vaśitā*). In the *Daśabhūmika Sūtra* (p. 46) the ten masteries are described in the following way: "1. [The bodhisattva in the eighth stage] achieves mastery over life (*āyuḥ-vaśitā*) because [the bodhisattva] sustains (*adhiṣṭhāna*) [the bodhisattva's] lifespan for utterly incalculable eons. 2. [The bodhisattva] attains mastery over mind (*ceto-vaśitā*) because [the bodhisattva] enters profound awareness (*nidhyapti-jñāna*) in innumerable concentrations (*samādhi*). 3. [The bodhisattva] attains mastery over personal belongings (*pariṣkāra-vaśitā*) because [the bodhisattva] manifests (*saṃdarśana*) the sustaining power (*adhiṣṭhāna*) to adorn all world systems with many magical arrays (*vyūha*). 4. [The bodhisattva attains] mastery over karma (*karma-vaśitā*) because [the bodhisattva] manifests (*saṃdarśana*) sustaining power (*adhiṣṭhāna*) over the time at which karma matures. 5. [The bodhisattva attains] mastery over birth (*utpatti-vaśitā*) because [the bodhisattva] manifests birth in all world systems. 6. [The bodhisattva attains] mastery over aspiration (*adhimukti-vaśitā*) because [the bodhisattva] manifests the filling of all world systems with Buddhas. 7. [The bodhisattva] attains mastery over vows (*praṇidhāna-vaśitā*) because [the bodhisattva] manifests enlightenment at any time and in any Buddha-field [the bodhisattva] wishes. 8. [The bodhisattva attains] mastery over power (*ṛddhi-vaśitā*) because [the bodhisattva] manifests powerful miracles (*ṛddhi-vikurvaṇa*) in all Buddha-fields. 9. [The bodhisattva] attains mastery over Dharma (*dharma-vaśitā*) because [the bodhisattva] manifests illumination (*āloka*) of the entrance (*mukha*) into infinitely numerous *dharmas*. 10. [The bodhisattva] attains mastery over insight (*jñāna-vaśitā*) because [the bodhisattva] manifests perfect enlightenment with regard to the [ten] powers of a Tathāgata (*tathāgata-bala*), the [four] convictions (*vaiśāradya*), the [eighteen] exclusive attributes of a Buddha (*āveṇika-buddha-dharma*), the [thirty-two] primary characteristics (*lakṣaṇa*), and the [eighty] secondary characteristics (*anuvyañjana*)." In the *Madhyamakāvatāra* (La Vallée Poussin ed., p. 349), Candrakīrti quotes this description of the masteries in *DBh* in his account of the eighth bodhisattva stage, with only two small changes in the order. He switches numbers 6 and 7, and

numbers 9 and 10. Bhāvaviveka also reverses the order of numbers 9 and 10, but his biggest change is to remove the mastery of power from its place in *DBh* as item 8 and give it special treatment at the end of the list. The *MS* (pp. 269ff.) and *AA* VIII.4 treat the masteries as properties of the Dharma Body.

31. In the explanation of this verse and the verses that follow, Bhāvaviveka generally concludes the commentary by quoting the short, one-sentence explanation of each of the masteries in the *DBh*. The differences in wording are usually very slight. For the *DBh* version, see the preceding note.
32. The *DBh* speaks only of Buddhas. Bhāvaviveka adds the qualification "Buddha-manifestations" (*buddha-nirmāṇa*).
33. The *DBh* identifies the *dharmas* as the different attributes of a Buddha.
34. The Peking version of the commentary adds the following passage: "Because [the bodhisattva] has power, [the bodhisattva] exercises power over the whole world. [The bodhisattva] has the mastery of power (*ṛddhi-vaśitā*) because [the bodhisattva] instantly manifests innumerable manifestations to teach individually innumerable sentient beings, just as the moon gives rise to innumerable, simultaneous reflections." This seems to have been added by someone who did not understand that Bhāvaviveka has moved the mastery of power to the end of the list of masteries for separate treatment. Bhāvaviveka's revised order is made clear in the commentary on verse 329.
35. Bhāvaviveka devotes the next sixteen verses (313–29) to the mastery of power (*ṛddhi-vaśitā*). His classification of the different types follows a scheme that is discussed in detail in chapter 5 of *BBh* (pp. 40–46). In that text, the scheme is applied to the superknowledge that consists of power (*ṛddhy-abhijñā*), not to the mastery of power. Here Bhāvaviveka adapts the scheme to the list of masteries and develops his own framework later (in verses 336–45) to describe the superknowledge of power. The *BBh* distinguishes two kinds of power (*ṛddhi*): the power to transform (*pariṇāmikī ṛddhi*) and the power to manifest (*nairmāṇikī ṛddhi*). The power to transform is divided into sixteen subcategories. Bhāvaviveka seems to make use of fourteen of these categories. Listed, with the numbers of the verses in which they appear, they are: shaking (313ab), burning (313cd), glowing (314ab), making visible (314cd–315), changing (316), coming and going (317), putting things inside his own body (318), shrinking and expanding (319), entering assemblies (320), appearing and disappearing (321ab), overwhelming the power of others (321cd), taking control (322ab), giving confidence, memory, and pleasure (322cd and commentary), and releasing rays (323). The power to manifest is introduced in verse 324, then is divided into three subcategories: manifestations of body (325), manifestations of place (326), and manifestations of voice (327–29). A somewhat abbreviated account of the sixteen varieties of the power to transform is found in *MS*, pp. 221–22.
36. Literally, "Innumerable three thousand great thousands of innumerable hundreds of *koṭis*." Lamotte comments on the numerical system in Mahāyāna cosmology in his note on "Buddha-fields" in the Appendix to *The Teaching of Vimalakīrti* (p. 275). According to Lamotte, "three thousand great thousands" (*trisāhasra-mahāsāhasra*) is the equivalent of one billion. See also W. Kirfel, *Die Kosmographie der Inder nach den Quellen dargestellt* (Bonn and Leipzig: Kurt Schroeder, 1920), pp. 178–207; and W. Randolph Kloetzli, *Buddhist Cosmology: Science and Theology in the Images of Motion and Light* (Delhi: Motilal Banarsidass, 1983), ch. 3.
37. Bhāvaviveka's explanation equates the bodhisattva's "yawn" (*jṛmbhana*) with "play" or "easy mastery" (*vikrīḍana*). (He actually gives two synonyms—Tibetan *rnam par rtse ba* and *rnam par rol ba*, but both are equivalent to the Sanskrit *vikrīḍana*.) As Edgerton explains in the *BHSD*, "the lion's yawn" (*siṃha-vijṛmbhana*) and "the lion's play" (*siṃha-vikrīḍita*) can be used to name specific states of concentration and also specific Tathāgatas. Lewis Lancaster has commented on the same connection in "Samādhi Names in Buddhist Texts," *Malalasekera Commemoration Volume*, ed. O. H. de A. Wijesekera (Columbo: Malalasekera Commemoration Volume Editorial Committee,

1976), pp. 196–202. The classic example of an "action" that shakes the world is found in the opening pages of *The Large Sūtra on Perfect Wisdom*: "Thereupon the Lord, seated on that very Lion Seat, entered into the concentration called 'The Lion's Play.' With his supernatural power he shook this great trichiliocosm in six ways . . ." (Conze trans., p. 40). In the language of many of the Mahāyāna sūtras, the Buddha's "yawn" or "act of play" is but another example of his effortless power. It is closely related and in many cases almost synonymous to "sustaining power" (*adhiṣṭhāna*) and even "magical array" (*vyūha*), as in *The Lotus Sūtra* (ed. Kern and Nanjio, p. 426): "By the Tathāgata's sustaining power, by an application of the Tathāgata's force, by the Tathāgata's play, by the Tathāgata's magical array, by the Tathāgata's great knowledge. . . ."

38. On the bases of power (*ṛddhi-pāda*), see *Mppś*, pp. 1124–25, 1177–79. Among other things, the bases of power allow a person to prolong the span of life. See Étienne Lamotte, ed. and trans., *La concentration de la marche héroïque* (*Śūraṃgamasamādhisūtra*), (Brussels: Institut Belge des Hautes Études Chinoises, 1965), pp. 121–22.
39. This half verse is missing in the Tibetan but is the subject of the commentary that follows. The *saṃvega* of the Sanskrit ("violent excitement or agitation") is explained by *'gyod* in the Tibetan ("remorse"). In the form of a verb (*saṃvejanīya*), *saṃvega* plays a role in the account of Buddhist holy sites in the Pali *Mahāparinibbāna Sutta*: The four holy sites associated with the life of the Buddha are "to be seen" (*dassanīya*) and "powerfully experienced" (*saṃvejanīya*). Here the same two elements are present: the gods are given a vision of hell and are deeply moved. On the significance of *saṃvega* in an aesthetic and religious context, see A. K. Coomaraswamy, "*Saṃvega*: Aesthetic Shock," *Harvard Journal of Asiatic Studies* 7 (1943), pp. 174–79, and Gregory Schopen, "Burial '*Ad Sanctos*' and the Physical Presence of the Buddha in Early Buddhism," *Religion* 17 (1987), p. 195.
40. Bhāvaviveka's description of the hells presents a number of textual problems. The list of places that begins (in the Tibetan word order) with *ral gri'i nags tsal* (*asivana*) corresponds roughly to the list of four *utsadas* (secondary hells) in the commentary on *Kośa* III.59. The third of these *utsadas* is divided into three separate regions to produce a list of six. These six separate regions are called *kukūla* ("a pit of coals"), *kuṇapa* ("mud made of excrement"), *kṣuramārga* ("a road made of knives"), *asipattravana* ("a forest where the leaves are swords"), *ayaḥśalmalīvana* ("a forest with spines"), *vaitaraṇī* ("a river with boiling water"). Bhāvaviveka appears to list five of these six but in an order different from the order of the *Kośa*. He begins with a series of clauses that constitute a description of the hells. These can be matched with the five regions at the end of the passage but only with difficulty and only by rearranging the order of the different elements. The results of that rearrangement will be evident in the translation that follows. Since the passage requires such extensive rearrangement to make sense, I have taken the further liberty of putting the five *utsadas* in the order followed by the *Kośa*. The text that we have available to us omits the *kṣuramārga* ("the road made of knives") from the list of *utsadas*. I have tentatively identified this as the item that is "guarded by Yama's cruel hosts."
41. It is possible that the iron-beaked ravens associated later with the Śalmalī trees actually belong here, although Lamotte is probably right when he says that the creatures in this realm who have iron beaks and penetrate the body from the nose to the soles of the feet are actually insects (*Mppś*, pp. 961–62). In the list that appears in the *Kośa*, *kuṇapa* is followed by *kṣuramārga*, a road paved with knives. Bhāvaviveka seems to have omitted it.
42. Bhāvaviveka sometimes uses the ten powers (*bala*), four convictions (*vaiśāradya*), and four infallible penetrations (*pratisaṃvid*) to represent the qualities of a Buddha. On the qualities themselves, see *Mppś*, pp. 1505–1624.
43. This seems to be the meaning of *'bigs byed*. The *BBh* says only that he is able to pass through walls, mountains (*śaila*), and ramparts (p. 42).
44. The description of the bodhisattva's ability to "enter assemblies" (*sabhāgatopasaṃ-*

krānati in the *BBh* (p. 43) shows that this ability is not limited to assemblies of the gods. It also includes assemblies of kṣatriyas and brāhmaṇas in the human realm. Compare also *DBh*, p. 45, where the bodhisattva takes the form also of vaiśyas and śūdras. This suggests indirectly some of the beings Bhāvaviveka has in mind when he uses the word "fortunate" (*bhavya*) in the next sentence.

45. On "fortunate beings" (*bhavya*) see the commentary on verse 268.
46. The first half of the verse describes the bodhisattva's power to "take control" (*vaśitva-karaṇa*). Lamotte defines this power (*MS*, p. 222) by saying, "Il fait aller, venir, s'arrêter, parler à sa volonté les créatures de tous les mondes." This follows the definition found in the *BBh* (p. 43): "He causes the entire realm of beings to engage in actions such as going, coming, and standing. If he thinks, 'Let it go,' it goes; 'Let it stay,' it stays; 'Let it come,' it comes; and 'Let it speak,' it speaks." This would seem to indicate that *gati-sthānoktiṣu* is a *dvandva* compound naming three activities—going, standing, and speaking—in which the bodhisattva places the world. The Tibetan translator, however, translates the compound as "speaking about places to go" (*'gro ba'i gnas ni brjod*).
47. The second half of the verse seems to cover the powers to give confidence (*pratibhāna-dāna*), to give memory (*smṛti-dāna*), and to give pleasure (*sukha-dāna*), although the commentary adds the fourth element "intelligence."
48. The commentary on the first half of the verse begins with several sentences that seem to have confused the Tibetan translator and whose meaning is obscure. Bhāvaviveka says, "'A place to go' (*gati-sthāna*) is a continent and so forth. Things distinguished by particular words that refer to these [continents and so forth] are cities and so forth. These cities [and so forth] are what is meant by 'places to go.'"
49. These are the eight great hells listed in the commentary on *Kośa* III.58 and in *MV* 4920–27. For a discussion of the classification of these hells in Buddhist literature, see *Mppś*, pp. 955–68.
50. On the eight cold hells, see *Kośa* III.59 and *Mppś*, pp. 955–57. Bhāvaviveka's list of the cold hells begins with an item called simply *gas pa*. The word *gas pa* occurs as an element in the names of several of the cold hells, but it does not appear separately in the list found in *MV* 4929–36. Bhāvaviveka's partial list of cold hells also contains a hell called Kumuda (*ku mu ta ltar gas pa*) that is not found in the *MV* list and is not mentioned in Lamotte's analysis of the sources.
51. See *Kośa* III.69 on the different categories of gods who inhabit the Realm of Desire (*kāma-dhātu*).
52. Ejima reads *romakūpebhyaḥ stūpebhyo* ("from pores and from stūpas"). The Tibetan version of the verse and commentary does not mention stūpas, but speaks instead of musical instruments (*rol mo*) and drums (*rṅa*). The correct reading of the verse is most likely *romakūpebhas tūryebhyo* ("from pores and from musical instruments").
53. The Tibetan sentence starts with an explanation of the first part of the verse (*adhimuktīndriyavaśāt*), then skips to the second part of the verse without an appropriate transition. Something has probably been omitted, perhaps because of the similarity between the *bźin* that ends the first *pāda* and the *źi ba* that begins the second.
54. See particularly *MMK* XVII.31.
55. *Ratnamegha Sūtra* (*Ārya-ratna-megha-nāma-mahāyāna-sūtra*), in *The Tibetan Tripitaka: Peking Edition*, ed. Daisetz T. Suzuki, (Tokyo-Kyoto: Tibetan Tripitaka Research Institute, 1956–61), no. 897, vol. 35, pp. 171–220, folios *Dzu* 1–121a.
56. The standard treatment of the superknowledges (*abhjñā*) gives a list of six: the superknowledge of power (*ṛddhyabhijñā*), the superknowledge of clairaudience (*divyaś-rotra*), the superknowledge of other minds (*paracittābhijñā*), the superknowledge in which one remembers previous lives (*pūrvanivānusmṛtyabhijñā*), the superknowledge of death and rebirth (*cyutyupapādābhijñā*), or clairvoyance (*divyacakṣus*), and the superknowledge of the extinction of defilements (*āsravakṣayābhijñā*). Lamotte discusses the sources of this list in an extended note in *Mppś*, pp. 1809–17. He

points out that the sixth superknowledge, the extinction of defilements, posed a problem for Mahāyāna authors, since a bodhisattva has to retain at least a vestige of defilement to remain on the bodhisattva path. Mahāyāna sources apparently responded to the problem in two ways. One was to say that the bodhisattva only attained the first *five* super-knowledges as part of the bodhisattva path. The sixth superknowledge was then attained at the level of Buddhahood. This option is followed in *Mppś*, pp. 328–33 (and in the portion of *The Perfection of Wisdom Sūtra* on which it is based). The second option was to explain that extinction of defilements applies only to certain categories of defilements and leaves others intact. This option is followed in *Mppś*, pp. 1817–18. Bhāvaviveka chooses the first option and omits the sixth superknowledge altogether. He also changes the order in several ways, the most important of which is to move the superknowledge of power (*ṛddhy-abhijñā*) from the beginning of the list to the end. This mirrors the move he made with the mastery of power in the preceding section and allows him again to give the concept special treatment. He also discusses clairvoyance (*divya-cakṣus*) twice as a result of an ambiguity in the concept itself. Other changes will be apparent from the text that follows.

57. Instead of "defiled" (*kliṣṭa*), the Tibetan of the verse and commentary reads "lower" (*dman pa*). It seems unlikely that this is correct, since "lesser" (*hīna*) is mentioned in the second half of the verse.
58. *Kleśa* and *upakleśa*.
59. Perhaps at the time of a Buddha.
60. BHSD (s.v. *praṇīta*) lists a number of places where *hīna* ("lesser") is contrasted with *madhya* ("middle") and *praṇīta* ("higher"). It is possible that Bhāvaviveka also has in mind an additional three-part subdivision of each category.
61. Clairvoyance (*divya-cakṣus*) is interpreted in two ways. In the list of five superknowledges that appears in *Mppś*, pp. 328–33, clairvoyance is defined as the ability to see beings and substances in the six realms of rebirth—that is, forms that are close, far away, gross, or subtle. In other accounts of the six superknowledges (discussed by Lamotte in *Mppś*, pp. 1809–27, and mentioned in *The Large Sūtra*, p. 81), clairvoyance is defined as the ability to see death and rebirth. Bhāvaviveka discusses this second kind of clairvoyance in verse 335. In the commentary on verse 335, Bhāvaviveka says that it is possible to group both forms of vision together under the category of clairvoyance, or to treat the first form of vision as a function of the physical eye (*māṃsa-cakṣus*) and only the second as clairvoyance (*divya-cakṣus*). The problem is that the sources Bhāvaviveka accepts as authoritative do not speak with a single voice.
62. The same point is made in the discussion of the five "eyes" in *The Large Sutra on Perfect Wisdom* (Conze trans., p. 77).
63. Ejima's reading of *bhāñji* is somewhat problematic. The manuscript reads *ābhāṃji* or *abhāṃji*. In the verse the word is translated as *gyur pa* ("to become"). The commentary seems to take it as "gross" (*rags pa*), in contrast to the word "subtle" (*sūkṣma*) in the first *pāda*. I am following the explanation of the commentary.
64. The Sanskrit word *ghana* means simply a lump or solid mass, but it is translated by the Tibetan word *bkod pa*, which also translates the Sanskrit *vyūha* ("magical array").
65. It is possible that Bhāvaviveka is referring to the arrays that come from the Buddha of the eastern direction, King of Illumination, Splendor, and Radiance (*Vairocanaśrītejorājā*) at the beginning of the *Gaṇḍavyūha Sūtra* (Vaidya ed., p. 6). But Bhāvaviveka seems to be speaking of Vairocana Buddha in a more general sense, as he is spoken of, for example, in the Vairocana section of the *Avataṃsaka Sūtra*. See the verses spoken in praise of Vairocana of the throne of enlightenment in *The Flower Ornament Scripture*, trans. Thomas Cleary, vol 1 (Boulder: Shambhala, 1984), pp. 257–58.
66. This formula is similar to the one quoted from the *DBh* in *Mppś*, p. 1811.

67. *Sa bla sa steng* is a puzzling phrase for which the dictionaries and indices give little help.
68. Some Buddhist schools, particularly the Sāṃmitīyas, took the position that there is an "intermediate state" (*antarābhāva*) between the end of one life and the beginning of another. Others said that the new birth follows directly after the end of the previous life. The topic is discussed in *Kośa* III.10–14. For further references, see *Mppś*, p. 745.
69. As in the scriptural accounts of the superknowledges quoted in *Mppś*, pp. 1809–1814.
70. As in *The Large Sutra on Perfect Wisdom* (Conze trans., pp. 76–77).
71. The four bases of power (*ṛddhi-pāda*)—namely, the concentrations of mind, energy, zeal, and investigation (*citta-*, *vīrya-*, *chanda-*, and *mīmāṃsā-samādhi*)—are discussed in *Mppś*, pp. 1124–25, 1177–79. See also the note in the commentary on verse 313ab.
72. Compare *Mppś*, pp. 1939–1940: "The bodhisattva who resides in the tenth stage and has entered the concentration of the hero's march (*śūraṃgama-samādhi*) is present in the great trichiliocosm, and there he sometimes manifests the first arising of the aspiration to enlightenment and practices the six perfections, and so forth." (Translation adapted from Lamotte's French.) The same point is made in *Śgs*, p. 132. In the introduction to his translation, Lamotte explains that the concentration of the hero's march should be understood less as a particular concentration than as an aspect of concentration in general. The concentration derives its name from the fact that someone who attains it can go anywhere like a hero, without meeting any resistance.
73. This item is substituted for the usual "childhood games" (*kumārakrīḍā*), which is found in the *DBh* and in the commentary on verse 268.
74. The Tibetan inserts a half verse between these two verses. Ejima suggests that it be omitted.
75. This paragraph and the verses that follow develop an image of the bodhisattva that appears in the tenth chapter of the *DBh*: "At will, in a single moment, he manifests as many bodies as there are grains of sand in countless world systems. In each body he reveals an equally vast number of hands. And with these hands he offers worship to the Buddhas in the ten directions. Each hand offers clusters of flowers as [numerous] as the sands of the Ganges to the Lord Buddhas. Like the flowers, [he also offers clusters of] perfumes, garlands, ointments, powders, robes, parasols, banners, flags, and all arrays. In each body he sustains (*adhitiṣṭhati*) equally vast numbers of heads. In each head he creates equally vast numbers of tongues. With these he speaks praise to the Lord Buddhas" (Vaidya ed., pp. 61–62).
76. This verse describes the flowers with which (instrumental case) the bodhisattva offers worship to the Buddha in the next verse. If it were not necessary to accommodate the commentary, we would start this verse with the word "with" and let it simply run on into verse 340.
77. The Tibetan translation simply repeats "fine" (*mchog*) and "sweet" (*bzan̄*), but it is likely that in the Sanskrit different synonyms are used to define the words in the verse.
78. On the significance of peaked dwellings (*kūṭāgāra*), see Ananda K. Coomaraswamy, "Indian Architectural Terms," *JAOS* 48 (1928), pp. 250–75; K. de Vreese, "Skt. Kūṭāgāra," in *India Antiqua* (Leiden: Brill, 1947); Willem B. Bollee, "Le *kūṭāgāra* ou de la maison des hommes au manoir dans l'Inde orientale et l'Asie du Sud-Est," *Bulletin dÉtudes Indiennes* 4 (1986), pp. 189–214.
79. The Sanskrit manuscript of the verses contains a similar series of phrases (*maṇikāñcanasopānarucirāmalavedikaiḥ*) inserted between the two halves of the next verse. As Ejima points out in a note to his edition of the text, the line interrupts the flow of the text. It is most likely a part of the commentary that has been inserted by mistake in the text of the verses.
80. On the word "accomplished" (*kṛtin*), see the commentary on verse 301.
81. Compare *DBh* (Vaidya ed.), pp. 59–60, where the tenth bodhisattva stage (called the

Dharma cloud) is defined as one in which the bodhisattva "bears, receives, appropriates, and preserves the immeasurable great Dharma teachings, great Dharma illuminations, and great Dharma clouds of the Lord Buddhas."

NOTES TO SECTION 3

1. Bhāvaviveka refers to this aspect of the bodhisattva vow in *MHK* I.7–8: "It is right for someone who is wise . . . , when he has seen that all ordinary people have their wisdom-eye concealed, should first save himself from the unholy hell of samsara and then save them."
2. According to the Tibetan of the commentary, the compound that Ejima reads as *janmāvṛto* should mean "birth and transmigration" and be combined in a compound with *duḥkha* ("suffering"). The manuscript comes closer to the text of the commentary when it reads *janmāvarttādduḥkha*, but it should be emended to *janmāvarttaduḥkha*.

   The image of the Dharma as a boat also occurs in *Buddhacarita* I.70: "With the mighty boat of knowledge, he will bring the world, which is being carried away in affliction, up from the ocean of suffering, which is overspread with the foam of disease and which has old age for its waves and death for its fearsome flood" (translation quoted from E. H. Johnston, *The Buddhacarita or Acts of the Buddha* [Lahore, 1936; reprint ed., Delhi: Motilal Banarsidass, 1972], p. 15).
3. Compare *Buddhacarita* I.71: "The world of the living, oppressed with the thirst of desires, will drink the flowing stream of his most excellent Law, which is cooled by concentration of thought and has mystic wisdom for the current of its water, firm discipline for its banks and vows for its Brahminy ducks" (Johnston, p. 15). Bhāvaviveka combines this image of the teaching as thirst-quenching water with the image of jewels that remove poverty. The juxtaposition of these two images in the same verse makes it difficult to give a graceful translation.
4. The Tibetan translation of the verse and commentary suggests a reading of *avidyāmārgadeśikaṃ* ("for whom ignorance is what shows the way") for *avidyādharmadeśikaṃ* ("for whom the Dharma that shows [the way is concealed] by ignorance"). Compare *Buddhacarita* I.72: "For to those who, finding themselves on the desert-tracks of the cycle of existence, are harassed by suffering and obstructed by the objects of sense, he will proclaim the way of salvation, as to travellers who have lost their road" (Johnston, p. 15).
5. The Tibetan of the verse takes *jñāna* ("knowledge") as the subject of *cikitsati* ("cure") and translates it as *ye śes sman*, "knowledge-medicine." This is consistent with the introduction to the verse, which compares the Buddha to the medicine rather than to the doctor who uses it.
6. Compare *Acintyastava* 55 (Lindtner, *Nagarjuniana*).
7. Compare *Buddhacarita* I.74–75.
8. The diamond-like concentration (*vajropama-samādhi*) is the moment on the path to liberation that immediately precedes enlightenment. See Lamotte, *The Teaching of Vimalakīrti*, pp. 298–303.
9. On Bhāvaviveka's understanding of the "ambrosia of wisdom" (*prajñāmṛta*) see the note on verse 300.
10. Read *durddānta* with the manuscript. On the lion's roar that frightens heretics, compare *Acintyastava* 54.
11. As Bhāvaviveka explains in the commentary that follows, the word "passion" (*mada*) also can mean the rut of an elephant.
12. According to *Kośa* VII.47ab, the three miracles (*prātihārya*)—power (*ṛddhi*), proclamation (*ādeśanā*), and delivery of the teaching (*anuśāsanī*)—correspond to the first, third, and sixth superknowledges—namely, the superknowledge of power (*ṛddhyabhijñā*), the superknowledge of other minds (*paracittābhijñā*), and the super-

knowledge of the extinction of defilements (*āsravakṣayābhijñā*). Bhāvaviveka discusses the first five of the six superknowledges in the context of the bodhisattva path (verses 330–45). The sixth superknowledge belongs only to the Buddha and occurs, by implication, only in this verse.

13. The four bases of mindfulness (*smṛty-upasthāna*) are the first of thirty-seven auxiliaries of enlightenment (*bodhipākṣika-dharma*). See *Mppś*, pp. 1150–76.
14. Bhāvaviveka quotes, with only two variations, the standard list of the sixty attributes (*aṅga*) of the Buddha's voice found in *MV* 445–504 and in the commentary on *MSA* XII.9.
15. This attribute, "like the sound of a stormy ocean," is missing from the list in *MV* 445–504 and from the list quoted in the commentary on *MSA* XII.9.
16. After "comprehensive" (*prasṛta*) and before "fulfilling all sounds" (*sarvasvarapūraṇī*), *MV* lists "complete" (*sakhilā* / *chub pa*), "continuous" (*saritā* / *rgyun chags pa*), and "charming" (*lalitā* / *'brel ba*). Bhāvaviveka adjusts for the addition of the sound of the ocean earlier by omitting the second of these three attributes. The Tibetan terms for the other two also differ from the Tibetan equivalents given in *MV*. Bhāvaviveka's "beneficial" (*phan pa daṅ bcas pa*) corresponds to "complete" (*sakhila*), which the quotation in *MSA* explains by saying that the Buddha's voice accomplishes the aims of all sentient beings. For the word "charming" (*lalita*), it is necessary to follow the Peking version's reading of *rol pa daṅ bcas pa* rather than the Derge's reading of *pha rol pa daṅ bcas pa*.
17. The Tibetan translation of Bhāvaviveka's text identifies the source as the *Guhyamati Sūtra* (*gsaṅ ba blo gros kyi mdo*). The text is better known as the *Guhyādhipatinirdeśa Sūtra*, as in the commentary on *MSA* XII.9.
18. *MHK* I.5abc, the titles of the first three chapters of this text.
19. Compare the "ten infinitely varied Buddha-*dharmas*" (*anantamadhya-buddha-dharma*) in *MV* 369: *an-anta-madhya-buddha-bhūmi-samatādhigataḥ*. These occur in a list of "names of the Tathāgata's majesty mentioned in the sūtras" (*sūtrānta-uddhṛtāni tathāgata-māhātmya-nāmāni*).
20. Special Buddha-attributes (*āveṇika-buddha-dharma*) occur in various lists, the most common of which has eighteen members (see *BHSD*). Lamotte discusses the traditional source of the list of eighteen in *Mppś*, pp. 1625–28. He also mentions a list of 140 that is found in the *Yogācārabhūmi*, but he does not mention a list of 300. In the text that has come down to us, Bhāvaviveka's list of 300 qualities contains only 290 items. The *Tathāgata-daśabhūmika Sūtra*, from which Bhāvaviveka quotes his list, does not appear in the Tibetan canon. Without the text of this sūtra, the gap, unfortunately, remains unfilled.

BIBLIOGRAPHY

Akṣayamatinirdeśa Sūtra. In *The Tibetan Tripitaka: Peking Edition*, edited by Daisetz T. Suzuki, vol. 34, no. 842, 35–74 (folios *Bu* 82b-180a). Tokyo-Kyoto: Tibetan Tripitaka Research Institute, 1956–61.

Anantamukhanirhāradhāraṇī. See Inagaki.

Anesaki, M. "Docetism (Buddhist)." In *Encyclopedia of Religion and Ethics*, edited by James Hastings, vol. 4, 835–40. Edinburgh: T & T. Clark, 1911.

Aparimitāyur-jñāna-nāma-mahāyāna-sūtram. Edited by Max Walleser. Sitzungsberichte der Heidelberger Akademie der Wissenschaften: Philosophisch-historische Klasse, vol. 12. Heidelberg, 1916.

Apte, V. S. *Sanskrit-English Dictionary*. 2 vols. Poona: Prasad Prakashan, 1957.

Āryadeva. *Catuḥśataka*. Translated by Karen Lang. *Āryadeva's Catuḥśataka: On the Bodhisattva's Cultivation of Merit and Knowledge*. Indiske Studier 7. Copenhagen: Akademisk Forlag, 1986.

Asaṅga. *Bodhisattvabhūmi*. Edited by Nalinaksha Dutt. Tibetan Sanskrit Works Series, vol. 7. Patna: K. P. Jayaswal Research Institute, 1966.

Cecil Bendall and Louis de La Vallée Poussin. "Bodhisattvabhūmi: Sommaire et Notes." *Le Muséon* 30 (1911): 155–91.

——. *Mahāyānasaṃgraha*. Tibetan and Chinese versions edited and translated by Étienne Lamotte. *La Somme du Grand Véhicule d'Asaṅga*. 2 vols. Louvain-la-Neuve: Institut Orientaliste, 1973.

The Realm of Awakening: A Translation and Study of the Tenth Chapter of Asaṅga's Mahāyānasaṃgraha. Edited by Paul J. Griffiths, et al. New York: Oxford University Press, 1989.

Asmussen, Jes Peter, ed. and trans. *The Khotanese Bhadracaryādeśanā*. Historisk-filosofiske Meddelelser Det Kongelige Danske Videnskabernes Selskab 39, no. 2. Copenhagen, 1961.

Aṣṭasāhasrikā Prajñāpāramitā. Edited by P. L. Vaidya. Buddhist Sanskrit Texts, no. 4. Darbhanga: Mithila Institute, 1960.

Translated by Edward Conze. *The Perfection of Wisdom in Eight Thousand Lines and Its Verse Summary*. Bolinas, California: Four Seasons Foundation, 1973.

Atiśa. *Lamp for the Path to Enlightenment* (*Bodhipathapradīpa*). Edited by Helmut Eimer. *Asiatische Forschungen* 59. Wiesbaden: Otto Harrassowitz, 1978.

Bodhipathapradīpapañjikā. sDe-dge Tibetan Tripiṭaka bsTan-ḥgyur preserved at the Faculty of Letters, University of Tokyo (Dbu-ma), no. 3948, vol. 16, 121–47 (folios *Khi* 241a-293a). Tokyo, 1979.

Translated by Richard J. Sherburne, S. J. *A Lamp for the Path and Commentary*. Wisdom of Tibet Series, no. 5. London: George Allen & Unwin, 1983.

Atthasālinī. Edited by E. Müller. 1897. Revised ed. London: Pali Text Society, 1979.

Attwater, Donald. *The Penguin Dictionary of Saints*. Harmondsworth, Middlesex: Penguin Books, 1965.

Auboyer, Jeannine. *Le trône et son symbolisme dans l'Inde ancienne*. Annales de Musée Guimet, vol. 55. Paris: Presses Universitaires de France, 1949.

Avataṃsaka Sūtra. Translated by Thomas Cleary. *The Flower Ornament Scripture*. Vol. 1. Boulder: Shambhala, 1984. Vols. 2, 3. Boston: Shambhala, 1986–87.

Bakhtin, M. M. *The Dialogic Imagination*. Edited by Michael Holquist. Austin: University of Texas Press, 1981.

Bareau, André. *Les sectes bouddhiques du petit véhicule*. Paris: École Française d'Extrême-Orient, 1955.

———. "Le site de la Dhānyakaṭaka de Hiuen-tsang." *Arts asiatiques* 12 (1965): 21–52.

———. "Le stūpa de Dhānyakaṭaka selon la tradition tibétaine" and "Recherches complémentaires sur le site probable de la Dhānyakaṭaka de Hiuan-tsang." *Arts asiatique* 16 (1967): 81–100.

———. *Recherches sur la biographie du Buddha dans les Sūtrapiṭaka et les Vinayapiṭaka anciens: les derniers mois, le parinirvāṇa et les funerailles*. 2 vols. Paris: École Française d'Extrême-Orient, 1970–71.

———. "Le site bouddhique de Guntupalle," *Arts asiatique* 23 (1971): 69–92.

———. "Le parinirvāṇa du Buddha et la naissance de la religion bouddhique." *BEFEO* 61 (1974): 293–99.

———. "Les récits canoniques des funerailles du Buddha et leur anomalies: nouvel essai d'interprétation." *BEFEO* 62 (1975): 151–89.

———. "La composition et les étapes de la formation progressive du *Mahāparinirvāṇasūtra* ancien." *BEFEO* 66 (1979): 45–103.

———. "The Place of the Buddha Gautama in the Buddhist Religion During the Reign of Aśoka." In *Buddhist Studies in Honour of Walpola Rahula,* edited by Somaratna Balasooriya et al., 1–9. London: Gordon Fraser, 1980.

———. "The Superhuman Personality of Buddha and Its Symbolism in the *Mahāparinirvāṇasūtra* of the Dharmaguptaka." In *Myths and Symbols: Studies in Honor of Mircea Eliade,* edited by Joseph M. Kitagawa and Charles H. Long, 9–21. Chicago: University of Chicago Press, 1969.

Barrett, Douglas. *Sculptures from Amaravati in the British Museum*. London: The Trustees of the British Museum, 1954.

———. "The Later School of Amarāvatī and Its Influences." *Art and Letters* 28 (1954): 41–53.

Barrett, T. H. "Exploratory Observations on Some Weeping Pilgrims." In *The Buddhist Studies Forum, vol. 1: Seminar Papers 1987–1988,* edited by Tadeusz Skorupski, 99–110. London: School of Oriental and African Studies, University of London, 1990.

Basso, Keith. "'Stalking with Stories': Names, Places, and Moral Narratives among the Western Apache." In *Text, Play, and Story: The Construction and Reconstruction of Self and Society,* edited by Stuart Plattner, 19–55. Proceedings of the American Ethnological Society, 1983.

Bechert, Heinz. "The Date of the Buddha Reconsidered." *Indologica Taurinensia* 10 (1982): 29–36.

Beyer, Stephan. "Notes on the Vision Quest in Early Mahāyāna." In *Prajñāpāramitā and Related Systems: Studies in Honor of Edward Conze,* edited by Lewis Lancaster, 329–40. Berkeley Buddhist Studies Series 1. Berkeley: Berkeley Buddhist Studies Series, 1977.

———. *The Cult of Tārā: Magic and Ritual in Tibet*. Berkeley: University of California Press, 1978.

Bhagavad Gītā. Edited by Dinker Vishnu Gohkale. Poona Oriental Series, no. 1. Poona: Oriental Book Agency, 1950.

Bhattacharya, Kamaleswar. "Mādhyamika et Vaitaṇḍika." *JA* 263 (1975): 99–102.

Bhāvaviveka. *The Verses on the Essence of the Madhyamaka* (*Madhyamakahṛdayakārikā*) with the autocommentary entitled *The Flame of Reason* (*Tarkajvālā*).

Tibetan translation *in sDe-dge Tibetan Tripiṭaka bsTan-ḥgyur Preserved at the Faculty of Letters, University of Tokyo (Dbu ma)*, no. 3856, vol. 3, 20–163 (folios *Dza* 40b-329b). Tokyo, 1977.

The Sanskrit manuscript of the verse portion of the text was discovered by Rahula Samkrtyayana in Źa-lu monastery in Tibet and published in part in the works listed below. References to chapters 4 and 5, which have not been published, are based on photographs of the manuscript provided by Dr. Jiang Zhongxin of the Academy of Social Sciences, Beijing.

Chapter 1. Edited and and translated by V. V. Gokhale and S. S. Bahulkar. "Madhyamakahṛdayakārikā Tarkajvālā: Chapter I." In *Miscellanea Buddhica*, edited by Christian Lindtner, 76–107. Indiske Studier 5. Copenhagen: Akademisk Forlag, 1985.

Chapter 2. Edited and translated by V. V. Gokhale. "The Second Chapter of Bhavya's Madhyamakahṛdaya (Taking the Vow of an Ascetic)." *IIJ* 14 (1972): 40–45.

Chapter 3, verses 1–136 with commentary. Edited and translated by Shotaro Iida. *Reason and Emptiness: A Study in Logic and Mysticism*. Tokyo: The Hokuseido Press, 1980. Verses of the entire chapter edited with Japanese translation by Yasunori Ejima. *Development of Madhyamaka Philosophy in India: Studies on Bhāvaviveka*. Tokyo, 1981.

Chapter 8. Edited and translated by Olle Qvarnström. *Hindu Philosophy in Buddhist Perspective: The Vedāntaviniścaya Chapter of Bhavya's Madhyamakahṛdayakārikā*. Lund Studies in African and Asian Religions, vol. 4. Lund: Plus Ultra, 1989.

Chapters 9 and 10. Edited by Shinjo Kawasaki. "The Mīmāṃsā Chapter of Bhavya's *Madhyamaka-hṛdaya-kārikā*—Text and Translation—Pūrva-pakṣa." *Studies 1976*, Institute of Philosophy, University of Tsukuba, 1977: 1–16; "The Mīmāṃsā Chapter of Bhavya's *Madhyamaka-hṛdaya-kārikā*—Sanskrit and Tibetan Texts." *Studies 1986, 1987, 1988*, Institute of Philosophy, University of Tsukuba, 1990: 1–23.

——. *The Lamp of Wisdom* (*Prajñāpradīpa*). Tibetan translation in *sDe-dge Tibetan Tripiṭaka bsTan-ḥgyur Preserved at the Faculty of Letters, University of Tokyo (Dbu ma)*, vol. 2, no. 3853, 23–130 (folios *Tsha* 45a-259b). Tokyo, 1977.

Chapter 25 (appendix). Edited by Christian Lindtner. "Bhavya's Controversy with Yogācāra in the Appendix to Prajñāpradīpa, Chapter XXV." In *Tibetan and Buddhist Studies Commemorating the 200th Aniversary of the Birth of Csoma de Körös*, edited by Louis Ligeti, 77–97 Bibliotheca Orientalis Hungarica 29. Budapest: Akademiai Kiado, 1984.

——. *A Summary of the Madhyamaka* (*Madhyamārthasaṃgraha*). Translated with Sanskrit restoration by Ayyaswami Sastri. "*Madhyamārthasaṃgraha of Bhāvaviveka." *Journal of Oriental Research (Madras)* 5 (1931): 41–49.

——. *The Jewel in the Hand* (**Karatalaratna*). Translated from Chinese by Louis de La Vallée Poussin. "Le joyau dans le main." *MCB* 2 (1932–33): 68–138.

——. *The Jewel Lamp of the Madhyamaka* (*Madhyamakaratnapradīpa*). Tibetan translation in *sDe-dge Tibetan Tripiṭaka bsTan-ḥgyur Preserved at the Faculty of Letters, University of Tokyo (Dbu ma)*, no. 3854, vol. 2, 130–45 (folios *Tsha* 259b-289a). Tokyo, 1977.

Chapter 1. Translated by Christian Lindtner. In "Atiśa's Introduction to the Two Truths, and Its Sources." *JIP* 9 (1981): 169–77.

Chapter 3. Translated by Christian Lindtner. In "Materials for the Study of Bhavya." In *Kalyāṇamitrarāgaṇam: Essays in Honour of Nils Simonsson*, edited by Eivind Kahrs, 182–91. Oslo: Norwegian University Press, 1986.

Chapter 4. Edited by Christian Lindtner. In "Materials for the Study of Bhavya," 192–202.

Translated by Christian Lindtner. "Bhavya's Critique of Yogācāra in the Madhyamakaratnapradīpa, Chapter IV." In *Buddhist Logic and Epistemology*, edited by B. K. Matilal and R. D. Evans, pp. 239–63. Dordrecht: D. Reidel, 1986.

Birnbaum, Raoul. *The Healing Buddha*. Rider: London, 1980.

———. "Buddhist Meditation Teachings and the Birth of 'Pure' Landscape Painting in China." *SSCR Bulletin* 9 (1981): 42–58.

———. *Studies on the Mysteries of Mañjuśrī*. Society for the Study of Chinese Religions, Monograph no. 2. 1983.

———. "Thoughts on T'ang Buddhist Mountain Traditions and Their Context." *T'ang Studies* 2 (1984): 5–23.

Bodhisattva Stages (*Bodhisattvabhūmi*). See Asaṅga.

Bolle, Kees W. "Speaking of a Place." In *Myths and Symbols: Studies in Honor of Mircea Eliade*, 127–39. Edited by Joseph M. Kitagawa and Charles H. Long. Chicago: University of Chicago Press, 1969.

Bollee, Willem B. "Le *kūṭāgāra* ou de la maison des hommes au manoir dans l'Inde orientale et l'Asie du Sud-Est." *Bulletin d'Études Indiennes* 4 (1986): 189–214.

Booth, Wayne C. *A Rhetoric of Irony*. Chicago: University of Chicago Press, 1974.

Buddhabhūmi Sūtra. Tibetan translation edited by Nishio Kyōo. *Buddhabhūmi-sūtra and Buddhabhūmi-vyākhyānā of Śīlabhadra*. Vol. 1. 1939. Reprint ed. Tokyo: Kokusho Kankōkai, 1982.

Buddhaghosa. *Visuddhimagga of Buddhaghosācariya*. Edited by Henry Clarke Warren. Harvard Oriental Series, vol. 41. Cambridge: Harvard University Press, 1950.

Translated by Bhikkhu Ñyāṇamoli. *The Path of Purification*. 2 vols. 1956–64. Reprint ed. Boulder: Shambhala, 1976.

Bühnemann, Gudrun. *Der allwissende Buddha: ein Beweis und seine Probleme*. Wiener Studien zur Tibetologie und Buddhismuskunde, vol. 4. Vienna: Arbeitskreis für Tibetische und Buddhistische Studien Universität Wien, 1980.

Burks, Arthur W. "Icon, Index, and Symbol." *Philosophy and Phenomenological Research* 9 (1949): 673–89.

Candrakīrti. *Madhyamakāvatāra*. Edited by Louis de La Vallée Poussin. Bibilotheca Buddhica 9. St. Petersburg, 1907–12. Reprint ed. Osnabrück: Biblio Verlag, 1970.

Chapter 1-chapter 6, verse 165. Translated by Louis de La Vallée Poussin. *Le Muséon* 8 (1907): 249–317; 11 (1910): 271–358; 12 (1911): 235–328.

Chapter 6, verses 166–226. Translated by Helmut Tauscher. *Candrakīrti: Madhyamakāvatāra und Madhyamakāvatārabhāṣyam (Kapitel VI, Vers 166–226)*. Wiener Studien zur Tibetologie und Buddhismuskunde, vol. 5. Vienna: Arbeitskreis für Tibetische und Buddhistische Studien Universität Wien, 1981.

———. *Prasannapadā*. Edited by Louis de La Vallée Poussin. *Mūlamadhyamakakārikās (Mādhyamikasūtras) de Nāgārjuna avec la Prasannapadā Commentaire de Candrakīrti*. Bibliotheca Buddhica 4. St. Petersburg, 1903–1913. Reprint ed. Osnabrück: Biblio Verlag, 1970.

Chapters 5, 12–16. Translated by Stanislaw Schayer. *Ausgewählte Kapitel aus der Prasannapadā*. Cracow: Polska Akademja Umiejetności, 1931.

Chapters 18–22. Translated by J. W. de Jong. *Cinq chapitres de la Prasannapadā*. Paris: Librairie Orientaliste Paul Geuthner, 1949.

Chapters 2–4, 6–9, 11, 23–4, 26–7. Translated by Jacques May. *Candrakīrti Prasannapadā Madhyamakavṛtti*. Paris: Adrien Maisonneuve, 1959.

Carter, John Ross. *Dhamma: Western Academic and Sinhalese Buddhist Interpretations: A Study of a Religious Concept*. Tokyo: Hokuseido Press, 1978.

Collins, Steven. *Selfless Persons: Imagery and Thought in Theravāda Buddhism*. Cambridge: Cambridge University Press, 1982.

Conze, Edward. *Materials for a Dictionary of the Prajñāpāramitā Literature*. Tokyo: Suzuki Research Foundation, 1973.

———. The *Prajñāpāramitā Literature*. 2d ed. Tokyo: Reiyukai, 1978.

Coomaraswamy, Ananda K. "The Origin of the Buddha Image." *The Art Bulletin* 9 (1927): 287–329.

———. "Indian Architectural Terms." *JAOS* 48 (1928): 250–75.

———. "*Saṃvega*: Aesthetic Shock." *Harvard Journal of Asiatic Studies* 7 (1943). Reprinted in *Coomaraswamy: Selected Papers*, vol. 1, edited by Robert Lipsey, 179–85. Princeton: Princeton University Press, 1977.

Culler, Jonathan. *On Deconstruction: Theory and Criticism after Structuralism*. Ithaca, New York: Cornell University Press, 1982.

Dallapiccola, Anna Libera. *The Stūpa: Its Religious, Historical and Architectural Significance*. Beiträge zur Südasien-Forschung Südasien-Institut Universität Heidelberg, vol. 55. Wiesbaden, 1980.

Daśabhūmika Sūtra. Edited by P. L. Vaidya. Buddhist Sanskrit Texts, no. 7. Darbhanga: Mithila Institute, 1967.

Dayal, Har. *The Bodhisattva Doctrine in Buddhist Sanskrit Literature*. London: Routledge & Kegan Paul, 1932. Reprint ed. Delhi: Motilal Banarsidass, 1970.

Demiéville, Paul. "Les versions chinoises du Milindapañha." *BEFEO* 24 (1924): 1–264.

———. "La *Yogācārabhūmi* de Saṃgharakṣa." *BEFEO* 44 (1954): 339–436.

Derrida, Jacques. *Margins of Philosophy*. Translated by Alan Bass. Chicago: University of Chicago Press, 1982.

Descent to Laṅkā Sūtra. See *Laṅkāvatāra Sūtra*.

Descombes, Vincent. *Modern French Philosophy*. Cambridge: Cambridge University Press, 1980.

Dhammapada. Translated by John Ross Carter and Mahinda Palihawadana. New York: Oxford University Press, 1987.

Diamond Sūtra. Translated by Edward Conze. In *Buddhist Wisdom Books*. New York: Harper & Row, 1972.

Dīgha Nikāya. Edited by T. W. Rhys Davids, et al. 3 vols. London: Pali Text Society, 1889–1910.

Translated by T. W. Rhys Davids. *Dialogues of the Buddha*. 3 vols. 1899. Reprint ed. London: Pali Text Society, 1977.

Dignāga. *Ālambanaparīkṣā*. Edited and translated by F. Tola and C. Dragonetti. *JIP* 10 (1982): 105–34.

———. *Epitome of the Perfection of Wisdom* (*Prajñāpāramitāpiṇḍārtha*). Edited and translated by Giuseppe Tucci. "Minor Sanskrit Texts on the Prajñā-pāramitā: 1. The Prajñā-pāramitā-piṇḍārtha of Dignāga." *JRAS* (1947): 53–75.

Distinction between the Middle and the Extremes (*Madhyāntavibhāga*). See Maitreyanātha.

Divyāvadāna. Edited by P. L. Vaidya. Buddhist Sanskrit Texts, no. 20. Darbhanga: Mithila Institute, 1959.

Dorson, R. M. "The Eclipse of Solar Mythology." In *Myth: A Symposium*, edited by Thomas A. Sebeok, Bibliographical and Special Series of the American Folklore Society, vol. 5. Philadelphia: American Folklore Society, 1955.

Eck, Diana L. *Darśan: Seeing the Divine in India*. Chambersburg, Pennsylvania: Anima Books, 1981.

Eckel, Malcolm David. "Bhāvaviveka and the Early Mādhyamika Theories of Language." *PEW* 28 (1978): 323–37.

———. "A Question of Nihilism: Bhāvaviveka's Response to the Fundamental Problems of Mādhyamika Philosophy." Ph.D. diss. Harvard University, 1980.

———. "Gratitude to an Empty Savior: A Study of the Concept of Gratitude in Mahāyāna Buddhist Philosophy." *HR* 25 (1985): 57–75.

———. "Bhāvaviveka's Critique of Yogācāra Philosophy in Chapter XXV of the Prajñāpradīpa." In *Miscellanea Buddhica*, edited by Christian Lindtner, 25–75. Copenhagen: Akademisk Forlag, 1985.

———. "Bhāvaviveka's Vision of Reality: Structure and Metaphor in a Buddhist Philosophical System." *JAAR* 65 (1987): 39–54.

———. *Jñānagarbha's Commentary on the Distinction between the Two Truths*. Albany: State University of New York Press, 1987.

Edgerton, Franklin. *Buddhist Hybrid Sanskrit Grammar and Dictionary*. 2 vols. New Haven: Yale University Press, 1953. Reprint ed. Delhi: Motilal Banarsidass, 1970–72.

Emmerick, Ronald, trans. *The Book of Zambasta*. London: Oxford University Press, 1968.

Flame of Reason (Tarkajvālā). See Bhāvaviveka.

Folkert, Kendall Wayne. "Two Jaina Approaches to Non-Jainas: Patterns and Implications." Ph.D. diss., Harvard University, 1975.

Foucher, Alfred. *La vie du Bouddha d'après les textes et les monuments de l'Inde*. Paris: Payot, 1949.

Foucault, Michel. *The Order of Things*. New York: Vintage Books, 1973. A translation of *Les mots et les choses*. Paris: Gallimard, 1966.

Franz, Heinrich Gerhard. "The Origins of the Temple-Tower in India." In *South Asian Archaeology 1981*, edited by Bridget Allchin, 280–84. Cambridge: Cambridge University Press, 1984.

Gaṇḍavyūha Sūtra. Edited by P. L. Vaidya. Buddhist Sanskrit Texts, no. 5. Darbhanga: Mithila Institute, 1960.

Translated by Thomas Cleary. In *The Flower Ornament Scripture*, vol. 3. Boston: Shambhala, 1987.

Giles, H. A., trans. *The Travels of Fa-hien (399–414 A.D.)*. London: Routledge & Kegan Paul, 1956.

Gokhale, Balakrishna Govind. "Buddhism in the Gupta Age." In *Essays on Gupta Culture*, ed. Bardwell Smith, pp. 129–53. Delhi: Motilal Banarsidass, 1983.

———. "'Āloko Udapādi' The Imagery of Illumination in Early Buddhist Literature." Paper delivered at the annual conference of the International Association of Buddhist Studies, Berkeley, California, August, 1987.

Gokhale, V. V. "Masters of Buddhism Adore the Brahman through Non-adoration." *IIJ* 5 (1961–62): 271–75.

Gombrich, Richard F. "The Consecration of a Buddhist Image." *JAS* 26 (1966): 23–36.

———. *Precept and Practice: Traditional Buddhism in the Rural Highlands of Ceylon*. Oxford: Oxford University Press, 1971.

———. "The Significance of Former Buddhas in the Theravādin Tradition." In *Buddhist Studies in Honour of Walpola Rahula*, edited by S. Balasooriya et al., 62–72. London: Gordon Fraser, 1980.

Gómez, Luis O. "The Bodhisattva as Wonder-worker." In *Prajñāpāramitā and Related Systems: Studies in Honor of Edward Conze*, edited by Lewis Lancaster, 221–61. Berkeley Buddhist Studies Series 1. Berkeley: Berkeley Buddhist Studies Series, 1977.

———, ed. *Barabuḍur: History and Significance of a Buddhist Monument*. Berkeley Buddhist Studies Series 2. Berkeley: Asian Humanities Press, 1981.

——. "Indian Materials on the Doctrine of Sudden Enlightenment." In *Early Ch'an in China and Tibet*: 393–434. Edited by Whalen Lai and Lewis R. Lancaster. Berkeley Buddhist Studies Series 5. Berkeley: Asian Humanities Press, 1983.

——. "The Direct and Gradual Approaches of Zen Master Mahāyāna: Fragments of the Teaching of Mo-ho-yen." In *Studies in Ch'an and Hua-yen*: 69–167. Edited by Robert M. Gimello and Peter N. Gregory. Honolulu: University of Hawaii Press, 1983.

Gonda, Jan. *Eye and Gaze in the Veda*. Verhandelingen der Koninklijke Nederlandse Akademie van Wetenschappen, Afd. Letterkunde, vol. 75, no. 1. Amsterdam: North-Holland Publishing Co., 1969.

Griffiths, Paul. *On Being Mindless: Buddhist Meditation and the Mind-Body Problem*. LaSalle, Illinois: Open Court, 1986.

——. "Buddha and God: A Contrastive Study in Ideas about Maximal Greatness." *The Journal of Religion* 69 (1989): 502–29.

——. "Omniscience in the Mahāyānasūtrālaṃkāra and Its Commentaries." *Indo-Iranian Journal* 33 (1990): 85–120.

Grousset, Réné. *In the Footsteps of the Buddha*. Translated by Mariette Leon. London: George Routledge & Sons, 1932.

rGyal-tshab Dar-ma Rin-chen. *Rnam bśad sñiṅ po rgyan*. Sarnath: Gelugpa Students' Welfare Committee, 1980.

Halbfass, Wilhelm. "Observations on Darśana." *WZKS* 23 (1979): 195–203.

——. *India and Europe: An Essay in Understanding*. Albany: State University of New York Press, 1988. Translation of *Indien und Europa. Perspektiven ihrer Geistigen Begegnung*. Basel: Schwabe & Coag, 1981.

Haribhadra. *Light on the Ornament of Realization* (*Abhisamayālaṃkārālokā*). Edited by U. Wogihara. *Abhisamayālaṃkārālokā Prajñāpāramitāvyākhyā*. 3 vols. Tokyo: Toyo Bunko, 1932–37.

——. *Sphuṭārthā*. Tibetan text with Sanskrit restoration. Edited by Samdhong Rinpoche. *Acāryaharibhadraviracitā Abhisamayālaṃkāravṛtti Spuṭārthā*. Bibliotheca Indo-Tibetica 2. Sārnāth: Center for Higher Tibetan Studies, 1977.

Harrison, Paul M. "Buddhānusmṛti in the Pratyutpanna-buddha-saṃmukhāvasthita-samādhi-sūtra." *JIP* 6 (1978): 35–57.

Heart Sūtra. Translated by Edward Conze. In *Buddhist Wisdom Books*. New York: Harper & Row, 1972.

Hōbōgirin: Dictionnaire encyclopédique du Bouddhisme d'après les sources chinoises et japonaises. Tokyo: Maison Franco-Japonaise, 1929-.

Horner, I. B., trans. *The Collection of the Middle Length Sayings (Majjhima Nikāya)*. 3 vols. London: Pali Text Society, 1954–59.

Hsüan-tsang. *Si-Yu-Ki: Buddhist Records of the Western World*. Translated by Samuel Beal. Reprint ed. Delhi: Munshiram Manoharlal, 1969.

Mémoires sur les contrées occidentales. Translated by Stanislas Julien. 2 vols. Paris: Imprimerie Impériale, 1857–58.

——. *Vijñaptimātratāsiddhi: Le siddhi de Hiuan-tsang*. Edited and translated by Louis de La Vallée Poussin. 2 vols. Paris: Librairie Orientaliste Paul Geuthner, 1928–29.

Hui-li. *The Life of Hiuen-tsiang by the Shaman Hwui-li*. Translated by Samuel Beal. London: Kegan Paul, Trench, Trübner & Co., 1911.

Histoire de la vie de Hiouen-thsang et de ses voyages dans l'Inde. Paris: Imprimerie Impériale, 1853.

Huntington, C. W., Jr. "The System of the Two Truths in the Prasannapadā and the Madhyamakāvatāra: A Study in Mādhyamika Soteriology." *JIP* 11 (1983): 77–106.

—— and Geshe Namgyal Wangchen. *The Emptiness of Emptiness: An Introduction to Early Indian Mādhyamika*. Honolulu: University of Hawaii Press, 1989.

Huntington, Susan L. *The Art of Ancient India: Buddhist, Hindu, Jain*. New York: Weatherhill, 1985.

Iida, Shotaro. *Reason and Emptiness: A Study in Logic and Mysticism*. Tokyo: Hokuseido Press, 1980.

Inagaki, Hisao. *The Anantamukhanirhāra-Dhāraṇī Sūtra and Jñānagarbha's Commentary*. Kyoto: Nagata Bunshodo, 1987.

Ingalls, Daniel H. H. "Śaṅkara on the Question 'Whose Is Avidyā?'" *PEW* 3 (1953): 69–72.

I-tsing. *A Record of the Buddhist Religion as Practiced in India and the Malay Archipelago (A.D. 671–695)*. Translated by J. Takakusu. Oxford, 1896.

Jackson, John Brinckerhoff. *Discovering the Vernacular Landscape*. New Haven: Yale University Press, 1984.

Jaini, Padmanabh S. "On the Buddha Image." In *Studies in Pali and Buddhism*, edited by A. K. Narain, 183–88. Delhi: B. R. Publishing Corp., 1979.

Jātaka. Ed. V. Faussbøll. *The Jātaka together with Its Commentary*. 6 vols. London: Trübner & Co., 1875–96.

Jhalakīkar, Mahāmahopādhyāya Bhīmācārya. *Nyāyakośa or Dictionary of Technical Terms of Indian Philosophy*. Rev. ed. Mahāmahopādhyāya Vāsudev Shāstrī Abhyankar. Poona: Bhandarkar Oriental Research Institute, 1978.

Jñānagarbha. *Satyadvayavibhaṅga*. See Eckel.

———. *Anantamukhanirhāradhāraṇīṭīkā*. See Inagaki.

Johnston, E. H. *The Buddhacarita or Acts of the Buddha*. Lahore, 1936. Reprint ed. Delhi: Motilal Banarsidass, 1972.

Jong, J. W. de. "La légende de Śāntideva." *IIJ* 16 (1975): 161–82.

———. "The Problem of the Absolute in the Madhyamaka School." *JIP* 2 (1972): 1–6.

Joshi, Lalmani. *Studies in the Buddhistic Culture of India (During the 7th and 8th Centuries A.D.)*. Delhi: Motilal Banarsidass, 1967.

Kajiyama, Yuichi. "'Thus Spoke the Blessed One . . .'" In *Prajñāpāramitā and Related Systems: Studies in Honor of Edward Conze*, edited by Lewis Lancaster, 93–99. Berkeley Buddhist Studies Series 1. Berkeley: Berkeley Buddhist Studies Series, 1977.

———. "Later Mādhyamikas on Epistemology and Meditation." In *Mahāyāna Buddhist Meditation: Theory and Practice*: 114–43. Honolulu: University of Hawaii Press, 1979.

———. "Stupas, the Mother of Buddhas, and the Dharma-body." In *New Paths in Buddhist Research*, edited by A. K. Warder, 9–16. Durham, North Carolina: The Acorn Press, 1985.

Kakar, Sudhir. *Shamans, Mystics, and Doctors*. Boston: Beacon Press, 1982.

Kalupahana, David. *Buddhist Philosophy: A Historical Analysis*. Honolulu: University Press of Hawaii, 1976.

Kamalaśīla. *Bhāvanākrama I*. In *Minor Buddhist Texts*, Part II, edited by Giuseppe Tucci. Serie Orientale Roma 9. Rome: Istituto Italiano per il Medio ed Estremo Oriente, 1958.

———. *Bhāvanākrama III*. In *Minor Buddhist Texts*, Part III, edited by Giuseppe Tucci. Serie Orientale Roma 43. Rome: Istituto Italiano per il Medio ed Estremo Oriente, 1971.

Karpelès, Suzanne. "*Lokeśvaraśatakam* ou cent strophes en l'honneur du seigneur du monde, par Vajradatta." *JA* (1919): 357–465.

Katz, Nathan. "Does the 'Cessation of the World' Entail the Cessation of Emotions? The Psychology of the Arahant." *Pāli Buddhist Review* 4 (1979): 53–65.

Kaviraj, Gopinath. "Nirmāṇakāya." *The Princess of Wales Saraswati Bhavana Studies* 1 (1922): 47–58.

Kirfel, W. *Die Kosmographie der Inder nach den Quellen dargestellt*. Bonn and Leipzig: Kurt Schroeder, 1920.

Kirk, K. E. *The Vision of God: The Christian Doctrine of the Summum Bonum*. 2nd edition. London: Longmans, Green and Co., 1932.

Kloetzli, W. Randolph. *Buddhist Cosmology: Science and Theology in the Images of Motion and Light*. Delhi: Motilal Banarsidass, 1983.

Kloppenborg, Ria. *The Paccekabuddha: A Buddhist Ascetic*. Leiden: E. J. Brill, 1974.

Kramrisch, Stella. *The Hindu Temple*. Calcutta, 1949. Reprint ed. Delhi: Motilal Banarsidass, 1976.

Lakoff, George and Johnson, Mark. *Metaphors We Live By*. Chicago: University of Chicago Press, 1980.

Lalitavistara. Edited by P. L. Vaidya. Buddhist Sanskrit Texts, no. 1. Darbhanga: Mithila Institute, 1958.

Translated by Philippe Edouard Foucaux. *Le Lalita Vistara*. Paris, 1884.

Lalou, Marcelle. "Le culte des Nāga et la thérapeutique." *JA* (1938): 1–19.

——. "Notes à propos d'une amulette de Touen-houang." *MCB* 4 (1936): 135–49.

Lamotte, Étienne. "La critique d'interpétation dans le bouddhisme." *Annuaire de l'Institut de Philologie et d'Histoire Orientales et Slaves* 9 (1949): 341–61.

——. *Le traité de la grande vertu de sagesse de Nāgārjuna* (*Mahāprajñāpāramitāśāstra*).

Vols 1, 2. Bibliothèque du Muséon, vol. 18. Louvain: Institut Orientaliste, 1949. Reprint ed. 1966–67.

Vols. 3–5. Publications de l'Institut Orientaliste de Louvain 2, 12, 24. Louvain-la Neuve: Institut Orientaliste, 1970–80.

——. "Sur la formation du Mahāyāna." *Asiatica* (Festschrift Weller): 377–96. Leipzig, 1954.

——. "Mañjuśrī." *T'oung Pao* 48 (1960): 1–96.

——. "Vajrapāṇi en Inde." In *Mélanges de Sinologie offerts à Monsieur Paul Demiéville*: 113–59. Bibliothèque de l'Institut des Hautes Études Chinoises. Vol. 20. Paris: Presses Universitaires de France, 1966.

——. *Histoire du bouddhisme indien: des origines à l'ère Śaka*. Louvain: Institut Orientaliste, 1958. Reprint ed. 1967.

——. "Lotus et Buddha supramondain." *BEFEO* 69 (1981): 31–44.

Lancaster, Lewis R. "An Early Mahāyāna Sermon about the Body of the Buddha and the Making of Images." *Artibus Asiae* 36 (1974): 287–91.

——. "The Story of a Buddhist Hero." *The Tsing Hua Journal of Chinese Studies*, n.s. 10 (1974): 83–89.

——. "The Oldest Mahāyāna Sūtra: Its Significance for the Study of Buddhist Development." *Eastern Buddhist* 8 (1975): 30–41.

——. "Samādhi Names in Buddhist Texts." *Malalasekera Commemoration Volume*, edited by O. H. de A. Wijesekera, 196–202. Colombo: Malalasekera Commemoration Volume Editorial Committee, 1976.

——. "The Bodhisattva Concept: A Study of the Chinese Buddhist Canon." In *The Bodhisattva Doctrine in Buddhism*, edited by Leslie S. Kawamura, 153–63. Waterloo, Ontario: Wilfred Laurier University Press, 1981.

Laṅkāvatāra Sūtra. Edited by Bunyiu Nanjio. Bibliotheca Otaniensis, vol. 1. Kyoto: Otani University Press, 1923.

Translated by Daisetz Teitaro Suzuki. *The Lankavatara Sutra*. London: Routledge & Kegan Paul, 1932. Reprint ed. 1973.

Large Sūtra on Perfect Wisdom. Trans. Edward Conze. Berkeley: University of California Press, 1975.

La Vallée Poussin, Louis de. "Studies in Buddhist Dogma: The Three Bodies of a Buddha (Trikāya)." *JRAS* (1906): 943–77.

———. "Notes sur les corps du Bouddha." *Le Muséon* 14 (1913): 257–90.

Legge, James. *A Record of Buddhistic Kingdoms.* Oxford: Oxford University Press, 1886. Reprint ed. New York: Paragon Book Reprint Corp. and Dover Publications, 1965.

Lindtner, Christian. "Apropos Dharmakīrti—Two New Works and a New Date." *Acta Orientalia* 41 (1980): 27–37.

———. "Atiśa's Introduction to the Two Truths, and Its Sources." *JIP* 9 (1981): 161–214.

———. *Nagarjuniana: Studies in the Writings and Philosophy of Nāgārjuna.* Indiske Studier 4. Copenhagen, 1982. Reprint ed. *Master of Wisdom: Writings of the Buddhist Master Nāgārjuna.* Oakland: Dharma Publishing, 1986.

———. "Adversaria Buddhica." *WZKS* 26 (1982): 167–94.

———. "On Bhavya's Madhyamakaratnapradīpa." *Indologica Taurinensia* 12 (1984): 163–84.

———. "Bhavya the Logician." *Adyar Library Bulletin* 50 (1986): 58–84.

Lopez, Donald S., Jr. *A Study of Svatantrika Madhyamika.* Ithaca, New York: Snow Lion Publications, 1987.

———, ed. *Buddhist Hermeneutics.* Honolulu: University of Hawaii Press, 1988.

Lotus Sūtra. See *Saddharmapuṇḍarīka Sūtra.*

Macdonald, A. W. "La notion de *saṃbhogakāya* à la lumière de quelques faits ethnographiques." *JA* 243 (1955): 229–39.

Mahābhārata. Edited by Vishnu S. Sukthankar, et al. 19 vols. Poona: Bhandarkar Oriental Research Institute, 1933–1959.

Mahāparinibbāna Sutta. See *Dīgha Nikāya.*

Mahāparinirvāṇa Sūtra. Edited by Ernst Waldschmidt. Vol. 1. Abhandlung der Deutschen Akademie der Wissenschaften zu Berlin: Philosophisch-historische Klasse, 1949, no. 1. Berlin: Akademie-Verlag, 1950.

Vol. 2. Abhandlung der Deutschen Akademie der Wissenschaften zu Berlin: Klasse für Sprachen, Literatur, und Kunst, 1950, no. 2. Berlin: Akademie-Verlag, 1951.

Vol. 3. Abhandlung der Deutschen Akademie der Wissenschaften zu Berlin: Klasse für Sprachen, Literatur, und Kunst, 1950, no. 3. Berlin: Akademie-Verlag, 1951.

Mahāvastu. Edited by Émil Senart. 3 vols. Paris: Société Asiatiques, 1882–97.

Translated by J. J. Jones. Sacred Books of the Buddhists, vols. 16, 18, 19. London: Luzac & Co., 1949–56. Reprint ed., London: Pali Text Society, 1973–76.

Maitreyanātha. *Ornament of Realization* (*Abhisamayālaṃkāra*). Edited by U. Wogihara. See Haribhadra.

Translated by Edward Conze. Serie Orientale Roma 6. Rome: Istituto Italiano per il Medio ed Estremo Oriente, 1954.

———. *Dharmadharmatāvibhāga.* (*Chos daṅ chos ñid rnam par 'byed pa*). In *sDe-dge Tibetan Tripiṭaka bsTan-ḥgyur Preserved at the Faculty of Letters, University of Tokyo (Sems-tsam),* no. 4022, vol.1, 23–5 (folios *Phi* 46b-49a). Tokyo, 1979.

———. *Distinction between the Middle and the Extremes* (*Madhyāntavibhāga*). Edited by Gadjin M. Nagao. Tokyo: Suzuki Research Foundation, 1964.

Chapter 1. Translated by Th. Stcherbatsky. *Madhyāntavibhaṅga: Discourse on Discrimination between Middle and Extremes.* Bibliotheca Buddhica 30. Leningrad, 1936.

———. *Ornament of the Mahāyāna Sūtras* (*Mahāyānasūtrālaṃkāra*). Edited and translated by Sylvain Lévi. *Mahāyāna-Sūtrālaṃkāra: Exposé de la doctrine du grand véhicule selon la système Yogācāra.* 2 vols. Bibliothèque de l'École des Hautes

Études, sciences historiques et philologiques, fasc. 159 and 190. Paris: Librairie Ancienne Honoré Champion, 1907–11.

Edited by S. Bagchi. *Mahāyānasūtrālaṃkāra*. Buddhist Sanskrit Texts, no. 13. Darbhanga: Mithila Institute, 1970.

——. *Ratnagotravibhāga*. Edited by E. H. Johnston. "The Ratnagotravibhāga Mahāyānottaratantraśāstra." *Journal of the Bihar Research Society* 36 (1950): 1–129.

Translated by E. Obermiller. "The Sublime Science of the Great Vehicle to Salvation, being a Manual of Buddhist Monism." *Acta Orientalia* 9 (1931): 81–306.

Majjhima Nikāya. Ed. V. Trenckner. Vol. 1. London: Pali Text Society, 1888.

Malamoud, Charles. "On the Rhetoric and Semantics of Puruṣārtha" In *Way of Life: King, Householder, Renouncer*, edited by T. N. Madan, 33–54. New Delhi: Vikas Publishing House, 1982.

Masson-Oursel, M. P. "Les trois corps du Bouddha." *JA* (1913): 581–618.

Mātṛceṭa. *Praṇidhānasaptati*. Edited and translated by Christian Lindtner. *Asiatische Studien* 38 (1984): 100–28.

——. *One Hundred and Fifty [Verses] (Śatapañcāśatka)*. Edited and translated by D. R. Shackleton Bailey. The *Śatapañcāśatka of Mātṛceṭa*. Cambridge: Cambridge University Press, 1951.

May, Jacques. "Āryadeva et Candrakīrti sur la permanence." In *Indianisme et bouddhisme: mélanges offerts à Mgr Étienne Lamotte*, 215–32. Publications de l'Institut Orientaliste de Louvain 23. Louvain-la-Neuve: Institut Orientaliste, 1980.

——. "Āryadeva et Candrakīrti sur la permanence (II)." *BEFEO* 69 (1981): 75–96.

Middle Length Sayings. See *Majjhima Nikāya*.

Milindapañho. Edited by V. Trenckner. London: Williams and Norgate, 1880.

Translated by T. W. Rhys Davids. *The Questions of King Milinda*. Sacred Books of the East, vols. 35, 36. Oxford: Clarendon Press, 1890–94. Reprint ed. New York: Dover Publications, 1963.

Murti, T. R. V. *The Central Philosophy of Buddhism*. London: George Allen & Unwin, 1960.

Mus, Paul. "Le bouddha paré." *BEFEO* 28 (1928): 153–278.

——. *Barabuḍur: Esquisse d'une histoire du bouddhisme fondée sur la critique archéologique des textes*. 2 vols. Hanoi: Imprimerie d'Extrême Orient, 1935.

——. "The Iconography of an Aniconic Art." *Res* 14 (1987): 5–26.

Nagao, Gadjin. "The Silence of the Buddha and Its Madhyamic Interpretation." In *Studies in Indology and Buddhology Presented in Honour of Professor Susumu Yamaguchi*: 137–51. Kyoto: 1955.

——. "On the Theory of the Buddha-body (*Buddha-kāya*)." *Eastern Buddhist* 6 (1973): 25–53.

——. "'What Remains' in Śūnyatā: A Yogācara Interpretation of Emptiness." In *Mahāyāna Buddhist Meditation: Theory and Practice*, edited by Minoru Kiyota, 65–82. Honolulu: University Press of Hawaii, 1978.

——. "From Mādhyamika to Yogācāra: An Analysis of MMK, XXIV.18 and MV, I.1–2." *JIABS* 2 (1979): 29–43.

——. "The Bodhisattva Returns to the World." In *The Bodhisattva Doctrine in Buddhism*, edited by Leslie S. Kawamura, 61–79. Waterloo, Ontario: Wilfred Laurier University Press, 1981.

Nāgārjuna. *Root Verses on the Middle Way (Mūlamadhyamakakārikās)*. Edited by J. W. de Jong. *Mūlamadhyamakakārikāḥ*. Madras: Adyar Library and Research Center, 1977.

Trans. See the translations of Candrakīrti's *Prasannapadā*.

——. *Jewel Garland (Ratnāvalī)*. Edited by Michael Hahn. *Nāgārjuna's Ratnāvalī*. Bonn: Indica et Tibetica Verlag, 1982.

Translated by Jeffrey Hopkins and Lati Rinpoche. *The Precious Garland and the Song of the Four Mindfulnesses.* London: George Allen & Unwin, 1975.

———. *Resolution of Difficulties* (*Vigrahavyāvartanī*). Edited by E. H. Johnston and A. Kunst. "The *Vigrahavyāvartanī* of Nāgārjuna." *MCB* 9 (1948–51): 99–152.

Translated by Kamaleswar Bhattacharya. "The Dialectical Method of Nāgārjuna." *JIP* 1 (1971): 217–61.

———. On Nāgārjuna's other works, see Lindtner, *Nagarjuniana.*

Nagatomi, Masatoshi. "The Framework of the Pramāṇavārttika, Book I," *JAOS* 79 (1959): 263–66.

Niddesa I: Mahāniddesa. Edited by Louis de La Vallée Poussin and E. J. Thomas. 2 vols. London: Pali Text Society, 1916–17.

Nishida, Kitarō. "The Logic of the Place of Nothingness and the Religious Worldview." In *Last Writings: Nothingness and the Religious Worldview,* translated by David A. Dilworth. Honolulu: University of Hawaii Press, 1987.

Nishitani, Keiji. *Religion and Nothingness.* Translated by Jan Van Bragt. Berkeley: University of California Press, 1982.

Oberhammer, Gerhard. *Offenbarung: Geistige Realität des Menschen.* Vienna: Indologische Institut der Universität Wien, 1974.

Obermiller, E. "The Doctrine of the Prajñāpāramitā as Exposed in the *Abhisamayālaṃkāra* of Maitreya." *Acta Orientalia* 11 (1932): 1–133.

O'Flaherty, Wendy Doniger. *Dreams, Illusions, and Other Realities.* Chicago: University of Chicago Press, 1984.

Ornament of Realization (*Abhisamayālaṃkāra*). See Maitreyanātha and Haribhadra.

Ornament of the Mahāyāna Sūtras (*Mahāyānasūtrālaṃkāra*). See Maiteyanātha.

Owen, Stephen. *Remembrances: The Experience of the Past in Classical Chinese Literature.* Cambridge: Harvard University Press, 1986.

Pas, Julian F. "The *Kuan-wu-liang-shou Fo-ching*: Its Origin and Literary Criticism." In *Buddhist Thought and Asian Civilization,* edited by Leslie S. Kawamura and Keith Scott, 194–218. Emeryville, California: Dharma Publishing, 1977.

———. "The Meaning of Nien-fo in the Three Pure Land Sutras." *Studies in Religion* 7 (1978): 403–13.

Path of Discrimination. See *Paṭisambhidāmagga.*

Paṭisambhidāmagga. Edited by Arnold C. Taylor. 2 vols. London: Pali Text Society, 1905–7.

Pelliot, Paul. Review of Thomas Watters, *On Yuan Chwang's Travels in India, 629–645 A.D. BEFEO* 5 (1905): 423–57.

Perfection of Wisdom in Eight Thousand Lines. See *Aṣṭasāhasrikā Prajñāpāramitā.*

Pollock, Sheldon. "The Theory of Practice and the Practice of Theory in Indian Intellectual History." *JAOS* 105 (1985): 499–519.

Poppe, Nicholas. *The Twelve Deeds of the Buddha.* Asiatische Forschungen, vol. 23. Wiesbaden: Otto Harrassowitz, 1967.

Prajñākaramati. *Bodhicaryāvatārapañjikā.* See Śāntideva.

Prajñā-pāramitā-ratna-guṇa-saṃcaya-gāthā. Edited by Akira Yuyama. Cambridge: Cambridge University Press, 1976.

Pye, Michael. *Skilful Means: A Concept in Mahāyāna Buddhism.* London: Duckworth, 1978.

———. and Morgan, Robert, eds. *The Cardinal Meaning: Essays in Comparative Hermeneutics: Buddhism and Christianity.* The Hague: Mouton, 1973.

Python, Pierre. "Le rituel du culte mahāyanique et le traité tibétain *'phags pa Phuṅ po gsum pa* (sanscrit: *Ārya-Triskandhaka*)." *Asiatische Studien* 35 (1981): 169–84.

Rahder, Jean. "La carrière du saint bouddhique." *Bulletin de la Maison Franco-Japonaise* 2 (1929): 1–22.

Raja, K. Kunjunni. *Indian Theories of Meaning.* Madras: Adyar Library and Research Centre, 1963.

Ratnagotravibhāga. See Maitreyanātha.

Ratnamegha Sūtra (*Ārya-ratna-megha-nāma-mahāyāna-sūtra*). In *The Tibetan Tripitaka: Peking Edition,* edited by Daisetz T. Suzuki, no. 897, vol. 35, 171–220 (folios *Dzu* 1–121a). Tokyo-Kyoto: Tibetan Tripitaka Research Institute, 1956–61.

Rawlinson, Andrew. "The Position of the *Aṣṭasāhasrikā Prajñāpāramitā* in the Development of Early Mahāyāna." In *Prajñāpāramitā and Related Systems: Studies in Honor of Edward Conze,* edited by Lewis Lancaster, 3–34. Berkeley Buddhist Studies Series 1. Berkeley: Berkeley Buddhist Studies Series, 1977.

———. "The Ambiguity of the Buddha-nature Concept in India and China." In *Early Ch'an in China and Tibet,* edited by Whalen Lai and Lewis R. Lancaster, 259–79. Berkeley Buddhist Studies 5. Berkeley: Asian Humanities Press, 1983.

Renou, Louis. "Sur le genre du sūtra dans la litterature sanskrite." *JA* (1963): 165–216.

Reynolds, Frank E. "The Many Lives of Buddha: A Study of Sacred Biography and Theravada Tradition," in *The Biographical Process,* edited by Frank E. Reynolds and Donald Capps. The Hague, 1976.

———. "The Several Bodies of Buddha: Reflections on a Neglected Aspect of Theravada Tradition." *HR* 6 (1977): 374–89.

———. and Hallisey, Charles. "Buddha." In *The Encyclopedia of Religion,* edited by Mircea Eliade, vol. 2, 319–32. New York: Macmillan, 1987.

Rorty, Richard. *Philosophy and the Mirror of Nature.* Princeton: Princeton University Press, 1979; 2nd printing, with corrections, 1980.

Ruegg, David Seyfort. "Ārya and Bhadanta Vimuktisena on the Gotra-Theory of the Prajñāpāramitā." *WZKS* 12–3 (1968–69): 303–17.

———. *La théorie du tathāgatagarbha et du gotra.* Paris: École Française d'Extrême Orient, 1969.

———. "Le Dharmadhātustava de Nāgārjuna." *Études tibétaines dediées à la mémoire de Marcelle Lalou*: 448–71. Paris, 1971.

———. "The Uses of the Four Positions of the *Catuṣkoṭi* and the Problem of the Description of Reality in Mahāyāna Buddhism." *JIP* 5 (1977): 1–71.

———. "The Study of Tibetan Philosophy and Its Indian Sources: Notes on Its History and Methods." *Bibilotheca Orientalis Hungarica* 23 (1978): 377–91.

———. "Towards a Chronology of the Madhyamaka School." In *Indological and Buddhist Studies: Volume in Honour of Professor J. W. de Jong on his Sixtieth Birthday,* edited by L. A. Hercus et al., 505–30. Canberra: Faculty of Asian Studies, 1982.

———. *The Literature of the Madhyamaka School of Philosophy in India.* Wiesbaden: Otto Harrassowitz, 1981.

———. "Über die Nikāyas der Śrāvakas und den Ursprung der philosophischen Schulen des Buddhismus nach den tibetischen Quellen." In *Zur Schulgehrigkeit von Werken der Hīnayāna-Literatur,* edited by Heinz Bechert, 111–26. Göttingen: Vandenhoeck & Ruprecht, 1985.

———. *Buddha-nature, Mind and the Problem of Gradualism in Comparative Perspective: On the Transmission and Reception of Buddhism in India and Tibet.* London: School of Oriental and African Studies, University of London, 1989.

———. "On the Authorship of Some Works Ascribed to Bhāvaviveka/Bhavya." In *Earliest Buddhism and Madhyamaka*: 59–71. Edited by David Seyfort Ruegg and Lambert Schmithausen. Leiden: E. J. Brill, 1990.

Saddharmapuṇḍarīka Sūtra. Edited by H. Kern and Bunyiu Nanjio. Bibliotheca Buddhica 10. St. Petersburg: Imprimerie de l'Académie Impériale des Sciences, 1912.

Edited by P. L. Vaidya. Buddhist Sanskrit Texts, no. 6. Darbhanga: Mithila Institute, 1960.

Translated by H. Kern. *Saddharmapuṇḍarīka or The Lotus of the True Law.* Sacred Books of the East, vol. 21. Oxford: Clarendon Press, 1884. Reprint ed. New York: Dover Publications, 1963.

Saṃyutta-Nikāya. Translated by F. L. Woodward. *The Book of the Kindred Sayings (Saṃyutta-Nikāya).* London: Pali Text Society, 1930. Reprint ed. 1965.

Śaṅkara. *Brahmasūtrabhāṣya.* Edited by J. L. Shastri. *Brahmasūtra-śaṃkarabhāṣyam.* Delhi: Motilal Banarsidass, 1980.

Translated by George Thibaut. *The Vedānta Sūtras of Bādarāyaṇa with the Commentary of Śaṅkara.* Sacred Books of the East, vols. 34 and 38. Oxford: Clarendon Press, 1890–96. Reprint ed. New York: Dover Publications, 1962.

Śāntideva. *Introduction to the Bodhi[sattva] Practice* (*Bodhi[sattva]caryāvatāra*). Edited by P. L. Vaidya. *Bodhicaryāvatāra of Śāntideva with the Commentary Pañjikā of Prajñākaramati.* Buddhist Sanskrit Texts, no. 12. Darbhanga: Mithila Institute, 1960.

Translated by Ernst Steinkellner. *Eintritt in das Leben zur Erleuchtung: Poesie und Lehre des Mahayana-Buddhismus.* Düsseldorf: Eugen Diederichs Verlag, 1981.

———. *Compendium of Instruction* (*Śikṣāsamuccaya*). Edited by P. L. Vaidya. Buddhist Sanskrit Texts, no. 11. Darbhanga: Mithila Institute, 1961.

Sāyaṇa Mādhava. *Sarva-darśana-saṃgraha of Sāyaṇa Mādhava.* Edited by V. S. Abhyankar. 3d ed. Poona: Bhandarkar Oriental Research Institute, 1978.

Schmithausen, Lambert. *Der Nirvāṇa-Abschnitt in der Viniścayasaṃgrahaṇī der Yogācārabhūmiḥ.* Vienna: Österreichische Akademie der Wissenschaften, 1969.

———. *Ālayavijñāna: On the Origin and the Early Development of a Central Concept in Yogācāra Philosophy.* 2 vols. Studia Philologica Buddhica 4. Tokyo: International Institute for Buddhist Studies, 1987.

Schopen, Gregory. "The Phrase '*sa pṛthivīpradeśaś caityabhūto bhavet*' in the Vajracchedikā: Notes on the Cult of the Book in Mahāyāna." *IIJ* 17 (1975): 147–81.

———. "Sukhāvatī as a Generalized Religious Goal in Sanskrit Mahāyāna Literature." *IIJ* 19 (1977): 177–210.

———. "Mahāyāna in Indian Inscriptions." *IIJ* 21 (1979): 1–19.

——— and Salomon, Richard. "The Indravarman (Avaca) Casket Inscription Reconsidered: Further Evidence for Canonical Passages in Buddhist Inscriptions." *JIABS* 7 (1984): 107–23.

———. "The Bodhigarbhālaṅkāralakṣa and Vimaloṣṇīṣa Dhāraṇīs in Indian Inscriptions: Two Sources for the Practice of Buddhism in Medieval India." *WZKS* 29 (1985): 119–49.

———. "Two Problems in the History of Indian Buddhism: The Layman/Monk Distinction and the Doctrines of the Transference of Merit." In *Studien zur Indologie und Iranistik*: 9–47. Reinbeck: Verlag für Orientalistische Fachpublicationen, 1985.

———. "Burial '*Ad Sanctos*' and the Physical Presence of the Buddha in Early Indian Buddhism: A Study in the Archaeology of Religions." *Religion* 17 (1987): 193–225.

———. "On the Buddha and His Bones: The Conception of a Relic in the Inscriptions of Nāgārjunikoṇḍa." *JAOS* 108 (1988): 527–37.

Schrader, F. O. "On Some Tibetan Names of the Buddha." *Indian Historical Quarterly* 9 (1933): 46–48.

Se-ra rJe-btsun-pa. *Bstan bcos mṅon par rtogs pa'i rgyan 'grel ba daṅ bcas pa'i rnam bśad rnam pa gñis kyi dka' ba'i gnad gsal bar byed pa legs bśad skal bzaṅ klu dbaṅ gi rol mtsho źes bya ba las skabs brgyad pa'i spyi don*. Modern blockprint. Bylakuppe: Sera Je Monastery, n.d.

Śīlabhadra. *Buddhabhūmivyākhyānā. Buddhabhūmi-sūtra and Buddhabhūmi-vyākhyānā of Śīlabhadra*. Tibetan translation edited by Kyōo Nishio. Vol. 1. 1939. Reprint ed. Tokyo: Kokusho Kankōkai, 1982.

Sivaramamurti, C. *Amaravati Sculptures in the Madras Government Museum*. Bulletin of the Madras Government Museum, n.s., general section, vol. 4. Madras: Government Press, 1942.

Snellgrove, David. *Indo-Tibetan Buddhism*. 2 vols. Boston: Shambhala, 1987.

Sontag, Susan. *On Photography*. New York: Dell Publishing Co., 1977.

Soper, Alexander Coburn. *Literary Evidence for Early Buddhist Art in China*. Ascona, Switzerland: Artibus Asiae Publishers, 1959.

Sponberg, Alan. "Meditation in Fa-hsiang Buddhism." In *Traditions of Meditation in Chinese Buddhism*, edited by Peter N. Gregory, 15–43. Honolulu: University of Hawaii Press, 1986.

Steinkellner, Ernst. "Buddhaparinirvāṇastotram." *WZKS* 17 (1973): 43–48.

Sthiramati. *Madhyāntavibhāgaṭīkā*. Edited by Sylvain Lévi. Tokyo: Suzuki Research Foundation, 1966.

Translated by David L. Friedmann. *Sthiramati: Madhyāntavibhāgaṭīkā*. Utrecht, 1937.

———. *Sūtrālaṃkāravṛttibhāṣya (Mdo sde rgyan gyi 'grel bśad)*. In *sDe-dge Tibetan Tripiṭaka bsTan-ḥgyur Preserved at the Faculty of Letters, University of Tokyo (Sems-tsam)*, no. 4034, vol. 3, 1–131, vol. 4, 1–117 (folios *Mi* 1b-283a, Tsi 1b-266a). Tokyo, 1980.

Streng, Frederick. *Emptiness: A Study in Religious Meaning*. Nashville: Abingdon Press, 1967.

Strong, John S. *The Legend of King Aśoka: A Study and Translation of the Aśokāvadāna*. Princeton: Princeton University Press, 1983.

Subāhuparipṛcchā Sūtra (*Ārya-subāhu-paripṛcchā-nāma-mahāyāna-sūtra*). *The Tibetan Tripitaka: Peking Edition*, edited by Daisetz T. Suzuki, vol. 24, no. 760 (26), 63–76 (folios *Zi* 153b-184b). Tokyo-Kyoto: Tibetan Tripitaka Research Insititute, 1956–61.

Sukhāvatīvyūha (*vistaramātṛkā* and *saṃkṣiptamātṛkā*). Edited by P. L. Vaidya. In *Mahāyāna-sūtra-saṃgraha*. Buddhist Sanskrit Texts, no. 17, pt. 1. Darbhanga: Mithila Institute, 1961.

Śūraṃgamasamādhi Sūtra. Tibetan translation edited and translated by Étienne Lamotte. *La concentration de la marche héroïque*. Brussels: Institut Belge des Hautes Études Chinoises, 1965.

Sūtra of Golden Light. See *Suvarṇaprabhāsa Sūtra*.

Sutta-nipāta. Edited by Dines Andersen and Helmer Smith. London: Pali Text Society, 1965.

Translated by K. R. Norman The *Group of Discourses (Sutta-nipāta)*. London: Pali Text Society, 1984.

Suvarṇaprabhāsa Sūtra. Ed. Johannes Nobel. *Suvarṇaprabhāsottamasūtra: Das Goldglanz-sūtra*. Leipzig: Otto Harrassowitz, 1937.

Translated by Ronald Emmerick, *The Sūtra of Golden Light*. Sacred Books of the Buddhists, vol. 27. London: Pali Text Society, 1970. Reprint ed., 1979.

Takasaki, Jikido. "Description of the Ultimate Reality by Means of the Six Categories in Mahāyāna Buddhism." *Indogaku Bukkyōgaku Kenkyū* 9 (1961): 731–40.

———. *A Study on the Ratnagotravibhāga (Uttaratantra): Being a Treatise on the Tathāgatagarbha Theory of Mahāyāna Buddhism*. Serie Orientale Roma, no. 23. Rome: Istituto Italiano per il Medio ed Estremo Oriente, 1966.

———. "Dharmatā, Dharmadhātu, Dharmakāya, and Buddhadhātu: Structure of the Ultimate Value in Mahāyāna Buddhism." *Indogaku Bukkyōgaku Kenkyū* 14 (1966): 903–19.

Tambiah, Stanley Jeyaraja. *The Buddhist Saints of the Forest and the Cult of Amulets.* Cambridge: Cambridge University Press, 1984.

———. "Purity and Auspiciousness at the Edge of the Hindu Context—in Theravāda Buddhist Societies." In *Purity and Auspiciousness in Indian Society,* edited by John B. Carman and Frédérique Apffel Marglin, 94–108. Leiden: E. J. Brill, 1985.

Tāranātha. *History of Buddhism in India.* Translated by Lama Chimpa and Alaka Chattopadhyaya. Edited by Debiprasad Chattopadhyaya. Simla: Indian Institute of Advanced Study, 1970. Reprint ed. Calcutta: K. P. Bagchi & Co., 1980.

Tathāgataguhya Sūtra (*Ārya-tathāgata-acintya-guhya-nirdeśa-nāma-mahāyāna-sūtra*). In *The Tibetan Tripitaka: Peking Edition,* edited by Daisetz T. Suzuki, vol. 22, no. 760 (3), 47–95 (folios *Tshi* 113b-233a). Tokyo-Kyoto: Tibetan Tripitaka Research Institute, 1956–61.

Tathāgatajñāmudrāsamādhi Sūtra (*Ārya-tathāgata-jñāna-mudrā-samādhi-nāma-mahāyāna-sūtra*). In *The Tibetan Tripitaka: Peking Edition,* ed. Daisetz T. Suzuki, no. 799, vol. 32, 60–72 (folios *Thu* 250b-276a). Tokyo-Kyoto: Tibetan Tripitaka Research Institute, 1956–61.

Tatz, Mark. "The Life of the Siddha Philosopher Maitrīgupta," *JAOS* 107 (1987): 695–711.

Teaching of Vimalakīrti. See *Vimalakīrtinirdeśa Sūtra.*

Thera- and Therīgāthā. Edited by Hermann Oldenberg. London: Pali Text Society, 1883.

Thomas, Edward J. *The Life of the Buddha as Legend and History.* 3d ed. revised. London: Routledge & Kegan Paul, 1949.

Thurman, Robert A. F. *Tsong Khapa's Speech of Gold in the Essence of True Eloquence.* Princeton: Princeton University Press, 1984.

Treasury of the Abhidharma (*Abhidharmakośa*). See Vasubandhu.

Tucci, Giuseppe. "A Propos Avalokiteśvara." *MCB* 9 (1948–51): 173–219.

———. "Nomina Numina." In *Myths and Symbols: Studies in Honor of Mircea Eliade,* edited by Joseph M. Kitagawa and Charles H. Long, 3–7. Chicago: University of Chicago Press, 1969.

Vajracchedikā. Edited by Edward Conze. Rome: Istituto Italiano per il Medio ed Estremo Oriente, 1957.

Van der Leeuw, G. *Religion in Essence and Manifestation.* Translated by J. E. Turner. 2 vols. New York: Harper & Row, 1963.

Vasubandhu. *Abhidharmakośabhāṣya.* Ed. Prahlad Pradhan. 2d ed., rev. Aruna Haldar. Tibetan Sanskrit Works Series, vol. 8. Patna: K. P. Jayaswal Research Institute, 1975.

———. *Abhidharmakośa & Bhāṣya of Acharya Vasubandhu with Sphuṭārthā Commentary of Ācārya Yaśomitra.* 4 vols. Edited by Swami Dwarikadas Shastri. Varanasi: Bauddha Bharati, 1970–73.

———. *Madhyāntavibhāgabhāṣya.* See Maitreyanātha.

———. *Triṃśikā* and *Viṃśatikā.* Edited and translated by Sylvain Lévi. *Vijñaptimātratāsiddhi: Deux traités de Vasubandhu: Viṃśatikā (La Vingtaine) et Triṃśikā (la Trentaine).* Paris: Bibliothèque de l'École des Hautes Études, 1925.

Vimalakīrtinirdeśa Sūtra. Translated by Étienne Lamotte. *The Teaching of Vimalakīrti.* Translated by Sara Boin. London: Pali Text Society, 1976.

Vinaya Piṭakaṃ. Edited by Hermann Oldenberg. 5 vols London: Williams and Norgate, 1879–83.

Vinaya-viniścaya-upāli-paripṛcchā. Edited and translated by Pierre Python, O.P. Paris: Adrien-Maisonneuve, 1973.

Vreese, K. de. "Skt. Kūṭāgāra." In *Indian Antiqua: A Volume of Oriental Studies Presented to Jean Philippe Vogel*, 323–25. Leiden: E. J. Brill, 1947.

Waldschmidt, Ernst. *Die Überlieferung vom Lebensende des Buddha*. Abhandlungen der Akademie der Wissenschaften in Göttingen: Philologisch-Historische Klasse, nos. 29–30. Göttingen, 1944–48.

———. "Beiträge zur Textgeschichte des Mahāparinirvāṇasūtra." In *Von Ceylon bis Turfan*: 80–119. Göttingen: Vandenhoeck & Ruprecht, 1967.

———. *Der Buddha preist die Verehrungswürdigkeit seiner Reliquien*. Nachrichten der Akademie der Wissenschaften in Göttingen: Philologisch-Historische Klasse, No. 11. Göttingen, 1961.

Waley, Arthur. *The Real Tripitaka and Other Pieces*. London: George Allen and Unwin, 1952.

Watson, Burton, trans. *The Complete Works of Chuang-tzu*. New York: Columbia University Press, 1968.

Watters, Thomas. *On Yuan Chwang's Travels in India*. 2 vols. London: Royal Asiatic Society, 1904–5.

Wayman, Alex. "The Mirror-like Knowledge in Mahāyāna Buddhist Literature." *Asiatische Studien* 25 (1971): 353–63.

———. "The Mirror as a Pan-Buddhist Metaphor-Simile." *HR* 13 (1974): 264–81.

Yu, Anthony, trans. *The Journey to the West*. 4 vols. Chicago: University of Chicago Press, 1977–83.

Zwalf, W., ed. *Buddhism Art and Faith*. London: British Museum Publications, 1985.

Index